BUS
4/6/00

MANAGEMENT
2000

THE PRACTICAL

GUIDE TO

WORLD CLASS

COMPETITION

MANAGEMENT
2000

THE PRACTICAL

GUIDE TO

WORLD CLASS

COMPETITION

Harry K. Jackson, Jr.
Normand L. Frigon

VNR VAN NOSTRAND REINHOLD
New York

I(T)P   Van Nostrand Reinhold is an International Thomson Publishing company. ITP logo is a trademark under license.

Printed in the United States of America

Van Nostrand Reinhold
115 Fifth Avenue
New York, NY 10003

International Thomson Publishing GmbH
Königswinterer Str. 518
5300 Bonn 3
Germany

International Thomson Publishing
Berkshire House, 168–173
High Holborn, London WC1V 7AA
England

International Thomson Publishing Asia
38 Kim Tian Rd., #0105
Kim Tian Plaza
Singapore 0316

Thomas Nelson Australia
102 Dodds Street
South Melborune 3205
Victoria, Australia

International Thomson Publishing Japan
Kyowa Building, 3F
2-2-1 Hirakawacho
Chiyada-Ku, Tokyo 102
Japan

Nelson Canada
1120 Birchmount Road
Scarborough, Ontario
M1K 5G4, Canada

16 15 14 13 12 11 10 9 8 7 6 5 4 3 2 1

CONTENTS

FOREWORD

This portion of *Management 2000* might be better entitled "FORWARD," because that's what this book is all about—going forward.

I am honored that the authors suggested that I write the Foreword/Forward for *Management 2000*. My first reason for agreeing to do so is that it's a damn good book. It says all the right things, in such a way that even the most ardent resisters will be hard pressed to disagree with their ideas, methods, and recommendations. And beyond the written word, their graphics go a long way towards helping the reader to comprehend fully their technical commentary.

Secondly, I am writing this because I admire and respect both gentlemen. They devoted an extraordinary amount of their time to researching, discussing, writing, rewriting, editing, and continuously polishing what you have in your hands, the final product. I am convinced that you and your organization will both be winners as a result of your insights gained from reading *Management 2000*.

No one in business today needs to be reminded of the multitude of dramatic shifts that have occurred in the past decade. The transition to a world marketplace and the end of the cold war have dramatically changed our individual and collective views of business, industry, and the world. There continue to be many casualties as a part of this transition; they include companies that once held preeminent positions in their markets, but which have failed to make the transition successfully. In my mind, the future belongs to those persons and those companies who are able to focus their activities quickly, adapt to rapidly changing markets, capitalize on chaos, and provide superior customer satisfaction.

After decades of failed quick fixes and "programs du jour," we now have a clear path to what it takes to become a world class competitor capable of not just surviving but thriving in the new world. This path is the model developed by the authors. It is a cross-functional application of tools and techniques in an integrated system, not as individual paradigms and certainly not as academic exercises. Mr. Frigon and Mr. Jackson clearly understand the practical aspects of business and the application of the improvement tools and techniques.

In *Management 2000*, the authors have provided us with a practical guide that I believe will be the definitive desk reference for executives, managers, supervisors, and entrepreneurs who are committed to thriving in the marketplace today and well into the 21st century.

I commend you for acquiring your copy of *Management 2000*. It is the first of many steps to achieving world class status.

Jack B. ReVelle, Ph.D.
Orange, CA

PREFACE

Today all businesses are faced with international competition. The evidence is that international companies are bringing world class management and technical resources into local and regional markets. World class competitors are moving into such local markets as real estate sales, construction, and light industry. These international world class competitors include many small businesses as well as the traditional multinational corporations. Clearly a business may be local, but its business activities are international. All businesses need, therefore, to produce world class quality products and services.

This international competition among business and industry can have national effects. This competition takes on the scope of an international conflict in the effects it has on national economies. Barely has the cold war ended when this economic conflict has risen to take its place.

The results of losing the economic conflict are the same as losing an armed conflict—cities that appear to be bombed out, homelessness, refugees, and economic despair. The evidence is in the abandoned inner cities such as Detroit, Manchester, Newark, Los Angeles, and London. It is in the increasing numbers of business failures, bank failures, and home and farm foreclosures. It is in the missions feeding the homeless in Los Angeles and New York. It is in the crisis of the thousands of unemployed workers.

The triad of strategic bombers, intercontinental ballistic missiles, and submarines provided the West's deterrence force during the cold war. Just as this strategic triad served the West during the cold war, there is need for a new strategic triad. This new strategic triad consists of government, business, and the financial institutions.

The government leg of the triad must provide the infrastructure (education, transportation, economic policy), trade policies and tax structure to create the environment in which businesses can not only compete globally, but thrive in the world marketplace. The business leg must consist of companies that produce high quality, low cost goods and services that can compete in the world marketplace. The financial institutions leg must provide long term investment, equity for capital formation and credit for capital purchases.

Management 2000 addresses the business element of this triad. It is a structured approach to using the management and technical resources needed to achieve a world class competitive status. The book provides a model that features a step-by-step procedure for implementation of these management and technical tools. We focus here on understanding and responding to customer needs. At the core of all our activities is translating those customer needs and expectations into products and services.

Our objective in writing this book is to offer a single comprehensive guide to businesses at all levels, small and large. We provide a coherent, well structured strategy for any business to achieve world class competitive status. This is done not by attempting to copy Japanese technology or EEC market manipulation, but by optimizing your human and technical resources, without abandoning your values or individual identity.

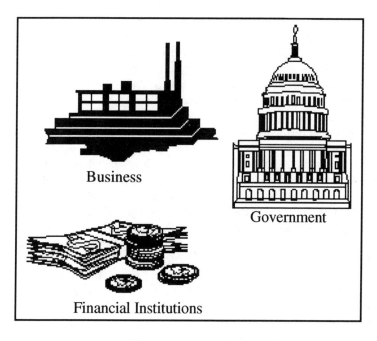

Business

Government

Financial Institutions

The New Strategic Triad

ACKNOWLEDGMENTS

This book is the result of the accumulation of our life experiences; both in the workplace and in the business of life. In our journeys we have struggled to understand and to apply the many tools that lead to Kaizen - continuous improvement in all aspects of life. We have found that there is no single tool nor technique that is appropriate for all situations. We have developed a philosophy that provides focus and helps us choose the appropriate tool or technique for a given situation. This resulting philososphy is more than Total Quality, continuous improvement, or any other technique, tool or methodology that we have encountered. We call it Management 2000.

This is the way we view life and the way we approach business. It is a view of life and business that is constantly evolving as we study what others have done; cuss and discuss with those individuals that are struggling along with us; and as we learn from our successes and failures in applying what we are learning on this journey. It is this constant learning, interaction, and experience that has brought to this point.

There are many individuals that have contributed to our knowledge and understanding by their example, advice and teachings. We could not possibly enumerate them all; we would like, however, to especially acknowledge: Mr. Louis A. Arcangelo, Manager, Product Support Division, Hughes Aircraft Company; and Jack ReVelle, Ph.D., Chief Statistician, Hughes Aircraft Company.

MANAGEMENT
2000

THE PRACTICAL

GUIDE TO

WORLD CLASS

COMPETITION

1

Introduction
to
Management 2000

MANAGEMENT 2000
THE PRACTICAL GUIDE
TO
WORLD CLASS COMPETITION

THE WORLD IS TRANSITIONING from domestic, nationally centered economic systems to the global marketplace. Like the shift that occurred during the industrial revolution, from an agrarian economy to an industrial system, this transition will witness the disappearance of many old organizations and the emergence of new ones that are better prepared to challenge this new global economy. Organizations, businesses and entire industries, that we barely envisioned a few years ago are coming into existence. Many of the more traditional local, regional, and national business organizations are faltering. They are sustaining themselves by selling off assets, preparing only for short term survival and waiting for the inevitable end. The business world is not coming to an end, but it is transitioning and growing on a global scale never before imagined. It is critical

1

to your business, whether it is local, regional or national in scope, that you clearly understand that you are being challenged by world class competitors.

If you seize the opportunity, rather than lament the change, you can be well positioned to take advantage of the transition to a global market place. This book is your first step in the process of placing that opportunity within your grasp.

HISTORICAL PERSPECTIVE

The transitional economic and industrial situation we face today has its roots in attitudes fostered during the industrial revolution. Manufacturing equipment, techniques and processes were imported and innovated during the last half of the nineteenth century. There was a problem, however; this Industrial Revolution created a large demand for unskilled labor. The nature of the manufacturing processes, the attitudes of management, and the historic view of the labor force as essentially unskilled are still with us today. These attitudes fostered the organization of labor unions and brought about labor - management strife.

It was during this period that Frederick Winslow Taylor (1856-1915) developed the theory of "Scientific Management". Taylor theorized that employee performance could be defined by work standards and then controlled by rules enforced by management. He recommended time-and-motion studies for each task to enable management to divide jobs into small, simple, repeatable tasks. This approach would, Taylor thought, minimize complexity and maximize efficiency. It would also improve labor relations and productivity by eliminating the arbitrary use of power. This philosophy prevailed for decades and is still evident today.

About 1931 Dr. Walter A. Shewhart applied statistical tools to work processes. He used these tools to define the limits of random variation in all aspects of tasks. These limits could then be used to define acceptable highs and lows for variation. Points outside of the acceptable limits would be studied for corrective action. An added benefit of Dr. Shewhart's methods was that workers could use their own charting, and thereby gain control over their jobs. This ability to make adjustments on their own would increase job satisfaction, all in all, a win-win situation.

From 1927 to 1940 Dr. W. Edwards Deming pioneered the use of statistics and sampling methods at the U.S. Department of Agriculture. During those early years he also studied with Dr. Shewhart. It was a natural outcome therefore, when Dr. Deming was recruited to head up the new statistical sampling program for the 1940 census, the first time that the U. S. census was conducted using statistical methods. As the head of the sampling program, Dr. Deming also applied Dr. Shewhart's statistical control techniques to clerical tasks.

When World War II began, the work force changed as the world geared up for war. W. Allen Wallis of Stanford University contacted Dr. Deming about methods to improve productivity for the U.S. war effort. Dr. Deming proposed teaching Dr. Shewhart's methods to engineers, inspectors, and other key personnel at companies involved in wartime production. The idea was accepted, and eventually 31,000 people were trained in statistical methods. With this national focus on quality, the American Society for Quality Control was founded at the end of the war. The work force changed again as the American warriors returned.

During the post-war years there was an unparalleled demand for consumer goods. In addition, the management and leadership skills learned in the military created an environment where Taylor's scientific management flourished. The work of Shewhart and Deming, statistical control charts disappeared from the American work place - they were considered time-consuming and unnecessary.

The lesson from this for Dr. Deming was that there had not been total commitment to quality. They had trained only the technical people. The workers and management did not understand the value of what they were discarding. Furthermore, he recognized that it took pressure from management to implement and sustain statistical quality control.

Meanwhile, in Japan most industry was imported and the emphasis was on quantity, not quality. There was a lack of concern for the customer and the intended use of the product. Consequently, manufacturing processes were out of control and there was wide variation in material quality. It was during this time (1946) that W. G. Magil and H. M. Sarasohn taught quality control to the Japanese telecommunications industry.

In 1948, the Japanese Union of Scientists and Engineers (JUSE) established a five member research team for quality control which eventually became the Quality Control Group. In 1949 JUSE began teaching quality control.

In 1947, Dr. Deming was asked to join the statistical mission planning the 1951 Japanese census. The Japanese Union of Scientists and Engineers took that opportunity to ask Dr. Deming to conduct a statistical quality control seminar for them. He conducted his first eight day seminar in 1950. The lecture series was published as a book, and the royalties were donated to JUSE, which in turn used the proceeds to establish the now famous Deming Prize.

Later, the Japanese government awarded Dr. Deming the Order of the Sacred Treasure, second class, by the Japanese government for his contributions to the development of quality control in post World War II Japan.

Meanwhile, Dr. J. M. Juran also was invited to conduct quality control courses in Japan. Dr. Juran, stressing the role of management in quality control, began his work in Japan in 1954. The work of Dr. Juran and Dr. Deming accelerated the movement of Japanese industry into the statistical quality control phase of improvement. The next phase began with the recognition, by Japanese industry, that improvement must involve all functions within a company, and that there must be cross-functional management as well as vertical management. This phase is referred to as Total Quality Control.

Dr. A. V. Feigenbaum first coined the term *Total Quality Control* (TQC) in 1961, when he published his now famous book *Total Quality Control*. Dr. Feigenbaum's premise is that all functions of the company must join their efforts to build quality into its products instead of "inspecting" quality in. Many Japanese manufacturers recognized that TQC was in line with their management efforts and adopted this term for their own quality movement. Some Japanese managers preferred to call it *Company Wide Quality Control* (CWQC); in either case, the meaning is the same. The managers of these companies demonstrated a commitment to this philosophy which resulted in staggering growth in sales and productivity.

For the Japanese TQC is a thought revolution and is best summed up in the Japanese word *KAIZEN*. This word means continuous improvement in personal life, home life, social life, and work. At work, this translates to continuous improvement involving everyone in all aspects of the workplace. This never-ending search for improvement has been applied to TQC itself. The result is that Japanese companies have evolved to a point beyond the original understanding of TQC. They are using what we now refer to as the New Quality Technology, which includes Quality Function Deployment (QFD) and Design of Experiments (DOE). These tools enable manufacturers to (1) ensure coordination of improvement efforts throughout the company, (2) ensure product design meets customers' needs, (3) identify potential problems and correct them before manufacturing begins, and (4) optimally make economically sound process adjustments.

These strides and innovations have helped to bring the economies of Japan and many European countries to the forefront of world class competition; however the "quality programs" have not accomplished this alone. The strongest business groups in the world today are the Mitsubishi Group and Daimler Benz. They are groups whose makeup would be illegal in many countries with antitrust laws. Yet they are not only competing in the global marketplace, they are defining the playing field. They are organizations with the direct involvement of government and financial institutions. World Class Competition is not a game that will be played by any nation's rules; the rules for world class competition will be played under "international rules."

In each successful industrial system there is a triad of support that has brought that success about. That triad is: industry, government and finance. It is critical that each leg of this strategic triad be strong. The industrial leg of the triad must bring high quality goods and services at competitive prices, the government leg must provide the trade policies, infrastructure and taxing system that promote business, and the financial institutions must bring capital with a long term vision.

MANAGEMENT 2000 VISION

The Management 2000 Vision is the integration of all cross-functional management and technical resources necessary to become a world class competitor. This Management 2000 Vision is the integration of continuous improvement tools into a system that ensures implementation in a participative environment. It is this integrated approach that is necessary to achieve world class competition.

Most companies have not even fully entered the SQC phase much less moved into Total Quality Control. A few, however, are moving ahead. They are struggling with the concept of World Class Competition and attempting to leapfrog their progress by piloting projects in QFD and DOE. Others have teamed with Japanese firms; (e.g. Toyota and General Motors), to establish pilot plants where industry can learn the Japanese methods and the Japanese company can learn to operate in the U. S. union environment.

Participative management, a cornerstone of continuous improvement, is in relative infancy, despite the "democratic-participative" leadership principles popularized in the early 1960s. The chief results of that movement was a facade of workplace collaboration. Quality Circles were formed. Organizational development specialists conducted encounter groups and sensitivity training, industrial psychologists provided group counseling and job-enrichment programs. In the end, the workers may have felt better, but productivity and quality were not enhanced.

Today, with the attempts to implement TQM in the U.S. and elsewhere, there are efforts to implement a wide range of management and technical approaches. These are usually in the form of work cells and generally yield dramatic improvements in quality, schedule, and cost. Frequently these start as pilot projects and proliferate in a non-systematic manner. There are, however, very few examples of self-managing work cells and very few examples of effective cross-functional management. There is, therefore, a need for a model to integrate the continuous improvement tools into a system that ensures cross-functional implementation in a participative environment. It is this integrated approach that is necessary for American industry to compete in world markets.

This need has been recognized at the national level. The Malcolm Baldrige National Quality Award, established in 1987, is given to those who demonstrate that they have achieved a level of world class competition through quality management of products and services. Since its inception, it has been awarded to only one or two companies each year. The reason that so few attain it is that so few understand how to develop the corporate infrastructure necessary to create the culture of a world class competitor. Implementing the Management 2000 model is the way to develop the infrastructure to become a world class competitor. The

Management 2000   Vision is, in fact, to become a World Class competitor where continuous improvement is a way of life.

ACHIEVING THE VISION

The management necessary to thrive in the world marketplace includes the application of the tools and concepts of Total Quality Management (TQM), Quality Function Deployment (QFD Cross Functional System), and Design of Experiments (DOE) in an integrated cross-functional system.   The concepts of TQM, QFD, and DOE are hazy and usually shrouded in jargon.   The terms used to describe them, such as *cultural change, continuous improvement, participative management, and statistical process control*, although accurate, often seem difficult to comprehend.   The situation is further complicated by the fact that the experts and the literature focus on what TQM, QFD and DOE are and what others are doing.   They may even provide a Benchmarking matrix so you can judge if you are there.   But they do not provide the specific steps to take, in such a manner that one knows what to do next.

Most companies struggle with these concepts, trying to understand them and to relate to what others are doing.   Until they achieve understanding of what the concepts are, there is a great deal of frustration.   They literally do not know what to do next.   This frustration is caused by the fact that American industry is product oriented and that each organization has a unique culture and set of processes.   These new concepts are process centric and require a different attitude, a new way of thinking.   This frustration frequently is expressed in comments like: "Our process is different."   "We build small quantities."   "I know how to do my job."   "This is good stuff, but it doesn't apply to our situation."   "We are a union shop and you can't do that in a union shop."   "What do I do now?"

The key to overcoming these frustrations and unlocking the mystery lies in the understanding that our goal is to make continuous improvement a way of life for everyone in the company, and that continuous improvement is process oriented.   It is independent of product, service or even quantity.   But even this level of understanding is not enough.   It doesn't tell you what to do to apply the concepts and tools to a specific situation.   The course of action to take is highly dependent on the culture of the organization and the nature of its processes.   This relationship is evidenced by the differences among successful companies: some have improvement teams, some have work cells, or team advisors, some have steering councils, some have pilot projects.   Some call the same elements by different names.   Some companies have these elements but do not know that this is what they are doing.

These differences, in what successful companies are doing, create confusion for an organization attempting to decide on a course of action to change its culture.   The key to determining what specific steps to take lies within the individuals in the organization. It is not the same for any two situations. The task, then is to determine the system that will enable the work force to decide what to do and how to do it. The system must involve the entire work force, as a team, working for continuous improvement, in a cross-functional, participative environment.

Achieving this Management 2000 Vision, of becoming a world class competition, is what this book is all about. It is structured around the Management 2000 Implementation Model demonstrated in Figure 1-1. This model provides the required vision, structure, control, and improvement processes to achieve the goal of world class competitiveness.

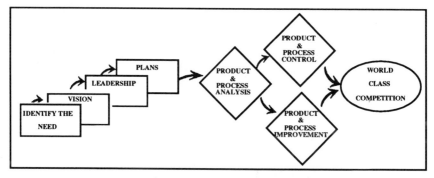

Figure 1-1. Management 2000 Implementation Model

The need to implement Management 2000 is driven by the trauma we are undergoing in industry today. That trauma is evident at all levels within an organization. Workers, supervisors, managers, and corporate executives all are personally affected. As demonstrated in Figure 1-2, the understanding of this trauma leads to the decision that a change is required.

Once again: competing in today's environment requires an integrated change. Management 2000 provides the model to facilitate this change, achieve world class competition, and sustain that achievement through continuous improvement.

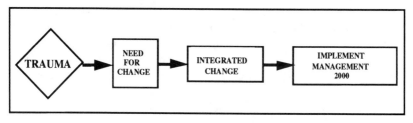

Figure 1-2. Decision to Implement Management 2000

The guiding principles for Management 2000 include participative manage-ment, which means accountability, responsibility and authority in the hands of the individuals accomplishing the tasks. These principles are implemented through the cross-functional application of this systematic integrated model for continuous improvement. The integration of total quality activities and the cross-functional nature of the model may create the perception that this is a mysterious and complicated procedure. It is not. The model depicted in Figure 1-3 is Management 2000 Transition Strategy.

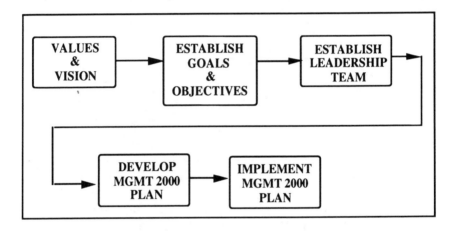

Figure 1-3. Transition Strategy

The Management 2000 Transition Strategy is a guide to facilitate the culture change specific to your organization. The nature of each step varies from orga-nization to organization, but all of the steps are included.   To explain the Transition Strategy we need a company model for reference. The model we use (Figure 1-4) is typical of many companies before they implement Management 2000. Some companies are more complicated with additional layers of manage-ment and supervision: others are simpler. The important issue is to extrapolate the concepts to your organization and not to mold your organization to this company model. This model is in fact a guide to lead your organization, no matter how big or small, to a culture of continuous improvement capable of competing in the world marketplace.

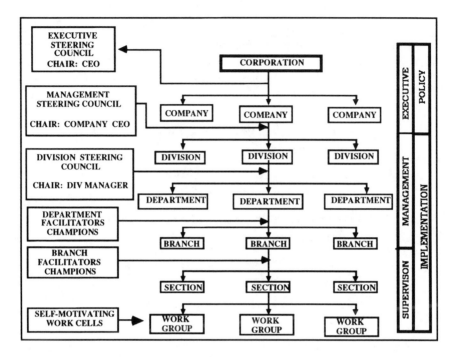

Figure 1-4. Management 2000 Business Implementation Model

Our company model is a collection of divisions organized into layers of management, from the corporate offices to the first-level working group. At the top of the organization are the corporate or company executives. The next stratum consists of the major business units. For our model, these are called divisions. In a matrix organization they are functionally arranged: Manufacturing Division, Engineering Division, Contracts Division, etc. For the purposes of our discussions the Divisions are complete business units. Each division is composed of functional departments, such as Production Operations, Engineering, Finance, Contracts, and Marketing. Each departments is a collection of smaller working groups called branches. Each branch has two or more sections consisting of two or more working groups.

The executive level is corporate/company and division management. The department, branch and section managers are the middle management level, while the working group supervisor is the first level of supervision. It is necessary to provide leadership at all levels to implement Management 2000. Policy and guidance is provided at the corporate, company and division level by Executive Steering Councils. Steering Councils at the department level lead the implementation of the corporate/company policies and guidance.

The Management 2000 Transition Strategy is designed to assist an organization to implement continuous improvement, and to align all company strategy and performance requirement programs into a single, integrated system, thereby focusing its efforts to become a World Class Competitor. The transition strategy consists of 5 tactics:

> **Determining the underlying individual and organizational values**

> **Establishing a company vision with associated goals and objectives**

> **Establishing a leadership team to accomplish the transition**

> **Deploying the vision, goals and objectives throughout the organization**

> **Developing and implementing plans**

The action necessary for each tactic depends on where you are on the journey to a Management 2000 culture. This is a continuous cycle, analogous to the Shewhart cycle. In Phase 1, planning is done to create the infrastructure necessary to achieve the Management 2000 culture. This is followed by deploying the plan (Phase 2). In Phase 3, you periodically assess progress and revise the plans. This action is then followed by deployment of the revised plans.

The beginning efforts in implementing the Management 2000 culture are the development of processes or systems that provide Management 2000 leadership and ensure deployment of Management 2000 plans. After the systems are defined, they are implemented. At this point you are in a maintenance activity for the system. This phase requires different activities for each specific tactic.

The following chapters describe specific details for each tactic. Chapter 1 describes the leadership skills necessary to achieve and sustain a Management 2000 culture. It then outlines actions your organization can take to establish the leadership required for implementation of Management 2000. Chapter 2 presents the Management 2000 method for establishing a corporate/company vision and the goals and objectives necessary to achieve it. It also defines a Management 2000 vision and the specific goals necessary to achieve it. Chapter 3 presents the Management 2000 method for deploying a vision throughout an organization. Chapter 4 presents the Management 2000 Plan, what it is and how it works, and how to develop the required plans for your own organization.

Chapter 5 provides the link between the management and technical tools through Knowing and Understanding your Processes. Chapters 6, 7, 8, 9, and 10 are the technical resources needed to quantify, control and improve the processes needed to achieve the Management 2000 Vision.

STRATEGY OF THE BOOK

The text of this book is arranged to coincide with the sequence of the Management 2000 Model presented in Figure 1-1. As indicated in Figure 1-5, the ten chapters of the text provide the management and technical skills needed to implement each phase of the model. The book is written specifically for managers, supervisors, entrepreneurs and business people of all levels of experience and education.

Topics are discussed in a logical progression which builds to the detailed steps that enable a company to become a world class competitor. The book is intended as a reference handbook, to be used on the shop floor as well as in the offices of supervisors and managers.   It is not merely the what, but the how, to develop and manage a company today and into the 21st century. The structure is intended to enable the reader to follow sequentially through the chapters or to enter at whatever point is relevant to the stage of transformation for your specific organization. The cross-referencing and indexing are designed to enable the user to refer to sections for help as required.

Management 2000 is all about the efficient effective use of management and technical resources to guide your organization to meet the challenges of World Class Competition. This book is the primer for understanding the need to integrate the management and technical resources in a well structured process. The process begins with a clear understanding of you and your organization's underlying values; the establishment of a vision based upon the realities of the marketplace; the leadership and organizational infrastructure needed to achieve that vision; and the planning necessary to implement the programs that will get you there.

The bridge between the management and technical resources is the understanding of your processes; you must know and understand your processes in great detail in order to implement the technical tools effectively. These technical tools enable you to control of your processes using the 7 Quality Control Tools and Statistical Process Control Charts. The stage is then set for process development and process improvement strategies using The seven Management and Planning Tools and the advanced techniques of Quality Function Deployment and Design of Experiments.

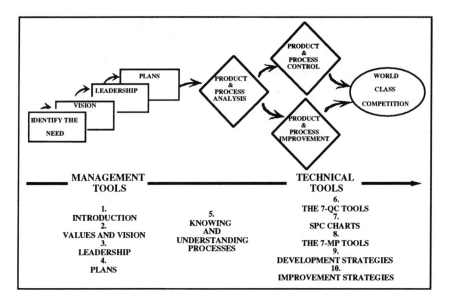

Figure 1-5.   Management 2000 Model

2

Values and Vision

**WORLD CLASS COMPANIES
DEMONSTRATE CLARITY,
CONSENSUS, AND INTENSITY
ABOUT THEIR VALUES AND VISION.**

EVERY BUSINESS BEGINS WITH A VISION, and with the hope that what is an idea today can one day become a reality. Each company's vision is a unique, ideal image of a possible future. It is what the company will look like, feel like, and act like, when the destination is reached. The vision may begin with the entrepreneur that founds the company, or it may be the product of the leadership team of an existing company. In many instances it changes over time. These changes often result from technological advances, changes in the marketplace or changes in the economic or political climate.

13

BUSINESS VISION AND VALUES

In order to achieve a vision, all members of the organization must focus on that vision. They need to understand the vision and believe in the possibility of achieving it. Moreover the vision must be founded on a set of values held by the members of the company. If attaining the vision requires action that is contrary to the values of the members of the organization, they will become dissatisfied and demoralized. Conversely, if the members agree with the values of the company, and if the vision is consistent with that value set, then achieving the vision is possible. The company leadership team must, therefore, begin by establishing the values of the company. After there is consensus about the organizational values, the vision can be developed and deployed throughout the company. This chapter describes how to establish the values necessary for developing the company vision.

Frequently companies publicly espouse values such as " people are our most valuable asset," or the "customer is king," but their actions contradict these stated values. When the actions of a company are inconsistent with the stated values, it is clear that the stated values are not consistent with the true values of the company leadership. This inconsistency leads to a lack of constancy of purpose, lack of confidence, and an atmosphere of chaos, stress, and low morale. Maximum effectiveness in a company can exist only, when the stated company values are consistent with the personal values of the leadership.

For an existing company, the values may already be established. These values may be written, or they may just be "understood." In any case, the actions of the leadership team show what its members really value. When their actions are consistent with stated company values, these values serve as unifying principles upon which all organizational policies and actions are based. This is a focused approach to achieving the company's vision.

Company values, as demonstrated by the actions of all of the members of the organization, form the foundation of the organization's corporate culture. If any group in the company demonstrates a set of values contradictory to those of any other group in the company, the two groups will be working against each other, even though they may have the same goals in mind. The company values provide a prism through which all behavior is ultimately viewed. Groups with different values will, therefore, not have the same perspective in any given situation.

Shared values foster strong feelings of personal effectiveness among the members of the organization. They promote high levels of company loyalty, develop consensus about organizational goals, and develop a strong sense of ownership and caring about the company. These shared values are the foundation for focusing the organization to achieve a vision. Hence, the vitality of the organization depends on, and is directly proportional to, the existence of a set of values that are shared by all. It is imperative, therefore, that every member of the organization know and subscribe to the company values.

DEVELOPING ORGANIZATIONAL VALUES

The company needs to develop its organizational values as soon as possible. Even if the company has already been established but the organizational values have not, it is never too late to start. The organizational values should be basic truths that are virtually impossible to refute. In addition, the values need to be simply stated so they can be easily understood and implemented. These values become the gauge by which the organizational vision is measured, and by which the employees judge the action of the leaders of the company.

The leaders of the organization have the responsibility of establishing its values. The leaders are also responsible for ensuring that all employees know and understand the values. The set of organizational values is made up of two subsets: (1) values that are peculiar to your organization, business, or market, and (2) core values that are necessary for implementation of Management 2000 in any business environment. The leadership team establishes the first subset, called supplementary values, by determining what is important to them and to their constituents. These values are usually business-specific. Often they refer to products, capabilities, or markets. The brainstorming method described in Chapter 8 can be used for establishing these values. The following are examples of business-specific values established by some U.S. firms:

> **Focus on Global Markets.**

> **Maintain commercial product lines instead of military.**

> **Sell by demonstration.**

> **Provide high-technology solutions to Department of Defense requirements.**

Successful world class leaders and their organizations need to subscribe to the following core values, which are defined and discussed below:

> **Be ethical in all dealings with customers, suppliers, and   one another.**

➤ Practice participate management at all   levels.

➤ Ensure fact-based decision making.

➤ Practice collaborative goal and objective   setting.

➤ Maintain a commitment to customer satisfaction.

Be Ethical

In an ever-expanding global economy, the trust bond between you, your customers, your suppliers, your employees, and your community is critical to your success. This trust bond is based upon your ethical behavior, and your reputation for integrity. A company must demonstrate the highest standards of social and professional ethics to be a world class competitor.

This level of ethical behavior extends beyond what is required by law, to doing what is right. A high ethical standard must form the foundation of the business practices of the world class competitor. This recommendation is not just a cliché. It is based on sound business principles:

➤ Relationships with suppliers, customers, and employees are more effective.

➤ Individuals are anxious to deal with you.

➤ Ethical behavior prevents harmful legal and business entanglements.

➤ Ethical behavior prevents adversarial relationships with suppliers, customers, employees, and the community.

Practice Participative Management

Participative management is the active involvement of employees in the management process. It is an interactive process in which the leader is a listener and coach. Leaders do not abrogate their responsibilities, but recognize that each person has unique talents and can make significant contributions to the organization. Therefore, participative management empowers the individuals at every level in the organization to implement continuous improvement.

The leader in a participative environment is challenged to manage groups and teams effectively. The results of this effective leadership will be:

> **Strong employee/management relationships.**

> **Improved employee job satisfaction.**

> **Improved upward and downward communications.**

> **Active employee support for company vision, goals, and objectives.**

> **Improved business environment.**

> **Improved quality and productivity.**

Keep in mind, however, that supervisors, managers, and executives retain the responsibility to provide leadership.

Ensure Fact-Based Decision Making

Decisions are only as good as the facts on which they are based. A world class competitor needs to apply the most appropriate quantitative methods and problem solving tools (statistical quality control, statistical process control, design of experiments, and quality function deployment), for continuous improvement in all aspects of the business-all processes, and all functions. The benefits of fact-based decision making include the following:

> **It focuses on problem solving, using a rational rather than an emotional basis for decision making.**

> **It provides a systematic method for identifying priorities for action.**

> **It helps individuals do their jobs better, faster and with less cost.**

Practice Collaborative Goal and Objective Setting

The Management 2000 model requires that the vision, goals, and objectives are developed at the top of the organization and systematically deployed throughout the company. In this manner, every action, and decision can be traced back to the company vision. This leadership practice ensures that:

> The company's vision cascades from the top to the bottom of the organization.

> All goals and objectives are focused to achieve the company's vision.

> All individuals and activities are focused on achieving the company's goals and objectives.

> The members of the organization have maximum cross-functional synergy.

> Everyone in the organization knows what is expected and why.

Maintain a Commitment To Customer Satisfaction

Satisfaction of the internal and external customers is a driving passion for the world class competitor. Satisfying the customers means giving them products and services that meet their expectations. It means that the customers believe you are responsive to their needs when they have a problem or complaint. For implementation of the Management 2000 model, this means establishing formal systems for determining customer requirements; using the appropriate tools to translate requirements into products and services; and ensuring responsiveness to customers' inquiries. Ensuring customer satisfaction results in:

> Larger market share.

> Increased customer loyalty.

> Fewer warranty returns.

> Minimal dissatisfaction of the internal and external customers.

➤   **Increased ownership and teamwork among the internal customers and suppliers who satisfy the external customers.**

Establishing the company's values is not a one-time event. Periodically, the leadership team needs to review all of the organizational values. This review is necessary to validate them in light of cultural, social, economic, and political developments. The leadership team may elect to leave the values as they are, or it may choose to refine or restate them. This periodic review will keep them fresh and alive.

It is strongly recommended that everyone in the organization have a copy of the values, and that the leadership team reinforce them continually by their actions and their words. This communication helps to establish the sense of ownership and caring that is an important aspect of the culture of a world class competitor.

DEVELOPING THE BUSINESS VISION

It has been said, "When there is no vision, there is no business." Conversely, when individuals with a shared vision come together, extraordinary things happen. The executives and managers of the company must communicate their vision to their followers. They must convince employees that they too have a stake in the vision, and that it is in their best interest to help the company achieve the vision. Each member of the organization is a stake-holder in the vision.

The most effective method for developing a vision is through participative management. This method involves the key staff members using the seven management and planning tools defined in Chapter 8. The very process of defining the vision this way increases ownership among the executives and managers, and reduces the time and energy required to communicate the vision throughout the company. In fact, it creates a body of visionaries and marketers for the vision.

Visions Need to be Collaborative and Supportive

The vision of becoming a world class competitor can be achieved only if the proper infrastructure is in place, and if this company business vision is synchronized and effectively deployed throughout the entire company. Management 2000 Phase 4, Planning, defines the necessary infrastructure and leads you to develop the specifics that create it. Phase 4 also leads you to the requirement to develop the specific vision for the business and all it's organizational elements. In this way, the vision to become a world class competitor is integrated with the company business vision and the result becomes the future of the company.

With this method, it is possible to establish a vision for any organization or element in a company and then deploy it throughout that part of the organization. Although it is possible to enter this process at any level in the organization, it is most effective if it begins at the top of the company. Only in that way can the entire company be fully integrated. The result of these actions is the integration of goals and objectives that support one another and ensure success in achieving the company vision. These vision statements, goals, and objectives are used in Phase 4 for developing the improvement plans.

The development of a vision is a process like any other. It has inputs, points where the input is processed, and outputs. It is also a repetitive activity, in that the vision is constantly reviewed, clarified, revised, and improved. For Management 2000, developing the company business vision begins at the top of the organization with the executives. The leadership team establishes the company vision, and this vision is then deployed systematically throughout the entire organization.

In the absence of top-down deployment, the Management 2000 technique for developing a vision can be used at any point in the organization. That is, an individual or single organizational element can develop it's vision and deploy it throughout the organization that it controls or affects. In this situation, however, the effectiveness of the vision is limited by the lack of congruence with the vision of the executives, organizations above, and other elements within the company.

The Past Shows the Way to the Future

To develop the company business vision, the team must project itself ahead in time. That is, the team members need to become compulsive about the future. They need to focus on the vision and ideas of possibilities. Their challenge is to develop an image of a possible and desirable future state of the company. This is not a trivial activity; it requires extensive effort, and it often takes a long period of time to accomplish it.

One activity that enhances the ability to project the future is examination of what we know. What do our experiences tell us about the trends in our industry, our technologies, our markets, our customers, our resources? This study of the past is an essential element of the process of developing a vision, for the past is a prologue for the future. Just as the past is a resource of knowledge and experience, the present is an opportunity to apply these resources in developing the vision of the future.

Intuition Plays an Important Role in Developing a Vision. Developing a vision requires that the logical, rational, and calculating (left) side of the brain assimilate data. The intuitive, creative, and verbally inarticulate side develops insight or makes decisions. The left side of the brain then arranges and puts into words the insights or decisions of the right half. The use of intuition is, therefore, crucial to developing a vision.

At work, however, many people act as if they were afraid that their peers would look down on them if they use their intuition for decision making. Intuition is sometimes viewed as a soft, mystical subject that suggests "touchy-feely stuff." Consequently, at work we usually do not admit or discuss using our intuition. The use of intuition is very common in the workplace, just as it is in our everyday lives.

A vision or intuitive insight results from picturing and imagining. This is the process of bringing together knowledge and experience to produce new insights. This knowledge is that gained through experience. It is an understanding of how and why things happen, and who gets them done. It is true, therefore, that the longer and more varied the experience, the more likely it is that the individual will develop a deep understanding of a given set of facts or circumstances.

Intuiting is the conscious or subconscious act of drawing upon past experiences to view a set of facts, perceptions, or circumstances. The process includes selecting the relevant information, making appropriate comparisons, integrating the information, seeing patterns of change, and extrapolating from the present trends to future possibilities. This is right-brain thinking: scanning possibilities over space as opposed to time, thinking in images, seeing wholes, and detecting geometric patterns. The intuiting process is, therefore, an important part of developing our vision. The Management 2000 model for developing your vision is designed to capitalize on the intuiting process through the selective application of the appropriate new quality technology tools and techniques.

When there is no involvement, there is no commitment. The team approach to developing visions ensures that there is commitment by those responsible for leading the company. The team approach also capitalizes on the experience, knowledge, and synergy of your management team. Unless you use the team approach to develop the company business vision, you will need to sell "your" vision to the leadership responsible for achieving it. Using the team approach builds a team of employees who feel ownership for the vision, and who are also "marketers" of the vision for the rest of the company.

The first requirement for establishing your vision is, therefore, to charter the leadership team that will develop the vision. It is essential to use the leadership team so that the vision reflects the entire company. In large companies there may be several collaborative visions, one for each independent business unit.

This requirement to establish collaborative visions exists at each level of the organization. The organization's stake holders must be involved in the process of developing the vision. This involvement builds commitment and ownership, and it minimizes resistance. It is, therefore, best if this begins with the leadership team of the company. They develop the vision for the company first, and then this vision is deployed throughout the company—each organizational element developing, in turn, its own vision, that is collaborative and supportive of the company vision.

You can develop a vision independently at any level in an organization. In this situation, using the same tools and methods described in this chapter, you work with what you know and what you are given. The resulting vision provides improved focus and direction, and can be deployed throughout the elements of the organization you control or influence. This effort will advance your organization toward world class status, but will be limited by a possible of a lack of continuity with company executives and the other elements of the organization.

DEVELOPING A BUSINESS VISION

The process of developing a business vision can be complex and confusing. Here we will develop a structured approach for developing your world class business vision. This process begins with understanding your business and all of the associated business, social, economic, and political environmental factors. This data is organized and evaluated using a unique brainstorming method. This evaluation provides the basis for drafting the company vision. These three steps are described as follows:

❶   **Data   Collection**

❷   **Brainstorming**

❸   **Creating   the   Vision**

Step 1.   Data   Collection

As you reflect on the past and project to the future, the vision will not reveal itself perfectly formed. It needs to be carefully stated, periodically validated, and continuously refined and clarified. To achieve these results, the team members need to establish what they know about their business, their customers, their constituents, their past, their markets, their suppliers, their products and services, and the trends regarding all of these. It is also necessary to establish what the team and it's constituents desire.

The data collection activities are of three types: determining what you know about your business; conducting surveys; and brainstorming. As the data is collected, a team member is responsible for updating a master file and ensuring that each team member has the latest set of data. Each team member then reviews the data prior to each meeting and for completing his or her action items.

Begin the data collection by gathering the "givens." For an existing organization this is information about the business which already exist in one form or another. Some of this information is "understood," and some is formally defined. If any required items are not formalized, you should develop them from the facts you know about your business as it operates now, and write them down.

For a new business this information is developed or the first time in this step. If any items are unknown and cannot be determined, do not despair. All of this information will be verified, validated, and revised in the process of developing the vision. The missing items will be developed as products of the process. Examples of the data items you will need include the following:

➤ **Statements of guiding values**

➤ **Mission statements**

➤ **Firm future business (such as orders and contracts)**

➤ **Plant facilities plans**

➤ **Manufacturing strategies and plans**

➤ **Current market survey**

➤ **Lists of customers (internal and external)**

➤ **Customer (internal and external) requirements and level of satisfaction**

➤ **Lists of organizational and personnel expertise and specialties (core competencies)**

➤ **Employees' desires and expectations**

Although for an established company this information may already exist, it must be periodically tested and validated. If any element of information has not been developed or formalized, now is the time to do so. The team needs to develop the guiding values, list the customers, list the constituents, and perform any necessary surveys.

The team must then review all of this information, discuss it, analyze it and reach consensus about it. For the pieces that already exist, or those that are handed to the team, it is wise to discuss the meaning and implications of each. For example, you could write a short paragraph that describes the meaning of a given item. This understanding serves as the baseline for the next step: brainstorming the vital issues.

Step 2.   Brainstorming

The recommended method for brainstorming is free association. Each person presents his or her idea or response to a given item. The ideas are not evaluated at this point. All discussion is focused on clarification and drawing out additional ideas. Procedurally, each idea or response is written on a single Post-it™ note. After you have exhausted the questions, usually after one hour, the responses are affinitized and an interrelationship digraph is developed. The affinity diagram, as explained below, develops association among the ideas. The interrelationship digraph applies logic to the ideas.

To develop the affinity diagram, have the team arrange the Post-it™ notes on a flat surface like a wall, white-board, or window. The idea is to group together related ideas. It is important that every member of the team participate in this activity. During this phase, there should be no discussion and everyone can move the Post-it™ notes around as they desire. This may seem chaotic, but if you set a time limit (such as 15 minutes) and encourage participation, soon there will be order and agreement.

The next step is to decide on a title for each group of ideas. This title needs to be an action statement. In some instances, naming the groups will require a compromise among the ideas in order to include all of the ideas in a particular grouping. Then you review each of the items under each title, to see if they still fit or if they should be included under a different title. At the same time, review the titles to ascertain if any of the groupings can be consolidated. The resulting affinity diagram will bring order to a collection of apparently unrelated ideas. (Figures 2-1 through 2-4 illustrate how this process works.)

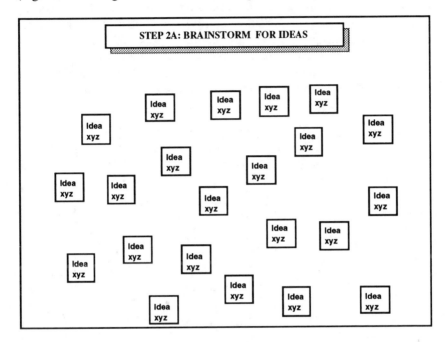

Figure 2-1. Result of Initial Brainstorming for Ideas About the Business.

The next step is to take the titles from the affinity diagram and develop an interrelationship digraph. This is a powerful tool that reveals the relationship among the action statements. In essence, the affinity diagram produces the action to be taken, and the interrelationship digraph reveals the importance and the priority for each. The method we recommend for the interrelationship digraph is a matrix, as illustrated in Figure 2-5.

List the titles along the vertical and horizontal axis. For every item on the vertical axis, compare it with each item along the horizontal axis asking the question: Does this item depend on the item on the horizontal axis? If the answer is no leave the block empty. Otherwise, enter the corresponding symbol. This will result in a matrix with a pattern of symbols. This makes the qualitative analysis of the matrix very easy; strengths and weakness jump out at us. We can easily determine if there are issues that have been overlooked, or if we are heavily concentrated in one area as opposed to another.

When you have completed this determination, give each symbol the numeric weight indicated and sum the columns. The result will be a quantitative matrix that you can use to set priorities. The item with the largest column total will have the greatest impact or effect, since more items depend on it.

The result of this process is a powerful insight into the data you have developed. You can act on this information directly, or use it to develop a plan of action. Remember, this process develops information from brainstormed issues or questions. The value of this analysis is in developing information. How you act on it is up to your knowledge, experience, or intuition. You can elect to ignore the relationships, or you can use them as the basis for decisions.

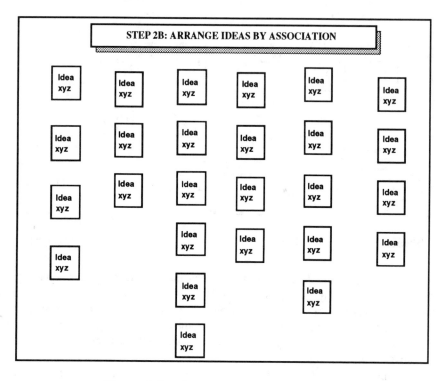

Figure 2-2. Ideas Arranged by Association.

Brainstorm the vital issues   The leadership team, establishing the vision, needs to brainstorm a series of questions. This process develops supplementary information about the vital issues affecting the business or organization. Brainstorming can occur prior to, parallel with, or after analysis of the "givens" and the results of the survey efforts. Before the final vision statement is established, however, the brainstorming results must be integrated with the

survey results and the analysis of the "givens." The following questions are recommended to focus on the vital issues affecting your business, your market, and
your future:

> **What are the technological trends that could affect your industry or business?**

> **What are the environmental issues that are likely to affect your industry or business in the near term and in the future?**

> **What are the economic and resource issues that will affect your industry or business in the future?**

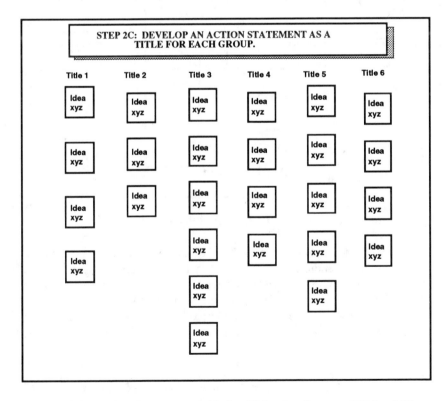

STEP 2C: DEVELOP AN ACTION STATEMENT AS A TITLE FOR EACH GROUP.

| Title 1 | Title 2 | Title 3 | Title 4 | Title 5 | Title 6 |

Figure 2-3. Action Statements Added as Titles for Groups of Related Ideas.

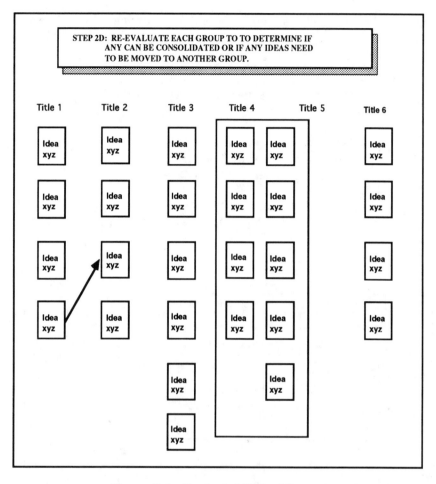

Figure 2-4.   Revised Affinity Diagram.

Brainstorm Personal Desires and Ambitions   A separate brainstorming session is needed to address some important questions concerning the personal desires and ambitions of the leadership team.   This session will develop an understanding of the personal desires of the team members, and will lead to consensus about the desired nature of the future organization and its culture.   It will also help define the future roles and relationships of the members of the leadership team.

> ➤   **What do you want the organization of the future to look like or act like?**

➤ What future would you invent for the organization and yourself?

➤ What is your personal agenda?

➤ What contributions would you like your organization to make to society ?

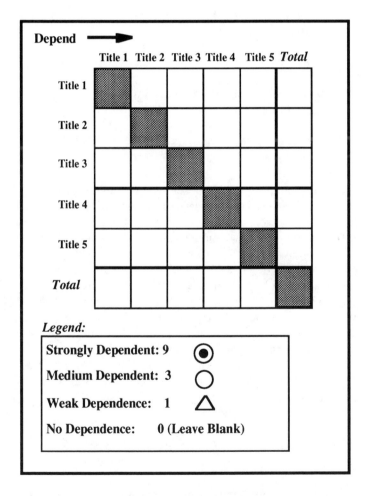

Figure 2-5. Interrelationship Digraph.

Step 3.   Creating the Vision

At this point in the process of developing a vision, the leadership team has a large amount of data about the business. The analysis of the following data will provide the information necessary for developing the company's vision:

> The "givens."

> Customer requirements.

> Suppliers' and employees' desires and expectations.

> Core competencies.

> Vital issues affecting your business and organization.

> Personal desires and ambitions of the leadership team.

The leadership team is now ready to start formulating the vision. Reflect on the information collected and begin articulating a vision. Reach consensus about it, and then draft a statement of this vision, remembering that it is a statement of what you want to do—not how you are going to do it. Those details are developed in the deployment of the vision throughout the company, through the Management 2000 plans developed in later chapters.

The vision statement requires time to take shape. Focus on what you want the company to be and do and the company values upon which all action will be based. Write out the vision statement, realizing that it will become clearer as you move toward it. The length of the vision statement will vary, depending on the organizational structure, nature of the business, and size of the company. It is not cast in stone; rather, it is a living document, continually held before the organization, continually tested, and continually modified to adapt to changes in the market and business information.

Effective Vision Statements Challenge and Excite the Organization

The purpose of the vision is to provide the foundation upon which evolutionary, opportunistic change can take place. The vision statement needs to be articulated in clear and exciting language. It is most effective if it is challenging but provides the latitude for flexibility and innovation in day-to-day operations. The vision statement needs to empower the employees. It is the basis for developing strategies and mission statements and for making decisions between conflicting courses of action.

The Management 2000 method ensures that each element of the organization develops a unique vision statement that is collaborative and supportive with the company vision. This uniqueness fosters pride and boosts self-esteem and self-respect. It is very important for a Management 2000 company to establish the employee teamwork and ownership necessary to become a world class company. An effective vision statement is, therefore, unique. It differentiates the company or organization from others, and tells those inside and outside the organization what is unique about it.

KEY   POINTS

All business begins with the belief that what is an idea today can one day become real.

Effective visions are founded on a set of organizational values.

Company values must be consistent with the personal values of the leadership. These values should be basic truths.

Supplementary values are peculiar to your organization; core values are necessary for implementation of Management 2000. The core values are:

> **Be ethical in all dealings with customers, suppliers, and each   other.**

> **Practice participative management at all   levels.**

> **Ensure fact-based decision making.**

> **Practice collaborative goal and objective setting.**

> **Maintain a commitment to customer satisfaction.**

The development of a vision is a process.

The Management 2000 method ensures that each element of the organization develops a unique vision statement that is collaborative and supportive with the company vision.

Developing the company business vision begins with the executives.

The Management 2000 technique for developing a vision can be used at any point in the organization, but the effectiveness of a vision is limited if there is a lack of congruence with the vision of the executives and organizations above.

To develop the company business vision, the leadership team must focus on the future.

The study of the past is essential element to developing a vision.

Intuition is an important element in the vision development process.

The team approach to developing visions ensures commitment by those responsible for leading the company.

Data collection is an essential step for developing your vision. Data collection activities include determining what you know about your business and brainstorming vital issues.

The vision statement defines what you want to do, not how you will to do it.

Focus on what you want the company to be and do and on the company values upon which all action is based.

Effective vision statements challenge and excite the organization.

EXAMPLE

The President of Leander Wiles Company Inc. (LWCI), Mr. Ohmar Leander, has determined that he needs to implement the Management 2000 Model. In order to establish a world class vision for his company, he must first determine the underlying values of the company leadership. He has established a team to make this determination, including the principal staff members and the managers of the three operating divisions.

LWCI LEADERSHIP TEAM

Mr. Ohmar Leander: President, Team Leader

Mr. Hurbert Wiles: Vice President and General Manager, Machine Tool Division.

Mr. Lester Hammond: General Manager, Electronics Division

Mr. Jeffrey Bernstein: General Manager, Production Machinery Division

Ms. Rita Sanches: Company Controller

Ms. Lucille Rowan: Manager, Human Resources

Mr. Frank Barret: Manager, Company Safety

Mr. George Kickncount: QA Manager

Ms. Linda Johnston: Marketing Manager

In preparation for this event Mr. Leander and Mr. Wiles requested that all managers and principal staff members read *Management 2000*. The team is, therefore, familiar with the methods and approaches in this model. Mr. Leander and Mr. Wiles are training the company staff and division managers using the text. Mr. Leander plans to lead and facilitate the team through the first phases of implementation.

In the course of the first meeting they discussed what their objectives as the leadership team were; how they would operate as a team; what the time frame for actions was; and what their respective roles would be. In two subsequent meetings, they were able to develop their values into clear statements describing the underlying values of the leadership team. These statements define the company's underlying values.

Example Figure 2-1 reflects the results of the initial brainstorming session. These results reflect the team members' individual values, ranging from the Management 2000 core values to such personal values as power and personal position.

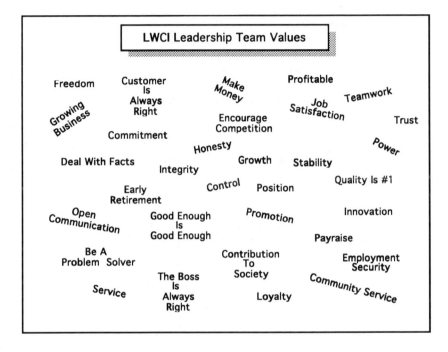

Example Figure 2-1. Result of brainstorming individual values.

From these individual values, the team was able to gain consensus on a set of company values that include the required core values. The company values are:

➤ **Being ethical in all dealings with customers, suppliers, and one another.**

➤ **Practicing participative management at all levels.**

➤ **Ensuring fact-based decision making.**

➤ Practicing collaborative goal and objective setting.

➤ Maintaining a commitment to customer satisfaction.

➤ Providing a stable work environment.

➤ Promoting customer, supplier, and employee loyalty.

➤ Ensuring profitability.

➤ Providing a positive contribution to society.

LWCI has identifying several important company values, in addition to the core values required to implement Management 2000. The additional values were explained by the team as follows:

Providing a stable work environment. This value includes the stability of the organization, job security, and promotion opportunities.

Customer, supplier, and employee loyalty.   Building loyalty is an important part of the way we do business at LWCI. Loyalty is a commodity that can be banked and traded.

Profitability. LWCI is in business to make money.

Providing a positive contribution to society. This company provides products and services that are needed and useful to our society. We accomplish this result in a safe and environmentally conscious manner. Collectively, these core and supplemental values are the standard against which the vision, goals, and objectives of LWCI are established and measured.

The President of Leander Wiles Company Inc., (LWCI), Mr. Ohmar Leander, can now establish a corporate vision. To accomplish this he led his management team in determining the underlying values of the company leadership. In subsequent meetings they focused on collecting the information necessary for developing the vision:

> Statement of guiding values

> Existing mission statements

> Orders and contracts

> Plant facilities plans

> Manufacturing strategies and plans

> Current market survey

> Lists of customers (internal and external)

> Customer (internal and external) requirements and level of satisfaction

> Lists of organizational and personnel expertise specialties (core competencies)

> Employees' desires and expectations

Based on the evaluation of this information, the leadership team concluded that there were three critical elements for LWCI business: the existing customers, the customer requirements, and the core competencies of the company.

Customer Requirements

- High-quality machinery equipment
- Tight tolerance manufacturing equipment
- High reliability
- Low-cost equipment
- Digital controlled machinery
- High-quality tooling
- Tight tolerance tooling

Customers

- U.S. auto makers (65%)
- U.S. electronics industry (25%)
- U.S. aerospace and defense (10%)

Core Competencies

- Machine tool & die design
- Production of machine tools & dies
- CAM design & production
- Design & production of electronic controllers

The LWCI leadership team reviewed all of this information, discussed it, analyzed it and reached consensus about it. With this information in mind, the leadership team brainstormed a series of specific questions:

> **What are the technological trends that could affect our business?**

> **What are the environmental issues that will affect our industry in the near term and in the future?**

> **What are the economic and resource issues that will affect our business in the future?**

> **What do we want LWCI of the future to look like or act like?**

> **What future would we invent for LWCI and ourselves?**

> **What is our personal agenda?**

> **What contributions would we like LWCI to make to society ?**

The results of this brainstorming effort were arrayed using the Post-it™ method, as described below. The information on LWCI's existing customers, their requirements, and core competencies were added to the brainstorming results for developing the affinity diagram.

They further refined the titles and distilled this data into five categories, as indicated in the results of Step 2D below:

The interpretation of the interrelationship digraph is used to establish the important factors for the vision for LWCI. The highest priority item is the most important element of the vision statement.   The second highest priority is the second most important, and so forth. In the interrelationship digraph above, the most important element of the vision statement is profitability. The next most important items are world class competitiveness and the focus on the production of manufacturing equipment. These are followed by access to global markets and, finally being a publicly responsible company.

The dependence of these elements is indicated by the vertical score on the right-hand side of the interrelationship digraph. This score is used to determine how dependent any given element is upon the accomplishment of all of the other elements. The highest score indicates the highest level of dependency. In the LCWI example above, access to global markets is the element most dependent upon the accomplishment of the other vision elements.

STEP 2A: BRAINSTORM FOR IDEAS.

Forecast declining business within existing market.

Market share is flat.

U.S. market narrowing.

Technology is flattening.

Foreign competition is growing.

Cost of doing business is increasing.

LWCI is in a good cash position.

LWCI has good credit.

We want to make money.

Increase in size.

Survive.

Stabilize size.

Be competitive.

Keep foreign companies out of our markets.

Challenge foreign companies in global markets.

Provide a stable work environment.

Go public.

Avoid EPA problems.

Develop environmentally safe products.

Expand production overseas.

Consolidate facilities at one site.

Do something worthwhile.

Help U.S. Economy.

Create jobs.

Expand company equity.

Minimize risk.

Become recognized as a world class competitor.

Increase return on net assets.

Increase return on investments.

Maintain a safe work environment.

Example Figure 2-2. Brainstorming for ideas.

STEP 2B: ARRANGE IDEAS BY ASSOCIATION.

- Cost of doing business is increasing.
- LWCI is in a good cash position.
- LWCI has good credit.
- We want to make money.
- Increase in size.
- Expand company equity.
- Increase return on net assets.
- Increase return on investments.
- Consolidate facilities at one site.
- Go public.

- Maintain a safe work environment.
- Do something worthwhile.
- Help U.S. economy.
- Create jobs.
- Avoid EPA problems.
- Develop environmentally safe products.

- Forecast declining business within existing market.
- Market share is flat.
- U.S. market narrowing.
- Be competitive.
- Keep foreign companies out of our markets.
- Technology is flattening.

- Foreign competition is growing.
- Challenge foreign companies in global markets.
- Expand production overseas.
- Become recognized as a world class competitor.

- Machine tool & die design.
- Production of machine tools & dies.
- CAM design & production.
- Design & production of electronic controllers
- High quality machinery equipment.
- Tight tolerance manufacturing equipment.
- High reliability.
- Low cost equipment.
- Digital controlled machinery.
- High quality tooling.
- Tight tolerance tooling.

- Survive.
- Stabilize size.
- Minimize risk.
- Provide a stable work environment.

- U.S. automakers (65% of LWCI business)
- U.S. electronics industry (25% of LWCI business)
- U.S. aerospace and defense (10% of LWCI business)

Example Figure 2-3. Arrange ideas by association.

STEP 2C: DEVELOP AN ACTION STATEMENT AS A TITLE FOR EACH GROUP.

Be profitable.

- Cost of doing business is increasing.
- LWCI is in a good cash position.
- LWCI has good credit.
- We want to make money.
- Increase in size.
- Expand company equity.
- Increase return on net assets.
- Increase return on investments.
- Consolidate facilities at one site.
- Go public.

Be publicly responsible.

- Maintain a safe work environment.
- Do something worthwhile.
- Help US Economy.
- Create jobs.
- Avoid EPA problems.
- Develop environmentally safe products.

Become a World Class Competitor.

- Forecast declining business within existing market.
- Market share is flat.
- US market narrowing.
- Be competitive.
- Keep foreign companies out of our markets.
- Technology is flattening.

Compete in the global marketplace.

- Foreign competition is growing.
- Challenge foreign companies in global markets.
- Expand production overseas.
- Become recognized as a world class competitor.

Design & produce manufacturing equipment.

- Machine tool & die design.
- Production of machine tools & dies.
- CAM design & production.
- Design & production of electronic controllers.
- High quality machinery equipment.
- Tight tolerance manufacturing equipment.
- High reliability.
- Low cost equipment.
- Digital controlled machinery.
- High quality tooling.
- Tight tolerance tooling.

Become recession proof.

- Survive.
- Stabilize size.
- Minimize risk.
- Provide a stable work environment.

Our existing customer profile.

- U.S. automakers (65% of LWCI business)
- U.S. electronics industry (25% of LWCI business)
- U.S. aerospace and defense (10% of LWCI business)

Example Figure 2-4. Develop action statement for each group.

**STEP 2D: REEVALUATE EACH GROUP TO DETERMINE IF ANY CAN
BE CONSOLIDATED OR IF ANY IDEAS NEED TO BE
MOVED TO ANOTHER GROUP.**

1. **LWCI will become a world class competitor.**

   Foreign competition is growing.

   Technology is flattening.

   LWCI is in a good cash position.

   LWCI has good credit.

   LWCI is in a good cash position.

   Be competitive.

   Challenge foreign companies in global markets.

   Become recognized as a world class competitor.

2. **LWCI will be a publicly responsible company.**

   Provide a stable work environment.

   Avoid EPA problems.

   Develop environmentally safe products.

   Do something worthwhile.

   Help U.S. economy.

   Create jobs.

   Maintain a safe work environment.

3. **LWCI will be profitable.**

   We want to make money.

   Cost of doing business is increasing.

   Go public.

   Consolidate facilities at one site.

   Expand company equity.

   Minimize risk.

   Increase return on net assets.

   Increase return on investments.

4. **LWCI will focus on the design & production of manufacturing equipment.**

   Machine tool & die design.

   Production of machine tools & dies.

   CAM design & production.

   Design & production of electronic controllers.

   High quality machinery equipment.

   Tight tolerance manufacturing equipment.

   High reliability.

   Low cost equipment.

   Digital controlled machinery.

   High quality tooling.
   Tight tolerance tooling.

5. **LWCI will compete in the global marketplace.**

   Forecast declining business within existing market.

   Market share is flat.

   U.S. market narrowing.

   Survive.

   Keep foreign companies out of our markets.

   LWCI is in a good cash position.

   LWCI has good credit.

   Expand production overseas.

   U.S. automakers (65%)

   U.S. electronics industry (25%)

   U.S. aerospace and defense (10%)

Example Figure 2-5. Review and consolidate ideas.

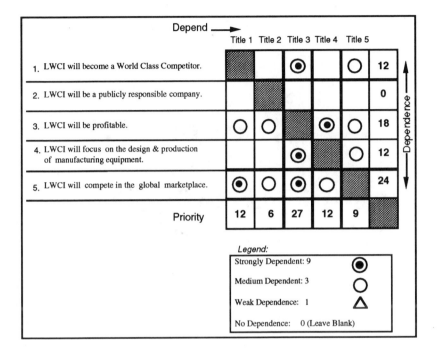

Example Figure 2-6. Interrelationship Digraph.

LWCI used this information to build the following vision statement for the company:

The Leander Wiles Company, Inc. will be a highly profitable enterprise producing world class quality products and services. We are focused on the design and production of manufacturing equipment. We will challenge the global marketplace, and do so while remaining committed to being a socially responsible company.

3

Transition to Management 2000 Leadership

```
┌─────────────────────────────────────┐
│                                      │
│            LEAD PEOPLE               │
│                                      │
│           MANAGE THINGS              │
│                                      │
└─────────────────────────────────────┘
```

TO MEET THE CHALLENGES of a global economy and achieve the vision of being a world class competitor, you must have world class employees. To have world class employees, you must be a world class leader. To be a leader you must challenge yourself first, challenge people, and challenge systems in pursuit of excellence. This active process of leadership gives you the ability to lead change and remake your corporate culture in the Management 2000 model.

44

LEADERSHIP

Leadership is the art and science of getting others to perform what needs to be accomplished. Ideally, a leader challenges, encourages, enables, and provides a model for employees. Leadership is a personal relationship between the leader and followers. The final test of leadership is in the actions of the followers, as their performance is a direct reflection of the leader's capability. Followers desire leadership that is honest, forward looking, competent, and inspiring. The leader works to create an atmosphere of trust among the employees, supervisors, and management. Some basic leadership practices are common to all effective leaders:

> **Always challenge people, challenge systems, and challenge yourself.**

> **Be willing to change.**

> **Provide a shared vision that is inspirational.**

> **Facilitate others to act.**

> **Win respect rather than command authority.**

> **Encourage workers with positive reinforcement. Instill commitment and enthusiasm.**

Leadership is an active process requiring a pioneering spirit and the willingness to take risks and be innovative. All good leaders are learners, students of past mistakes who benefit from all that has gone before, rather than autocrats who need to fix blame. Workers will not follow a leader without a common vision that is inspirational. The Management 2000 leader inspires a shared vision that is accepted by all employees. Inspired leadership is a passion that can ignite an organization to extraordinary accomplishments. Today's managers are all too often naysayers, the source of the final no that dampens innovation and progress. The Management 2000 leader is a proactive leader who challenges the process and the system. Leaders cannot achieve success for their companies unless they achieve success for the employees. Every employee has a vital contribution to make to the company, and the Management 2000 leader facilitates that contribution. By facilitating others to act, you instill a sense of teamwork that will go far beyond the individual relationship of the employee and the leader.

As a leader you must earn respect, as your every action and word is appraised by followers. If you are not the model that they are looking for, all the authority in the corporate world cannot make you a successful leader. People do not undertake a job, profession, or skill without a desire to succeed. All employees potentially are good, successful workers; encouragement is the key to unlocking that potential. Frequent, positive reinforcement, publicly acknowledged, is the best form of encouragement.

THE CORPORATE CULTURE

The ability to lead change in the corporate culture is the most significant skill needed in industry. A corporate culture is the pattern of activities in a company which has been used to influence the employees, establish goals, perform planning and make decisions. It determines the way people perceive, and feel about their organization, its infrastructure, and its leadership. The corporate culture is the formal and informal way things get done. Inherent in this definition is its intangibility. You cannot touch, feel, taste, or read about the corporate culture, but you can certainly see its results in the workplace.

Our current corporate culture is closely associated with the classic autocratic approach to management. In today's developing business world, however, the pure autocrat has become an increasingly ineffective leader. This dinosaur makes decisions without consultation, then gives orders and expects immediate obedience. Since the autocrat does not seek the opinion of subordinates, creativity and innovation are held to a minimum.

The current corporate culture requires close supervision and motivates through negative reinforcement. The work force has reacted to this form of leadership by doing only what is compulsory, seeking protection in unions and attempting to suppress its frustrations. Often we have seen these frustrations result in aggressive behavior, verbal abuse, work stoppage, and sometimes sabotage. In this environment, the basis for legitimate leadership is formal authority. This system is task oriented and places little value on consideration for subordinates; therefore, the development of working relationships with subordinates is superfluous.

To be successful at leading change, you must be able to assess the current culture for your company. You need to establish a baseline of "where we are now." You probably have an opinion of the corporate culture you work in, but this opinion may not be based on fact. The most effective method of assessing corporate culture is to perform a cultural assessment survey. This survey can be verbal or written, formal or informal. Typically it contains some of the following questions:

➤ **What is your career path in this company?**

➤ **What must you accomplish to succeed in that career path?**

➤ **What does your supervisor expect of you?**

➤ **What are the company taboos?**

➤ **What are the company rivalries?**

➤ **Who holds the power in this company?**

➤ **How do you get ahead?**

➤ **How do you stay out of trouble?**

➤ **What does this company really value?**

The challenge for Management 2000 is to be a principal cause of positive change in this corporate culture. This change will turn the autocrat into a leader of people, and autocratic companies into leaders of industry in the new global economy. There is nothing more difficult to accomplish, less likely to succeed, and more hazardous to a career than to initiate change. Therefore, ability to lead change is the most significant management skill needed in business today. Those leaders who develop the skill to facilitate change in an organization will be the guiding force for the next two decades.

Change and reorganization are universally feared. Change upsets the established order; change includes risk; change disturbs the status quo. Due to this fear, change and reorganization are often deferred. The results include a loss of effectiveness, quality, and throughput, and an increase in cost.

Now we will consider the various causes of resistance to change. We will systematically determine the best strategy for implementing change and building an effective leadership team.

EVALUATING RESISTANCE

Managers, supervisors, and employees resist change in every organization. Experienced managers are aware of this fact; however, rarely do these managers perform a systematic analysis to determine who might resist and for what reasons. To anticipate what form resistance, managers need to understand its most common causes. Stated in the most direct terms, these causes of resistance are:

> **Narrow-minded motivation.**

> **Lack of understanding and confidence.**

> **Different analysis of the situation.**

> **Low tolerance for change.**

Each of these causes has distinct motivations and must be understood separately when leading change. By understanding the four causes of resistance to change, we can determine which ones apply to any situation and use that knowledge to determine how to counter the resistance.

Narrow-Minded Motivation

The fear of losing something of value (position, salary, status) is always a motivation to resist change. Self-interest causes people to consider first their personal situations and not that of the organization. The following changes can be expected to result in resistance:

> **Changes that alter an individual's status.**

> **Changes that reduce decision-making power.**

> **Changes that interfere with existing relationships.**

> **Changes that affect salary.**

People often attempt to subvert change before and during planning and implementation. This reaction occurs whenever an individual or group does not view the proposed change as personally beneficial. The resulting political behavior rarely takes the form of open resistance. Instead, very subtle approaches are used and tend to occur beneath the surface, using back channels of communication.

Lack of Understanding and Confidence

Individuals and groups also resist change when they do not understand its implications, and when they perceive that it will cost them more than they will gain. These situations occur most often where there is a lack of trust between the individual initiating the change and the employees. Rarely is there a high level of trust among executives, managers, supervisors, and employees. Unless clear and precise communication, cooperation, and coordination accompany change, these misunderstandings surface when the following types of change are introduced:

> ➤ **Changes in individual status that are not clearly defined.**

> ➤ **Changes that require a level of trust between the change agent and individuals.**

> ➤ **Changes that have been poorly communicated and coordinated.**

Misunderstandings must be recognized and resolved rapidly, for if they are not addressed they often lead to resistance. The assumption cannot be made that resistance occurs only due to the narrow motivation of self-interest.

Different Analysis of the Situation

Commonly, people resist organizational change when they evaluate the situation differently from the change agent. Assumptions are the damaging elements here. Frequently, those initiating change assume that they have all the relevant data necessary to conduct a thorough analysis, and that everyone in the organization is working with the same data. This problem arises when:

> ➤ **Change data and information are not thoroughly disseminated.**

> Evaluation of change data is performed using different methods.

> Assumptions leading to the need for change are not clear.

Low Tolerance for Change

People also resist change because they fear that they will not be able to cope with the new skills and behavior that will be required. Organizational changes sometimes require people to adapt more rapidly than they are able. There are human limitations to the ability to absorb change. Changes that conflict with:

> Changes that require skills beyond individual perceived capabilities.

> Changes that are beyond the training and education of individuals.

> Changes that are beyond the human ability to absorb change.

> Changes implying that previous actions and decisions were incorrect.

This limited tolerance can be the cause of resistance to change. The resistance is emotional, even when the change is clearly in the individual's, and organization's best interest. This low tolerance also surfaces when individual egos are threatened by a belief that the change is an admission that previous decisions and methods were wrong.

COUNTERING RESISTANCE

To fully implement Management 2000 principles, methods, and techniques, it is necessary to overcome resistance to change within an organization. To counter this resistance, the organization must achieve a transition from traditional leadership and management methods to a world class leadership team. During this transition period, all the causes of resistance must be overcome. It may be necessary to apply some forceful methods to overcome this resistance. The following are four strategies designed to overcome resistance to change. The situation will determine which strategy is used.

Communication, Cooperation and Coordination (3C)

The most effective method of dealing with potential resistance to change is through communication, coordination and cooperation—the three Cs of achieving the Management 2000 vision. This method of countering resistance is the most effective because it frequently eliminates resistance before it starts.

Figure 3-1. Management 2000 3Cs of Countering Resistance

Communication   In overcoming potential resistance to change, it is crucial to communicate effectively with everyone involved early in the process. The method is a process of one-on-one discussions, presentations to organizational groups, clearly defined and formally stated goals, and sharing of the facts leading to the necessity for change. The goals stated for effecting the change must be clearly collaborative with the goals and objectives of the organization and individuals. The need for change and the logic leading to a change decision should be outlined, explained, and documented. This documentation transforms the needed change from someone's idea to an organizational reality. Finally, for maximum effectiveness a broad dissemination of all the factors affecting the change is necessary. The communication process involves one-on-one discussions, formal reports, presentations, and memorandums. The ability of a change agent to communicate effectively will directly affect his or her ability to lead change successfully.

Cooperation The direct involvement of potential resisters in the design and implementation of change can forestall resistance. Form a network of those potential resisters who may have something positive to contribute to the change. This strategy is practical if those individuals can perceive some benefit from the change, or if they can limit the negative effects of the change on them personally. It is not very practical to involve employees who are potential net losers in the change process. In the spirit of cooperation the change leader must display some flexibility. Be prepared to compromise with the change network, and do not expect 100% acceptance of your recommendations. Cooperation of potentially affected personnel as part of a change network can bring about their whole hearted commitment. Also, be aware that anticipation of change has some drawbacks. It can lead to a compromise solution if the process is not expertly led, and it can be time consuming.

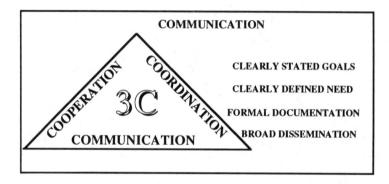

Figure 3-2. The Communication Process as a Component of the 3C Method

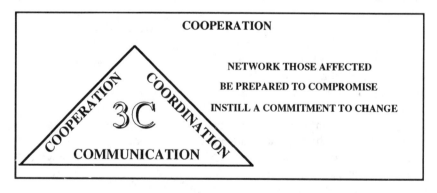

Figure 3-3. Cooperation as a Component of the 3C Method.

Coordination A well-coordinated change effort can help deal with resistance to change by being supportive of the elements required to implement change. This process includes providing the support needed to facilitate change among the individuals and elements of the organization; providing the training and education necessary to implement new skills and standards; planning and structuring the change so that it can be effectively transitional; and, finally, executing the planned change, rather than just allowing it to happen in a haphazard way.

A 3C program can be very effective when resistance is based upon inadequate information or incomplete data. The program facilitates the change agent's acquisition of help from all employees, including potential resisters. It fosters a good relationship between the change agent and the resisters. The program also requires time and effort, however, and it will not negate all resistance to change. The change will always have a negative effect on some individuals and parts of an organization. In those cases, it is sometimes necessary to implement other methods indicated in the following paragraphs.

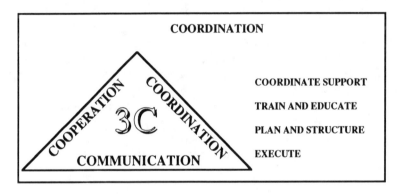

Figure 3-4. Coordination as a Component of the 3C Method

Negotiation and Agreement

Offering incentives to potential or active resisters is another way of countering resistance to change. This method is frequently used throughout industry. Changes in work rules, benefits, and productivity can be balanced with higher wages, early retirement, and production incentives. Negotiation is an effective way of dealing with change when there is clearly someone who will lose and when that individual has the power to resist. Negotiating agreements can be an easy way to overcome resistance, but like some other processes they can be time consuming and expensive. This strategy is:

> Used with employees who have power to resist change.

> Used to avoid major causes of resistance.

> Expensive in time, cost, and assets.

Manipulation and Coopting

The manipulation and selective use of information is an effective way to deal with resistance to change. Manipulation, in this context, involves the very selective use of information and the conscious structuring of events.

Coopting an individual usually involves giving the person a role in the design or implementation of change. Similarly, coopting a group involves giving one of its leaders a key role in the design or implementation of change. This is not a form of participation, however, because the initiators of change do not want the participation of the person coopted, merely his or her passive endorsement.

Coopting can be a relatively easy and inexpensive way to gain an individual's or group's support. This method is quicker than participation and cheaper than negotiation, but there are some drawbacks. If individuals and groups feel they are being tricked into not resisting, are not being treated equally, or are being lied to, they often respond in a very aggressive and negative way. Another serious drawback to manipulation and coopting is that, if a manager develops a reputation as a manipulator, it can undermine his or her ability to use other needed approaches such as the Management 2000 3C method. The coopting strategy is:

> Used when other strategies have not worked.

> Used when change is urgent, and there is insufficient time to implement the first two strategies.

> Not preferred because it can lead to future problems with personnel.

Coercion and Termination

In the final instance, managers must at times deal with resistance coercively. They must force people to accept change by explicitly or implicitly threatening them with loss of jobs, promotion, position, or authority. The employee may actually be transferred or terminated. Like manipulation, coercion is a risky process. Inevitably, people strongly resent forced change. These employees must be terminated (or retired, or transferred) to facilitate the change and to establish a Management 2000 Leadership Team. In some situations, where speed is essential and where change will not be popular regardless of how it is introduced, coercion sometimes is the manager's only available tool. Some employees, supervisors, and managers always resist change no matter what leadership efforts are exerted. In these cases, termination sometimes is necessary to facilitate the needed change. This strategy is:

> **A last resort when all other strategies have failed.**

> **Able to overcome all sources of resistance very quickly.**

> **Very risky, because it always damages the trust bond and leaves people angry and alienated.**

> **One that almost always leads to the necessity to terminate an employee.**

Strategy to Overcome Resistance

Successful change is always characterized by skillful leadership in the application of a combination of these approaches, as presented in Figure 3-5. The approaches must be applied in various combinations, depending on the situation. Most successful efforts share two distinct characteristics:

> **Leaders employ the approaches with a sensitivity to their strengths and limitations.**

> **Leaders appraise the situation realistically.**

The most common mistake managers make is to use only one approach or a limited set of them, regardless of the situation. It is surprising how many managers have this problem. Typical examples are the hard-boiled boss who often coerces people, the people oriented manager who constantly tries to be (over) involved with his people; and the cynic who always manipulates and coopts. The point is that leadership cannot be confined to a single principle. Application of the proper approach depends on situation variables.

COUNTERING RESISTANCE			
STRATEGY	SITUATION	STRENGTHS	LIMITATIONS
3C Communicate Cooperate Communicate	Insufficient information data.	Team building creates change agents and advocates.	Requires significant time and effort.
Negotiation & Agreement	People with clear power to resist.	Easy way to avoid major resistance.	Can be expensive.
Manipulate & Co-option	When other tactics will not work or are too expensive.	Relatively quick and inexpensive.	Can lead to future problems with personnel.
Coercion & Termination	Used when speed is essential and the initiators have power and authority.	Can very quickly overcome all types of resistance.	Very risky; always leaves angry people. Always requires termination.

Figure 3-5. Strategies for Countering Resistance

A second common mistake that managers make is to approach change in an unstructured way, rather than as part of a clearly considered strategy. The approaches to change and the urgency for its implementation indicate the change strategy for countering the resistance. This relationship is demonstrated in Figure 3-6.

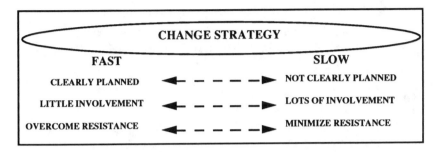

Figure 3-6.   Strategy to Overcome Resistance

Change Factors

The greater the anticipated resistance, the more difficult it is to overwhelm it, and the more leaders need to move to the right of Figure 3-6 to find ways to deal with resistance. This rule is especially true in regard to organizational position and power. The less powerful the initiator in respect to the resisters the farther to the left of Figure 3-6 he or she must move. The stronger the position of the change agent, the farther to the right he can move. This is especially true with organizational position and power. The greater the short-run risk for organizational performance and survival if the present situation is not changed, the more the initiator must move to the left of the strategy. The strategic change approaches depend on four basic factors:

> **The amount and kind of resistance that is anticipated.** If resistance is strong, move to the right of the strategy; if there is less resistance, move to the left of the strategy.

> **The position of the initiator with respect to the resisters.** If it is a strong position, move to the left of the strategy; for a weaker position, move to the right of the strategy.

> **The availability of relevant data.** If there is excellent, well documented basis for change, move to the left of

the strategy; for poor or limited documentation, move to the right.

➤ **The stakes involved.** Higher stakes for the individual and the company require that you move the strategy to the right; for lower risk, move the strategy to the left.

Implications for Managers

All of the factors previously discussed have implications for managers leading change. To determine what these implications are and how they will affect your change efforts, you need to conduct an analysis of the factors relevant to producing the needed change. This analysis focuses on the potential resistance to change:

➤ **Determining how and where within an organization each of the methods for countering resistance needs to be applied.**

➤ **Selecting a change strategy, based upon the previous analysis, specifying where on the strategic continuum the strategy will lie.**

➤ **Monitoring the implementation process.**

No matter how well the initial strategy and tactics are planned, something unexpected will occur. It is always necessary to adjust the strategy and methods as the change process progresses. The leader of any change effort can significantly improve their chances of success by:

➤ **Conducting an organizational analysis.**

➤ **Evaluating the factors relevant to producing the needed change.**

➤ **Selecting the methods to be applied.**

➤ **Selecting a change strategy.**

➤ **Monitoring the implementation process.**

Interpersonal skills are a key to this method, but not even the most outstanding leadership will make up for a poor choice of strategy, lack of planning, or ineffectively applied methods for overcoming change. And in an industrial world that is becoming more and more dynamic, the consequences of poor change leadership will become increasingly severe.

MANAGEMENT 2000 LEADERSHIP

Four basic principles facilitate the implementation of a Management 2000 leadership team. These principles are aimed at developing the trust necessary to lead change successfully. This special relationship between the leader and the follower is in sharp contrast to the traditional relationship of autocrat and employee.

> ➤ **The trust bond.** The entire leadership process is built around an open and honest relationship on the part of both the supervisor and the employee.

> ➤ **Understanding.** Employees comply not because they are made to do so, but because they understand the requirements and are in turn understood by the manager.

> ➤ **Self-Government.** People strive for the right and privilege to make their own decisions. They resent being manipulated, controlled, or coerced into making a decision, even if it is a good decision.

> ➤ **Problem Solving.** Let employees be problem solvers. Do not solve all problems by fiat. Employees will resent such solutions and resent the manager who imposes them. Let the employees be part of the problem solving team.

These principles allow employees to exercise optimum expression at work and to become active, contributing members of the organization. When employees are more active than passive; when they are more independent than dependent; exercise control rather than being controlled, they feel accepted and respected. As a result, they maximize their contributions to the company. As employees experience these management principles, a trust bond is formed that facilitates effective team building.

It may be difficult for managers who are held responsible for results and who are "in-charge movers," to drop old habits and suddenly become interactive leaders. There must be a realization, gradual or sudden, that change is necessary. Like all change, this does not come easily. It is a process of mistakes and failures, an opportunity to learn and grow. Always keep in mind that "actions speak louder than words." Do not attempt interactive management unless you are capable of trusting your employees and can give them the opportunity to be team members.

Transition Process

There is a four-step process to structure the transition to world class leadership. This structure makes it easier to establish an effective team, lead change, and overcome resistance.

❶   Form the trust bond.

❷   Establish a leadership transition team.

❸   Develop the transition plan.

❹   Follow through.

Step 1. Form the Trust Bond   Mutual respect and understanding are prerequisites to team building and joint problem solving. The development of a firm trust bond relationship with your employees is the foundation of interactive management. Under these conditions, employees can participate without the concern of being exploited. These extraordinary levels of trust are not always required in routine work situations, but trust is always required within the leadership team to accomplish change.

To develop and deepen a trust relationship, the leader must take the initiative. The foundation of mutual trust is the belief that the other person has integrity. This belief is demonstrated by keeping commitments and delivering on promises. The leader must initiate this demonstration of trust. The commitment to trust must be public, visible, and tangible.

➢   **Be inclusive. Always say "we" or "the team."**

➤   **Create ways for people to collaborate and work together.**

➤   **Take a clear risk to demonstrate your trust in others.**

➤   **Delegate authority and responsibility.**

➤   **Focus on the opportunity to succeed.**

➤   **Always demonstrate integrity, by keeping your commitments and promises.**

Trust is a two-way function. You must display that you have trust in others and keep your commitments and promises before they will, in turn, trust you. Sowing the seeds of trust will reap a rich harvest of collaboration and lead to accomplishing extraordinary things in change and transition.

Step 2. Establish a Transition Team Involvement leads to commitment. It is essential, therefore, that you involve the company's leaders in the transition to Management 2000 leadership. This involvement needs to be accomplished immediately after a strong trust bond has been established. Involvement also reinforces the trust bond.

In forming the leadership transition team, involve employees from every level of the company. The more leaders and employees are involved, the broader the buy-in will be for the new culture. This approach increases the number of advocates and reduces the resistance for the new culture. The team relationship provides for symbiotic change in that it provides support for the change process from the top down and from the bottom up. It also provides for synergistic change, in that the some of the whole is greater than the sum of the parts.

The most effective method of involving others in the transition process is the Management 2000 3C strategy. In this strategy, effective communication, cooperation, and coordination are used as tools to build the framework to accomplish the change necessary for the transition. This strategy also provides a clear charter for the transition team.

Once this team is formed, you must provide training in the company vision, the underlying values of the company, and Management 2000 leadership. The following specific actions can be used to build a transition team:

➤   **Assign company leaders at all levels to the transition team.**

➤   **Provide a clear charter for change.**

➤   **Provide training and facilitating.**

Step 3. Develop a Plan of Action The company leadership team works together to plan the change. The major role of the leader here is to facilitate, to keep the process on track, and to allow the team to solve the transition problems. The newly derived plan of action will be mutually beneficial to the extent that it is founded on the goals and objectives of the team. It is important that the interactive manager act as a guide in this process, not as a controller, manipulator, or director. A solution discovered by the transition team is personally meaningful to each employee, and is likely to be implemented enthusiastically.

➤   **Perform a cultural survey.**

➤   **Compare the survey results to the Management 2000 leadership principles.**

➤   **Develop transition strategy to establish the Management 2000 leadership principles.**

➤   **Implement the strategy.**

Step 4. Follow Through This must be the leader's commitment to the transition team. In Step 3 the team developed a plan for accomplishment of the transition. You must now provide the resources and personal commitment to make it happen. The progress of the transition team must be periodically reviewed in relationship to the plan. The team efforts to accomplish the leadership transition must be publicly recognized and rewarded. This recognition reinforces, for the employees, the company's commitment to the Management 2000 leadership principles. Reinforcement encourages others in the company to emulate these leadership principles and reduces potential resistance.

➤   **Periodically review the status of the transition and measure that against the plan.**

➤ **Provide the needed resources for the transition team.**

➤ **Provide awards and recognition for the transition team.**

THE MANAGEMENT 2000 LEADERSHIP CHALLENGE

The challenge to the Management 2000 leader is in the transformation from a manager to a leader, with the ability to lead teams effectively so that every group can identify and make decisions related to its activity. We can no longer be sustained by superior technology alone; we must become superior leaders. This leadership must be a managed process, for participation will not occur by itself, nor can it be forced. Responsibility and involvement are the keys. Successful teams are fully integrated into the business goals and objectives of an organization, and every team member has collaborative individual goals. Management 2000 leadership involves all employees.

As an organization, you must be prepared for a deluge of participation. Do not implement Management 2000 leadership unless you want to be extensively involved. If Management 2000 leadership is to work, there are several things you should be prepared to do:

➤ **Be prepared to share power, authority, and responsibility.**

➤ **Build mutual trust and respect.**

➤ **Provide formal training in team building, process analysis, and problem solving.**

➤ **View all tasks as a cooperative undertaking with participation of management, supervisors, and employees. Be willing to accept consensus decisions, and at the same time be willing to reject solutions that are not beneficial.**

➤ **Be willing to decentralize the decision-making process.**

➤ **Get out of the finger-pointing mode of fault finding. You will learn quickly that progress is much more important than authority.**

➤ **Believe that everyone can have good ideas, and that combining these good ideas into consensus is productive and profitable.**

➤ **Chase fear out of your workplace. The work environment is conducive to developing employee loyalty. That loyalty is a hard currency that is banked, saved, and traded upon, just as cash receivables are.**

➤ **Organized labor is an interactive part of the program and participates in the leadership team.**

➤ **This is a long-term commitment, just as the acceptance of the Management 2000 vision is a strategic business decision.**

With the implementation of these methods and the Management 2000 leadership team, quality and productivity will be improved, and two way communication will improve. A stronger leader/employee relationship will also develop, and overall morale will improve. Problem solving will occur at all levels of the organization, and problems will be solved before they become priority issues for management.

When you become a Management 2000 leader and decide to implement this leadership team, do not assume that employees and unions will be roadblocks. In fact, in case after case, rank and file employees and their unions have willingly participated in these programs. Supervisors and front-line managers typically offer the most resistance. They resist these programs for several reasons: they feel threatened by the loss of authority; they do not understand the program or its effects; they perceive this as a high-risk activity to them personally; and, finally, they do not see the benefit to themselves.

You can avoid this problem by the methods explained here. Remember that these supervisors and managers are individuals, just like the other employees in the company. The Management 2000 process cannot be dictated to them. First, lead the change by using the 3C method and gain the support of these supervisors and managers. It cannot be over-emphasized that the active participation of this level of management is crucial to successful Management

2000 leadership. You can effectively implement a Management 2000 leadership team by taking the following actions:

➤ **Education.** Managers, supervisors, and employees must be working from the same plans, with the same tools, and using the same process. Training in the problem-solving and decision-making processes will accomplish this result.

➤ **Clearly defined structure.** All employees at all levels must clearly understand where they fit in the organization and its structure. They must know what is expected of them and how results will be measured. The supervisor's and manager's job descriptions must reflect the need for Management 2000 leadership.

➤ **Rewards.** A system of rewards and corrective action must be implemented. Top management needs to review very carefully the company reward and corrective action programs. In a Management 2000 environment, the responsibility of the manager is not always clearly visible, so it can be difficult to recognize poor performance by managers. This disadvantage is offset by fewer clear errors being made by consensus decision making.

➤ **Get everyone aboard early.** It is important to involve all levels of management and supervision from the beginning.

➤ **Networking.** The most convincing argument for the implementation is made by the peer group. Establishing networks that encourage peer groups to review and interchange ideas about Management 2000 is an effective way of convincing others of its value.

➤ **Live it.** The best way to convince everyone, at all levels, of the value of Management 2000 management is to become a part of Management 2000 yourself.

➤ **Domino Theory.** As the work-related decision responsibility moves lower and lower in an organization,
authority also must move down. This delegation of
authority will strengthen the position and prestige of the
employees.

CAUTION

DO NOT CONFUSE MANAGEMENT 2000 LEADERSHIP WITH PERMISSIVENESS !

LEADERSHIP INFRASTRUCTURE

Steering councils, facilitators, and Implementation Teams are needed to provide the leadership to create a Management 2000 company culture.   Steering
councils function at the executive and management levels of an organization.
These councils develop the vision for the organization, and provide the policy
and guidance to deploy the vision throughout the company.   Facilitators provide the technical assistance. Implementing teams provide front-line emphasis
for implementation as the organization makes the transition to a world class
competitor.

The steering councils function at the executive and management levels of
an organization. The executive steering council establishes the Management
2000 vision for the company. This vision is translated into policy to be deployed throughout the company. In larger organizations a division steering
council is also as an executive council, they also providing policy and guidance. The management steering councils provide the planning and actions necessary to implement the company vision and the executive policy and guidance.
The activities at this level are the "nuts and bolts" implementation and are,
therefore, of interest to the department managers and their staff. These are, after all, the day-to-day responsibilities and activities of the department managers, branch heads, section heads, and supervisors.

Executive Steering Council

The members of the company executive steering council are the company executives, division managers, and a corporate total quality manager. The
council is chaired by the chief executive or by his or her designated alternate.

The company total quality manager is a non-voting member and serves as the council facilitator. The company executive steering council is responsible for developing the corporate and company vision. This council also is responsible for developing the infrastructure to ensure deployment and implementation of the vision throughout the organization. Additionally, the executive steering council identifies and implements appropriate company-level improvement projects.

Division Steering Councils

The division councils parallel the company executive steering council. The division level of executive council is used in larger organizations where divisions are independent business units. The difference is that the company executive council is concerned with broad company-wide goals, whereas the division councils are concerned with specific business goals for their business units. These goals, in turn, support the company-wide goals. The division councils, therefore, create the infrastructure within their divisions to implement the company vision. The division council members are the division manager, department managers, key staff members, and the division total quality manager. The council is normally chaired by the division manager. The division total quality manager is a non-voting member and serves as the facilitator.

Management Steering Councils

The department steering councils are responsible for developing and implementing Management 2000 plans for departments and branches. The department council members are the department manager, key staff members, and the department total quality facilitator. The council is normally chaired by the department manager. The department total quality facilitator is a non - voting member and serves as a facilitator at the pleasure of the council.

Steering Council Operation

Each steering council is responsible for preparing plans to carry out its goals and measuring progress against the goals. Each steering council has the mission to:

> **Establish total quality management policy for the division, and create the infrastructure to implement the policy.**

> Coordinate establishment of goals and objectives for the division, consistent with the corporate or company vision.

> Coordinate preparation of plans to carry out the objectives.

> Review progress against goals.

> Review, approve, and provide resources for cross- functional continuous improvement projects.

The following guidelines are suggested for all councils. The chair conducts the meetings and publishes the minutes and the agenda. It is recommended that the council initially meet weekly. Periodically, the council should review the adequacy of its meetings. Are they accomplishing their objectives? Are they covering the proper material? Are they participative? Are the council members working well together? Is the frequency of the meetings appropriate?

It is vital to publish the agenda prior to the meeting, and to publish the minutes immediately after the meeting. In addition to annotating the names of the presenters and speakers, the chair should indicate the time allotted for each agenda item and the type of item (announcement, discussion, or action item requiring a decision). It is also important that meetings start on time and that they end on time. It is the chair's responsibility to keep the meeting on track, sticking to the agenda. This is an important point that is often overlooked. Remember, the council members and presenters are busy people and do not want to feel they are wasting their time. If they do they will soon lose interest and stop participating.

As a member of the company executive steering council each division manager periodically reports to the executive council:

> Management plans for continuous improvement.

> Management progress toward continuous improvement.

> The activity of the management improvement project teams.

> Recommendations for management-level recognition of successes or outstanding performance.

A recommended agenda for steering council meetings is provided in Figure 3-7 as a guide.

NETWORK OF FACILITATORS

A sound transition strategy needs committed upper management support and requires organizational resources—people skilled in the total quality management tools. It is not feasible to shut the doors of your company, create the culture, and reopen for business. The transition must be made over time while you are still doing business. Although all supervisors and managers eventually will be skilled enough to facilitate and champion these activities in their respective organizations, during the transition phase it is necessary to develop champions for the transition. These individuals will operate as consultants, mentors, teachers, and confidants for the implementation of Management 2000 activities. They are the catalyst for the cultural change.

As a minimum, assign a company total quality manager, and a total quality manager for each division. Assign facilitators for each department, branch, or lower-level business unit. How these individuals operate and to whom they report will depend upon the realities of your specific organization. It is essential that their full time responsibility is facilitating. They will need to maintain a close network to coordinate their efforts, learn from one another successes, and console one another after the inevitable failures.

The company total quality manager leads the network of total quality managers. Each division total quality managers leads a network of facilitators. Each team of facilitators, must establish a written charter or mission statement for itself, and present the charter to its respective steering council for concurrence. A mission statement for a network of facilitators might be to promote total quality management by:

> ➤ **Providing training and support in the application and implementation of total quality management.**

> ➤ **Recruiting total quality champions.**

> ➤ **Providing total quality management links with inter- and intra-organizational activities.**

> ➤ **Publishing lessons learned.**

> ➤ **Facilitating improvement projects.**

Once its mission statement is established, a network of facilitators needs to develop a plan of action to ensure that the mission is accomplished. The plan must be consistent with the company vision and goals. Milestones and metrics need to be established, and individual responsibility must be assigned. Remember, what gets documented and measured gets done.

The total quality managers are the principal facilitators for the company and their respective divisions. These individuals need to be knowledgeable in the Management 2000 philosophy and skilled in its methodology. Each of these managers pulls together his or her respective network of facilitators, and provides the leadership to facilitate the transition of the company and division cultures to Management 2000.

When selecting facilitators, seek individuals inclined toward (1) people skills, (2) technical skills, and (3) training skills. Figure 3-8 shows curriculum designed to provide the minimum skills and areas of knowledge required for a facilitator. Most companies develop their own training in these areas, but there are also public seminars and workshops in these skills. It is prudent, therefore, to avoid the *not invented here* trap.

The level of expertise required in the listed topics depends on the involvement of the individual facilitator and the nature of the processes with which he or she is involved. Appendix B provides a bibliography of recommended reading.

IMPLEMENTATION TEAMS

The executive and management steering councils provide the vision, policy, and planning to accomplish the transition to a world class leadership team. The hands on transformation is accomplished by implementation teams. These implementation teams have the task of transforming the vision, policy, and planning into action. Implementation teams are formed at any level of an organization. The company staff establishes a team to transform staff functions; management teams are formed to enhance the decision making process and most frequently teams will be formed at the process level for products and services. There are also permanent project specific teams such as work cells, developing specific improvements or teams for continuously measuring, evaluating, and improving processes. Figure 3-9 demonstrates the relationship of these implementation teams to the leadership of the steering and management councils and facilitators.

Leander Wiles Company, Inc.
Steering Council
21 April 1993
8:00 - 10:00

1. **Old Business**	John Doe	5 Min. Discussion
2. **Department Manager Reports**	Jane Manager	5 Min. Discussion
3. **Improvement Project Teams Progress Reports**	# 1 Joe Leader	15 Min. Discussion
	# 2 Jane Leader	15 Min. Discussion
4. **Department Continuous Improvement Plans**	Bob Boss	15 Min. Discussion
5. **Improvement Project Team Proposal Report**	Harry Idea	15 Min. Discussion
6. **New business**	Norm LaDux	10 Min. Discussion
7. **Action items**	#1 Judy Smith	5 Min. Announcement
	#2 Lucille Jones	5 Min. Announcement

Figure 3-7. Agenda for Steering Council Meetings

EMPLOYEE TRAINING RECORD				
EMPLOYEE NAME:	ORG: DATE:			
TRAINING TOPICS\LEVEL	A AWARE	B APPLY	C FACIL	D TEACH
1. Total Quality Overview	X		X	X
2. Statistical Quality Control		X	X	
3. Just In Time (JIT)		X	X	X
4. New Quality Technology		X	X	X
5. Teamwork		X	X	X
6. Team Leadership		X	X	X
7. The Role Of Supervision		X	X	X
8. The Role Of Management		X	X	X

Figure 3-8. Sample Curriculum for TQM Facilitators.

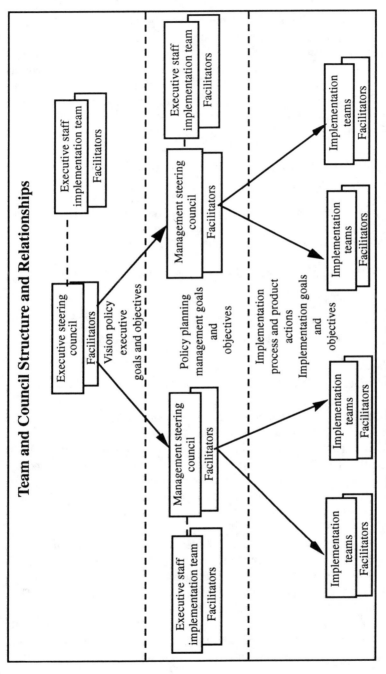

Team and Council Structure and Relationships

Figure 3-9. Team and council structure and relationships

The activities of implementation teams are focused on specific tasks to be accomplished in support of implementation of the vision, policy, planning, or process improvements. Ideally, the teams are formed during the process of implementation and are an integral part of the transformation. The teams are responsible for optimizing the implementation of the leadership team at the functional level where the work activity is being accomplished. As with all the teams you will use while implementing the Management 2000 model, these teams have the following characteristics:

> ➤ **Teams must be trained in the basic skills of team decision making.**

> ➤ **Teams are cross-functional and multi-disciplinary.**

> ➤ **Teams are focused with a specific mission.**

> ➤ **Teams understand the processes that produce their product or service.**

> ➤ **Teams effectively facilitate communication of the company vision and its goals and objectives.**

TEAM BUILDING

Team building skills are essential for successful leadership. In the movie Patton, George C. Scott, as General Patton, gives a poignant speech in which he states that the ". . . individuality stuff written about the Army, in the *Saturday Evening Post*, is a bunch of crap . . . An army is a team, it works as a team, eats as a team, sleeps as a team and fights as a team . . ." This same statement can be made about all organizational endeavors, no matter how large or small. Consequently, all important accomplishments are the result of a team effort.

Implementing the Management 2000 model, the challenge for the leader is in developing and achieving the organizational vision. He or she must determine and accomplish the long-term, intermediate, and short term goals and objectives, including improvement initiatives and problem resolution. These goals and objectives are usually inter-departmental, cutting across many functions and requiring special skills, knowledge, and abilities. The effective leader knows she or he cannot do everything alone. The leader must get others to perform what needs to be accomplished—this means teamwork.

Establishing teams (work groups, task forces, work cells, self-managing teams, councils) to accomplish a mission promotes a sense of collaborative goals. Furthermore, tasks that require people to exchange ideas and resources reinforce the notion that the participants have collaborative goals. This team-work creates a sense of ownership, and people will feel empowered. When people feel empowered, they are more likely to use their energies to produce extraordinary results.

The effective leader builds teams and empowers others to act. The leader actively involves others in planning and gives them discretion to make their own decisions. Exemplary leaders enlist the support and assistance of all those who must live with the results, and make it possible for others to do good work. It is imperative, therefore, that leaders understand the team building process and team dynamics.

Types of Teams

There are two basic types of teams: functional and cross-functional. We define a functional team as one composed of individuals who all do the same type of job in a given process, such as circuit card assemblers, in-process inspectors, or purchasers. A cross-functional team is composed of individuals who have dif-ferent jobs but contribute to the same process. An example of a cross-func-tional team would be all the individuals in the process of building circuit cards or all the department managers in a division, etc. A cross-functional team is preferred for all activities because it brings together all of the individuals nec-essary to understand the entire process.

Depending on its mission, a team is considered to be a management team, a project or improvement team, a work cell, or a self-managing work team. In any case, a team is a means to an end, not an end in itself. It is established to contribute to the accomplishment of the business goals of the organization.
A management team is a cross-functional team that addresses organizational issues, such as planning, policy, guidelines and infrastructure. These teams typically are comprised of a manager or executive and her or his direct reports. Steering councils are examples of management teams.

A project team or improvement team is a cross-functional team established to perform a specific mission, such as resolving a specific problem, improving a specific process, or achieving a specific goal. This type of team has a finite life span. Once the team has accomplished its mission, it disbands. The solu-tions, products, services, or improvements developed by the team are main-tained by the work group that has cognizance of the affected process or pro-cesses.

Work cells and self-managing work teams are cross functional teams composed of all the members of a particular process. They are responsible for completing a well-defined segment of a finished product or service. For our purposes, a work cell maintains the traditional hierarchical management structure. A self-managing work team, by contrast, is a group of employees that assumes a major role in such activities as planning, priority setting, organizing, coordinating, problem solving, scheduling, and assigning work. Regardless of the type of team, the team dynamics are the same.

Team Dynamics

As defined here, team dynamics include (1) team structure, (2) team activities, and (3) team phases. Team structure is the fundamental organization of a team—who the members are, what their relationships are, and what their roles are. Team activities are the generic actions each team must take for success. The team phases are the predictable stages each team goes through during its life.

Team Structure

Studies and experience have repeatedly demonstrated that a successful team begins with a well established structure. This structure includes active management support and a membership with clearly defined roles. Additionally, companies find that teams are more effective if they are assisted by people with extra training in project management, group process, statistical process control, and the scientific method. In the Management 2000 model, each member of a successful team performs one of four roles:

> **Manager/Supervisor/Senior Advisor**

> **Team Leader**

> **Facilitator**

> **Team Members**

Manager/Supervisor/Senior Advisor   Too often, in American business, improvement activities and teamwork are simply allowed to happen. Such activities are permitted, or at most encouraged. This level of support is not sufficient to become a world class competitor. As Dr. Jack ReVelle of Hughes Aircraft Company says: "If there is a problem with finance, the president of the company calls in the VP for Finance, rolls up his sleeves and they resolve the problem. If there is a production problem, the president of the company calls in the Operations VP, rolls up his sleeves and they resolve the problem. If there is a quality problem, the president of the company calls in the VP for Quality, and instructs him to "Fix it!" The executives and managers must be proactive in their leadership role, and this includes improvement activities and establishing teamwork.

Effective teams begin with active management support. This could be a single supervisor or manager who sees the need for a team activity, such as a improvement team or work cell. Or it could be a steering council that determines the need. In either case, the management responsibilities are to develop a draft mission statement for the team with preliminary goals and to assign a team leader and assign a facilitator. Management must work with the team leader to ensure that the resources necessary to accomplish the mission are available, and they must clear the organizational paths for action when necessary.

When a manager or supervisor establishes a team, he or she has a vested interest in the success of the team. Accordingly, the effective manager or supervisor talks with the team leader from time to time to determine how the team is progressing, and to provide guidance and ensure that resources are available as required. This relationship is analogous to a mentorship. When a steering council establishes a team, it is desirable to assign one of its members as a senior advisor to the team. The role of the Senior Advisor is also that of mentor. Again, this is an individual who has a stake in the team as well as organizational experience and clout.

Team Leader The team leader manages the team. He calls and facilitates meetings, handles and assigning administrative tasks, orchestrates team activities, and oversees preparation of reports and presentations. When selecting the team leader, it is important to choose an individual who has a stake in the process. He or she needs to be interested in solving the problems, and must be reasonably good at working with individuals and groups. It is also important to ensure that the team leader is trained in the tools and techniques of the team process.

Facilitator. The facilitator is a specialist trained in all the total quality tools. His or her role is to work with the team leader and the team to help keep them on track, to provide training as needed, and to facilitate the application of the appropriate tools. The facilitator must possess a broad range of skills—group process, effective meetings, conflict resolution, effective communications, the total quality tools, and training. These tools are all presented in this book.

Team Members   The team members are the individuals who form the bulk of the team. They are the individuals who carry out assignments and make improvements. The team members usually are individuals from the functions involved in the process, but the team may also include people from functions necessary to make changes developed by the team. The standing team members are those individuals who meet regularly with the team and who are essential for the team's activities. There may be others, called ad hoc members, who contribute to the success of the team but do not meet regularly with them. Ad hoc members possess specialized skills or knowledge that the team needs to address particular issues or actions. The standing team members should be kept to the minimum necessary to accomplish the mission, usually fewer than eight.

Team Activities

The team activities can be divided into three parts: preparation, process, and results.

Team Preparation   Each team needs to be well prepared for success. The planning stage and includes:

>   **Ensuring that the mission, goals, and objectives of the team support those of the organization.**

>   **Selecting the right team members.**

>   **Training the team members.**

>   **Developing sound plans of action and milestones.**

>   **Obtaining the resources necessary for achieving the goals and objectives of the team.**

The individual or group (steering council) that establishes the team develops the draft mission statement and preliminary goals for the team, and appoints the team leader, facilitator, and senior advisor (as appropriate). The mission for the team must support the business goals of the organization. The mission statement needs to be worded such that it is related back to the vision of the organization (see Chapter 2). If the mission statement does not support the organization's vision, clearly there is no justification for expending your precious resources on it.

The team leader meets with the facilitator to determine the membership of the team. At this time, they review the mission statement to determine the functions affected, as well as those necessary to achieve the goals as they are understood at the time. A preliminary team membership list is developed. As appropriate, the team leader discusses the membership list with the cognizant supervisors of the candidate members, and enlists their support for the participation of their employees.

The team leader and facilitator next review the list of candidate team members, their past experience in team activities, and their training in the team process and related skills and knowledge. Based on this evaluation, the team leader and facilitator agree on a plan for training the team. Training in all cases should be just-in-time training; the team should receive only the training it needs to perform the tasks at hand. Eventually all managers, supervisors, team members, facilitators, and team leaders will have the needed skills. But this is not practical nor desired in the beginning. Remember, all training has a half-life; if it isn't used, it decays.

The team leader calls the first meeting of the team, ensuring that all can attend. At this meeting the team members are introduced to one another and to the team process by the team leader and facilitator. The team establishes ground rules regarding attendance, schedules for meetings, how assignments will be handled, and participation. Training for the team is also discussed and scheduled as appropriate. After these administrative matters have been completed, the first order of business for the team is to review the mission statement and goals assigned to them. They must refine these as they understand the process.

At this time, the team takes the mission statement and goals and develops the scope for the team. The scope for the team addresses to the time frame for the team, specifics of the process(es), details about the authority of the team to make changes, and completion criteria. Quality function deployment (QFD) has numerous tools to aid in this action, such as affinity diagrams, interrelationship digraphs, and tree matrices. The application of the QFD tools is a very effective and efficient method for planning. Additionally, these tools provide a good, traceable record of the team's planning actions. It is imperative that the mission statement, goals, and scope for the team be documented to ensure a common understanding among all of the team members.

The mission statement, goals, and scope are then used to develop the team's plan of action and milestone chart (POA&M). This is the action the team members will be taking. The team must next determine the resources it will need to accomplish its tasks. All of these details must, therefore, be well documented, and accountability needs to be assigned for all activities. Figures 3-8 through 3-11 present some team planning sheets that can be used to document the team's plan. They cover the information that the authors have found necessary for planning team activities they have guided, led, facilitated, or participated in. These sheets are presented as a guide, and the reader is encouraged to modify them for his or her specific situation.

The next step is for the team leader and facilitator to meet with the manager, supervisor, steering council that established the team. At this meeting, they review the team's mission statement, goals, scope, and POA&M to develop consensus. Periodically thereafter, the team leader meets with the manager, supervisor or steering council to assesses the team's progress, discuss resource requirements, and request management assistance as needed. It is also recommended that the entity that established the team meet periodically with the entire team to discuss progress, demonstrate management interest, and recognize the contributions of the team members to the success of the company.

Team Process   This is the stage where the POA&M is implemented. Each team performs according to its own POA&M, and the specific steps taken are unique for that team and the subject process(es). In general these steps are:

> **Record keeping.**

> **Process definition.**

> **Data collection and analysis.**

> **Determination of courses of action.**

> **Action.**

Record keeping is the administrative aspect of the teams responsibilities, and it is very important. It is recommended that the Team Leader maintain a master file for the team. This file typically includes:

> **Copies of meeting agendas and minutes.**

> **Written mission statement, goals, and objectives.**

> **Team planning sheets (POA&M).**

➤ **Action logs.**

➤ **Copies of all presentations.**

➤ **Copies of all support documentation, including data and charts.**

This data is vital for reviewing the progress of the team, developing presentations about the team, retracing steps, educating others about the team and reviewing decisions. In the early stages of the team, it is advisable to discuss the record keeping in order to develop consensus about what is needed and who will maintain it. You may want to designate a team member as a permanent scribe, to take minutes, publish meeting agendas, and keep action logs; or you may want to rotate the job among all the members. In either case, this is a critical job on the team and needs to be addressed promptly. Because this job is so vital to the success of the team, the individual serving as scribe deserves the full support of the entire team.

Regardless of the type of team or its mission, the implementation of the POA&M begins with a process definition—a statement that defines and describes the process assigned to the team. This may be obvious for a team that has been established to develop a work cell, solve a problem, or exploit an improvement opportunity. A team focusing on policies, guidelines or planning also must develop a process definition. A process is best defined with a flowchart (see Chapter 5).

After the process is defined the team determines what information it needs to refine its POA&M and to accomplish its goals. The team collects the appropriate data and performs data analysis. This step requires the application of statistical process control (SPC) for product and service oriented teams, or QFD tools for planning teams (see Chapters 5 and 9). The results of the data analysis are used to derive conclusions and to determine courses of action, recommendations, and corrective actions. At this point, the team is taking direct action to achieve its goals.

Team Results There is a tendency to focus exclusively on the results of a team activity by measuring the return-on-investment in order to justify the investment in resources. This focus can be a fatal pitfall. Effective leaders understand that teamwork is a balance of preparation, process, and results. It is important, however, to measure results, to report them, and to celebrate them as appropriate. Results are what keep us motivated and reassured that our investments in time and money are worthwhile.

As the team implements its POA&M, therefore, it needs to measure its results. Is it accomplishing the expected results? What is the magnitude? Are the results permanent? What are the future expectations for the process(es) affected? The answers to these questions are best determined by the customer(s), internal or external, of the team and the process(es) affected. This information can be derived from surveys or SPC, and it is vital to the implementation of Management 2000.

The leadership of the company needs to recognize the results of the team efforts. This is called cheer leading by some. In reality, it is honoring the team members and sharing with them the taste of success. When you honor a team, focus on the key values that its members embodied in their efforts. Give them public and visible recognition and make sure upper management is being personally involved.

Some companies have public ceremonies or annual recognition days, whereas others have luncheons with the boss. There are numerous variations that you can implement. The message is: do something, but make it personal. All of these ideas are easy to implement and inexpensive, but they are very well received by employees and greatly appreciated. They will contribute significantly to your efforts to develop a sense of ownership by all of the employees.

Team Phases

There are four stages or phases that each team passes through as it matures. The time it takes to get through each phase varies from team to team, as does the intensity of each phase. It is important to understand these stages of team development so that you won't be caught off guard when the normal teaming problems arise. It will also guide your expectations for the teams.

Forming   In the beginning of the team's life, the members are learning what is the acceptable group behavior. They are getting acquainted and struggling with the transition to their new roles. It is also common for members to test the leadership of the team leader and facilitator. There may be some excitement and optimism about the team, but there is also some uncertainty and cautiousness among some of the members.

During this stage, there is little progress toward the team's goals, but this is a normal and necessary phase for the team to go through.

Storming   is a very difficult stage to work through. At this point in the team's life, often there is impatience at the lack of progress. There is arguing, defensiveness, and competition among members or groups of members of the team. There is, however, good news in this phase. The team members are beginning to understand one another and beginning to think of themselves as a team.

Norming In this phase, the conflict has been reduced and the members accept the team norms. They are working together and starting to make significant progress toward the team goals.

Performing In this phase the team members are a cohesive unit, working in concert. They understand the team process and accept and appreciate individual differences. They are performing as a team.

Each time you change the structure of the team, you start over in Phase 1 and repeat all the other phases. The duration of the phases will be shortened, and the intensity will be lessened, but you will still have to do it again!

The following forms are provides in Figures 3-10 to 3-13 to assist you in your team building efforts. These blank forms are also provided as tear out sheets in the work book.

➤   **Team Planning Summary Sheet**

➤   **Team Activities Schedule/Milestone Chart**

Team Planning Summary Sheet

Team Name:_____   Date:_____
                                                Revision:
Organization:_____   _____

1. Team Members:	2. Mission Statement:

3. Goal(s):	4. Method(s) of Measuring Success:

6. Completion Criteria:

7. Achievements:

* Attach continuation sheets if necessary.

Figure 3-10. Team Planning Summary Sheet (blank).

Team Planning Summary Sheet

Team Name: _____   Date: _____

Organization: _____   Revision: _____

1. Team Members:	2. Mission Statement:
List all team members and their respective org. codes. Indicate if they are a Team Leader (L), Facilitator (F), Senior Advisor (S).	Provide a brief mission statement for the team. This addresses why the team exists and may refer to the process and/or problem(s) to be addressed.

3. Goal(s):	4. Method(s) of Measuring Success:
List the goal(s) established by this team. If they are "TBD", indicate that in this space and reference the schedule , which would then include,"establishing goals" as one of the tasks listed.	List the metrics established by this team. If they are "TBD", indicate that in this space and reference the schedule, which would then include "determining metrics" as one of the tasks listed.

6. Completion Criteria:

List the completion criteria for each goal identified. This is where you establish the products and/or services that must be completed for this team to perform its mission.

7. Achievements:

List actual accomplishments, relative to each goal listed in #3 (above).

* Attach continuation sheets if necessary.

Figure 3-11. Team Planning Summary Sheet (annotated).

Team Activity Schedule/Milestone Chart

Date: _____
Revision: _____

Team Name: _____

TASKS	J	F	M	A	M	J	J	A	S	O	N	D

Remarks:

Figure 3-12.   Team Activity Schedule/Milestone Chart (blank).

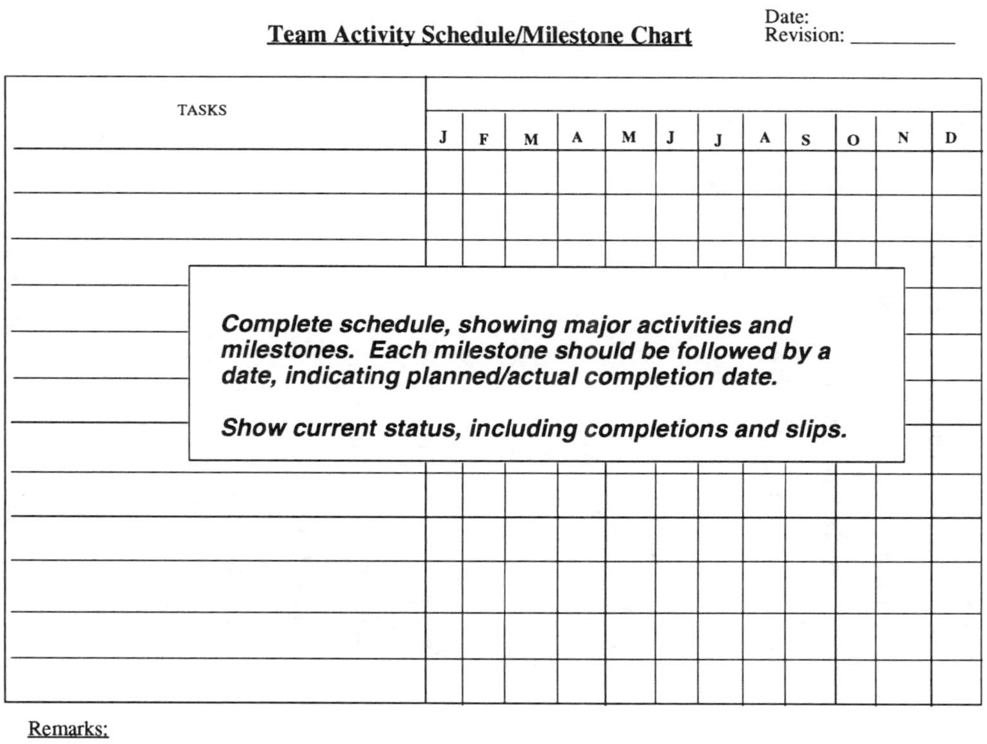

Team Activity Schedule/Milestone Chart

Date: _____
Revision: _____

TASKS	J	F	M	A	M	J	J	A	S	O	N	D

Complete schedule, showing major activities and milestones. Each milestone should be followed by a date, indicating planned/actual completion date.

Show current status, including completions and slips.

Remarks:

Figure 3-13.   Team Activity Schedule/Milestone Chart (annotated).

KEY POINTS

The final test of leadership is in the actions of the followers.

All good leaders are learners, students of past mistakes who benefit from all that has gone before, rather than autocrats who need to assign blame.

The ability to lead change is the most significant skill needed in industry.

The best leaders are effective change masters.

Resistance to change exists at all levels in every organization.

The most effective method of dealing with resistance to change is through 3C:

> **Communication:**
  Clearly stated goals
  Clearly defined needs
  Well documented
  Broad dissemination

> **Cooperation:**
  Network those effected
  Compromise
  Commitment to change

> **Coordination:**
  Coordinate support
  Train and educate
  Plan and structure
  Execute

The four basic principles that facilitate implementation of world class leadership are :

> **The trust bond. The entire leadership process is
  built around an open and honest relationship.**

> **Understanding. Employees comply because they
  understand the requirements .**

> **Self Government. People strive for the right and
>   privilege to make their own decisions.**

> **Problem Solving. Let employees be problem solvers.**

There is a four-step process to structure the transition to world class leadership:

❶ **Form the Trust Bond**

❷ **Establish a Leadership Transition Team**

❸ **Develop the Transition Plan**

❹ **Follow Through**

Steering councils and facilitators are necessary to provide the leadership to create a Management 2000 company culture.

The transition strategy demands committed upper management and requires organizational resources—people skilled in the total quality management tools.

People that feel empowered are more likely to use their energies to produce extraordinary results.

There are two basic types of teams:

> **Functional team: Composed of individuals who do
>   the same type of job in a given process.**

> **Cross-functional team: Composed of individuals
>   who have different jobs but contribute to the same
>   process.**

In the Management 2000 model there are four team roles necessary for maximum success:

> **Manager/supervisor/senior advisor**

> **Team leader**

➤   **Facilitator**

➤   **Team members**

The team phases are the predictable stages each team goes through during its life: Forming, Storming, Norming, and Performing.

During Forming the members learn the acceptable group behavior, get acquainted, and struggle with the transition to their new roles.

During Storming there is arguing, defensiveness, and competition among members or groups of members of the team. The team members are beginning to understand one another and beginning to think of themselves as a team.

In the Norming phase, conflict has been reduced and members accept the team norms.

In the Performing phase, team members are a cohesive unit, working in concert.

Each time you change the structure of the team you start over in phase 1 and work through each phase again.

EXAMPLE

LWCI has established its company vision of becoming a world class competitor. To meet the challenges of a global marketplace and achieve its vision, LWCI must now transition the company to Management 2000 leadership.

Mr. Leander and Mr. Wiles first decided on a method to assess LWCI's corporate culture. They performed a formal, written cultural survey administered by the company staff. This survey was developed from the information provided in this chapter, and was administered separately to each of the three operating divisions and the company staff. The table on the facing page contains some of the questions on the survey:

Having reviewed the survey, the company history, and its current management and leadership team, Mr. Leander and Mr. Wiles concluded that the company retains the same basic top down nature that developed while it was a small business. The basic management style is pragmatic. The corporate cultures of the Tool and Die Division and the Production Machinery Division are both pragmatic, with a structured decision-making process reflecting the company's top down nature. The corporate culture of the Electronics Division is autocratic, and its leadership is viewed as authoritarian.

The potential resistance to LWCI's planned transition will be dependent upon the specific culture within each division.   In the division that demonstrates an autocratic culture and authoritarian management, resistance is expected due to **narrow-minded motivation** caused by changes in individual status and reduction of decision making power. Additionally, the limited communication within this division creates a **lack of understanding and confidence.** This factor will cause additional resistance to the planned changes.

The resistance expected from the other two divisions will be different, by virtue of their cultures and management styles. Within these divisions, some of the required changes will challenge individual skills, training, and education. Therefore, a **low tolerance** to the planned change is anticipated. It is also anticipated that the nature of the overall company, the dissemination of change data, and its evaluation will create a **different analysis of the situation.** This factor will compound the expected resistance.

Mr. Leander and Mr. Wiles, having evaluated the potential causes for resistance to the change, have determined to counter that resistance by implementing three strategies as needed for the 3C program—negotiation where required, and coercion and termination.

What division are you in?	Do you have the authority to make decisions regarding your job?
What is your current position?	
	Does your immediate supervisor have the authority to make decisions regarding your job?
How many years have you been with LWCI?	
How long have you been in your current position?	What level of management has the authority to provide you the resources necessary to perform your duties?
When have you last had technical training ?	
What do you see as your promotion potential within LWCI?	Is meeting production quotas important to LWCI?
What must you do to be promoted?	Is meeting quality standards important to LWCI?
Are promotions at LWCI based on good performance?	Are customers' needs important to LWCI?
Are merit raises at LWCI based on performance?	Have you had training in Total Quality programs?
At LWCI, under no circumstances are you to	Do you participate in decisions about the quality of products or services at LWCI?
At LWCI you **must**	Is it important to be a member of a team at LWCI?
Do you work in a process? The management style at LWCI is :	
a) Autocratic	Do you know the external customers for your products or services?
b) Authoritarian	
c) Participative	Do you know the internal customers for your products or services?
d) Pragmatic	
e) None of the above	

Example Figure 3-1.   LWCI Questionnaire

The LWCI 3C Program

Mr. Leander and Mr. Wiles have decided to implement the Management 2000 3C program as the centerpiece of their change effort. Communication cooperation, and coordination will constitute the first phase of their implementation strategy. The detailed approach to implementing this program includes the following:

> ➤ **Mr. Leander and Mr. Wiles will meet with each division and branch periodically to discuss the need for change and progress of the transition.**

> ➤ **LWCI will establish a newsletter to keep staff informed regarding the status of the change process.**

> ➤ **Changes throughout the company will be documented and published for all employees.**

> ➤ **Cooperation will be promoted by using the company's formal and informal networks.**

> ➤ **Although the basic need for change will not be compromised LWCI will demonstrate its ability to compromise when it is in the best interest of the company and the employees to do so.**

> ➤ **The required support for the transition will be coordinated throughout the company and training and education will be provided where required.**

Negotiation and Agreement

The second strategy used by LWCI will be negotiation and agreement. The Electronics Control Division has recently been unionized, and gaining the cooperation of these employees is viewed as a difficult achievement. Mr. Johnston's abrasive nature and autocratic management style were a principal factors in bringing the union to this division. The LWCI approach to implementing negotiation and agreement will include the following:

➤ Where the 3C program is not sufficient to prevent resistance, LWCI will implement negotiation and agreement with selected employees.

➤ LWCI will maintain a positive attitude toward the unionized employees, and will negotiate an agreement with their union so that LWCI can:

- develop a "pay for skills and knowledge" program

- make changes in work rules to provide greater latitude in work assignments

- develop improvement teams and work cells

➤ LWCI will implement the same changes in its non-union divisions, as a preventive measure to counter resistance there.

Coercion and Termination

LWCI will, as a last resort, use coercion and termination to effect this transition. This method will be used only when the first two measures failed. Coercion and termination will be employed under the following circumstances:

➤ After the first two strategies have failed to alter an employee's resistance.

➤ When a leader's management style and approach are clearly contrary to Management 2000 leadership.

➤ When there is clear and open resistance, by an individual, that will have a damaging effect on LWCI's becoming a world class competitor.

Mr. Leander had several meetings with Mr. Johnston and his staff about the implementation of Management 2000. Mr. Johnston continuously maintained an openly contemptuous attitude toward his employees, and maintained that he knew best how to run his division. After numerous personal counseling efforts by Mr. Leander, Mr. Johnston still saw no need to implement any new programs. He also asserted that he would not allow his position, nor his authority, to be, diminished. Reluctantly, Mr. Leander consulted with Mr. Wiles about terminating Mr. Johnston. Mr. Johnston was subsequently asked to leave the company, and was replaced by Mr. George Kickncount. Mr. Frank Barrett was promoted to QA manager, and his former position was advertised throughout the company as a merit promotion opportunity.

Establishing Management 2000 Leadership

Mr. Leander and Mr. Wiles are now prepared to establish Management 2000 leadership at LWCI. They have decided to use the four-step process to transition their company to this new leadership style. The four phase approach is:

❶   Form the trust bond

❷   Establish a leadership transition team.

❸   Develop the transition plan.

❹   Follow through.

In the first phase LWCI has the difficult task of forming a trust bond among its leadership team and employees. Mr. Leander and Mr. Wiles have personally taken the initiative to accomplish this first step, as follows:

> ➤   **LWCI will conduct regular, periodic meetings with the division managers to tell them about their plans for implementing Management 2000.**

> ➤   **LWCI will conduct "all hands meetings" with each of the divisions, focusing on the opportunities to succeed.**

> ➤   **Mr. Leander and Mr. Wiles will delegate the responsibility and authority for implementation of this transition directly to the three division managers and to a select leadership team from each division.**

Mr. Leander and Mr. Wiles have established the transition team for developing and implementing the transition strategy. The team includes:

➤ **The three division managers.**

➤ **Members of the company staff.**

➤ **Selected first line supervisors from each of the divisions.**

➤ **Selected non-supervisory personnel (from both the bargaining unit and the non-bargaining unit).**

Mr. Leander and Mr. Wiles have given the team the charter to develop and implement Management 2000 leadership throughout LWCI. Professional training has been provided in Total Quality Management (tools and techniques) as well as in team building. A facilitator, skilled in the application of the TQM tools and techniques and in teaming, has been assigned to assist the team.

The team is now ready to develop its plan of action for implementing Management 2000 leadership. The team's responsibilities, at this point, are to develop and document the plan by:

➤ **Performing a comparative analysis of the cultural survey and the Management 2000 leadership principles.**

➤ **Developing the documentation for the transition strategy to bring the LWCI culture in line with these principles.**

➤ **Deploying and implementing the strategy throughout the company (see Chapters 7-9).**

The company leaders will demonstrate their commitment and follow through on this process by:

➤ **Reviewing weekly the status of the transition. At the status review, progress will be measured against the plan.**

➤ **Providing a small budget, within the limited resources of LWCI, as well as basic administrative support.**

➤ **Committing to provide personal recognition and awards when transition milestones are met.**

Through these actions, Mr. Leander and Mr. Wiles have provided for the transition of LWCI to Management 2000 leadership. They are now in a position to create the leadership infrastructure to become a world class competitor. Mr. Leander and Mr. Wiles next established a single executive steering council along the lines of the leadership team. This steering council was assigned the responsibility to develop the vision and the infrastructure to implement the vision. The executive steering council then determined that a division steering council would be established for each division. The executive steering council members were assigned as follows:

Co-Chairs: Mr. Leander and Mr. Wiles

Members: Mr. Hammond, Manager of the
               Electronics Division

               Mr. Kickncount, Manager of the
               Production Machine Division

               Mrs. Sanches, Company Controller

               Ms. Rowan, Manager Human Resources

               Mr. Barrett, QA Manager

               Ms. Johnston, Marketing Manager

               Mr. Frigon, Total Quality Manager
               (Facilitator)

The executive steering council then established a requirement for a division steering council in each of the operating division. The division steering councils members are:

Chairman: Division Manager

Members: Department managers
               Selected section supervisors
               The division total quality manager as facilitator.

In an organization of this size, it was determined that department steering councils were not appropriate. Each department manager, however, is still responsible for developing a plan of action for deploying the division's goals and objectives in his or her organization. Each department manager has available a facilitator to assist in the development and implementation of these plans, using implementation teams. The division steering council has made available to the department managers training in TQM, Management 2000, and facilitation, and will provide support to the department implementation teams.

LWCI established its network of facilitators on the company staff. There are three permanent full-time facilitators to provide for facilitating improvement projects, facilitating meetings, and training. Consultants are used to fill in where the work load exceeds the capability of these three facilitators.

A preliminary report from the company controller (Ms. Rita Sanches) revealed that 80% of LWCI costs are support related. A Pareto diagram of the support cost elements indicated that the cost of the procurement process is high. The procurement process originally was centralized at the company level to streamline this function, and it provided the controls desired by Mr. Leander and Mr. Wiles. As the company grew, procurement remained centralized as a section reporting directly to Mr. Leander.

In addition to the high cost of the procurement function, there have been several complaints from the operating divisions that the procurement process is slow and ineffective. The LWCI executive steering council, recognizing that it is necessary to reduce its overhead costs to be a world class competitor, decided to establish a team to improve the procurement process.

The team structure is:

> **Senior advisor to the team: Mr. Leander.**

> **Team leader: Ms. Eleanor Goodwill (supervisor for procurement).**

> **Facilitator: Mr. Robert W. Freeman (company facilitator from quality assurance).**

The mission statement given to the Team Leader is:

Evaluate LWCI's centralized procurement process, and implement improvements in quality, cost, and schedule.

Ms. Goodwill and Mr. Freeman met and discussed their assigned project. They reviewed the mission statement and developed a course of action:

➤ **Identify candidate team members, ensuring representation from all three production divisions.**

➤ **Determine initial training requirements for the team.**

➤ **Set the first meeting agenda, date, time, and location.**

The candidate team members included:

➤ **Mr. Joseph Dyer (accounts payable from controller's department).**

➤ **Mr. John Everett (line supervisor from the machine tool division).**

➤ **Ms. Jennifer Clausen (electronics engineer from the electronics division).**

➤ **Mr. Henry Beauchamp (industrial engineer and production planner from the production machinery division).**

At the first meeting of the Procurement Improvement Team, Ms. Goodwill explained the mission to the team members. This item was followed by storming by the members. The production folks complained about the procurement process, and the procurement folks complained about the production folks and how difficult it is to deal with the outside vendors. At this point the facilitator, Mr. Freeman, interrupted the discussion. He focused the team on its mission and the need to structure the team process.

Mr. Freeman then provided a short training session on the dynamics of team activities, the team process, and team phases. This short (one-hour) training program refocused the team on its mission, and provided a structured approach to accomplishing that mission.

The team reviewed and validated the mission statement. It defined the procurement process, from initiation of a material requirement through receipt of that material. Based upon the mission statement, the team then developed a series of goals and objectives as tasks for the team to accomplish. The team agreed that this should be a 90-day project.

The results of this meeting were used to initiate the Team Planning Summary Sheet and the Team Activity/Milestone Sheet. As the team progresses, it will continue to review, update, and refine these sheets.

The Team determined milestones and a schedule for this project, based on the Team Planning Summary Sheet. The schedule and milestones included accomplishment of the stated goals; biweekly reporting by the team leader to the senior advisor; and team reporting to the executive steering council. Additionally, the team recognized that continuous measurable improvement in this process would be an ongoing function and would be the responsibility of the individuals and functions within the overall procurement process.

Team Activity Schedule/Milestone Chart													2/22/93
Team Name: PROCUREMENT IMPROVEMENT													ORIG.
TASKS	1993												
	J	F	M	A	M	J	J	A	S	O	N	D	
INITIAL KICKOFF MEETING		▲											
PROCESS ANALYSIS			△—△										
DEVELOP IMPROVEMENT PLAN				△△									
IMPLEMENT IMPROVEMENTS				△△									
BIWEEKLY MEETING FOR TEAM LEADER AND SENIOR ADVISOR		△———————△											
TEAM REPORT TO EXECUTIVE STEERING COUNCIL					△△								
CONTINUOUS MEASURABLE IMPROVEMENT					△——————————————————▷								
Remarks:													

Example Figure 3-2. Milestone Chart

Team Planning Summary Sheet

Team Name: Procurement Improvement   Date: 2/22/93

Organization: Revision:
            Company   Orig.

1. Team Members:	2. Mission Statement:
MS. Goodwill MR. Freeman MR. Dyer MR. Everett MS. Clausen MR. Beauchamp MR. Leander (Sr. Advisor)	Evaluate LWCI's centralize procurement process, and implement improvemets in quality, cost, and schedule.

3. Goal(s):	4. Method(s) of Measuring Success:
• Perform process analysis • Reduce cost of this function • Improve responsiveness of this process	• Schedule to plan • Cost of procurement • Procurement cycle time • Quality (TBD)

6. Completion Criteria:
   • Process analysis

   • Improvement plan

   • Improvements implemented

7. Achievements:

   • Determined mission goals and objectives for the team

   • Instituted schedule and milestone chart

   • Trained team on teaming process

* Attach continuation sheets if necessary.

Example Figure 3-3. Procurement Improvement Planning Sheet

4

Planning

EXECUTIVE PLANS ESTABLISH POLICY AND
PROVIDE THE INFRASTRUCTURE TO DEPLOY
THE VISION

THREE SPECIFIC TYPES OF PLANS ARE REQUIRED to implement the Management 2000 model: executive, management and operating. An executive plan develops the company's policies and basic principles of operation, and develops the structure of the company; including the executive offices, company staff, subsidiaries, and company-level standing committees. The management-level plans establish the methods, practices, and procedures necessary to translate the company's policies into action. The operating plans use the methods, practices, and procedures, established through the management plans to focus the work activities and individual actions to achieve the overall company vision.

In simpler terms: executive plans provide for establishment of policy; management plans provide for the mechanisms to implement the policies; and operating plans use these mechanisms to implement the policies.

The level 1 matrix objectives are the broad, top level categories of action that must be accomplished to achieve the level 1 goal—the company vision. These level 1 objectives require the establishment of policies, guidelines, and infras-

102

tructure by the executive level of the company. The establishment of these policies, guidelines, and infrastructure is achieved by implementation of the executive plan.

The level 2 matrix provides the mechanism to transition the level 1 objectives to level 2 goals, which in turn are accomplished by the level 2 objectives.
At this point, the level 2 objectives become the level 3 goals. The level 3 objectives necessary to achieve the level 3 goals are specific actions. The level 2
matrix is, therefore, the transition level for the policies, guidelines, and infrastructure. At this level, the management plan is established—the plan that provides for the establishment of the methods, practices, and procedures necessary to
implement the policies, guidelines, and infrastructure. The actual implementation is accomplished at the operating level. These relationships are depicted in
Figure 4-1.

			Organization Level		
			Executive	Management	Operating
M a t r i x L e v e l	1 (Policy)	P L A N S	◇		
	2 (Transition)		◇	◇	
	3 (Action)		◇	◇	◇

Figure 4-1. Relationships Between Matrices and Organizational Levels.

At the executive level there is also a management plan and an operating plan.
The management plan and operating plan at the executive level address the company-level organization and its processes. At the executive level, the management plan addresses the implementation of the policies, guidelines, and infrastructure in the executive processes. Similarly, the operating plans at the executive level addresses the specific actions needed to implement the policies, guidelines, and infrastructure in the processes of the company offices.

A company with several business units might have more than one layer of
executive plan, but this complexity can be a trap. We need to avoid developing

"policies for policies" and creating unnecessary complexity and bureaucracy. We must strive for simplicity in becoming a world class competitor.

A company with only one business unit consolidates the executive and management plans into one plan. Figure 4-2 illustrates the relationships among the various types of Management 2000 plans, and how they deploy their requirements throughout the company

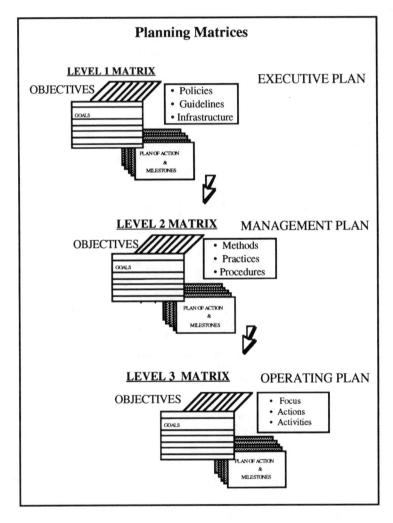

Figure 4-2. Relationships Among Management 2000 Plans.

ESTABLISHING POLICIES, GUIDELINE₍ INFRASTRUCTURE

An executive plan consists of a plan of action and milestones. It auur̲c̲s̲s̲c̲₋ ₋
major elements that are essential if one is to become a world class competitor.
For each of these elements, the plan needs to provide a systematic approach for:

> Identifying policies and guidelines.

> Defining infrastructure.

> Deploying the policies, guidelines, and infras-
  tructure.

The executive plan is developed by the executive steering council. This leadership team assigns task teams, as it deems necessary, to develop the elements of
the plan. Each team needs to be comprised of individuals who are knowledgeable
about the area or function being studied. Team membership should not, therefore, be restricted to executive steering council members.

Identifying Policies and Guidelines

The process for developing policies and guidelines can be complex and confusing. We will use the same structured approach that we used earlier for developing the company vision. This process begins with studying the area or topic
about which you wish to develop policies and guidelines, as well as the external
forces affecting it. This data is then organized and evaluated to provide the basis
for drafting the policy or guideline.

The first action is to define clearly the objective or purpose for the policy or
guideline. The purpose needs to be carefully stated, periodically validated, and
continuously refined and clarified as you work through this process. Each policy
or guideline needs to be consistent with the company values and vision. The
team members need to establish what they know about their business, the culture, including the traditions, and history of their company. Centric to this effort is a careful review of the existing policies, guidelines, and infrastructure for
implementation of those policies and guidelines.

The team needs to review all of this information, discuss it, analyze it, and
reach consensus about it. For the pieces that already exist or are handed to the
team, it is wise to discuss the meaning and implications of each, and to write a

short paragraph that describes the meaning of a each item. This understanding will serve as the baseline for the next step: brainstorming the vital issues.

The leadership team establishing a policy or guideline needs to brainstorm a series of questions. This process develops supplementary information about the vital issues affecting the business or organization. Before the policy statement or guideline is established, however, the brainstorming results must be integrated with the data collected earlier. The same brainstorming method used to develop the company vision is recommended for this step.

The following questions, although not all inclusive, are recommended to help you focus on the vital issues affecting a given element of the executive plan:

> **What are the control issues for this element of the executive plan?**

> **What action would be consistent with the Management 2000 model?**

> **What are the necessary authority, responsibility, and accountability levels for this issue?**

> **What requirements, if any, do my customers levy on me regarding this issue?**

> **How does this issue relate to the company vision?**

As with the development of the company vision, use an affinity diagram and an interrelationship digraph to analyze and integrate this data.

At this point in the process, the leadership team has a large amount of data about the issue. The leadership team is now ready to start formulating the policy or guideline. Reflect on the information collected, and begin articulating the policy or guideline.

The policy or guideline statement needs to state clearly what its purpose is, who has the authority for this issue, what action is required, and why it is necessary to provide this level of control.

Defining Infrastructure

Infrastructure refers to the facilities, personnel, training, systems, and core competencies. That are required for implementing the policies and guidelines. For each element of the executive plan a careful study must be done to define the infrastructure necessary to implement and deploy the policies and guidelines. A plan of action is then developed to ensure that these are developed. The answers to the following questions will provide the data necessary to define your infrastructure requirements:

> What facilities are required to implement the policy or guideline?

> What personnel, in what positions, are necessary to implement the policy or guideline?

> What support systems are required to implement the policy or guideline?

> What training is required to implement the policy or guideline?

> What budgets are required to implement the policy or guideline?

> What core competencies are required to implement the policy or guideline?

Use an affinity diagram and an interrelationship digraph to analyze and integrate this data. The result will be a document defining the infrastructure requirements for becoming a world class competitor.

Deploying Policies, Guidelines, and Infrastructure

The actual deployment of the policies, guidelines, and infrastructure is accomplished by the management plan and the operating plans. The management and operating plans are derived from the single executive plan, to ensure that collaborative planning is accomplished throughout the organization. These plans are deployed to lower-level organizations using a level 1 matrix, as indicated in Figure 4-3. This matrix provides for deployment of the company vision, by deploying goals and objectives to each lower-level activity in the organization. This method ensures that there is a link at each successive level in the organization to the activities above and below. In this manner one is able to trace the relationship of an activity to the vision of the company and each component organization.

DEVELOPING THE EXECUTIVE PLAN

As a minimum, an executive plan consists of a level 1 matrix (Figure 4-3) and a plan of action and milestones that address the following six elements:

➤   **Develop and deploy a company vision.**

➤   **Establish world class leadership.**

➤   **Establish a communication strategy.**

➤   **Establish a training program.**

➤   **Establish an awards and recognition program.**

➤   **Establish a commitment to customers.**

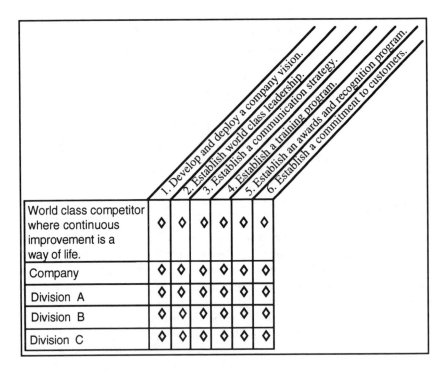

Figure 4-3.   Management 2000 Level 1 Matrix.

These six elements Provide the *how* required to accomplish the *what* of becoming a world class competitor, where continuous improvement is a way of life.

The following paragraphs discuss the level 1 matrix objectives and the actions required at the executive level of the company. These objectives are the planning elements that will enable your business to become a world class competitor. These policies, guidelines, and infrastructure need to be appropriate for your organization, business, and culture.

Develop and Deploy a Company Vision

The successful Management 2000 company is a focused business. Everyone in the company knows why it is in business, what its products and services are, what the goals and objectives are, and how he or she personally contributes to the attainment of these goals and objectives.

To ensure that the company is a focused business, there must be a company vision. If your company has no vision, or if the vision is not written or known by all the employees, then you need to establish a vision (see Chapter 2). The executive steering council assigns a team of its members the responsibility for developing the vision. While this "vision team" is accomplishing its task, the organization proceeds with the implementation of Management 2000: establishing goals and objectives, developing plans to implement them, training and making improvements—using what you already know about your business. As the vision is developed, your Management 2000 activities can be adjusted to meet the vision.

After the company's vision is established, the executive steering council assigns a team of its members to conduct an annual review the company vision, to adjust, modify, or otherwise revise it in light of changes in the marketplace, technology, or resources. This is a continuous process of determining where you are going as a business, evaluating your path, and making course corrections as necessary.

To ensure that the company's vision is deployed throughout the company, each organization must develop long-term goals that support the company's vision. At the company and corporate levels, this is the strategic vision; as you move throughout the organization, these goals become more and more specific and task-oriented. This process normally results in a long-term (for a period of 10 years or longer plan) for your organization in support of the company's vision.

Establish World Class Leadership

The success and the rate of progress in achieving a world class competitive business are directly proportional to the participation of its managers and executives. If they provide proactive leadership in the Management 2000 activities, the employees, subordinate managers, and supervisors will know they are serious. If they do not provide proactive leadership in the Management 2000 activities, the employees, managers, and supervisors will believe this is just another program—another phase that will go away in time.

The challenge for the management and executive steering councils is to develop a plan to ensure that the managers and executives provide proactive, participative leadership. The corporate executive steering council must assign a project team to establish policies and guidelines for management leadership of Management 2000 activities. Bonuses and promotions can be used to demonstrate proactive management 2000 leadership. The company and division executive steering councils and each of the management steering councils, in turn, must assign a project team to determine how they will implement the policies and guidelines established by the executive steering council. The policies, guidelines, and specific plans for ensuring Management 2000 leadership depend on the size of the company and the organizational culture.

After the policies and guidelines are established and plans are developed, they must be documented and must receive the widest distribution. Implementation of the policies and guidelines through the plans must be visible to the employees.   Only then will your employees will know you are serious about Management 2000.

Establish a Communication Strategy

Dr. W. Edwards Deming has repeatedly stated that one of the main deficiencies of American managers is that they provide inadequate work instructions to their employees. For Management 2000, work instructions are called command media and are of two types. The first includes technical guidance such as statistical process control; the second type takes the form of guidance for applications (policies, guidelines, bulletins). The action required here is to establish a system to develop, distribute, review, and revise the command media. The goal of this system is to provide employees the information necessary to perform their responsibilities and to provide consistent direction throughout the organization.

To establish a communication strategy, each executive steering council assigns a team of its members to establish a system for developing, reviewing, and revising command media. The system must be appropriate for its level of responsibility (corporate, company or division). Management steering councils take the details of the system and implement it within their own organizations.

One important aspect of the communication strategy is the dissemination of company news. This element of the corporate executive plan is designed to publicize the company's Management 2000 activities and to provide public recognition for those employees achieving your goals. Properly implemented, this effort will improve awareness of the company's activities and encourage participation in Management 2000. The first action is to establish a corporate newsletter. That addresses the news for the entire corporation. The editorial policy should focus on implementation of the Management 2000 strategy, news about the business, recognition of achievement of milestones, and significant successes. Most companies have a newsletter of some sort, so this is not a new concept. If one already exists, the action is to ensure that the editorial policy is consistent with the Management 2000 strategy.

If the corporation is large enough, it might require a newsletter for each subsidiary or division. This decision must be made on a case-by-case basis. In all instances, it is advisable to keep your publications simple, straightforward and published on a regular basis. Again, the purpose is communication: communication of the strategic vision; communication of the goals and objectives; communication of news affecting the business; communication of the successes; communication of the events affecting the Management 2000 strategy. The action, then, is to initiate a project to establish a newsletter, or, if one exists, to review the existing newsletter with respect to the Management 2000 strategy.

Experience has proven that displays in work areas showing the continuous improvement activities in critical processes is an important part of the communication strategy. In addition, displays are needed in central areas (such as building lobbies) for the divisions, companies and corporation. By presenting topical information on improvement activities at the respective organizational levels, these displays serve a multitude of purposes. They are good advertisements for customers and suppliers. They also tell employees how the processes are doing and recognize improvement achievements.

Establish a Training Program

We cannot overstate the importance of the training program for the organization. Successful implementation of the Management 2000 strategy requires an integrated, cross-functional approach to training and education. It must be integrated into the existing training program. If there is no formal training program in effect, start one now!

It makes no difference whether you develop a training curriculum of your own, have in-house trainers, or use a conglomerate of external sources. The important factors are (1) that you assess your needs, and (2) that you continuously evaluate the effectiveness of the training used and adjust your training program accordingly.

The training program should provide for reviewing the needs of the organizations, and making revisions as necessary based on feedback from students and instructors. For the Management 2000 company model, this means the corporate executive plan must include a corporate policy on training. The training program must be developed and coordinated at the corporate level but implemented at the company level, in order to minimize duplication of effort.

To ensure that course material satisfies the needs of the employees, they must complete evaluation forms by appropriate authority. This feedback is important for external training as well as internal training. It is also important to insist on meaningful testing. This step is often omitted from professional training, but it provides useful feedback for students, instructors, and management.

When developing the training program, consider how to communicate what training is available and when. One method that has proven effective is a training newsletter that provides company personnel with information on Management 2000 training (course availability, schedules) and selected topics. If you choose to do this, keep it simple. Ensure that the publication schedule is regular (whether it is monthly, quarterly, or annually) and that you reach the maximum distribution.

The supervisors and managers of a world class competitor are all capable of coaching continuous improvement activities in their own operations and providing facilitation for others. They are well trained, educated, and experienced in the principles of total quality leadership, statistical process control, team building, problem solving, the new quality technology. These results do not occur overnight. The successful implementation of continuous improvement, as embodied in Management 2000, requires that all organizations within the company have adequate facilitator support until the transition is made and the management 2000 culture is established.

The mission of the Management 2000 facilitators is to provide assistance in identifying and accomplishing improvement projects and maintaining a philosophy of continuous improvement throughout the business operations. The facilitators do not assume responsibility for the improvement activities, but provide advice, guidance, training, and assistance in improvement activities where and when needed.

The first decision to make is whether to employ outside consultants as facilitators or develop internal facilitators. Some companies use a combination of outside and internal consultants to get started. There are advantages to this plan. First, outside consultants have experience with various organizations, and this experience can be applied to your efforts. Second, the outside consultants are already trained, educated, and experienced. Third, as your management team becomes able to lead the efforts, you can easily phase out the consultants.

The downside is that the outside consultants are not familiar with the specifics of your business, processes, and culture. Also, consultants do not have to live with the changes that are implemented. In our experience, the optimum is a blend of internal and external resources. Employ the external consultants to assist in development of internal resources and to avoid reinventing ideas.

Establish an Awards and Recognition Program

This objective focuses on ensuring appropriate awards and recognition for continuous improvement activities. It is essential for encouraging participation in the implementation of the Management 2000 strategy. As you begin the journey to become a world class competitor, it is imperative that you establish systems to communicate, recognize, and reward the improvement activities. For the executive level plans, the action is to ensure that the systems are established and implemented. The management level plans provide the specific action to implement the systems.

The specifics of this program, again, depend on the nature of your business and organizational culture. Keep in mind that personal and public recognition is the best and most lasting award. Many companies have conducted extensive research in this area, and most have come to the same conclusion. It is equally important for the company to "put their money where their mouth is," but cash or prizes are soon forgotten. The personal and public recognition, preferably with photographs, is lasting. The combination is most effective.

Some employers give $100 bonds, some use $25 gift certificates, and some offer credits toward purchases at department stores. The important point is that the employees see that the company is willing to spend its hard-earned profit dollars to reward the employees' efforts. It is also important to provide methods for recognition at various levels, from corporate to supervisor. To this end, it is necessary to define and publish the award and recognition criteria.

The task here is to establish a corporate project team to develop the awards and recognition program for the entire company. The team must be empowered to develop and establish the program. This result can be accomplished by reviewing existing programs, evaluating their effectiveness, evaluating what others are doing, developing a tailored program, and establishing the appropriate command media.

One area most often overlooked is the status evaluation, scoring, and reporting of the improvement activities. The management plans provide the specifics at the management and operational levels within the organization. For the executive level plans, policies must be established requiring these activities defining their format and information content at each executive level, and outlining a schedule.

To accomplish this objective, each executive steering council assigns a team of its members to establish a system for status evaluation, scoring and reporting of the   improvement activities appropriate for its level of responsibility (corporate, company or division). The management steering councils take the details of the system and implement them within their own organizations.

Establish a Commitment to Customers

Customer satisfaction is the goal of your business. It is easy to say that the customer comes first —The customer is king—The customer is number one— but it is a difficult challenge to practice this philosophy. You need accurate information about your market, competition, customer expectations, and customer opinions of your products and services. Collecting this information is a complex process, especially since customers' demands and expectations are constantly changing.

There are two parts to this objective. The first addresses the internal customers, and the second the external customers. For the internal customers, there are the operating plans. These call for a process-centric approach to improvement which requires identifying internal customers and their expectations. (Chapter 5 provides the details.) For the second group, external customers, the corporate executive plan calls for a corporate-level project team to evaluate what customer satisfaction mechanisms already exist, what world class companies are doing, and what the competition is doing.

The product of this element of the executive plan is a corporate policy on customer satisfaction and the details for implementation throughout the company. The company's executive steering council and each management steering council are, in turn, responsible for the implementation of the company's customer satisfaction system, adapted to their specific situation. This may include establishing a toll-free telephone number, customer surveys, or incorporating feedback from field service engineers. The possibilities are limited only by your creativity and budget!

Management Plans

Management Plans are used to deploy the company vision and other elements of the executive plan to each business unit in the company. At this level, the plans provide the methods, practices, and procedures to translate the policies and guidelines of the Executive Plan to every operational level of the organization. The Management Plan also establishes the organizational infrastructure to implement Management 2000 Total Quality Management Programs in the organization. The Management Plans are derived from the level 1 matrix, and are defined in a set of level 2 matrices with their associated plan of action and milestones as indicated in Figure 4-4.

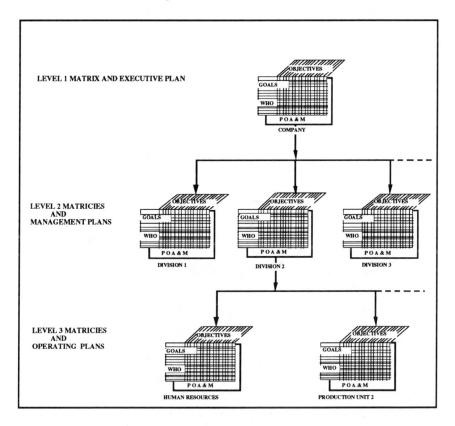

Figure 4-4. Deployment of Company Policy Using
Management Plans and Level 2 Matrices.

Each Management Plan takes the policies provided by the Executive Plan, in the level 1 matrix and its associated POA&M, and uses these policies to develop the organizational infrastructure to deploy the vision throughout the organization. This is accomplished by means of a series of implementation plans and level 3 matrices. This result is accomplished by using the five standard elements indicated in the level 2 matrix in Figure 4-5. This level 2 matrix shows the relationship between the level 1 objectives, as the level 2 goals, and the level 2 objectives. It is important to note that there is a weight attached to the relationships among the goals and objectives, but these are not to be interpreted as a priority scheme for deciding which objectives can be eliminated. The weighting provides an insight for the relationships; each objective, however, needs to be addressed if you are to create an organization that is a world class competitor. Depending on the specific requirements of the organization, additional objectives sometimes are added.

	Develop Operating Plans	Provide Facilitators	Implement Training Program	Implement Awards and Recognition	Establish Newsletter and Displays	Status, Score, and Report
1. Develop & Deploy a Company Vision	◉	◉	○	△	△	○
2. Establish World Class Leadership	◑	△	●	○		○
3. Establish a Communication Strategy	△	△	△	○	◉	○
4. Establish a Training Program	◉	○	●			△
5. Establish an Awards & Recognition Program	△			◑	○	◐
6. Establish a Commitment to Customers	◐		●		○	◉
Company	◇	◇	◇	◇	◇	◇
Division (s)	◇	◇	◇	◇	◇	◇
Functional Areas/Depts/Etc.						
Product Operations	◇	◇	◇	◇	◇	◇
Engineering	◇	◇	◇	◇	◇	◇
Material	◇	◇	◇	◇	◇	◇
Quality Operations	◇	◇	◇	◇	◇	◇
Marketing	◇	◇	◇	◇	◇	◇
Contracts	◇	◇	◇	◇	◇	◇
Personnel (Human Resources)	◇	◇	◇	◇	◇	◇
Finance & Administration	◇	◇	◇	◇	◇	◇

Figure 4-5. Management 2000 Level 2 Matrix.

The first matrix element is the Operating Plan, which is used to deploy the methods, practices, and procedures to implement the company vision to the operating levels of the organization. The other four elements are executed at the management-level to implement the infrastructure. Each of these elements is described as a step to establish the Management Plan and its associated plan of action and milestone chart.

➤   **Develop operating plans.**

➤ **Provide facilitators.**

➤ **Implement training programs.**

➤ **Maintain an awards and recognition program.**

➤ **Status, score and report.**

Develop Operating Plans

The operating plans are used to focus the work activities and operational planning of the level 3 matrix. Figure 4-6 presents a level 3 matrix that identifies a series of actions designed to achieve the goal: Develop Operating Plans. Your specific level 3 matrix can vary from this depending on the specifics of your organization, culture, products, or processes. There are 8 level 3 objectives for our sample.

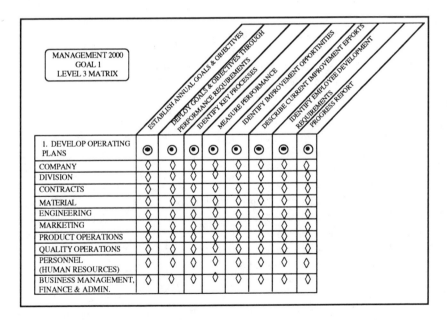

Figure 4-6. Operating Plan Matrix

Establish Annual Goals and Objectives   To ensure that the company's strategic vision, mission, goals, and objectives are deployed throughout the organization, each management business unit must focus its annual goals and objectives on present and future needs. Each organizational element needs to develop annual goals and objectives that are consistent with, and support, the company's strategic vision, and its goals and objectives. These goals and objectives are cascaded to each organization to develop organizational specific short-, intermediate- and long-term goals.

Deploy Goals and Objectives through Performance Requirements
One of the major obstacles to successful implementation of the Management 2000 Strategy is the misalignment of performance requirements. Frequently, goals are set for profit, cash flow, capital investment, manufacturing, schedule, and personal performance without regard to their relationships or effects on one another. The strength of the Management 2000 Strategy is in the deployment of mission, goals, and objectives from strategic vision to personal performance requirements. The matrices are used to align all performance requirements and reward programs so that they are mutually supportive and deploy the Management 2000 Strategy responsibilities.

As you develop your annual goals and objectives, establish plans of action and milestones to achieve them. Assign teams or individuals to be responsible for each action, and include metrics for measuring progress and completion. Each team and individual can then plan their action, and delegate as appropriate. This will align the performance requirements of all individuals within the company, and focus on achieving the vision.

Process Improvement   There are four objectives in the sample level 3 matrix that can be grouped as process improvement: Identify Key Processes; Measure Performance; Identify Improvement Activities; and Describe Current Improvement Activities. Improving the processes depends on first identifying the processes you should improve and then measuring their performance to gain the understanding necessary to control and improve the processes. The first step is to identify your key products and services. These are the products and services that are critical to achieving your mission. Next, identify the process that produces the key product or service, and determine the metrics for measuring the process. For each process element there are four performance measures to quantify its performance: quality, cost, effectiveness and efficiency.

> ➤   **Quality is measured by counting defects, yields, conformance to requirements, or some other index of product or service usefulness.**

➤ Cost can be measured in units of dollars, time, or facilities use.

➤ Effectiveness measures the ability of a process, service, or product ability to meet the required need.

➤ Efficiency is a measure of how well the process can meet the needed schedule, cycle time, and throughput requirements.

The metrics must be carefully chosen to ensure an accurate picture of the processes. Experience has demonstrated that systematic improvement in one of these measures causes improvement in others. It is essential, however, to monitor all four measures (quality, cost, effectiveness, and efficiency) to ensure that the improvements are systematic. The detailed discussion of process analysis in Chapter 5 explains the steps required to develop metrics and to measure the performance of key processes.

At this point in developing the operating plan you have identified your key products and services, identified the processes for producing them, and determined the metrics for measuring the processes. You need also to identify the improvement activities that are already in place, and document your plans for controlling and improving your processes.

Identify Employee Development Requirements   World Class competitive businesses require well-trained, well-educated employees. The task here is to establish the appropriate training and education requirements for each employee, along with a plan to satisfy those requirements. Typically, this task is thought of as job-specific training and education. For Management 2000, the training requirements include continuous improvement topics (SPC, JIT, DOE, QFD, teamwork) and job-specific topics. Collectively, these requirements provide the command media and tools; such as polices, procedures, methods, directives, planning, technical tools, and people skills.

Experience has proven that mass training is a mistake. The half life of most training is very short, so it is best to wait until it needs to be applied immediately. This concept is often referred to as Just-In-Time (JIT) Training. It is imperative, therefore, to develop and implement a strategy for training and educating employees.

Supervisors and managers must work with each of their subordinates to develop an understanding of his or her career goals, as well as to achieve a common understanding and agreement of the position requirements. This information provides the basis for individual training requirements (courses and training schedules), which are documented in training plans. These plans in turn are maintained as part of each employees personnel record and, as such, provide a plan for the future and a history of each employee's progress.

Develop a Management 2000 Progress Report   It is a fact of life that what gets measured gets done. Therefore, each organization needs to report on the status of its Operating Plan. This reporting enables the organization to establish its baseline for meeting short- and long-term goals: to determine requirements for revising its plans; and to provide a meaningful measure progress.

The format for the progress report depends on the specific nature of the business and its strategic vision. This format is usually established under the Executive Plan and passed down through the Management Plan. Until the format is established, begin periodic reporting of the (1) status of the improvement activities, (2) employee training summary, and (3) progress toward goals and objectives.

The periodicity for reporting also depends on the nature of the organization, and its processes, and on the dynamics of the marketplace. Initially branches report monthly to their department steering councils and that the departments report quarterly to their division steering councils. The divisions, in turn report quarterly to the company executive steering council. The reporting frequency should be adjusted as experience and progress dictate.

Provide Facilitators

Experience has repeatedly taught the value of a facilitator in teamwork. This is an individual well versed in the technical and organizational tools of Total Quality. The role of this individual is to assist managers, supervisors, and team leaders in the process of continuous improvement. This includes participating in team meetings to facilitate the application of the tools. This enables the team leader to participate as a full team member, and yet provides an individual that can focus on the process rather than the product of the team. This is important to achieve maximum results, and to keep the team focused on its goals. Figure 4-7 presents a sample level 3 matrix that identifies the objective s necessary to achieve the level 3 goal: Provide Facilitators.

The first objective of the level 3 matrix assumes that facilitators have been identified and trained. If they have not, identify candidate internal facilitators. Include a mix of employees with some supervisors and managers. These individuals will lead their organizations according to the Management 2000 model, and will develop others as internal resources to assist other organizations.

Determine Facilitator Needs for Each Organization Each year, quantify the facilitator needs for your organization. Discuss the support requirements for the coming year with the appropriate executives, managers and supervisors. Evaluate the effectiveness of the existing facilitators with the appropriate executives, managers, and supervisors. Determine how the facilitators can improve their effectiveness. Resolve concerns expressed by the facilitators, executives, managers, and supervisors. Assign or reassign facilitators as required. There are numerous styles of facilitating, and not all are equally effective in a given situation. Facilitators also vary in their levels of experience and skill. It is important to match the facilitator to the organization with which she or he will be working with. Recruit additional facilitators as needed.

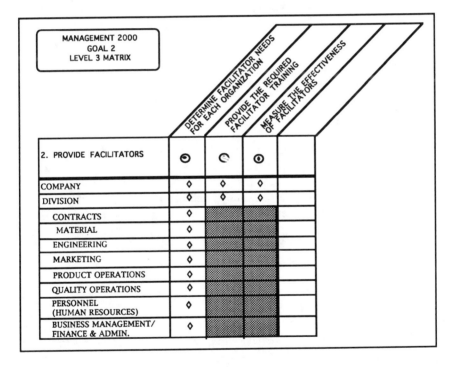

Figure 4-7. Facilitators

Provide the Required Facilitator Training It is important that all facilitators be fully trained and knowledgeable regarding all information needed to perform their roles. In addition to the technical skills, they must fully understand their responsibilities and their role in the organization and the Management

2000 Strategy. This training process takes time and money, but is essential to ensure consistent and uniform support for Management 2000 activities.

Establish a training record for each facilitator. Review each facilitator's training record and determine his immediate training needs. Identify sources of training for requirements, and schedule the training. Ensure that training is received on time and that facilitator training records are updated.

Measure the Effectiveness of Facilitators   The effectiveness of a facilitator does not depend on his or her knowledge and skills alone. It also depends on proactive management support and leadership. To ensure the effectiveness of each facilitator in meeting the needs of his or her assigned areas of responsibility, it is necessary to assess each facilitator's performance. A periodic documented evaluation of the facilitator's effectiveness is a good tool to help determine what training, education, experience, or management support is needed. This needs to be a no-fault evaluation. Its purpose is to help everyone identify and understand what needs to be done to optimize the continuous improvement efforts.

Remember: if a facilitator is not as effective as desired, it is a breakdown of the company's leadership team. Everyone has a responsibility to identify opportunities for improvement in implementation of the Management 2000 Strategy. There must be continuous, open, candid communication between facilitators, supervisors, and management. This is a team effort. If it fails, everyone loses.

Periodically review the facilitator support feedback forms from the assigned organizations. Review the training records for respective facilitators. Review task and project reports from the facilitators. Review the results of the preceding steps with the respective facilitators, and determine a plan of action and milestones (POA&M) to improve the effectiveness of each facilitator. Review the POA&M with the respective manager or supervisor and facilitator. Implement the POA&M with periodic reviews with the respective facilitators and managers or supervisors.

Implement Training Programs

As stated previously, training and education are crucial to your success in becoming a world class competitor. Figure 4-8 presents a sample level 3 matrix that identifies three objectives to achieve the level 3 goal: Implement Training Programs.

Perform a Needs Assessment   Before you can train or educate effectively, you must determine what is needed. The first step, therefore, is to perform a needs assessment. Determine the skills and knowledge necessary for your subordinates to perform their responsibilities, including implementation of the Management 2000 strategy. Each supervisor, manager, and executive reviews the training records for his or her subordinates and compares these to their goals and objectives and the skills and knowledge necessary to implement the Management 2000 strategy. The resulting needs are documented and used to establish the plan for developing your employees. At each level, there must be a consensus on the value of the training and a commitment to expend the resources.

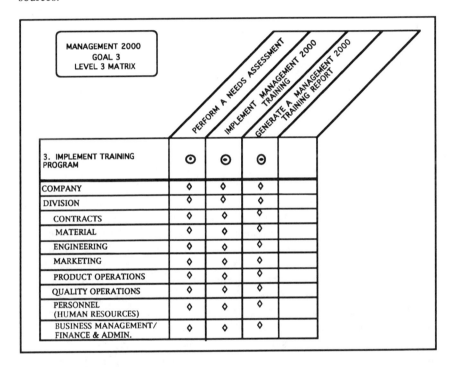

Figure 4-8. Training Program Implementation

Implement Management 2000 Training All too often, employees are sent to classes months before they can put in practice what they have learned. Training is a precious activity, consuming vital overhead dollars. It is best nurtured as a vital commodity of high value. The implementation of training, therefore, needs careful consideration and coordination.

The goal of everyone in this process, from the trainers to the trainees, is to provide training, just-in-time, to meet the needs of each organization. The individuals responsible for providing the training have a need to ensure that the curriculum is offered at appropriate times and locations. This planning function can be accomplished by the training coordinators, after analyzing the training needs assessment summaries. Supervisors have a responsibility to ensure employees are scheduled for training as it is needed in a planned, systematic manner. Each employee needs to be able to apply the training immediately upon returning to their duties.

To accomplish this objective the organizations coordinating the training periodically develop a master training schedule for all organizations to use. Supervisors, managers, and executives submit training requests as appropriate; individuals are trained; and each organization updates its employee training records.

Generate a Management 2000 Training Report   The action here is to develop and maintain individual training records for all employees and to report progress. This information is essential for individual as well as organizational planning, but it is frequently overlooked by supervisors and managers.

Maintain an Awards and Recognition Program

The definition of the awards and recognition program is accomplished in the corporate Executive Plan. The policy and methodology for implementation are developed in the company and division Executive Plans. The action here is to publicize the awards and recognition program, report monthly awards and recognition program status to the division steering council. The division steering councils periodically review the program to report status to the company and corporate levels and to recommend improvements. Again the purpose is to ensure that improvement activities are appropriately recognized and that participants' rewards are commensurate with their contributions.

Figure 4-9 presents a sample level 3 matrix for achieving the goal: Implement an Awards and Recognition Program. As a sample it is sparse, in that it only has two objectives. At this level the responsibility is to implement the company's Awards and Recognition Program, and support recognition of team and individual accomplishments.

Designate a point of contact for the awards and recognition program. These individuals are responsible for publicizing the program, reporting progress to the appropriate management, and providing assistance for implementation of the program. Quarterly, each division steering council reviews the results of the program. When it is appropriate, the council forwards recommendations for improvements.

In addition each organization can establish and maintain information centers to publicize progress to their employees and customers and to provide a method for public recognition of improvement activities. These centers can be as simple as small bulletin boards, or as elaborate as your imagination and budget allow.

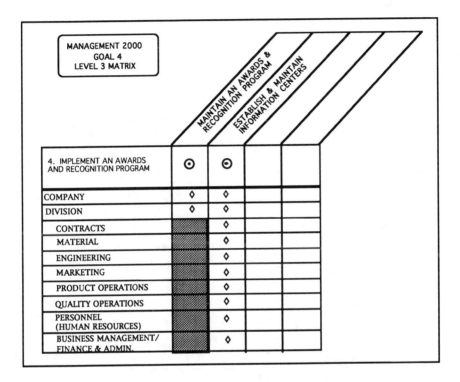

Figure 4-9. Awards and Recognition Program

Establish Newsletter and Displays

Newsletters and displays provide an excellent method for communication from management to the organization. The implementation and effectiveness of this objective will be highly dependent on the size and the culture of the organization. Small to medium companies may not need a newsletter, however, displays in the lobby and in the work areas are good methods to disseminate information. The displays need to be changed regularly, or they will fade from consciousness- and no one will notice them.

If you elect to implement a newsletter, it is important to focus on content not form. This is a good way to tell the employees what the goals of the company are, and to recognize the contributions of individuals and teams. The newsletter, like the displays, will be seen as a barometer of what is important to management. Ensure, therefore, that the message conveyed is consistent with and supports the implementation of the Management 2000 Model.

A blank sample level 3 matrix is presented for this objective in Figure 4-10. The details are so dependent on the specifics of your organization that we leave it up to you to fill in the details.

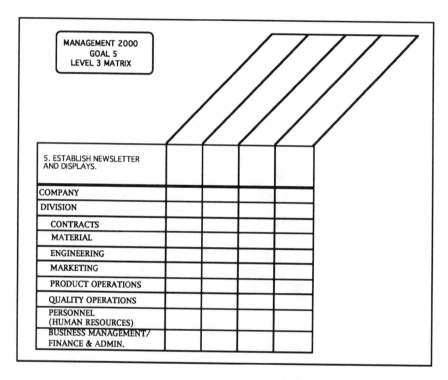

Figure 4-10. Newsletters and Displays

Measure Status Score and Report

The activities here need to have a priority. We must have sensitive, accurate measuring techniques to assess our progress, to decide where we need to make changes, and to determine if our corrections do what we intend them to do. This is a division-level activity that uses the inputs from the departments. The responsibility for this activity depends on the specific culture of the organization. The Total Quality Managers need to take a proactive role in these activities. Figure 4-11 presents a level 3 matrix that identifies the sample objectives that achieve the goal: Status, Score, and Report.

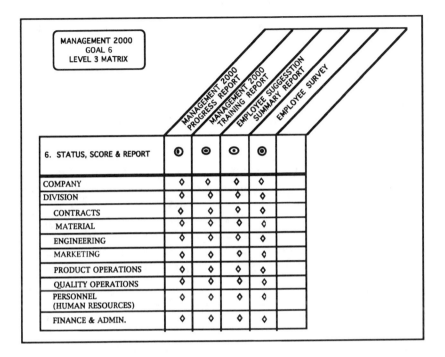

Figure 4-11. Status Score and Report.

Management 2000 Progress Report The basic progress reports performed as part of the first level 2 goal (Develop Operating Plans) are but one piece of the picture. They serve to inform the steering councils on what is happening throughout the individual departments. Each organization reports the status of all its Management 2000 related activities. These are then evaluated against the Management Plan in a recursive manner to provide a periodic progress report. This is normally an annual report that provides insight on progress toward goals and objectives.

Management 2000 Training Reports The training reports, from the training program need to be combined to develop department, division, and company training reports. This step is necessary for future planning and to determine if the employee development activities are implemented according to plan.

Employee Suggestion Summary Report An effective employee suggestion program is essential for successful implementation of Management 2000. It ensures that lessons learned are not lost. Periodic reports showing each organization's participation in the employee suggestion program can be a useful tool as well as good advertising of the progress being made.

Employee Survey   It is also important to receive and evaluate employee feedback. What the employees believe is the real measure of the progress in changing the culture. At least once a year, survey the employees. Find out what the think about the improvement activities, management, and the company.

Plan of Action and Milestone Charts
Complete a plan of action and milestones (POA&M) chart for each of the level 3 goals. The POA&M provides for a list of actions required and a schedule for their accomplishment. The POA&M shows a start date, dates for intermediate activities, and delivery dates, and indicates if tasks are continuing. The sample POA&M in Figure 4-12 below demonstrates how this tool can be used for organizing, planning, and tracking the accomplishment of the goals and objectives.

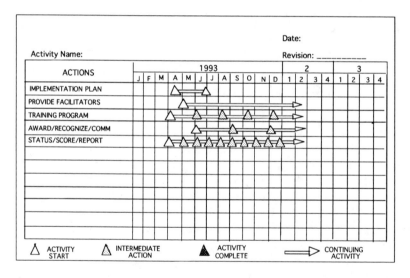

Figure 4-12.   Plan of Action and Milestone Chart.

MANAGEMENT 2000 OPERATING PLANS

The Management 2000 Executive and Management Plans provide the tools, mechanisms, and resources to become a world class competitor. The application of these tools, mechanisms, and resources creates the world class competitor. The vehicle for this is the Management 2000 Operating Plan. The need for this plan is derived from the level 3 matrix.

Each organization in the company needs to develop an operating plan. This plan is, in reality, a business improvement plan. It is not a plan to implement Total Quality Management, but rather a plan to improve your business using the appropriate Total Quality tools, mechanisms, and resources. As your organization evolves to a world class competitor, this operating plan becomes the business plan for your organization. Figure 4-13 shows how the Management 2000 Operating Plan is developed and implemented.

The action involved in developing the Management 2000 Operating Plan, as derived from the level 3 matrix, starts with establishing a strategic vision for your organization. This vision is specific to your organization. The method used to develop the vision, as described in Chapter 2, ensures that it is collaborative and that it deploys the top level strategic vision for the company. Long-term goals are then developed to achieve the vision thus establishing the future direction for your organization.

Periodically (annually or more often if conditions warrant) establish medium- and short-term goals and objectives to achieve the long-term goals. The level of detail necessary depends on the organizational level.

These goals will be derived from a self-assessment and the deployment of the company vision. Self-assessment is the process an organization uses to focus on its activities and to apply all of the Total Quality tools to manage its operations. You can use the following list of questions to get started. Consider them, discuss them, expand them, and decide upon the right questions for your specific organization and processes. (Remember this is a continuous cycle and there will be opportunities to rethink, rework, and refine each step of the self-assessment process.)

> **Define your mission. What are your critical products or services?**

> **What are the critical processes that produce the products or services?**

> **How do you describe the processes? Are there flowcharts? Can you flowchart the processes?**

> **What are the roles and responsibilities of your organization?**

> **Who are the internal and external suppliers and customers of your products and/or services?**

➤ How do you determine the requirements of your customers? How do you communicate your requirements to your suppliers?

➤ What metrics, in terms of quality, timeliness, throughput and cost, are appropriate for measuring your processes?

➤ What are the chronic problems that adversely affect your ability to perform your mission?

➤ What are the opportunities that you see for improving your processes and your competitiveness?

➤ How do your operations and improvement activities relate to the division's and company's vision?

The next step after the self-assessment is to set the goals. The goals need to support the vision and be consistent with the results of the self-assessment.

At this time you need to review your key processes, products and services and ensure that appropriate metrics are tracked to assess quality, timeliness, throughput, and cost. (Chapter 5 provides the methodology for process analysis and management.)

The results of your performance measurement are used to identify opportunities for improvement. It is also important to identify the perceived problems, prioritize them, and develop plans to make improvements. Perceived problems usually are more difficult to identify and resolve. These are the "we could perform better if we had less of, more of, or didn't have to . . ." issues. We recommend you brainstorm for the ideas, and use the affinity diagram to organize and refine the ideas; and the Interrelationship Digraph to prioritize the issues (Chapter 8 provides explanations of how to use these planning tools).

At this point, you have a collection of improvement activities determined from data on your processes and perceptions about your operations. These activities are prioritized by importance, and you can now decide what to do, who is to do it, and when. Your next responsibility is to ensure that they have the tools to do the job. It is, therefore, an opportune time to perform a needs assessment for training your employees.

To ensure success, you need to document the results of the planning, measure status, score, and report. The progress report is feedback for refining the strategic vision, the long- term goals and consequently the annual operating plan.

Development of the Management 2000 Operating Plans enables the members of the organization to evaluate its operations from the perspective of the company vision and the division's business goals. This evaluation is accomplished by (1) applying Statistical Process Control to your processes to manage their cost, quality, and schedule, (2) developing continuous improvement initiatives to support the goals and objectives developed from deployment of the company goals, and (3) identification of chronic problems and implementation of improvement activities. Collectively, the plans for the branches become the basis for each department's annual plan. The department plans collectively become the division's annual plan.

A typical Management 2000 Operating Plan consists of three sections. The first is the set of matrices that deploy the company vision throughout the organization. These matrices indicate the specific goals and objectives at each level of activity; milestone schedule charts for the actions identified in the matrices; and the name of those responsible for the tasks. The second section of the operating plan consists of Improvement Activity Sheets. The third section contains the employee development plans for the year. Remember that plans must be documented, individuals need to be responsible for accomplishing them, and regular, periodic monitoring is essential. Figures 4-14 through 4-18 present a sample operating plan. The "A" figures are sample blank forms, and the "B" figures are annotated with instructions for preparing the forms.

As you prepare your Operating Plan, these forms will provide a good planning document. Later as progress is made in accomplishing the plans, the updated forms provide a good record of the accomplishments. You also need to include appropriate support data such as run charts, Pareto charts, and cause-and-effect analysis. In this way you will have a complete record of what you are doing, why you are doing it, and how you are doing.

The activities identified in the plans become the performance requirements for the individuals assigned to them, including the supervisors and managers responsible for providing the leadership for their accomplishment. This process provides a mechanism to integrate awards, recognition, compensation, performance appraisals, merit reviews, and bonuses into a single system. It also makes continuous improvement an integral part of the company culture.

Periodically, the departments must present their Management 2000 plans and status to the division steering council. The purpose of the presentations is to provide an opportunity for the Council to:

> **Understand each department's processes.**

> **Understand each department's problems and their priorities.**

> **Understand what each department is doing to achieve continuous improvement.**

> **Understand what the division council can do to help each department overcome obstacles and capitalize on opportunities.**

The presentations improve interdepartmental communications and provide synergy for the implementation of the Management 2000 Strategy. It is important, therefore, that the meetings for these presentations be participative. These meetings are not the forum for working problems and issues; discussion is limited to understanding the continuous improvement activities and assigning action as required for advancing the efforts of the organization making the presentation.

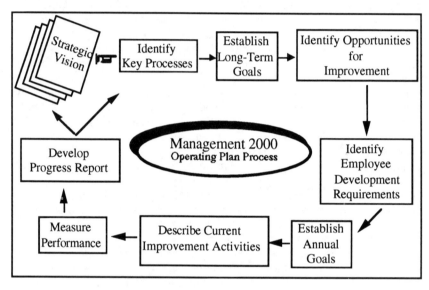

Figure 4-13. Management 2000 Operating Plan Process.

Department X

Management 2000

Operating Plan

Date:

Revised:

Figure 4-14. Cover Sheet for Sample Management 2000 Operating Plan

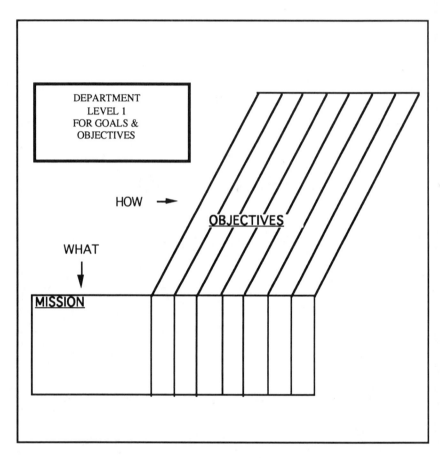

Figure 4-15. Sample Operating Plan Level 1 Matrix.

OPERATING PLAN
STATUS SUMMARY

IMPROVEMENT ACTIVITY		PROJECT DEFINED	ACTION INITIATED	TEAM TRAINED	PROCESS DOCUMENTED	IMPROVEMENT PLAN DEVELOPED	PROCESS METRICS DETERMINED	IMPROVEMENT GOALS DEVELOPED	COMPLETION DATE	COMMENTS
1.	PLAN									
	ACT									
2.	PLAN									
	ACT									
3.	PLAN									
	ACT									
4.	PLAN									
	ACT									
5.	PLAN									
	ACT									
6.	PLAN									
	ACT									
7.	PLAN									
	ACT									
8.	PLAN									
	ACT									
9.	PLAN									
	ACT									
10.	PLAN									
	ACT									

DEPT.　　　DATE　　　　PAGE— OF—

Figure 4-16A. Sample Operating Plan: Status Summary (Blank).

OPERATING PLAN
STATUS SUMMARY

IMPROVEMENT ACTIVITY		PROJECT DEFINED	ACTION INITIATED	TEAM TRAINED	PROCESS DOCUMENTED	IMPROVEMENT PLAN DEVELOPED	PROCESS METRICS DETERMINED	IMPROVEMENT GOALS DEVELOPED	COMPLETION DATE	COMMENTS
1.·List each activity/project that is part of the Implementation Plan	PLAN	*Indicate appropriate plan and actual status.*		*Change categories as appropriate for your specific plan.*						
	ACT									
2.	PLAN									
	ACT									
3.	PLAN									
	ACT									
4.	PLAN									
	ACT									
5.	PLAN									
	ACT									
6.	PLAN									
	ACT									
7.	PLAN									
	ACT									
8.	PLAN									
	ACT									
9.	PLAN									
	ACT									
10.	PLAN									
	ACT									

DEPT   DATE   PAGE   OF

Figure 4-16B. Operating Plan: Status Summary (Annotated).

```
┌─────────────────────────────────────────────────────────────┐
│                    Improvement Activity                       │
│                     Summary Sheet                             │
│ Improvement Activity Name:                                    │
│                                          Date:                │
│ Organization:                            Revision: _____  │
├──────────────────┬────────────────────────────────────────── │
│ 1. Team Members: │ 2. Summary Description:                    │
│                  │                                            │
│                  │                                            │
│                  │                                            │
│                  │                                            │
│                  │                                            │
├──────────────────┴──────────┬─────────────────────────────── │
│ 3. Improvement Goal(s):     │ 4. Method(s) of Measuring Improvement: │
│                             │                                 │
│                             │                                 │
│                             │                                 │
│                             │                                 │
├─────────────────────────────┴─────────────────────────────── │
│ 6. Task Completion Criteria:                                  │
│                                                               │
│                                                               │
├───────────────────────────────────────────────────────────── │
│ 7. Improvement Achievements:                                  │
│                                                               │
│                                                               │
│                                                               │
└─────────────────────────────────────────────────────────────┘
```
* Attach continuation sheets if necessary.

Figure 4-17A   Sample Operating Plan: Improvement
Activity Summary Sheet (Blank).

Improvement Activity
Summary Sheet

Improvement Activity Name: Include a title for the activity/project.

Organization: _____

Date:
Revision: _____

1. Team Members:	2. Summary Description:
List all team members and their respective org. codes. Indicate if each is a Team Leader (L), Facilitator (F), Senior Advisor (S).	Provide a brief description of the process improvement and/or problem(s) to be addressed. This description should take the form of a mission statement for this team.

3. Improvement Goal(s):	4. Method(s) of Measuring Improvement:
List the goal(s) established by this team. If they are "TBD", indicate that in this space and reference the schedule , which would then include,"establishing goals" as one of the tasks listed.	List the metrics established by this team. If they are "TBD ", indicate that in this space and reference the schedule, which would then include "determining metrics" as one of the tasks listed.

6. Task Completion Criteria:

List the completion criteria for each task identified. This is where you establish the products and/or services that must be completed for this activity.

7. Improvement Achievements:

List actual accomplishments, relative to each goal listed in #3 (above).

---

* Attach continuation sheets if necessary.

Figure 4-17B Sample Operating Plan:
Improvement Activity Summary Sheet (Annotated).

Improvement Activity Schedule/Milestone Chart

Improvement Activity Name:

Date: _____
Revision: _____

TASKS	J	F	M	A	M	J	J	A	S	O	N	D

Remarks:

Figure 4-18A. Sample Operating Plan: Improvement Activity Schedule/Milestone Chart (Blank).

Improvement Activity Schedule/Milestone Chart

Improvement   Activity   Name:

Date: _____
Revision: _____

TASKS	J	F	M	A	M	J	J	A	S	O	N	D

Complete schedule, showing major activities and milestones. Each milestone should be followed by a date, indicating planned/actual completion date.

Show current status, including completions and slips.

Remarks:

Figure 4-18B. Sample Operating Plan: Improvement Activity Schedule/Milestone Chart (Annotate).

KEY POINTS

Three types of plans are required to implement the Management 2000 model: Executive, management, and operating.

Executive plans provide for establishment of policy, guidelines, and infrastructure.

Management plans provide the mechanisms to implement the policies, guidelines, and infrastructure.

Operating plans use the mechanisms to implement the policies, guidelines, and infrastructure.

The process for developing policies and guidelines is a three-step process involving data collection, brainstorming, and creation of the policy or guideline statement.

Infrastructure includes the facilities, personnel, training, systems, and core competencies. Required for implementing the policies and guidelines.

The action is not complete until requirements are established for evaluating status, scoring, and reporting.

Management Plans provide the systems, methods, and activities necessary to deploy the policies established by the Executive Plans. The Management Plans are derived from the level 2 matrix and are defined in a set of level 3 matrices.

Training and education are crucial to your success. Supervisors and managers need to work with their subordinates to develop specific training requirements for each employee.

Ensure Management 2000 activities are appropriately recognized and participants' rewards are commensurate with their contributions.

You need to document the results of the planning, assess it status, and score and report to ensure success.

EXAMPLE

EXECUTIVE PLANNING AT LWCI

LWCI executive steering council took up the challenge to develop and implement the executive plan. The council decided to make the development and execution of the executive plan, a team effort. The council chartered six teams, one to address each of the six elements of the level 1 matrix (Example Figure 4-1).

	1. Develop & Deploy the Company Vision	2. Establish World Class Leadership	3. Establish a Communication Strategy	4. Establish a Training Program	5. Establish an Awards & Recognition Program	6. Establish a Commitment to Customers
LWCI will be a highly profitable enterprise producing world class quality products and services. We will challenge the global marketplace, and do so while remaining commited to being a socially and civically responsible company.	◉	◉	◉	◉	◉	◉
Company						
Production Machinery Division						
Electronics Division						
Machine and Tool Division						

Example Figure 4-1. Management 2000 Level 1 Matrix.

The council assigned its members to lead the teams as follows:

1.   Develop and deploy a company vision: Mr. Leander, President, Leander Wiles Co., Inc.

As the president and founder of the company, Mr. Leander should lead this team. The council recognized the imperative for the company vision to be led from the top of the organization.

2.   Establish world class leadership: Mr. Wiles, Vice President and General Manager, Machine and Tool Division.

In his position as vice president and division general manager, Mr. Wiles was the appropriate choice to lead this effort.

3.   Establish a communication strategy:
     Mr. Kickncount, General Manager, Production Machinery Division.

Mr. Kickncount has been with LWCI for 20 years. He has progressed through a series of increasingly responsible positions because of his technical expertise, knowledge of the business, understanding of the LWCI organization, and his outstanding interpersonal skills. Mr. Kickncount asked Ms. Holley, the Safety Manager, to work on this team with him.

4.   Establish a training program: Ms. Rowan, LWCI Human Resources Manager.

Ms. Rowan is currently responsible for employee development within LWCI. Since she already has cognizance over these policies and guidelines, she was the logical candidate to lead this team.

5.   Establish an awards and recognition program: Ms. Sanches, Company Controller.

Ms. Sanches volunteered for this objective. She has been very supportive of the total quality initiatives in the company. She has come to recognize the importance of the human element in all of LWCI's processes. Ms. Sanches believes a well-structured awards and recognition program could be heavily leveraged. It also seemed logical to the council that her department would oversee this program for the company.

6.   Establish a commitment to customers: Ms. Johnston, LWCI Marketing Manager.

Understanding customer requirements is ms. Johnston's responsibility. She recognizes, however, that this information is not useful if it is not acted upon. To ensure that the appropriate functions are represented, she asked Mr.. Hammond, general manager of the electronics division, and Mr. Barrett, quality operations manager, to work on this team with her.

Each team leader was given the charter to:

> ➤ **Identify the necessary policies and guidelines to achieve his or her element of the level 1 matrix.**

> ➤ **Identify the necessary infrastructure for implementing the policies and guidelines for his or her element of the level 1 matrix.**

> ➤ **Develop the plan of action and milestones for establishing the infrastructure and deploying the policies and guidelines to the three operating divisions and the company staff.**

> ➤ **Provide his or her team's plan of action and milestone chart for the executive plan.**

> ➤ **Provide a biweekly, summary status report to the executive steering council.**

The council decided not to assign senior advisors to these teams. It was the consensus that senior advisors would be redundant, since each of the team leaders was a member of the council. The council did, however, assign a facilitator to each team. Each team leader was given the authority to enlist team members from the entire company. The steering council agreed that each team would keep its membership to a minimum—no more than five, including the facilitator. They agreed there was a high degree of urgency for achieving the level 1 objectives, and set 30 days as the due date for the plans. They recognized that execution of the plans might take many months or even years. The important issue for them was to identify the plans and begin execution immediately.

Each of the six team leaders met with his or her facilitator and discussed their assigned project. Each team leader and facilitator reviewed the mission statement and developed a course of action to:

➤ Identify candidate team members, ensuring representation from appropriate functional areas.

➤ Determine the team's initial training requirements.

➤ Set the first meeting agenda, date, time, and location.

At the first meeting of each team, the team leader explained the mission to the team members. This explanation was typically followed by brainstorming by the members, who all had strong feelings and opinions about the adequacy of existing policies and procedures. The team leader and facilitator focused each team on its mission and the need to structure the team process. Each team's facilitator provided a introduction to the team process and teaming dynamics. This short one-hour training   session   refocused each team on its mission, and provided a structured approach to accomplishing the mission.   Each team reviewed and validated its mission statement, and developed a series of goals and objectives.

The results of these meetings were used to initiate team planning summary sheets and team activity/milestone sheets for each of the six level 1 matrix objectives. These sheets were presented to the executive steering council by the respective team leaders.   Collectively, these sheets form the executive plan as shown in Example Figure 4-2. Example Figure 4-3 presents the   team activity/milestone sheet for the first objective.

In reviewing the initial plan the executive steering council made numerous suggestions for refining the plan. These suggestions were evaluated by the teams and incorporated where appropriate. As the teams progress, they will continue to review, update, and refine these sheets.

The executive steering council completed the execution of the executive plan. This resulted in a new policy manual for guiding the leadership of the company. In addition, the executive steering council passed the level 1 and the level 2 matrices to the divisions. The level 2 matrix reflects the objectives that the divisions and the company offices must achieve to implement the policies, guidelines, and infrastructure established by the executive steering council. An example is shown in Example Figure 4-4.

The company offices and each division were required to develop the appropriate level 3 matrices to determine the specific action, required by their organizations, to achieve the level 2 objectives. In some instances the divisions developed task sheets below the level 3 matrix. The   management plans consisted of the level 1, 2, and 3 matrices, plans of actions and milestone charts for achieving the level 3 objectives.

The company offices and the divisions used the diamonds in the matrices to mark their progress. In this manner they were able to use the level 1, level 2, and level 3 matrices to track and status their progress in achieving the management plans.

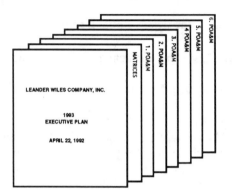

Example Figure 4-2. LWCI 1993 Executive Plan

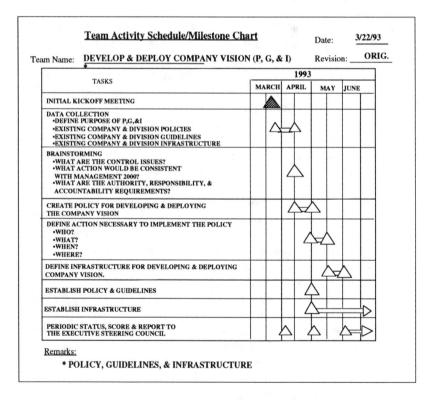

Example Figure 4-3. Team Activity Schedule/Milestone Chart

	1. Develop Implementation Plans	2. Provide Facilitators	3. Implement Training Program	4. Implement an Awards & Recognition Program & Communication Program	5. Status, Score & Report
1. Develop & deploy a company vision.	◉	◉	○	△	△
2. Establish world class leadership.	◉	◉	◉		
3. Establish a communication strategy.				◉	○
4. Establish a training program.	◉	◉	◉		
5. Establish an awards & recognition program.	◉			◉	
6. Establish a commitment to customers.	◉	◉	◉		○
Company					
Division					
Functional Areas/Depts.					
Engineering					
Product Operations					
Quality Operations					
Marketing					
Personnel (Human Resources)					
Finance & Administration					

Example Figure 4-4. Level 2 Matrix

MANAGEMENT PLANS AT LWCI

Mr. Hurbert Wiles, General Manager of the Machine Tool Division of Leander Wiles Co., Inc., established a management steering council for his division. The members of the council included his direct reports:

Mr. David Jackson, Engineering Manager
Ms. Linda Feld, Product Operations Manager
Mr. Bob Komatsu, Quality Operations Manager
Mr. James Orrin, Division Business Office Manager

Mr. Wiles decided to serve as the chairman of the council. He asked Mr. Robert Freeman, a Total Quality facilitator from the company offices, to serve as the facilitator for the council. Initially the council met on a bi-weekly basis to address the issues and actions necessary to establish its division as a world class business.

The Machine Tool Division Management Steering Council was given the level 1 and level 2 matrices from the Executive Steering Council. With these matrices, the newly published Company Policy Manual, and the level 3 matrices from Chapter 4 of *Management 2000,* the council developed level 3 matrices specific to their organization and operations. The council divided the Management Plan (Example Figure 4-5) into seven sections. The first section included the company's level 1 and 2 matrices. Sections 2 through 6 included the appropriate information for achieving the specfic level 3 objectives. The last section of the Management Plan was the annual training plan for the division.

Example Figure 4-5. Management 2000 Plan Organization

The Executive Steering Council had previously developed the policies and guidelines for the Level 1 objectives. The council had also established the requirements, and taken the necessary action, to establish the infrastructure to deploy the policies and guidelines.

The Division Management Steering Council used the level 2 matrix (Example Figure 4-6) derived from the level 1 matrix to develop the level 3 matrices. Their first action was to review the level 1 and level 2 matrices, the company policy manual, the technique for deploying the goals and objectives.

The Division Management Steering Council determined that for Goal 1, of the level 3 matrix (Example Figure 4-7), their action was to pass it to their operating functions as a requirement. In addition, they decided that they would develop an Operating Plan for the division. The division vision, goals, and objectives were developed so that they were collaborative with the company's. These were then passed to the operating organizations within the division for development of their Operating Plans. Quarterly and annual reviews were initiated for these Operating Plans.

The company has a cadre of three facilitators who are available to assist the divisions and company offices. These individuals are assigned primary responsibilities for specific divisions. The division will provide the company an estimate of its requirements for facilitator support for 1993, based on the operating plans for the division and each of its deparments.

The training and development of the facilitators occurs at the company level. In this relationship, the divisions are as customers to the company. The Machine Tool Division supports the efforts of the company in evaluating the effectiveness of the facilitators, but has no direct responsibility for this effort.

There is an established company policy that each supervisor and manager needs to maintain a current, accurate training record for each of her or his direct reports. The division management steering council has, therefore, established a requirement to develop and maintain a training record for all employees. These will be used to formulate employee development plans.

The Personnel representative in the Division Business Office will coordinate training for the Division. As part of the division's Operating Plan, they will establish a POA&M for ensuring that the Division Training Plan is properly developed and executed. Additionally, they will consolidate Training Requirements and Training Reports from the operating functions and the division offices.

The Company Awards Program has been established by the Executive Steering Council. The Division Management Steering Council, has assigned the responsibilty, authority, and accountability for implementation of the company's program to the Division Business Office. The Business Office will develop a POA&M for this program as part of their Operating Plan.

Each operating function within the Division has been given the requirement to develop and maintain an information display in their work areas. These displays are to include information about the organizations goals and objectives, performance of key processes, public recognition of the performance of the employees, and general information of interest to the employees.

Example Figure 4-6. LWCI Level 2 Matrix

The Executive Steering Council has established a library of selected Total Quality books, tapes, and magazines. These are being rotated around the divisions. The Division Quality Manager has volunteered to accept the responsiblity for providing the space for the Division Satelite Library. He will also ensure that information about the library and its holdings is posted in the work areas.

The Operating Plan Summary reports are integrated quarterly by the Quality Manager for the Quarterly Division Activity Report. The Quarterly Training Report is developed from the status reports provided by each of the Departments. This report is prepared by the Business Office. The Progress Report is an annual report prepared by the Division. It addresses the progress the Division is making achieving the company's vision. The Council has assigned the coordination of this report to the Quality Manager. He will receive inputs from each of the operating functions, and administrative support from the Business Office.

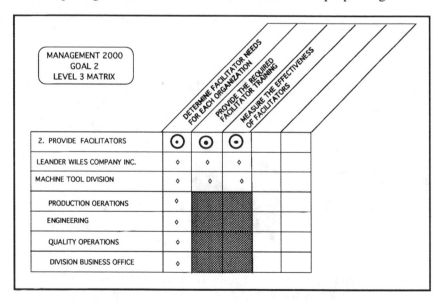

Example Figure 4-7. Level 3 Matrix , Goal #1: Develop Operating Plans

Example Figure 4-8. Level 3 Matrix Goal #2: Providing Facilitators

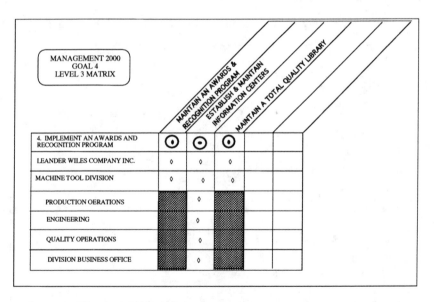

Example Figure 4-9. Level 3 Matrix, Goal #3: Implementing Training Program

Example Figure 4-10. Level 3 Matrix, Goal #4: Implement An Awards, Recognition, and Communication Program

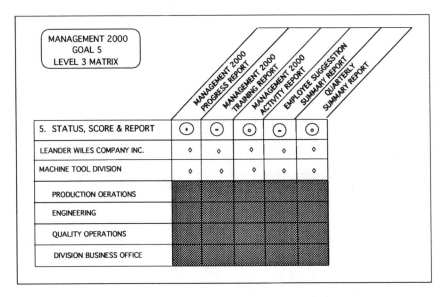

Example Figure 4-11. Level 3 Matrix Goal #5: Status, Score, and Report

OPERATING PLANS AT LWCI

The Production Planning Section of the Product Operations Department of the Machine Tool Division developed its Operating Plan using the Level 3 Matrix. Sample charts from the plan are presented in Example Figures 4-12 through 4-15. The Operating Plan consisted of:

1. **The vision statement for their organization:**

> **Provide world class production planning.**

2. **Operating Plan Status Summaries.**

3. **Improvement Activity Summary Sheets.**

4. **Improvement Activity Schedule/Milestone Charts.**

5. **Employee Training Records.**

OPERATING PLAN STATUS SUMMARY

IMPROVEMENT ACTIVITY		IDENTIFY OPPORTUNITY	INITIATE PLAN	PROCESS ANALYSIS	DEVELOP IMPROVEMENT STRATEGY	EXECUTE STRATEGY IMPROVEMENT	EVALUATE IMPROVEMENT	IMPLEMENT IMPROVEMENT	ESTABLISH CMI	COMMENTS
REDUCE PROCUREMENT LEAD TIME.	PLAN									
	ACT									
IMPROVE EFFECTIVENESS OF INSPECTION OPERATINS.	PLAN									
	ACT									
IMPLEMENT VARIABLITY REDUCTION IN MACHINING & MILLING	PLAN									
	ACT									
IMPLEMENT VARIABILITY REDUCTION IN FINISHING OPERATIONS.	PLAN									
	ACT									
IMPLEMENT VARIABILITY REDUCTION IN CASTING OPERATIONS.	PLAN									
	ACT									
IMPROVE MATERIAL PROCUREMENT SPECIFICATION PROCESS	PLAN									
	ACT									
REDUCE HAZARDOUS MATERIAL WASTE IN PRODUCTION OPERATIONS	PLAN									
	ACT									
	PLAN									
	ACT									
	PLAN									
	ACT									
ORG: PRODUCTION PLANNING	PLAN									
	ACT									

DATE: 3 MARCH 1993

PAGE 1 OF 1

Example Figure 4-12. Sample Operating Plan Status Summary

Improvement Activity Summary Sheet		
Improvement Activity Name: REDUCE PROCUREMENT LEAD TIME		
Organization: PRODUCTION PLANNING, PRODUCT OPERATIONS, MACHINE TOOL DIVISION		Date: **3/2/93** Revision: _____

1. Team Members:	2. Summary Description:
J. CHRISTENSEN (PRODUCTION PLANNER) **P. WHITE (ENGINEER)** **K. JONES (MACHINE OPERATOR)**	**PERFORM A PROCESS ANALYSIS AND IMPLEMENT IMPROVEMENTS IN THE PROCUREMENT PROCESS.**

3. Improvement Goal(s):	4. Method(s) of Measuring Improvement:
• **50% REDUCTION IN PROCUREMENT LEAD TIME.** • **25% REDUCTION IN COST TO PLACE ORDERS.** • **100% ACCURACY IN PROCUREMENT REQUESTS.**	• **IMPLEMENT PLAN TO SCHEDULE.** • **PROCUREMENT LEAD TIME.** • **COST TO PLACE MATERIAL ORDER.** • **ERRORS IN PROCUREMENT REQUESTS.**

6. Task Completion Criteria:

   • **PROCESS ANALYSIS OF THE PLANNING ORGANIZATION'S MATERIAL ORDERING PROCESS.**

   • **IMPLEMENTATION OF SPC IN THE PLANNING ORGANIZATION'S MATERIAL ORDERING PROCESS.**

7. Improvement Achievements:

* Attach continuation sheets if necessary.

Example Figure 4-13. Sample Improvement Activity Summary Sheet

Improvement Activity Schedule/Milestone Chart

Date: **12 MARCH 1993**
Revision: _____

REDUCE PROCUREMENT LEAD TIME

TASKS	F	M	A	M	J	J	A	S	O	N	D
INITIATE IMPROVEMENT PLAN											
PERFORM PROCESS ANALYSIS											
DEVELOP IMPROVEMENT STRATEGY											
EXECUTE IMPROVEMENT STRATEGY											
EVALUATE IMPROVEMENTS											
MODIFY AS REQUIRED											
ESTABLISH CMI - INSTITUTIONALIZE IMPROVEMENTS											
PERIODIC STATUS, SCORE, & REPORT											
FINAL PROJECT REPORT											

Remarks:

Example Figure 4-14. Sample Improvement Schedule/Milestone Chart

Org: Production Planning Date: 2 March 1993			EMPLOYEE TRAINING RECORD TRAINING COURSES						
NAME	TQM PRINCIPLES	STATISTICAL PROCESS CONTROL	DESIGN OF EXPERIMENTS	TEAM LEADER	TEAM MEMBER	MANAGING TOTAL QUALITY	7M TOOLS	QUALITY FUNCTION DEPLOYMENT
J. CHRISTENSEN	1	2	SCD 6/93	2	3		A	SCD 8/93
M. MOCHELS	1	1			2		A	
L. DELGADO	1	1			2		A	
K. JONES	1	1			2		A	

LEGEND

A   AWARENESS TRAINING
1. CAPABLE OF APPLYING SUBJECT MATTER
2. CAPABLE OF TEACHING SUBJECT MATTER
3. CAPABLE OF FACILITATING SUBJECT MATTER

Example Figure 4-15. Sample Training Record

5

Knowing and Understanding Processes

> **A PROCESS TRANSFORMS INPUTS INTO FINISHED PRODUCTS, THROUGH A SERIES OF VALUE-ADDED WORK ACTIVITIES.**

TO BECOME WORLD CLASS COMPETITORS BUSINESS MUST CAPITALIZE on the measurable factors of Quality, Cost and Schedule (Q$S). These controllable factors are the cutting edge of world class competition. To understand the impact of these factors we must first have the ability to describe, quantify and analyze them as part of a process. The first step in controlling these factors, and understanding the processes is to perform a process analysis. The properly completed process analysis provides the basis to implement a wide range of technical resources to accomplish the goal of becoming a world class competitor. Process Analysis is the tactical tool used to develop strategies to innovate and improve processes.

THE NATURE OF PROCESSES

This chapter provides guidelines and technical approaches for process analysis to achieve continuous measurable improvement. Each step and action must be viewed within the context of the specific process under study; not all steps or actions are appropriate for all processes. This methodology is based on the principle that all activities can be viewed as processes that are systematic, repetitive series of actions to develop or produce products or services. Improvement results from the proper management of these processes. There are three types of processes: industrial, administrative and managerial. Figure 5-1 shows that all three have the same characteristics: input >>>> process >>>>> output. These recursive characteristics enable us to apply the six phases of process analysis (Figure 5-2) to any process. We can also apply the other technical tools of the 7-MP Tools, Statistical Process Control Charts and the 7-QC tools to any of these processes.

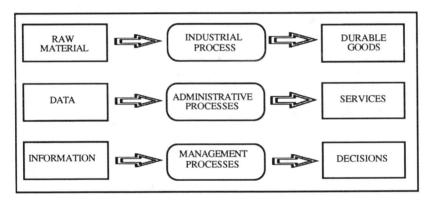

Figure 5-1. Three Types of Processes

A process is a transformation of inputs such as people, materials, equipment, methods, and environment into finished products, through a series of value-added work activities. In this section we will use the six phases of process analysis, presented in Figure 5-2, to provide a structured method of identifying and describing the elements of this transformation. The detailed understanding provided by a formal process analysis is a required precursor for the use of any technical resources. We must first understand a process, its elements, work activities and measurable parameters before applying any other technical tool. Once we have performed a process analysis, we can then use the other technical tools to quantify, control, and improve the process. The Management 2000 philosophy stresses continuous measurable improvement in Quality, Cost, and Schedule. A key factor in applying this philosophy is understanding the processes that affect these factors and customer satisfaction.

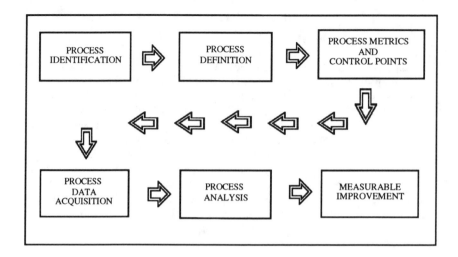

Figure 5-2. Six Phases of Process Analysis

PROCESS IDENTIFICATION

Implementing continuous measurable improvement begins with identifying the process we are going to analyze and determining who is specifically responsible for the process and who has the authority to change it. First, we must be able to distinguish between the three types of processes: industrial, administrative, and management.

Industrial Processes

Industrial processes come to mind immediately when we think of process analysis. These are the processes that produce things. The inputs to industrial processes are raw materials. These raw materials can be in the form of basic materials such as iron ore, steel, and coal; subassemblies, such as computer boards and engine parts or equipment for rework or repair, such as engines or automobiles that require overhaul, or aircraft requiring upgrade and modification. Industrial processes lend themselves most easily to the technical resources for process improvement. As indicated in Figure 5-3 the output from one industrial process can be the raw material of another industrial process. Processes such as repairing, rebuilding, or upgrading things are also industrial processes. In those cases, the items to be repaired, rebuilt, or upgraded, together with the new parts, rework kits, or upgrades, are the raw materials of the process.

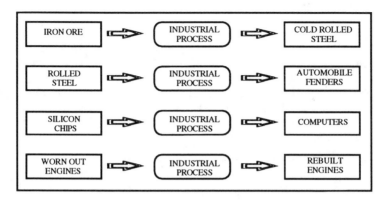

Figure 5-3. Industrial Processes

Administrative Processes

Administrative processes are the processes that frustrate customers (internal and external) most frequently. Administrative processes produce the paper, data and information that other processes use. They also produce products used directly by the customers, such as tax returns, pay checks, reports, and data. Figure 5-4 displays examples of administrative processes. These processes include some of the most complex and bureaucratic challenges in the pursuit of world class competitiveness. The streamlining of administrative processes affect all other processes in an organization. Special attention must be paid to the dilatory effect of inefficient and ineffective administrative processes on personnel morale, the team spirit, management processes, and industrial processes.

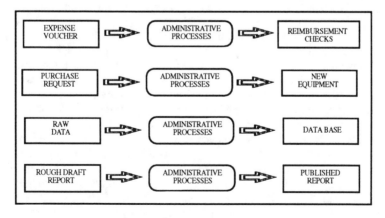

Figure 5-4. Administrative Processes

Management Processes

Management processes are the structured means by which businesses and individuals make key decisions. It is very important that we clearly understand that management is the process of using data to make decisions. That process works best when properly accomplished in organizations with a Management 2000 infrastructure. This structured, quantifiable approach to decision making insures fact based decisions. These fact based decisions are supported by quantifiable data derived from the application of the technical tools. Figure 5-5 illustrates the nature of Management Processes.

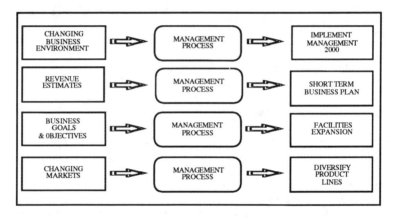

Figure 5-5.   Management Processes

Process Identification

To properly identify a process we must determine its initial input, its work activities, and its output. We must also identify process ownership. Every element of an organization can identify dozens of activities that are performed, include many that are important. To implement continuous measurable improvement, however, we must select those activities that are critical to the mission of the organization, business, and individuals. These, then, are the processes to be managed and improved. Resources for improvement activities are always limited; therefore, we must have a means of prioritizing those activities.

Many processes cross organizational boundaries, Therefore, in addition to identifying critical processes, it is equally important, to understand who is in charge of each process. The person who has the responsibility to manage the process irrespective of organizational boundaries, is the process owner. He or she must also have the means to effect changes and improve the process. In some instances, the person directly responsible for the activities that constitute the process is not in a position to detect the quality of the process product. In such cases process management teams (project teams or continuous improvement teams) should include individuals who can best influence and effect resolution of process issues as well as the persons responsible for the process activity.

The following two steps and their associated actions, provide a structured method for determining process identification, and the associated process ownership.

❶   **Acquire and review all process documentation.**

❷   **Determine process ownership.**

Step 1. Acquire and Review All Process Documentation.

Review the process specifications: These are documents such as the customer specifications for the process output; any other documentation provided by the customer; standard product specifications; and industry standards. What are the internal specifications for the product? Is specific equipment required? How do these specifications relate to input and output requirements? Are there any specifications for input to the process?

Review Process Procedures: What are the process procedures for the product or service? Who is responsible for the process documentation? Where was it written and by whom? Is specific equipment required for the process?

Review the Process Quality Assurance and Inspection Requirements: Are these requirements part of the overall QA manual? Where were these requirements obtained? Who is responsible for the QA manual and the QA program for this product?

Review the Process Input Requirements: What material or information is required as input to produce the product or service? Who are the suppliers? What are all the elements of the required input? How do they affect the output?

Review the Process Output Requirements: Who is the customer or customers? What are the output requirements, by type, volume, quality, and schedule? How do the output requirements affect the input requirements?

Step 2.   Determine Process Ownership

Who Has Direct Responsibility? Determine what specific individual or unit of the organization has direct responsibility for this process and its product.

Who Has Direct Contact?   Determine who has the most direct contact with the process. Who is the individual(s) performing the work activities? What individuals or elements of the organization are responsible for the activities?

Who Has The Authority?   Determine who has the ability and/or the authority to change the process.

In identifying the process, we have determined   several key factors:

➤   **What kind of process it is, Industrial, Administrative or Management.**

➤   **Where the process begins and ends.**

➤   **The input and output requirements.**

➤   **Information contained in all process documentation.**

➤   **Ownership of the process.**

Now that we understand the basic parameters of the process, the next step is process definition. We will look into the internal workings of the process in great detail.

PROCESS DEFINITION

After identifying a process, we need to develop a method for describing it so that we can understand what and how to measure. A very effective technique is to prepare a process flowchart. The process flowchart should be simple, with the minimum number of steps necessary to identify key activities.

Process Flowcharts

Before any system can be quantified, analyzed and subjected to continuous measurable improvement, the system must first be effectively described. The best method to provide a structured description of the system is the process flowchart. This flowchart traces the product through all steps and stages. It depicts how the streams of products (or services or materials) move, disperse, and converge during all processing stages. Such a process flowchart makes it easier for all concerned to understand the system under analysis and to identify the process elements to be evaluated. Figure 5-6 is an example of such a flowchart for a manufacturing process.

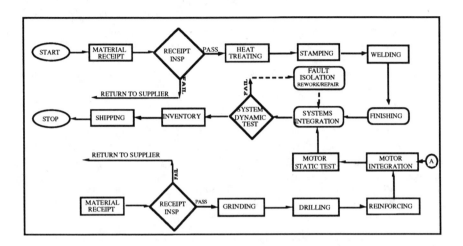

Figure 5-6. Process Flowchart

Flowcharts can be drawn at various levels in the process. Each level of system complexity adds an analytical burden in the amount and type of data taken at the various points in the process. Remember that the purpose of the flowchart is to describe the process properly so it can be quantified and analyzed. There are several steps in performing flowcharting that will provide the necessary understanding to quantify and analyze the process. These steps are discussed fully in the following sections.

Management often does not know or understand all the actions required in any process, and process documentation is often outdated and misleading.   To overcome this chronic problem, do not depend on the knowledge of managers, supervisors, or the process documentation. Instead form a cross-functional team to perform the process analysis. The members need to represent various engineering, analytical, administrative and technical skills, directly related to the process. Supervisory and working personnel have the best knowledge of their processes. Their in-depth knowledge and expertise should be utilized during the flowcharting phase and in all other phases of the process analysis.

Walking through the process is vital. This step provides new insight into the process, including indications of the process functions and criticality. A walk-through also familiarizes you with the personnel and physical layout involved in the process. The walk-through provides a first-hand understanding of the process, all its subprocesses, and the individual work activities associated with the process. This detailed understanding provides the basis for establishing which functions to flowchart and at what process level.

Flowcharts often become large and complex, so it is important to establish standard flowchart symbols and codes to describe the functions and criticality of each flowchart element. Flowcharts that are too large or detailed cannot be clearly understood or evaluated. Very large, complex processes should be broken down into manageable subprocesses. It is not necessary or desirable to reduce a process to each individual work activity, but only to identify the appropriate level to acquire the quality, cost and schedule measures of the critical points. These critical points usually are decision points that are measurable process functions or work activities.

Flowchart Symbols. A wide variety of flowchart symbols are available. Many are symbols specifically for electronic flowcharting, mechanical process flowcharting, computer program flowcharts among others.   Attempting to incorporate these symbols into process analysis can be very complex and confusing and it is also unnecessary. In performing flowcharting for process analysis, we will use only six symbols, as shown Figure 5-7 below.

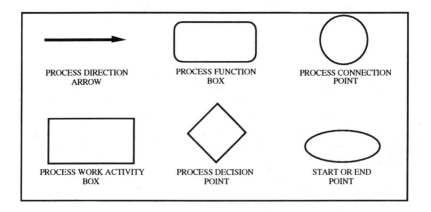

Figure 5-7. Flowchart Symbols

Process Direction Arrow. The process direction arrow shows the direction of the process flow. This arrow points to the next step in the process. The process flowchart in Figure 5-6 uses these arrows to demonstrate how the two processes flow from their start points, converge at system integration, and flow to the process completion at the stop point.

Process Function Box. This symbol represents a process function that contains more than one work activity that can be flowcharted separately.   A brief description of the function is written in the box. In the flowchart in Figure 5-6, this box is used to represent process functions such as system integration, finishing, fault isolation, rework, and repair. Each of these process functions has more than one work activity associated with it.

Process Connection Point. This circle will have a letter (A,B) within the circle. It is used when large complex flowcharts cover more than one page and is used to indicate where the process begins on the following page. In Figure 5-6 this symbol demonstrates that the process is continued from another page leading to motor integration.

Process Work Activity Box. This symbol represents a single work activity within the process flow. A brief description of the work activity is written in the box. Some of the single work activities represented in Figure 5-6 are grinding, welding, heat treating and others.

Process Decision Point. This is a process function or work activity that is a decision point. It has two or more process direction arrows, depending on the decision being made. The diamond contains a brief description of the process decision point. In Figure 5-6, this symbol is used to identify the receipt inspection decision points with the associated pass/fail arrows coming from the diamond. The symbol is also used to describe the decision point, of dynamic test with a "fail" arrow leading to the fault isolation rework/repair functional box and the "pass" arrow continuing the process to the inventory work activity box.

Start and End Points. This symbol signifies the start or stop points of a process. As indicated on the flowchart in Figure 5-6 there can be more than one start point for a complex process that includes the output of two or more converging processes. The number of start points depends on how you define the start of the process. Most processes have only one start point. The stop point is usually where the production of the product or service is complete.

Performing Process Definition

The following steps, provide a structured method to complete this phase and provide the basis for completing the flowcharts. In Steps 1-4 you develop lists of information that are used in Step 5 to create the flowchart.

❶   Define the internal elements and boundaries of the process.

❷   Identify the outputs and customers of the process.

❸   Identify inputs and suppliers of the process.

❹   Identify each work activity and   sub-process and the process flows.

❺   Document the process flows.

Step 1.   Define process internal elements and boundaries:
Within the overall process, what are the elements of the process? Are these elements themselves processes each with several work activities?   Define the element or work activity that begins and ends each process element. List the sub-processes or elements of the overall process.

Step 2.   Identify the process element outputs and customers:
List all the products and services produced by the process elements. List all internal and external customers of the process.

Step 3.   Identify process element inputs and suppliers: List all inputs the process receives. List all the suppliers, internal and external.

Step 4.   Identify each work activity and   sub-process and the process flow: For each input listed, define the work activity it feeds. For each work activity, define what outputs it produces. For each work activity output, define what process element it feeds. Determine who (specifically) performs each work activity.

Step 5. Document the process flow: Using the techniques described earlier, chart the process flow. Start at the initial element receiving process input. Diagram the flow of each process element and its associated work activity through the process. End at the process output that produces the final product or service associated with the process.

Sequentially number each process element. These numbers will be for future referencing. For each element, develop back up details to include, functional description, element criticality, ownership, performance measures, inputs, outputs, and other relevant information. In describing the process, we have looked closely at what is actually occurring:

➤   **What are the several elements of the process**

➤   **What are the inputs and outputs of these elements**

➤   **What are the work activities involved with the process**

We have also flowcharted the process at lower levels. The next question in this logical sequence is: "how do I measure this process?

PROCESS METRICS AND CONTROL POINTS

After identifying and defining the process the process analysis team must review the goals and objectives for the analysis and improvement of the process. Each goal must be concise and measurable, stressing one theme, such as cost reduction, improvement of quality, or schedule.   The objectives must then be established, documented, and clearly understood by all of the team members before the next step can be taken successfully. Some questions that help clarify goals include:

> **Is our objective to reduce defects?**

> **Is our objective to improve our process or activity?**

> **Is our objective to reduce the queue?**

> **Is our objective to improve the throughput?**

> **Is our objective to improve our timeliness?**

> **Is our objective to reduce the cost?**

Once the goals and objectives for the process analysis have been clearly and concisely written and agreed upon, the required control points and metrics can be identified.

Metrics are the measurements necessary to monitor the selected process and to determine if it is satisfying the requirements. These measurements should be based on customer requirements, easy to understand, and specific. In selecting control points, remember that they must be tied to results of critical operations and that they are at process decision points. The measures of process Q$S are of prime concern when measuring processes. We will next describe the step by step procedure to determine process metrics and control points.

Performing Process Measurement

The following five steps and their actions provide a structured method for determining what the process metrics and critical process elements to be measured are.

❶   Review process output requirements.

❷   Review process input requirements.

❸   Review all process elements.

❹   Define the measures of the process elements.

❺   Measures and control points.

Steps 1 and 2 collect data to be analyzed in step 3. The information derived from the analysis is used to make decisions in Step 4. In Step 5 we begin measuring the process.

Step 1.   Review process output requirements: Determine how process output requirements can be effectively measured. Can they be measured by:

➤   **Number of output units produced?**

➤   **Number of output units rejected at final inspection?**

➤   **Cost per output unit?**

➤   **Average warranty cost per output unit?**

➤   **Output units rejected by customers, internal and external?**

Step 2.   Review process input requirements: Determine how process input requirements can be effectively measured. A few commonly used measures are:

➤   **Number and type of inputs (raw material) received by the initial process element.**

➤   **Number, type and source of input units rejected at receipt.**

➤   **Cost per input unit.**

Step 3. Review all process elements: Determine what value added is derived from each work activity Determine effective measures for each process element and its associated work activity.

➤   Measure the cost of the element.

➤   Measure the process time of the element.

➤   Measure the scrap rate produced by the element.

➤   Measure the quality of material produced by the element

➤   Measure the timeliness and throughput of the element.

Step 4.   Define the measures of the critical process elements: The measures selected for the process inputs, outputs, and each critical process element should relate to the goals and objectives for the process analysis. Determine the measure of each critical element and control point by its direct relationship to the goals and objectives of the process analysis.

➤   Select a metric to calculate the measure of each selected element

•   **Quality (Q)**
•   **Cost ($)**
•   **Schedule**

➤   Design a statistic to be used in measuring the selected element

•   **Reject Rate**
•   **Warranty Returns**
•   **Cost of Scrap**
•   **Time to Complete a work Activity**

Step 5.   Measures and control points: Select a member of the team to be responsible for data collecting, monitoring, and reporting.   Evaluate the selection of measures and control points based upon the types of analysis that will be performed. Remember that you are attempting to control or improve quality, cost, schedule (Q$S). These measures can then be used to determine what the critical points in the process are. How those points can be measured and controlled for continuous measurable improvement are described in Process Data Acquisition and Analysis next.

PROCESS DATA ACQUISITION

After we have identified the process critical measures and control points, we must then collect data to facilitate the analysis of these points. To determine if the process is meeting customer needs and expectations requires measurable data. This data is also essential to determine if the process is in control and to ensure the success of improvement efforts.

Performing Process Data Acquisition

The following three steps and the associated actions describe the procedure to perform data acquisition.

❶ **Determine data media.**

❷ **Specify the scope of the data acquisition requirement.**

❸ **Gather data from the critical elements/control points.**

Step 1. Determine data media: Based upon the information obtained learned during the selection of metrics and control points, define the data that can be obtained from automated media. Define the data that must be manually acquired. Determine the most efficient and effective method for data acquisition.

Step 2.   Specify the scope of the data acquisition requirement: Define the size the data storage requirement. Will it be survey data, sampling data, or process control data already available in automated systems?   Can the data be effectively acquired, stored, and analyzed:

➤ **Manually?**

➤ **On a personal computer?**

➤ **On a computer network?**

➤ **On a Mainframe?**

Define how the data will be retrieved and used. Will we use automated analysis programs?   Will multiple access be required? Do we need this data on a network?

Step 3.   Gather data from the critical elements/control points:
Determine if the data will be surveyed or sampled. Gather the data from each
critical element and control point.

Now that the method and scope of data acquisition and retrieval have been determined, we are ready to analyze the process. The next phase, Process
Analysis, describes a structured approach to this effort.

ANALYSIS OF THE PROCESS

Many processes have evolved over time in response to specific needs. They have
been incrementally changed by additions or procedural modifications. The results, in some cases, are complex processes that do not fit the current needs of
the organization and are not compatible with the current business climate.
Process analysis is a systematic approach for examining the process to determine
improvement opportunities, develop cause-and-effect analysis, and prioritize corrective action. There are several steps in prioritizing opportunities. These steps
involve using all of the technical resources in this chapter and those discusses
under   Product and Process Control Chapter 7 and   Product and Process
Improvement in Chapter 10.

It is imperative that our activities be consistent with the stated objective for the
specific process improvement. Therefore after prioritizing opportunities, one
must base decisions for action on their fiscal, quality and/or schedule impact.

Performing Process Analysis

The following three steps and associated actions will aid in completing this
phase of process analysis.

    ❶   **Analysis of data using statistical techniques**

    ❷   **Compare performance and requirements**

    ❸   **Perform further analysis of selected elements**

Step 1.   Analyze data using statistical techniques: Build a table that
provides basic measures using the metrics developed previously. Using this
table, apply some of those basic statistical techniques.

Step 2. Compare performance and requirements: Establish control charts to monitor ongoing performance. Compare data acquired to process output requirements. Identify any difference between the analyzed process performance and requirements. Document all analysis findings.

Step 3. Perform further analysis of selected elements: Identify the critical problem elements or work activities and tie those problems directly to key metrics. Expand the quantitative analysis to include engineering and technical team members. Review process problem elements to determine:

> ➤ **Error sources**

> ➤ **Bottlenecks**

> ➤ **The need to clarify internal customer and supplier requirements and relationships**

> ➤ **The absence of adequate controls**

> ➤ **Process redundancies and other inefficiencies**

Gather additional qualitative data as required to further investigate and validate process performance.

MEASURABLE IMPROVEMENT

The culmination of all of the process analysis. It brings together the multi-disciplinary team of process operators, analysts, engineers, and management. The result is continuous measurable improvement. This is not, however, a one time event, process analysis and improvement represent a continuous effort. Developing and implementing the improvement plan of action can also be the most difficult part of process improvement.

Once the improvement action is in place, it is important to continue measuring the process. This effort necessary to determine the effects of the improvement actions, and to monitor for changes and other opportunities for improvement. This is also the time to develop the action that will institutionalize the improvement. This is essential, this is how we prevent having to solve the same problem over and over, ad infinitum.

Performing Continuous Measurable Improvement

The following steps and associated actions assist in the implementation of CMI:

❶   **Draw conclusions concerning the Process**

❷   **Provide recommendations for the conclusions**

❸   **Develop a continuous measurable improvement plan**

Step 1.   Draw conclusions concerning the process: Here we review the data and information about the process. Applying deductive reasoning we arrive at a logical inference about the process. This is where we predict performance, cause and effect, and influence.

➢   **Which process elements are critical to the goals of the process analysis.**

➢   **Which process metrics contribute significantly to Quality, Cost, Timeliness and Throughput.**

➢   **Which process elements are trending.**

➢   **Which process elements are in control and which process elements are not in control.**

Step 2. Provide recommendations based on the conclusions: The inferences drawn in Step 1 are just that, conclusions. They are not actions. All conclusions, therefore, need to be followed by a recommendation, even if it is to leave the process as is. It is the recommendations that lead to the specific actions for process improvements

Step 3. Develop a continuous measurable improvement plan: After the conclusions are drawn and the recommendations are developed, plans must be developed and executed to implement the improvements. This requires a plan of action and milestone chart.   This improvement plan also needs to include actions necessary for institutionalizing the improvements <u>and</u> the improvement process itself. The execution of the plan also requires statusing, scoring and reporting - remember, what gets measured gets done.

KEY POINTS

Before any system can be quantified, analyzed and subjected to continuous measurable improvement the system must first be effectively described. The method for providing a structured description of the system is the Process Flowchart. There are six phases to performing process analysis.

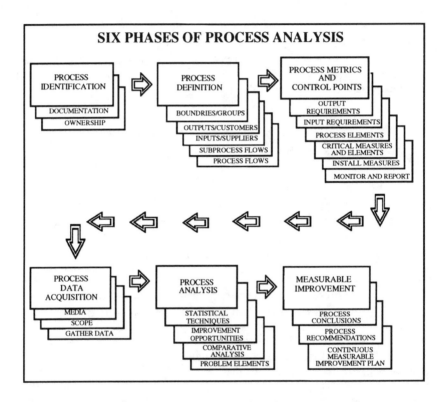

Figure 5-8. Six Phase Process Analysis

PROCESS IDENTIFICATION

Each of us can identify dozens of important activities that are performed in our organizations. To implement continuous measurable improvement, however, we must select those activities that are critical to the mission of the organization and, therefore, achieving the company's vision.

The identification process requires that we understand more than the name of the process, so that we can make an informed decision about which processes to manage. It is essential to collect preliminary information about a candidate process, inputs, outputs, who "owns" the process, etc.

PROCESS DEFINITION

We need to describe it so that we can understand what metrics need to be measured and how to measure them. This is where we add depth to the information gathered in identifying the process. This is where we develop the process flowchart.

DEFINING METRICS AND ESTABLISHING CONTROL POINTS

The process analysis team must define the goals and objectives for the analysis and improvement of the process. Each goal must be concise, stressing one theme, such as cost reduction, improvement of quality, enhances efficiency and effectiveness or improve timeliness and throughput. With this goal established, the team can determine what metrics are required to measure the process and its performance relative to the goal. They can also determine where in the process flow the measurements can be taken.

PROCESS DATA   ACQUISITION

After determining the process critical measures and control points, we must collect data to facilitate the analysis of these points. This data is also essential to determine if the process is in control and to ensure the success of improvement efforts.

ANALYSIS OF THE PROCESS

Process analysis is the systematic examination of the process to identify opportunities for improvement, develop cause and effect analysis, and prioritize corrective actions.

MEASURABLE IMPROVEMENT

The culmination of the process analysis. This is the phase where conclusions are drawn from the data analysis, recommendations are developed, and plans of action are established. The plans also need to include action to institutionalize the improvements. It is important to develop milestone charts, and status, score and report the execution of the plan.

EXAMPLE

LWCI, as part of its ongoing process of implementing Management 2000, is performing a process analysis of all company level critical processes. The Executive Steering Council determined that a critical process within LWCI is one that is necessary for achieving the company vision.

The Department Staff Steering Committee selected the Administrative Process of material procurement as a critical process. As you recall, as the company grew, this process remained consolidated at the company level, reporting directly to Mr. Leander. The cost of procurement has been a significant cost element within the company and there has been dissatisfaction, in the operating divisions with the process. Presently, there is a section within the company staff that performs the procurement of all raw material, equipment, and supplies.

LWCI established the team indicated in Example Figure 5-1 above. (Recall this team from chapter 6) to perform the analysis of the Procurement Process. The team consisted of one member from each of the operating divisions, a member from the company controller's staff, and the head of the company procurement section. The team used the six phase process analysis to accomplish the evaluation.

Process Identification

The first phase of the six step process analysis is to properly identify the process we desire to study by determining its inputs, work activities and outputs at the highest functional level. Here the team needed to determine when the procurement process began and when it was completed (Start and Stop). The two steps for process identification are to 1) acquire and review all process data and 2) determine the process ownership.

Step 1.   Acquire and Review all Process Documentation:

Process Specifications and Procedures: The Procurement Improvement Team first reviewed a wide range of information, relating to the procurement process. The requirements for raw materials are very well defined; however, there were no specifications for the procurement of equipment or supplies. The individual divisions specify the requirements for these items at the time a procurement request is initiated. The input to the procurement process is one of three company forms, one for raw materials that are required on a continuing basis for production, one for equipment with an associated justification sheet, and one for general supplies.

Process Quality Assurance and Inspection Requirements: There are three types of materials that are procured: metal for the machine tool

Team Planning Summary Sheet

Team Name: **PROCUREMENT IMPROVEMENT**   Date: **2/22/93**

Organization: **COMPANY**   Revision: _____ **ORIG.**

---

1. Team Members:

MS. GOODWILL
MR. FREEMAN
MR. DYER
MR. EVERETT
MS. CLAUSEN
MR. BEAUCHAMP
MR. LEANDER (SR. ADVISOR)

2. Mission Statement:

EVALUATE LWCI'S CENTRALIZED PROCUREMENT PROCESS, AND IMPLEMENT IMPROVEMENTS IN QUALITY, COST, AND SCHEDULE.

---

3. Goal(s):

• PERFORM PROCESS ANALYSIS

• REDUCE COST OF THIS FUNCTION

• IMPROVE RESPONSIVENESS OF THIS PROCESS

4. Method(s) of Measuring Success:

• SCHEDULE TO PLAN

• COST OF PROCUREMENT

• PROCUREMENT CYCLE TIME

• QUALITY (TBD)

---

6. Completion Criteria:
 • PROCESS ANALYSIS

 • IMPROVEMENT PLAN

 • IMPROVEMENTS IMPLEMENTED

7. Achievements:
 • DETERMINED MISSION GOALS AND OBJECTIVES FOR THE TEAM

 • INSTITUTED SCHEDULE AND MILESTONE CHART

 • TRAINED TEAM ON TEAMING PROCESS

* Attach continuation sheets if necessary.

Example Figure 5-1.   Team Planning Summary Sheet

division, components for the Electronic Controller Division, and assemblies and components for the Manufacturing Equipment Division. The requirements for these are documented in the separate division quality control manuals. There is no company quality assurance manual and no specific requirements for acceptance of equipment and supplies. The individual procurement request forms are filled out by the three divisions and the department staff, as required, with no specific instructions or written requirements, other than filling in the blanks on the form and providing specifications if required.

Process Input Requirements: There are no specific written procedures for the procurement process. A two year old policy memorandum from Mr. Leander indicates that all requests for procurement would be approved by the controller before any action was taken by the procurement section, and that all procurements over $10,000 in value would go to Mr. Leander for approval.

Process Output Requirements: The output of the procurement process is raw materials for production. The procurement process is required to provide raw materials five days before they are needed for production. This is indicated on the raw material procurement request form. There is no specific time requirement for equipment and supplies. The procurement section provides a weekly status report on all outstanding procurements and their expected delivery dates.

Step 2.   Determine Process Ownership:

Who has Direct Responsibility: The manager of the procurement section has the direct responsibility for the procurement process from the time she receives a procurement request through delivery of the requested material.

Who Has Direct Contact: Several individuals have direct contact with the procurement process:

> Individual workers first identify a need.

> Supervisors verify the need and provide specifications if required.

> Division managers or their staff prepare the appropriate form.

> The form is processed by the procurement section.

> The form is approved by the Controller.

> **The form may be approved by Mr. Leander.**

Who Has the Authority   Clearly there is only one individual with overall authority to change the process, Mr. Leander. All other employees, supervisors and managers have no direct authority over the procurement process.

Process Definition:

The next phase for the LWCI Procurement Improvement Team is process definition. They first looked at the upper level flow from a functional point of view. The resulting flow chart was very rough and displayed only process functions and did not provide any work activities or flow chart codes.

At this point in the process analysis, the team could identify the process only at the functional level as indicated in Example Figure 5-2. They could not perform any useful evaluation of the process because there was insufficient process detail, and there was no way to measure the work activities of the process. The team then used the process definition structure to clarify this flow chart and the charting level required to perform an evaluation. The first four steps of process definition were performed for each identified process function individually. The final step, documenting the resulting process flow chart, was performed as a separate step, consolidating the data from the first four steps. The Procurement Improvement Team systematically examined each of the 5 top level functions using the 5 Step process.

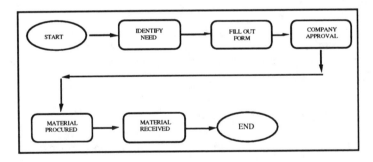

Example Figure 5-2.   LWCI Procurement Process

Step 1:   Determine Internal Elements and Boundaries

Step 2:   Identify Process Outputs and Customers

Step 3:   Identify Process Inputs and Suppliers

Step 4: Identify Work Activities, Sub-Processes and Flows

Step 5: Document Process Flows

The results of this activity for the Company Approval function are provided:

Internal elements and Boundaries:

Process Beginning: Process starts with the receipt of an approved material request form from one of the managers of the operating divisions.

Process Work Activities: The process work activities include the receipt and logging in of the request by the procurement section, forwarding the request for approval to Mr. Leander (if over $10K), forwarding to the controller for review and approval, return of the approved request to the procurement section.

Process Ending: The process ends when the procurement section receives the final approval from the controller.

Process Function Outputs and Customers:

Process Products and Services: The process produces a fully approved request for procurement.

Process Customers: Customers of this process are Mr. Leander and the controller who receive a properly completed request for materials and the procurement section which receives a fully approved request that is ready to go into the next phase of the process.

Process Function Input and Suppliers:

Process Inputs: The process input is a properly complete request form.

Process Suppliers: The supplier to this process function is the division manager who provides the original form.

Process Work Activities, Sub-Processes and Flows:

There are six work activities in the following flow to this process function:

1) **Receipt of a request form**

2)   Initial logging in the request form

3)   Logging out and forwarding the form to Mr. Leander for approval (if required)

4)   Receipt and logging in of the form from Mr. Leander

5)   Logging out and forwarding the form to the controller

6)   Receipt and logging in of the completely approved form from the controller.

LWCI's Procurement Improvement Team completed the process definition phase and developed the detailed flow chart for the process (see Example Figure 3).

Process Measures

The third phase for the LWCI Procurement Improvement Team is to determine the metrics for the processes. These are the process measures for managing the process. This phase will build on the information the team gathered during the process definition phase. The team reviewed the Team Planning Summary Sheet for the Procurement Improvement Team and confirmed that the goals of accomplishing a process analyses, reducing the cost of the process and improving the responsiveness of the process still were viable. The measures of success for the process are therefore:

➤   The overall cost of the procurement process and the cost of the sub-processes and process elements.

➤   The cycle times for the procurement process, the sub-processes and process elements.

➤   The quality of the material produced by the process.

The team then used the five steps of the Measuring Processes phase of process analysis.

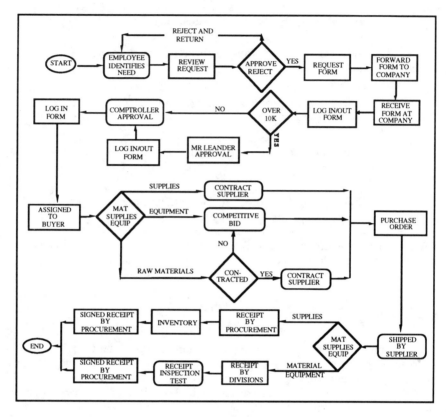

Example Figure 5-3. Detailed Process Flow

Review Process Output Requirements:

The team reviewed the process output requirements for the LWCI procurement process. The output requirements for the process are basically the requested supplies, equipment and raw materials. These outputs can be best measures by:

> **Accuracy: Are the supplies, equipment and raw materials received what is needed?**

> **The cost of the supplies, equipment and raw materials.**

> **The timeliness of the delivery of the supplies, equipment and raw materials.**

➤ **The internal cost to process the procurement requests.**

Review Process Input Requirements: There is but a single process input requirement. The form requesting procurement for supplies, equipment and raw materials. The best measures of these forms are:

➤ **Accuracy: Are the supplies, equipment and raw materials correctly specified on the form? Is the justification sufficient to process the request?**

➤ **Timeliness: Is the form submitted with sufficient lead time to meet the required delivery date?**

Review All Process Elements   Here is where numbering the process elements will be of great assistance to the team. The Procurement Improvement Team determined how to effectively measure each critical process work activity or function in terms of:

➤ **Time required to accomplish the element.**

➤ **Resulting cost in labor time.**

➤ **Rejection rate of the request form during the process.**

➤ **Rejection of requested material.**

➤ **Timeliness of the material receipt.**

The Procurement Improvement Team reviewed each of the 27 elements of the process. The details of this review for elements 5 and 9 are:

Process Element 5 (Forward Form to Company): The form is forwarded to the company using the internal mail process when it is completed and signed by the division manager. This is a critical process element as it provides the documentation necessary to initiate the procurement process at the company procurement section. This is a manual process and provides some specific data that is usable:

➤ The initiation date of the request form.

➤ The date the material is required.

➤ The estimated cost of the items requested.

Process Element 9 (Mr. Leander Approval): Mr. Leander approves all requests for procurements over $10,000. This is a residual practice from when the company was much smaller. Mr. Leander still wants to see all these requests "Just to Make Sure". Procurements over $10,000 are usually discussed at monthly management meetings and are not submitted until after that meeting. The data points here are:

➤ **The proportion of requests rejected by Mr. Leander, in a given period.**

Define the Measures of the Critical Process Elements

The team now has sufficient information to select the process critical elements and the measures to be used for each critical element. The team evaluated each process element to determine the appropriate measures. The measures for Process Element 5 are presented below to illustrate the results of the Team's efforts.

Process Element 5 (Forward Form to Company): As the process that initiates the whole procurement cycle, this is a very important element. The previous four elements were not sufficiently structured to provide for measures of any kind. Therefore, this is the first element that is critical to the process. It is measured by three criteria:

> **Quality:** How accurately is the form completed? This measure can be calculated as the proportion of forms that require correction when received at the company procurement section.

$$\text{Quality} = 1 - \frac{\text{Corrected Forms}}{\text{Total Forms}}$$

> **Timeliness:** Is the form submitted in sufficient time to provide the requested items on time based upon known lead time requirements?

$$\text{Timeliness} = 1 - \frac{\text{Short Lead Time Forms}}{\text{Total Forms}}$$

Cost: The cost of preparing and forwarding the form. This is primarily the cost of work hours required to gather the needed information, prepare the form and forward it to the company.

$$\text{Cost} = \text{Work Hours} \times \text{Salary or Wages}$$

Measures and Control Points

Now the team is at the last step of the measuring processes phase of process analysis. The team has selected Mr. Clausen and Ms. Goodwill as the team members in the best position, and with the most knowledge, concerning data acquisition and data base management. The process control points were selected based upon the availability of data to measure the points and their relevance to the goals of:

> ➤   **Reducing the cycle time of the process.**

> ➤   **Reducing the Cost of the Process.**

> ➤   **Improving the Quality of the product (the product being procurement services).**

The Following are the control points and their associated measures:

CYCLE TIME CONTROL POINTS

These control points are the points that can best be used to measure and therefore improve and control the process. Based upon all the information the team had gathered to date they chose the following process control points:

Process Element 12 (Logging In the form after company approval): This point will measure the total time expended in the higher level process function of company approval. The data on this cycle time will be determined as indicated previously by:

Total Time (7 to 12) = Log in Time at 12 − Log Out Time at 7

Process Element 19: This point will measure the overall time spent in the function of procurement. The data for this cycle time will be determined by using the statistic we have developed in Step 4, Define the Measures of the Critical Process Elements:

Total Time (12 to 19) = Purchase Order Date − Log Out Date at 12

Process Element 24: This element signals the final step in the procurement process for supplies. The team has decided to use this point as a measure of the material received. The measure taken from the work completed in Step 4 is:

$$\text{Average Time (22 to 24)} = \frac{\text{Invoice Signature Date} - \text{Receipt Date}}{\text{Total Supplies Forms}}$$

Process Element 27: This element signals the final step in the procurement process for equipment and raw materials. The team has decided to use this point as a measure of the material received. The measure taken from the work completed in step 4 is:

$$\text{Average Time (22 to 27)} = \frac{\text{Invoice Signature Date} - \text{Receipt Date}}{\text{Total Supplies Forms}}$$

These control points are the process control points the team has determined can best describe the cycle times of the overall process of procurement. The other elements they developed measures for in steps 3 and 4 can also be used in the analytical process, however, these points have been selected as the best measure of cycle times, the points where data is available for measurement and the points that indicate how well the process is and can be controlled.

QUALITY   CONTROL   POINTS

Quality control points are the points the team can use to measures the quality of the process product. The Procurement Improvement Team determined that the measures of quality could be measured by (1) the quality of the forms starting the process, from the operating divisions, and (2) the quality (in terms of the procurement process) of the material received at the completion of the process.

Process Element 6 (Receive form at company): This element begins the process at the company level. The quality of the forms used to begin this process are critical to the quality of the material produced by the process. The correctness and clarity of these forms is, therefore, the measure of their quality. Taking the measure developed during steps 3 and 4 the team will use:

$$\text{Forms Defect Rate} = \frac{\text{Corrected Forms at Element 7}}{\text{Total Forms}}$$

Process Elements 24 and 27 (Signed Receipt by Procurement): At these points the material is accepted. A measure of the process quality at this point is the correctness of the material received compared to what was needed as indicated by the original request forms:

$$\text{Procurement Defect Rate} = \frac{\text{Incorrect Items}}{\text{Total Items}}$$

These quality control points were selected by the team as the process elements that can best describe the quality of the procurement process. These points have been selected as the best measures of quality due to data availability at these points.

COST   CONTROL   POINTS

The cost control points needed to be separated into two distinct categories. First the cost of the process itself, as can be measured by the labor hours expended in the process and second, the actual cost of the material procured. Insufficient data and records were available to measure any of the costs during process elements 1 through 5. The costs accumulated during the company approval sub process are "negligible", (according to Mr. Leander), and there is no method to measure actual costs during that process. The single exception is process element 7, the initial logging in of the procurement forms. The team therefore decided on the following control points.

Process Element 7 (Log-in and log-out of original request forms on the procurement section automated tracking system): The entering of the original manual form to the automated system required a full-time clerk:

$$\text{Ave. Cost at Element } 7 = \frac{\text{Personnel Costs}}{\text{Total Procurement Forms}}$$

Process Element 19 (Purchase Orders): At this point, the team was able to accumulate the total internal cost (work hours) expended to produce the final purchase order. The cost of the procurement process element is best described in two ways: (1) the total cost of the process and (2) the average cost for each type of procurement.

$$\text{Ave. Cost } (13 - 19) = \frac{\text{Hours} \times \text{Personnel Costs}}{\text{Total Procurement Forms}}$$

$$\text{Ave. Supplies Cost} = \frac{\text{Summary of Purchase Order Costs}}{\text{Units Purchased}}$$

Process Elements 24 and 27   (Signed Receipt)   These process elements are used to accumulate the total costs of performing the receipt function for the supplies, equipment and raw materials received.

The cost control points were clearly the most difficult items for the team to define and describe. The original statement by the controller that procurement was a significant cost element within the company included the actual cost of supplies, equipment and raw materials. The internal company costs of procurement were not very well defined for some of the processes. The team decided to measure these costs and to apply improvement recommendations at those points.

At this point in the process analysis, the team decided to redraw the process flowchart to describe the process better . The resulting flowchart is displayed in Example Figure 5-4 below. In this chart the team integrated the first upper-level functional element of Identifying Need directly into the chart, replacing process elements 1 through 4 . The team also added the upper level process elements to the right side of the detailed flowchart adjacent to their associated subprocesses. These changes clarified the relationship of the two flowcharts.

Now the team is ready to move to the next of the six phases of process analysis, Process Data Acquisition.

Process Data Acquisition

As with the other phases, process data acquisition. This phase builds on the knowledge previously gained from the process, its measures, critical elements, and control points. The team employed the three steps associated with this phase: (1) determine data media, (2) specify the scope of the data acquisition requirement and (3) gather data from the critical elements and control points. The team then used these steps to structure the process data acquisition phase of the procurement process analysis.

Step 1. Determine Data Media The data available to the team was on automated and manual media. The primary sources of data were the manual procurement request forms, the manual purchase orders, and the manual signed receipts. Additionally, some data was available from automated tracing systems in the procurement section and automated payroll and accounting records from the controller's office.

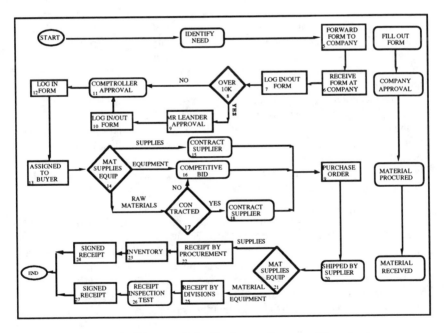

Example Figure 5-4. Redrawn Process Flowchart

The team needed to consolidate these manual and automated data sources into a single database for effective evaluation. The specific data items were are available on the following media:

➤ **Manual Procurement Request Forms**

➤ **Manual Purchase Orders**

➤ **Manual Material Receipt Forms**

➤ **Automated Procurement Tracking Records**

➤ **Automated Accounting Records of Costs**

➤ **Automated Financial Records for payroll**

Step 2.   Specify the Scope of the Data Acquisition Requirement
The team decided to sample the procurement process based upon the random selection of 25 procurements for each of the commodity areas, supplies, equipment
and raw materials. They would track these 75 procurements and consolidate the
data into a single database. From each of these procurements, the team would
draw data on the timeliness, quality, and cost of the procurement process.

This was not a very large data acquisition project. The members of the team
responsible for the data acquisition, Mr. Clausen and Ms Goodwill, estimated
that the data could be stored, sorted and evaluated using a standard PC spreadsheet
program. The manual data would be keyed into the spreadsheet program and the
automated data integrated using a small conversion program written by Mr.
Clausen. The team would then use the resulting statistical summary data to
evaluate the process and make recommendations.

**Step 3.   Gather Data From the Critical Elements and Control
Point** The 75 procurements were randomly selected from the previous year's
procurements, to ensure that the data acquired describes the current process. Mr.
Clausen and Ms Goodwill determined that the data gathering, data integration
and programming would require about two weeks with one data entry person
doing most of the work. Example Figure 5-5 shows one of these data tables.
After this work was accomplished, the team was prepared to start the analysis of
the process.

Analysis of the Process

The analysis phase uses all the data and information gathered to this point. The
team performs the evaluation of information necessary to achieve the goals of

the process analysis. Based upon the scope of this process analysis, the administrative nature of the process, and the (sufficient and not too complex) the LWCI team modified the steps for this phase. They deleted Step 2, Compare Performance and Requirement, and Step 3, Perform Further Analysis of Selected Elements. They deleted these steps because were no stated process requirements for the process to meet, and because the process was simple enough that it was not necessary to perform further iterations of selected subprocesses.

	EQUIPMENT			RAW MATERIAL			SUPPLIES		
	OUT AT 7	IN AT 12	TIME	OUT AT 7	IN AT 12	TIME	OUT AT 7	IN AT 12	TIME
1	66	72	6	68	73	5	65	69	4
2	66	72	6	68	73	5	65	69	4
3	70	86	16	72	87	15	69	83	14
4	71	76	5	73	77	4	70	73	3
5	90	96	6	92	97	5	89	93	4
6	92	96	4	94	97	3	91	93	2
7	92	99	7	94	100	6	91	96	5
8	97	101	4	99	102	3	96	98	2
9	100	104	4	102	105	3	99	101	2
10	100	105	5	102	106	4	99	102	3
11	105	110	5	107	111	4	104	107	3
12	110	116	6	112	117	5	109	113	4
13	110	114	4	112	115	3	109	111	2
14	119	127	8	121	128	7	118	124	6
15	122	131	9	124	132	8	121	128	7
16	125	145	20	127	146	19	124	142	18
17	150	157	7	152	158	6	149	154	5
18	155	161	6	157	162	5	154	158	4
19	156	167	11	158	168	10	155	164	9
20	190	199	9	192	200	8	189	196	7
21	195	203	8	197	204	7	194	200	6
22	200	211	11	202	212	10	199	208	9
23	205	212	7	207	213	6	204	209	5
24	230	236	6	232	237	5	229	233	4
25	245	255	10	247	256	9	244	252	8
		TOTAL	190		TOTAL	165		TOTAL	140
		AVERAGE	7.6		AVERAGE	6.6		AVERAGE	5.6

Example Figure   5-5. Sample Data Table

Step 1. Analysis of Data Using Statistical Techniques The team used some basic summary statistics translated into the tables and graphs in Example Figures 5-6, 5-7 and 5-8. This data was evaluated by the team.

Cycle Times: As indicated in Example Figure 5-6 below, the highest overall contributor to procurement cycle time was the equipment procurement process. This process also has the longest cycle time for the sub process of processing in the procurement section.

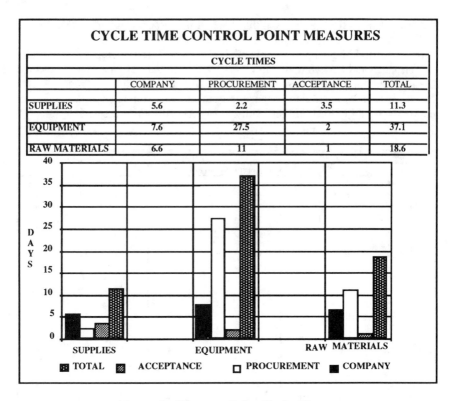

Example Figure 5-6. Cycle Times

Process Costs: Example Figure 5-7 below displays the data on process costs. There were no costs accumulated from the company sub process, and there were no direct cost records for that process element. The hands-on time at the company level was described as "negligible." However, referring back to Example Figure 5-6, substantial cycle time was spent during that process (a lot of time in in/out baskets?). The highest overall contributor to procurement cost was the equipment procurement process which also had the longest cycle time. Also of interest is the relatively high cost of processing the acceptance of supplies. The team attributed this cost to the tedious inventory process and repackaging of supplies for forwarding to the operating divisions.

Quality Measures: The quality measures evaluated by the team were described in Example Figure 5-8. Clearly the most problematic element of the process was the required corrections to initial procurement request forms. A very low percentage of supplies, raw materials, and equipment was rejected during the receipt phase of the procurement process.

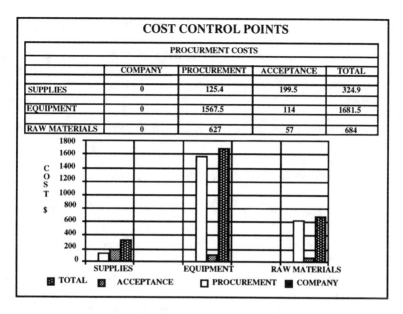

COST CONTROL POINTS

PROCURMENT COSTS				
	COMPANY	PROCUREMENT	ACCEPTANCE	TOTAL
SUPPLIES	0	125.4	199.5	324.9
EQUIPMENT	0	1567.5	114	1681.5
RAW MATERIALS	0	627	57	684

Example Figure 5-7. Process Costs

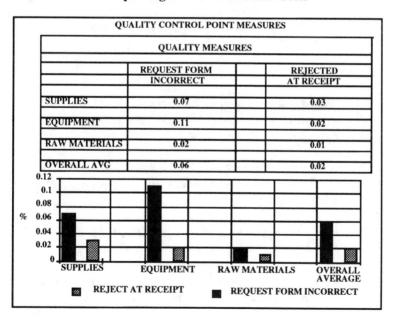

QUALITY CONTROL POINT MEASURES

QUALITY MEASURES		
	REQUEST FORM INCORRECT	REJECTED AT RECEIPT
SUPPLIES	0.07	0.03
EQUIPMENT	0.11	0.02
RAW MATERIALS	0.02	0.01
OVERALL AVG	0.06	0.02

Example Figure 5-8. Quality Measures

Conclusions, Recommendations, and Improvement Opportunities

The Procurement Improvement Team reviewed their data and decided that this process was indeed a good opportunity to enhance LWCI's competitiveness. They decided that the implementation of Statistical Process Control at each of the measurement points would enable them to manage the procurement process.

The Procurement Improvement Team identified the following improvements as immediate needs:

> ➤ **Automation of the procurement process.**

> ➤ **Streamlining the Company Approval Process.**

> ➤ **Decentralizing the Supplies Procurement Process.**

> ➤ **Implementing competitive bidding for raw materials.**

Step 1.   Draw Conclusions Concerning the Process   T h e Procurement Improvement Team concluded that the metrics they established were appropriate for the goals they set for their activity. They also decided that they should continue and implement Statistical Process Control throughout the process.

The Team also concluded that:

> ➤ **The Company Approval process is unnecessarily complex, and caused unnecessary delays in the process.**

> ➤ **The centralization of the supplies procurement introduced unnecessary opportunities for delays, and errors.**

> ➤ **The manual nature of the procurement process provided unnecessary opportunities for errors.**

> ➤ **The contracts for raw materials were not managed, and had not been reviewed in many years.**

Step 2.   Provide Recommendations The Procurement Improvement Team recommended that the LWCI implement Statistical Process Control throughout the procurement process. And, that this effort be the responsibility of the cognizant work groups.

The Team also recommended that:

> The company contract with a distributor for supplies but that the individual divisions order their own materials and have them shipped directly to them.

> The ordering system be automated, and that information copies be directed to the Company Controller and Mr. Leander (for purchases over $10,000.00).

Step 3. Develop CMI for the Process The Procurement Improvement Team developed a plan of action and milestone chart for implementing their recommendations. This plan required execution at the division level as well as the company level. The Team's plan called for statusing, scoring, and reporting to the Procurement Improvement Team which in turn reported progress to the LWCI Executive Steering Council.

LEANDER WILES COMPANY, INC.

PROCUREMENT IMPROVEMENT TEAM

The execution of the plan resulted in a streamlined process as indicated in Example Figure 5-9:

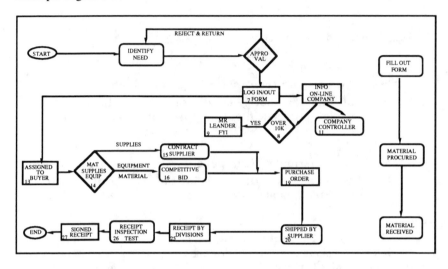

Example Figure 5-9.   Streamlined process

6

The Seven Quality Control Tools

STATISTICS BRINGS ORDER TO DATA
AND
GIVES MEANING TO LIFE.

THE AUTHORS HAVE HUMOROUSLY SAID, "STATISTICS BRINGS ORDER TO DATA and gives meaning to life." Although this comment is made with tongue in cheek, it is true that statistics is the source of all product and process control and improvement tools. These tools enable us to take sample measurements of our processes, draw conclusions, and make decisions and predictions with a strong degree of confidence.

STATISTICS AND MANAGEMENT 2000

Over the years, statistical methods have become prevalent throughout business, industry, and science. With the availability of advanced, automated systems that collect, tabulate, and analyze data, the practical application of these quantitative methods continues to grow. Statistics today plays a major role in all phases of modern business and is indispensable in the Management 2000 environment.

In Chapter 5 we discussed how to measure all business processes, and how the analysis of these measurements can guide us in choosing improvement activities. Next, we will take the analytical process one step further in sophistication by presenting the process and product control tools.

More important than the quantitative methods themselves is their impact on the basic philosophy of business. The statistical point of view takes decision making out of the subjective autocratic decision-making arena by providing the basis for objective decisions based upon quantifiable facts. This change provides some very specific benefits:

➢ **Improved process information.**

➢ **Better communication.**

➢ **Discussion based upon facts.**

➢ **Consensus for action.**

➢ **Information for process changes.**

Statistical Process Control (SPC) takes advantage of the natural characteristics of any process. All business activities can be described as specific processes with known tolerances and measurable variances. The measurement of these variances and the resulting information provide the basis for continuous process improvement. The tools presented here and in Chapter 11 provide both a graphical and measured representation of the process data. The systematic application of these tools, through the Management 2000 model, empowers business people to control products and processes to become world class competitors.

The basic tools of statistical process control are data Figures, Pareto analysis, cause and effect analysis, trend analysis, histograms, scatter diagrams, and process control charts. These basic tools provide for the efficient collection of data, identification of patterns in the data, and measurement of variability. Figure 6-1 shows the relationships among these seven tools and their use for the identification and analysis of improvement opportunities. We will review these tools and discuss their implementation and applications.

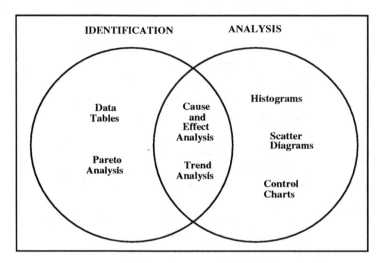

Figure 6-1. The Seven Quality Control Tools

In this chapter we will explain all of these tools except control charts, which are discussed in Chapter 7. We will explore how these tools are structured into a process analysis, and discuss how they are applied to industrial, administrative, and management processes.

DATA TABLES

Data Tables or data arrays, provide a systematic method for collecting and displaying data. In most cases, data tables are forms designed for the purpose of collecting specific data. These tables are used most frequently where data is available from automated media. They provide a consistent, effective, and economical approach to gathering data, organizing it for analysis, and displaying it for preliminary review. Data tables sometimes take the form of manual check sheets where automated data is not necessary or available. Data Figures and check sheets should be designed to minimize the need for complicated entries. Simple-to-understand, straightforward tables are a key to successful data gathering.

The effective use of data Figures requires that certain decisions must be made concerning the data to be collected, compiled, and analyzed. The following are some of these considerations:

> **PURPOSE.** Determine why you are collecting the
> data and what specific analysis and analytical meth-
> ods you will use.

> **REQUIREMENT.** Identify what type of data is
> needed to perform the analysis.

> **SOURCE.** Determine whether the data is currently
> available, and from what source, and on what media.

> **COLLECTION.** Identify where, when, and how the
> data will be collected, and by whom. Clearly define
> the data categories as you design your data Figure.

> **DATA REDUCTION.** Identify what data reduction
> tools you will use (automated, manual, programs)
> and how you will organize the data.

> **CONCLUSIONS AND RECOMMENDATIONS.**
> What actions are contemplated? Will the data col-
> lected support the planned conclusions and recom-
> mendations?

The flowchart in Figure 5-6 (Chapter 5) lends itself to the acquisition of
data using a check sheet. Figure 6-2 is an example of an attribute (pass/fail) data
Figure for the correctness of invoices derived from one element of that
flowchart. From this simple check sheet several data points become apparent.
The total number of defects is 34. The highest number of defects is from supplier A, and the most frequent defect is incorrect test documentation. We can
subject this data to further analysis by using Pareto analysis, control charts and
other statistical tools.

In this check sheet, the categories represent defects found during the
Material Receipt and Inspection functional element of the process. The following defect categories provide an explanation of the check sheet:

Incorrect Invoice: The invoice does not match the purchase order.

Incorrect Inventory: The inventory of the material does
not match the invoice.

Damaged Material: The material received was damaged and rejected.

Incorrect Test Documentation: The required supplier test certificate was not received and the material was rejected.

Defect	Supplier				
	A	B	C	D	Total
Incorrect Invoice	////	/		//	7
Incorrect Inventory	/////	//	/	/	9
Damaged Material	///		//	///	8
Incorrect Test Documentation	/	///	////	//	10
Total	13	6	7	8	34

Figure 6-2. Check sheet for Material Receipt and Inspection.

Figure 6-3 shows a data Figure developed for the same process. This Figure provides the data for failures of the several in-process inspections by work shift. An analysis of this data would reveal specific problem areas for personnel, training, documentation, and test equipment.

Defect	Shift 30 Day Period			
	1	2	3	Total
Run-up Test	15	10	30	55
System Integration	25	20	30	75
Motor Static Test	45	20	0	65
Motor Integration	5	50	60	115
Total	90	100	120	310

Figure 6-3. Data Figure of Failure During the Manufacturing Process by Work Shift.

The following defect categories provide an explanation of the data Figure in Figure 6-2.

Run-up test failures indicate that the system failed final acceptance dynamic test after integration of all assemblies.

System integration test failures indicate that the motor and associated assemblies failed continuity test at integration.

Motor static test failures indicate that the motor failed static test after integration with the carriage.

Motor integration test failure indicated a failure of the motor to mate with the carriage assembly.

This data Figure can provide a basis for further analysis using Pareto or cause and effect analysis. It is evident from the check sheet that motor integration and the third shift are potential problem areas. You should exercise caution in performing a direct analysis of this data, as will be explained in the following sections.

CAUSE AND EFFECT ANALYSIS

After identifying a problem, it is necessary to determine its cause. The cause-and-effect relationship is at times obscure. A considerable amount of analysis often is required to determine the specific cause or causes affecting the problem.

Cause and effect analysis uses diagramming techniques to identify the relationship between an effect and its causes. Cause-and-effect diagrams are also known as fishbone diagrams. Figure 6-4 demonstrates the basic fishbone diagram. The six steps used to perform Cause and Effect Analysis are:

❶   Identify the problem.

❷   Select an interdisciplinary brainstorming team.

❸   **Draw the problem box and prime arrow.**

❹   **Specify major categories.**

❺   **Identify defect causes.**

❻   **Identify effective corrective action.**

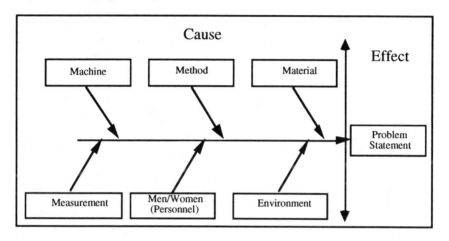

Figure 6-4.   Cause and Effect Diagram.

Step 1. Identify the Problem   This step often involves the use of other statistical process control tools, such as Pareto analysis, histograms, and control charts, as well as brainstorming. The result is a clear concise problem statement.

Step 2. Select Interdisciplinary Brainstorming Team   Select an interdisciplinary team, based upon the technical, analytical, and management knowledge required to determine the causes affecting the problem. Figure 6-5 displays the relationship between the development of the problem statement and the selection of a brainstorming team.

Step 3.   Draw Problem Box and Prime Arrow   The problem contains the problem statement being evaluated for Cause and Effect. The prime arrow functions as the foundation for the major categories. Establish the problem box and prime arrow, as indicated in Figure 6-6.

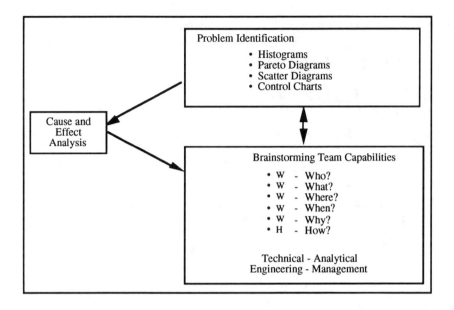

Figure 6-5. Problem Identification and Interdisciplinary Team Relationship.

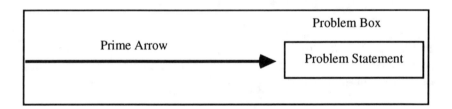

Figure 6-6.   Establish Prime Arrow and Problem Box.

Step 4.   Specify Major Categories   Identify the major categories of contributing to the problem stated in the problem box. The six basic categories for the primary causes of the problems are most frequently, personnel, method, materials, machinery, measurements and environment, as shown in Figure 6-7. Other categories may be specified based upon the needs of the analysis.

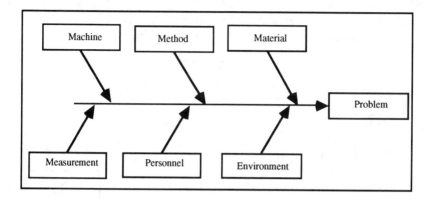

Figure 6-7. Specify Major Categories.

Step 5.   Identify Defect Causes   When you have identified the major causes contributing to the problem, then you can determine the causes related to each of the major categories. There are three methods to approach this analysis: the random method, the systematic method and the process analysis method.

Random Method   List all six major causes contributing to the problem at the same time. Identify the possible causes related to each of the categories, as shown on Figure 6-8.

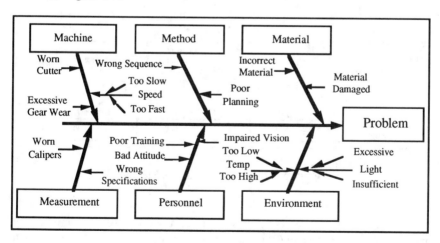

Figure 6-8. Random Method.

Systematic Method   Focus your analysis on one major category at a time, in descending order of importance.   Move to next important category only after completing the most important one.   This process is diagrammed in Figure 6-9.

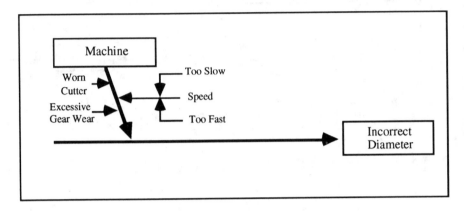

Figure 6-9.   Systematic Method.

Process Analysis Method   Identify each sequential step in the process and perform cause and effect analysis for each step, one at a time.   Figure 6-10 represents this approach.

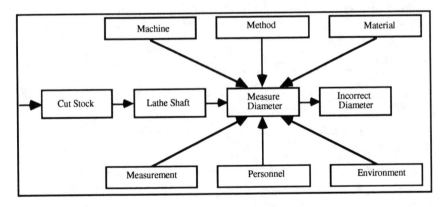

Figure 6-10.   Process Analysis Method.

Step 6.   Identify Corrective Action   Based upon (1) the cause and effect analysis of the problem and (2) the determination of causes contributing to each major category, identify corrective action.   The corrective action analysis is performed in the same manner as the cause and effect analysis. The cause and effect diagram is simply reversed so that the problem box becomes the corrective action box. Figure 6-11 displays the method for identifying corrective action.

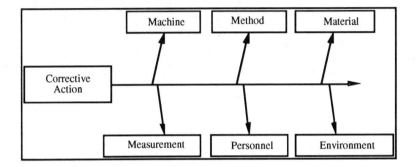

Figure 6-11. Identify Corrective Action.

HISTOGRAMS

A histogram is a graphical representation of data as a frequency distribution. This tool is valuable in evaluating both attribute (pass/fail) and variable (measurement) data. Histograms offer a quick look at the data at a single point in time; they do not display variance or trends over time. A histogram displays how the cumulative data looks *today*. It is useful in understanding the relative frequencies (percentages) or frequency (numbers) of the data and how that data is distributed.

Histograms for Attribute Data
Histograms for attribute data are easy to construct from data Figures and check sheets. The histogram in Figure 6-12 is based on the data Figure in Figure 6-3. A histogram of this data graphically demonstrates the relationships and frequencies of defects found in the manufacturing process.

The frequency of occurrence appears on the vertical (Y) axis and the attribute elements are on the horizontal (X) axis. This same data can be evaluated as a relative frequency distribution by converting the data to percentages (relative frequencies, as shown in Figure 10-13).

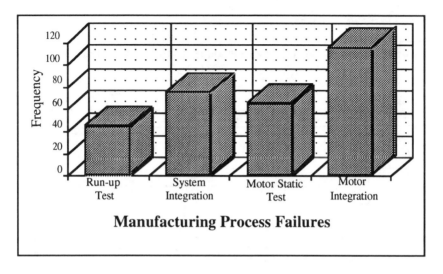

Figure 6-12. Histogram for Attributes.

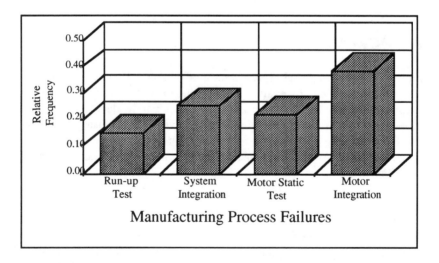

Figure 6-13. Relative Frequency Distribution.

Histograms for attribute data are sufficiently simple that it is not necessary to use the step-by-step approach to construct these charts. However, histograms for variable data are somewhat more complicated and require a structured approach.

Histograms for Variable Data

Histograms for variable data are similar to those for attributes, in that they provide a graphic demonstration of the data and its frequency distribution. The frequencies or relative frequencies are listed on the vertical (Y) axis, and the measurements (variables) are listed on the horizontal (X) axis. We will use the variable data in Figure 6-14 to construct a variable histogram. This data was derived from the soldering certification test scores of 50 employees. We are interested in the distribution of scores with respect to experience, stated in months.

Employee No.	Experience (Months)	Score (%)	Employee No.	Experience (Months)	Score (%)
1	120	0.88	26	69	0.72
2	119	0.92	27	66	0.77
3	118	0.90	28	64	0.86
4	118	0.86	29	58	0.76
5	114	0.76	30	52	0.69
6	114	0.99	31	51	0.78
7	113	0.72	32	48	0.81
8	112	0.76	33	48	0.82
9	97	0.87	34	48	0.86
10	96	0.82	35	46	0.79
11	96	0.92	36	46	0.75
12	96	0.88	37	44	0.74
13	94	0.76	38	43	0.73
14	86	0.83	39	40	0.80
15	88	0.85	40	36	0.77
16	76	0.66	41	36	0.76
17	77	0.72	42	32	0.70
18	74	0.73	43	28	0.88
19	73	0.75	44	28	0.90
20	73	0.88	45	22	0.86
21	73	0.77	46	22	0.94
22	73	0.80	47	21	0.97
23	70	0.72	48	12	0.86
24	69	0.88	49	12	0.87
25	69	0.62	50	6	0.88

Figure 6-14.   Solder Qualification Test Scores.

There are seven steps in preparing a variable histogram:

❶   Determine the number of columns.

❷   Establish the class boundaries.

❸   **Determine the intervals of classes.**

❹   **Identify the classes using the class mark.**

❺   **Determine the upper limit of the histogram.**

❻   **Place the data in a frequency distribution.**

❼   **Draw the completed histogram.**

Step 1 Determine The Number of Columns The number of columns in the variable histogram is dependent on the number of data points to be evaluated. Generally, a variable histogram should have a minimum of 5 columns and a maximum of 20. Figure 6-15 is derived from several sources and is generally accepted as a standard.

Data Points	Columns
< 50	5 – 7
50 – 100	6 – 10
100 – 250	7 – 12
>250	6 – 20

Figure 6-15.   Criteria for Determining the Number of Columns
in a Variable Histogram.

The data provided in Figure 6-14 has 50 data points, so this histogram should have 5 to 7 columns, or bars. We will use 5 columns since there are just 50 data elements.

➤   **50 Data Elements**

➤   **5 Columns**

Step 2 Establish the Class Boundaries The class boundaries are the highest and lowest measurements that are under evaluation. This measurement variable will be on the horizontal axis of the histogram. In the data set we are looking at, the class boundaries are 0.99 for employee 6 and 0.62 for employee 25. Therefore, the upper class boundary is 0.99, and the lower class boundary is 0.62.

Step 3 Determine the Class Intervals To determine the class intervals or group size, use the difference between the class boundaries divided by the number of columns.

$$\text{INTERVAL} = \frac{\text{Upper Class Boundary} - \text{Lower Class Boundary}}{\text{Columns}}$$

$$\text{INTERVAL} = \frac{(0.99) - (0.62)}{5} = \frac{(0.37)}{5} = 0.07$$

$$\text{INTERVAL} = 0.07$$

We have determined that there are 5 classes, each of 0.07 width. It would be difficult to identify each of these five columns by using the lower and upper boundaries for each class interval (i.e., 0.62 to 0.68, 0.69 to 0.75, and so on). It is easier and more effective to identify the column by its class mark, or mid point. The class intervals and the class marks also form the first two elements of the frequency distribution Figure. The class marks for our data are shown in Figure 6-16.

Class Interval		Class Marks
0.62 — 0.68		0.65
0.69 — 0.75		0.72
0.76 — 0.82		0.79
0.83 — 0.89		0.86
0.90 — 0.99		0.94

Figure 6-16.   Histogram Class Marks.

Step 5   Rearrange the Data in a Frequency Distribution   Using the data from Figure 10-16 determine the frequency of occurrence for each class interval as identified by the class mark. Place the data in a frequency distribution Figure, such as the one displayed in Figure 6-17.

Class Interval	Class Marks	Frequency (f)
0.62 — 0.68	0.65	2
0.69 — 0.75	0.72	11
0.76 — 0.82	0.79	15
0.83 — 0.89	0.86	15
0.90 — 0.97	0.94	7

Figure 6-17.   Distribution Frequency.

Step 6   Determine the Upper Limit of the Histogram   The upper limit of the histogram should be set at 1.5 times the highest frequency in the frequency Figure. In this case, the highest frequency is the number of employees (18) with a score identified by the class mark 0.855. Therefore, the upper limit of this histogram is 25.

Step 7   Draw the Completed Histogram   We are now prepared to draw the histogram. Figure 6-18 is the completed histogram, which demonstrates the relationship of test scores to their frequency of occurrence.

This same data can also be used to construct a relative frequency histogram. First, transform the numbers to percentages (relative frequencies) as in Figure 6-19. Then construct the histogram as demonstrated in Figure 6-20.

Many candidates for improvement can be identified using this one elementary tool. The frequency and shape of the data distribution provide insights that would not be apparent from the data alone. Histograms also form the basis for two other tools that we frequently use: Pareto analysis and process capability. We will present Pareto analysis in this chapter and process capability in the discussion of control charts in Chapter 7.

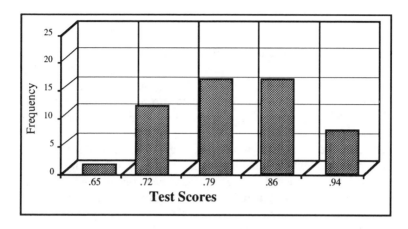

Figure 6-18.   Solder Certification Scores Histogram.

Class Intervals	Class Marks	Frequency (f)	Relative Frequency
.61 - .68	0.65	2	0.04
.69 - .75	0.72	11	0.22
.76 - .82	0.79	15	0.30
.83 - .89	0.86	15	0.30
.90 - .99	0.94	7	0.1

Figure 6-19.   Relative Frequency.

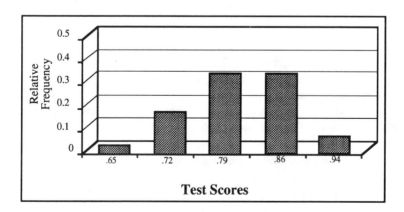

Figure 6-20.   Relative Frequency Histogram.

PARETO ANALYSIS

A Pareto diagram is a special type of histogram that helps us to identify and prioritize problem areas. The construction of a Pareto diagram may involve data collected from data Figures, maintenance data, repair data, parts scrap rates, or other sources. By identifying types of nonconformity from any of these data sources, the Pareto diagram directs attention to the most frequently occurring element.

There are three uses and types of Pareto analysis. The basic Pareto analysis identifies the vital few contributors that account for most quality problems in any system. The comparative Pareto analysis focuses on any number of program options or actions. The weighted Pareto analysis gives a measure of significance to factors that may not appear significant at first, such additional factors as cost, time and criticality. The following five steps apply to all types of Pareto analysis:

❶   **Identify the occurrence, measurement, or nonconformity for analysis.**

❷   **Determine the frequencies of the data.**

❸   **Calculate the frequency percentages and list the frequencies in descending order.**

❹   **Determine the scale for the Pareto diagram.**

❺   **Plot the results on a histogram.**

Step 1.   Identify the Occurrence, Measurement, or Nonconformity   In this step you identify the measure you wish to analyze.   This data can come from past control charts, data Figures, or other data sources. The data must be collected over some specific period of time before the analysis can be performed. Typically, Pareto analysis is performed to:

➤   **Identify significant measures of quality.**
     -Failures
     -Returns
     -Conformance to requirements
     -Warranty returns

-Frequency of repairs
-Rejects

➤   Identify measures of cost.
-Warranty cost
-Repair cost
-Facilities costs
-Labor costs
-Workman compensation cost

➤   Identify measures of effectiveness.
-Meeting customers expectations
-Returns
-Repeat customers
-Survey answers

➤   Identify measures of efficiency.
-Cycle times
-Throughput
-Unit cost
-Fixed costs
-Variable costs
-Meeting deadlines

Step 2. Determine the Frequencies of the Data   Determine the frequencies of the various data elements for Pareto analysis. Using the data from a check sheet, data table, or other data sources, construct a frequency Figure such as the ones used for histograms. Figure 6-19 is an example of a data table for basic Pareto analysis.

Step 3. Calculate the Frequency Percentages and List in Descending Order
Calculate the frequency percentage for each data category and the cumulative frequency. List the occurrences in descending order of frequency for the various elements (see Figure 6-19).

Step 4. Determine the Scale for the Pareto Diagram In Figure 6-19, the scale on the left side gives the frequency of occurrences and the right side gives the relative frequency as a percentage. Again, the scale should be 1.5 times the highest frequency. In this figure, the highest frequency is 13, so the upper limit of the Pareto chart is rounded to 20 (since we are not measuring 0.5 failures).

$$\text{Scale} = \text{Highest Frequency} * 1.5 = 13 * 1.5 = 19.5$$

$$\text{Scale} = 20$$

Step 5. Plot the Results on a Histogram   Plot the Pareto frequency bars and cumulative frequency percentages on a histogram, as indicated in Figure 6-19. This five-step process is used to develop the Pareto analysis charts for basic Pareto analysis, comparative Pareto analysis, and weighted Pareto analysis. The following discussion of these three types of Pareto analysis use the five-step process to develop the analysis.

Basic Pareto Analysis

The basic Pareto analysis chart provides an evaluation of the most frequent occurrences for any given data set. By applying the Pareto Analysis steps to the Material Receipt and Inspection process described in Figure 6-21, we can produce the basic Pareto analysis demonstrated in Figure 6-22. This basic Pareto analysis quantifies and graphs the frequency of occurrence for material receipt and inspection and further identifies the most significant based upon frequency.

A review of this basic Pareto analysis for frequency of occurrences indicates that supplier A is experiencing the most rejections with 37% of all the failures. The data demonstrated in Figure 6-21, and its associated Pareto analysis histogram in Figure 6-22 represent a basic Pareto for the frequency of occurrences. In Figures 6-23 and 6-24 below, the analysis is based on types of failing components. Other basic Pareto analyses can be based on time, cost, or production output factors.

Material Receipt and Inspection Frequency of Failures			
Supplier	Failing Frequency	Percent Failing	Cumulative Percent
A	13	38	37
B	6	17	55
C	7	20	75
D	9	25	100

Figure 6-21. Basic Pareto Analysis.

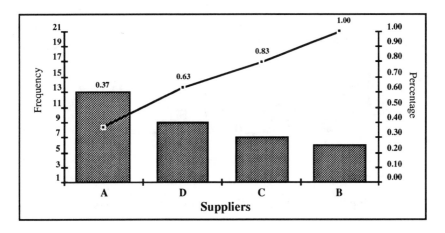

Figure 6-22. Basic Pareto Analysis.

Element	Component	Failing Frequency	% Failing	CUM %
A	Capacitor	700	39	39
B	Solder	400	22	61
C	Leads	300	17	78
D	Shorts	200	11	89
E	Others	200	11	100

Figure 6-23. Pareto Analysis for Frequency of Failure.

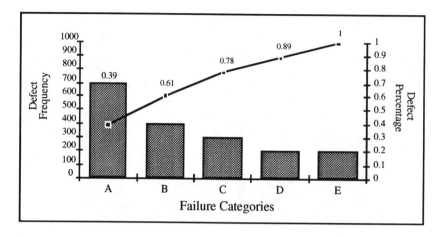

Figure 6-24.   Pareto Analysis for Frequency of Failures.

Comparative Pareto Analysis

Pareto analysis diagrams are also used to determine the effect of corrective action, or to analyze the difference between two or more processes and methods. Figure 6-25 displays the use of this Pareto method to assess the difference in defects after corrective action.

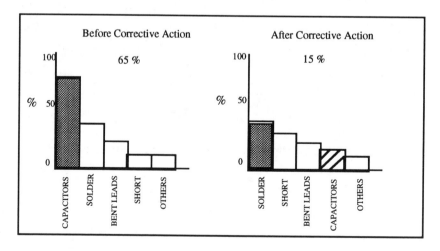

Figure 6-25.   Comparative Pareto Analysis.

Weighted Pareto Analysis

Weighted Pareto analysis provides the opportunity to consider other factors, such as cost and time. The weighted Pareto analysis uses a statistically weighted average to modify the frequency of occurrences. Using the data from Figure 6-24, we have modified the Pareto graphs to account for the cost of repairing the failures, as shown in Figures 6-26 and 6-27.

Weighted by Cost						
Element	Failure	Failing Frequency	% Failing	Unit Cost	Total Cost	Weighted Index
A	Capacitor	700	39	1.59	1113	434.07
B	Solder	400	22	0.13	52	11.44
C	Bad Leads	300	17	0.76	228	38.76
D	Short	200	16	17.10	3420	547.20
E	All Others	200	11	Various	76	8.36

Figure 6-26. Weighted Pareto Analysis.

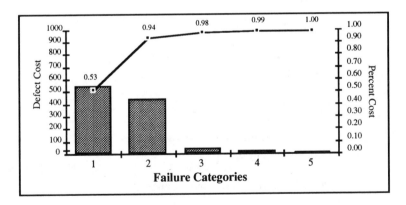

Figure 6-27. Pareto Analysis for Frequency.

A review of Pareto analysis, weighted for cost, indicates that shorts (D) are the most expensive failing component despite the fact that they are not the most frequent. The expense results from the intensive labor required to fault isolate a short.

SCATTER DIAGRAMS

Another pictorial representation of process control data is the scatter plot or scatter diagram. A scatter diagram organizes data using two variables: an independent variable and a dependent variable. This data is then recorded on a simple graph with X and Y coordinates showing the relationship between the variables. Figure 6-28 displays the relationship between two of the data elements from the solder qualification test scores in Figure 6-14. The independent variable, experience in months, is listed on the X axis. The dependent variable is the score, which is recorded on the Y axis.

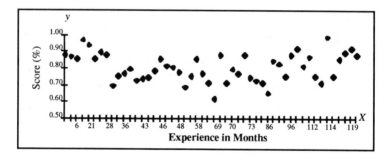

Figure 6-28. Solder Certification Test Scores.

Evaluating Scatter Plots

Some of the product and process control applications for scatter plots are:

> **Demonstrating the relationship between dependent and independent variables.**

> **Evaluating a variable's dependence.**

> **Determining if two dependent variables respond in the same way to an independent variable.**

> **Predicting the response of a dependent variable to a specific setting of an independent variable.**

These relationships fall into several categories, as shown in Figure 6-29 below. In the first scatter plot there is no correlation, the data points are widely scattered with no apparent pattern. The second scatter plot shows a curvilinear correlation demonstrated by the U shape of the graph. The third scatter plot has a negative correlation, as indicated by the downward slope. The final scatter plot has a positive correlation with an upward slope.

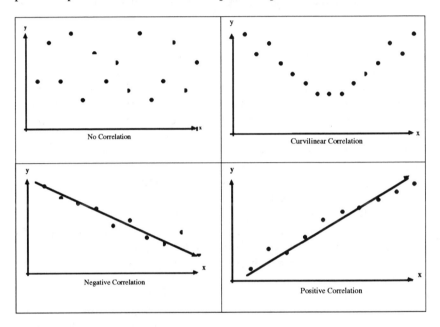

Figure 6- 29. Scatter Plot Correlation.

From Figure 6-28 we can see that the scatter plot for solder certification testing is somewhat curvilinear. The least and the most experienced employees scored highest, whereas those with an intermediate level of experience did relatively poorly. The next tool, trend analysis will help clarify and quantify these relationships.

TREND ANALYSIS

Trend analysis is a statistical method for determining the equation that best fits the data in a scatter plot. Trend analysis quantifies the relationships of the data, determines the equation, and measures the fit of the equation, to the data. This method is also known as curve fitting or least squares. Trend analysis has several values:

➤   **Identification of the optimal operating conditions.**

➤   **Qualitative understanding of the relationship of the variables.**

➤   **Forecasting.**

Trend analysis can determine optimal operating conditions by providing an equation that describes the relationship between the dependent (output) and independent (input) variables. An example is the data set concerning experience and scores on the solder certification test.

The equation of the regression line, or trend line provides a clear and understandable measure of the change caused in the output variable by every incremental change of the input or independent variable. Using this principle, we can predict the effects of changes in the process.

One of the most important contributions that can be made by trend analysis is forecasting. Forecasting enables us to predict what is likely to occur in the future. Based upon the regression line we can forecast what will happen as the independent variable attains values beyond the existing data.

Trend analysis is a natural outgrowth of process analysis and the other product and process control tools. Much of the work required for trend analysis is already accomplished during process analysis and in utilizing the other product and process control tools. There are four steps for performing basic linear trend analysis:

❶   **Define the metrics.**

❷   **Perform data acquisition.**

❸   **Plot the data on a scatter diagram.**

❹   **Calculate the equation of the trend.**

To demonstrate these four steps, we will use data derived from a study of the effect of training on failure rates. The following trend analysis is based on a sample of the data correlating solder certification test scores and quality of solder work performed, as measured by the pass rate of the soldering.

Step 1. Define the Metrics   This step is the same as for the process analysis. In fact, the measure often is selected during the process analysis. The metric or statistic that we define as the dependent variable is the Y variable on scatter plot. The measure of the trend is the independent variable and is represented by the X axis. The following kinds of measurements are used here, all with reference to some scale such as time, space, distance, score, or cycle:

> **Quality.** The measures of fitness of a process or product for its intended use.

> **Cost.** The cost of a process, process element, or product.

> **Timeliness.** The ability of a process to produce a product or service that meets some time requirement.

> **Throughput.** The amount of product or service that can be produced by a process per unit time, space, distance, score, or cycle.

For this example, the measure we use for the trend analysis is the quality of soldering (Y variable) compared to solder certification test score. This measure tells us whether the score employees receive in training is related to the subsequent quality of their work. The metric is therefore:

$$\text{Solder Quality} \; = \; \frac{\text{Pass}}{\text{Pass + Fail}}$$

Step 2. Perform Data Acquisition   Again, we collect the data in the same way as for process analysis. Data is collected from the existing process control points of processes, or you can develop check sheets or data arrays specifically for trend analysis if required. Once the data is collected, it must be placed in a data table such as the one in Figure 6-30.

We will use this data to construct the trend analysis. This data was derived from the soldering certification test scores of 50 employees and the quality of their work, as measured by the metric we designed in step 1. We are interested in the quality of the solder compared to the score on the certification test.

Step 3. Plot the Data on a Scatter Diagram   Using the standard scatter plotting methods provided in this chapter, we will produce a scatter plot of the data. In our example, Figure 6-31, the data points from Figure 6-30 are plotted on the graph.   The resulting scatter plot displays solder quality on the vertical plane on the left side of the chart (the Y axis).   The solder certification score is displayed on the horizontal axis of the scatter plot (the X axis).

Score	Quality	Score	Quality
0.62	0.86	0.81	0.96
0.66	0.85	0.82	0.97
0.69	0.83	0.82	0.96
0.70	0.85	0.83	0.97
0.72	0.86	0.85	0.97
0.72	0.88	0.86	0.96
0.72	0.86	0.86	0.95
0.72	0.88	0.86	0.96
0.73	0.85	0.86	0.94
0.73	0.87	0.86	0.96
0.74	0.89	0.87	0.97
0.75	0.90	0.87	0.98
0.75	0.90	0.88	0.98
0.76	0.92	0.88	0.98
0.76	0.92	0.88	0.99
0.76	0.91	0.88	0.98
0.76	0.93	0.88	0.98
0.76	0.94	0.88	0.99
0.77	0.93	0.90	0.99
0.77	0.94	0.90	0.99
0.77	0.94	0.92	0.99
0.78	0.95	0.92	1.00
0.79	0.93	0.94	0.99
0.80	0.95	0.97	0.98
0.80	0.96	0.99	1.00

Figure 6-30.   Trend Analysis Data Table

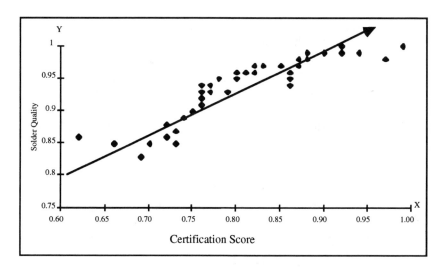

Figure 6-31.   Scatter Plot Solder Quality and Certification Score.

Step 4.   Calculate and Evaluate the Equation of the Trend   The equation of
the trend is also known as the regression equation or regression line. Here we
will study the linear regression line as it is represented by the equation:

$$y = ax + b$$

Where:

> **a** = The slope of the regression line
> **b** = The constant value of Y when X = 0
> **x** = The value of the independent variable
> **y** = The value of the dependent variable

To determine the equation of the line, we must first accomplish a few intermediate steps. We can calculate the slope of the regression line using the following equation:

$$a = \frac{\sum (X_i - \overline{X})(Y_i - \overline{Y})}{\sum (X_i - \overline{X})^2}$$

Where:

X = The value of the ith observation of the independent variable
$\overline{X}$ = The average value of the independent variable
y = The value of the ith observation of the dependent variable
$\overline{y}$ = The average value of the dependent variable

The next intermediate step is to determine the value of b, the constant value of y value when x is equal to zero:

$$b = \overline{Y} - aX$$

We can perform these calculations using a simple spreadsheet as demonstrated in Figure 6-32; this uses a sample of the data from Figure 6-30 to establish a trend line.

Sample	Score X	Quality Y	$(X-\overline{X})$	$(Y-\overline{Y})$	$(Y-\overline{Y})^2$	$(X-\overline{X})(Y-\overline{Y})$	$(X-\overline{X})^2$
1	0.62	0.86	-0.20	-0.08	0.01	0.02	0.04
2	0.69	0.83	-0.13	-0.11	0.01	0.01	0.02
3	0.72	0.86	-0.10	-0.08	0.01	0.01	0.01
4	0.74	0.89	-0.08	-0.05	0.00	0.00	0.01
5	0.75	0.90	-0.07	-0.04	0.00	0.00	0.00
6	0.76	0.92	-0.06	-0.02	0.00	0.00	0.00
7	0.76	0.93	-0.06	-0.01	0.00	0.00	0.00
8	0.77	0.94	-0.05	0.00	0.00	0.00	0.00
9	0.79	0.93	-0.03	-0.01	0.00	0.00	0.00
10	0.80	0.96	-0.02	0.02	0.00	0.00	0.00
11	0.82	0.97	0.00	0.03	0.00	0.00	0.00
12	0.83	0.97	0.01	0.03	0.00	0.00	0.00
13	0.86	0.96	0.04	0.02	0.00	0.00	0.00
14	0.87	0.98	0.05	0.04	0.00	0.00	0.00
15	0.88	0.98	0.06	0.04	0.00	0.00	0.00
16	0.88	0.99	0.06	0.05	0.00	0.00	0.00
17	0.90	0.99	0.08	0.05	0.00	0.00	0.01
18	0.94	0.99	0.12	0.05	0.00	0.01	0.02
19	0.97	0.98	0.15	0.04	0.00	0.01	0.02
20	0.99	1.00	0.17	0.06	0.00	0.01	0.03
Sum	16.340	18.830			0.048	0.082	0.173
Avg	0.817	0.942					

Figure 6-32. Trend Analysis Spreadsheet.

Using the Figure, we can now calculate the values for *a* and *b* in the trend equation. The slope (*a*) of the regression line is calculated using the equation shown earlier and the data from the Figure. The numerator in this equation is the sum of XY (=0.12) from the spreadsheet. The denominator in the equation is the sum of the last column in the spreadsheet. These operations can be accomplished easily using a manual or automated spreadsheet:

$$ a = \frac{\Sigma\ (X_i - \overline{X})\ (Y - \overline{Y})}{\Sigma\ (X_i - \overline{X})^2} = \frac{.082}{.173} = .47 $$

We calculated the value of Y when X is equal to zero (b) using the equation for that factor and the information derived from the spreadsheet. The average values ($\overline{Y}$ and $\overline{X}$) are taken directly from the spreadsheet. The value for a was just calculated, and the average value for x is shown in Figure 6-32.

$$ b = \overline{Y} - a\overline{X} = .94 - (.47)\,(.817) = .56 $$

Therefore, the equation of the trend (or regression) line is:

$$ Y = aX + b = (0.57)\,(X) + 0.47 $$

In Figure 6-33, we have drawn the line of the equation through the scatter plot of the data to clarify the relationship of the trend equation to the data.

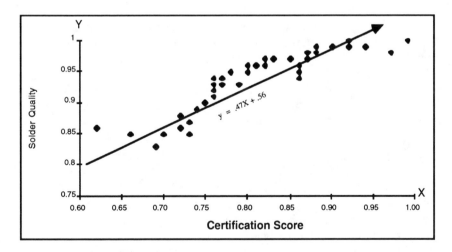

Figure 6-33. Scatter Plot: Solder Quality and Certification Score.

Evaluate the Equation of the Trend

Using the Trend Equation. Now that we have developed the trend equation and understand how it relates to the data on the scatter plot, we can use the equation to make projections. The *a* element of the equation is the slope of the trend line. For every unit of movement of the independent variable, the dependent variable moves *a* units. In this example, the value for *a* is 0.57. The units for both the independent (Y) and dependent (X) variables are percentages. Therefore, for every percentage point that is gained in the solder qualification score 0.57 percent (on average) is gained in quality. We can use the equation in this way to make projections. If we could improve the minimum standard for the solder qualification score from 0.75 to 0.85, what effect would this improvement have on the quality of the solder process?

$$Y = aX + b$$

$$Y = (0.57)(0.75) + 0.47$$

$$Y = 0.90$$

$$Y = (0.57)(0.85) + 0.47$$

$$Y = 0.95$$

We can project that requiring a minimum solder certification score of .85 for our employees will improve the minimum acceptable quality of soldering from 0.90 to 0.95.

Coefficient of Determination. Does the equation of the trend line really represent the data? How accurate is it? A test to answer these questions is a goodness-of-fit test. We will use the analytical technique called the coefficient of determination, represented by the symbol lower case r^2. (The square root of the coefficient of determination, *r*, is called the correlation coefficient.) The coefficient of determination measures the portion of the total variance in the dependent variable (*y*) that is explained by the independent variable (*x*). The explanation of the theory behind these statements could be demonstrated with elegant mathematical manipulations, but we will spare you that aggravation—let's get down to business. The coefficient of determination measures the explained variation in our trend equation, compared to the total variation:

$$r^2 = \frac{a\Sigma (X_i - \overline{X})(Y_i - \overline{Y})}{\Sigma (Y_i - \overline{Y})^2}$$

In this equation, the numerator represents the variation that can be explained by the relationship between the dependent and independent variables. The denominator represents the total variation of the dependent variable. Therefore, the ratio between these two elements measures what proportion of the variation is accounted for in the trend equation. A coefficient of determination of 0.50 or less indicates that there is not a correlation between the dependent and independent variables, and that the trend equation is not a good representation of what is occurring. A coefficient of determination of 0.50 or better indicates that we have a correlation and a coefficient of 0.75 or better indicates a strong relationship. Using this equation, and the data from the spreadsheet in Figure 6-32, we get:

$$r^2 = \frac{a\Sigma (X_i - \overline{X})(Y_i - \overline{Y})}{\Sigma (Y_i - \overline{Y})^2}$$

$$r^2 = \frac{(0.47)(0.082)}{0.048} = \frac{0.039}{0.048} = 0.80$$

The coefficient of determination at 0.80 indicates that there is a sufficient correlation to use the equation for forecasting and other decision making. Values of r^2 less than 0.50 may indicate that the best regression equation is a higher order polynomial. The methods used to find the trend equation in these cases are very rigorous, and we will reserve them for a more advanced text. Most data used in business can be described using linear trend analysis, and we will concentrate our efforts at that level.

KEY POINTS

CAUSE AND EFFECT ANALYSIS

Group together various causes. Organize the ideas resulting from the brain-storming session into the major categories. Do not overload the diagram; keep it as simple as possible, sorting out those ideas that are not direct causes of the problem.

Construct a separate diagram for each problem. Do not combine problems, but keep them separate and perform cause and effect analysis for each. Create a positive, solution-oriented atmosphere: "We are looking for a solution," *not* "let's find who caused this."

DATA FIGURES

Understand the analysis that you will perform on the data collected. Collect the data necessary for that analysis; avoid the trap of collecting all the data available.

Once you have identified the data that is required determine how the data is to be collected. Check sheets, data figures, manual or automated. Use the simplest method of collecting the data. Do not find a technology and try to fit an application to it, rather understand your application and find the appropriate technology.

PARETO ANALYSIS

Pareto analysis can be a very powerful tool in performing process analysis. There are three types of Pareto analysis, each applicable to specific analytical requirements:

Basic Pareto analysis is used to determine the most frequently occurring data element (area, process, item). This approach is useful when the actual number of occurrences is relevant to the analysis. It analysis identifies the significant few and the insignificant many, highlighting those areas, processes, and items that require the analyst's further attention.

Weighted Pareto analysis is employed when the significance of the data element is weighted by cost, time, quantity, or some other factor.

Comparative Pareto analysis is used to compare two or more data sets, such as data before and after process changes, comparison of different activities producing the same product, or the use of different equipment.

HISTOGRAMS

A histogram displays the cumulative data at a given point in time. The usefulness of histograms is in the understanding of the relative frequency (percentages) or frequency (numbers) of the data and how that data is distributed.

SCATTER DIAGRAMS

Scatter diagrams organize data using two variables, an independent variable (x) and a dependent variable (y). This data is then recorded on a simple two-dimensional graph showing the relationship between the variables.

TREND ANALYSIS

Trend analysis is a statistical method for determining the equation that best fits the data in a scatter plot. Trend analysis quantifies the relationships of the data, determines the equation, and measures the fit of the equation to the data. The equation of the regression or trend line provides a clear and understandable measure of the change caused in the output variable by every incremental change of the input or independent variable.

EXAMPLE

The manufacturing equipment division of LWCI maintains a service department to service the customers of the division. The department provides technical assistance, equipment setup service, and on-site repair for the manufacturing equipment produced by the division. In keeping with the LWCI goal of becoming a world class competitor, and to achieve implementation of continuous measurable improvement, the service department performs a process analysis of its key processes. For example, the customer service and support department formed an operating team to accomplish the process analysis. Here we will review how the team applied the product and process control tools to the field service of the LWCI 1587 coating machine.

The LWCI 1587 coating machine applies liquid preservative coatings to metal services using a closely controlled spray. The machine applies the spray through a high-pressure application system that uses a flow rate controller to measure the application of the product. The machine applies the coating to surfaces by moving a jointed arm around the item being preserved. An electronic motion controller controls the arm movements. The system operates on a low pressure hydraulic system that is run by electric motors. The system uses separate power supplies for the electronic controllers and drive motors. The application arm is driven by a central drive shaft.

As a part of the process analysis, the service department needed to determine what controls were in place within that department and how they were being employed to provide world class service for this equipment, both at the time of the analysis and in the future. This assessment was keyed to providing better service to the customers and feedback to the those responsible for the design and development of the coating machines.

> ➤   **Analysis of the service requirements of the LWCI 1587 system.**

> ➤   **Analysis to determine the out year requirements for the LWCI 1587 system.**

For the first analysis, the team members selected to perform data collection determined that they could accomplish the evaluation using service call data already on hand for the system. There were 725 LWCI 1587 systems in use. To provide data that represented recent requirements, and to smooth out any fluctuations in the data, the team decided to use the most recent 12 months of service reports. They placed these manual reports into a data Figure,   in

Example Figure 6-1. The data Figure provided a structured view of the data and provided the basis for further analysis.

Item	Name	Months												Total
		1	2	3	4	5	6	7	8	9	10	11	12	
A	Central Dive Shaft	4	4	4	5	4	5	6	3	5	5	7	4	56
B	Controller Board	0	0	1	2	0	0	0	2	2	0	3	0	10
C	Drive Motor	3	0	1	0	2	2	3	0	0	1	1	2	15
D	Hydraulic System	2	0	0	0	2	3	0	2	1	2	1	1	14
E	Power Supply	1	0	1	2	1	0	0	1	1	0	0	1	7
F	LWCI 1587 (Total)	13	14	7	12	14	18	13	14	12	13	15	17	102

Example Figure 6-1. LCWI 1587 System Service Calls.

From the data Figure, the team determined that 102 service calls were made for the LWCI 1587 during the previous 12-month period. The data Figure also provided totals for each assembly that required service, and the number of service calls during each of the 12 months.

The next tool the team used to evaluate the data was a histogram. They produced the histogram using a standard spreadsheet program on a personal computer. The resulting histogram is demonstrated in Example Figure 6-2. The letter code for each column of the histogram represents the associated name of the failing assembly from the data Figure in Example Figure 6-1.

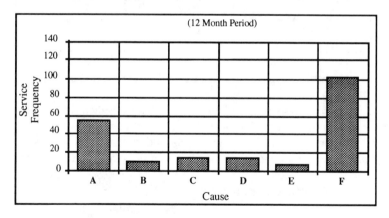

Example Figure 6-2. LWCI 1587 Service Calls.

The histogram further clarified the data. Since this was attribute data, no frequency distribution could be derived from the histogram. The team decided to employ the basic Pareto analysis tool for frequency of occurrence to analyze this data further. They used the same simple spreadsheet program to create the Pareto diagram in Example Figure 6-3.

From this Pareto analysis, the team determined several important facts concerning the service calls for the 725 LWCI 1587 systems currently being used by customers. The central drive shaft (A) accounted for the highest number of service calls with 51 failures or 55% of all service calls during the previous 12 months. Drive motor (C) failures were the next most frequent, with 15 failures or 15% of the service calls. The cumulative failure rate for central drive shafts and drive motors together is 70%. The hydraulic system (D) accounted for 14 service calls, or 13% of the total calls. The cumulative total of service calls for items A, C, and D is 83%. Compared to these, the failure rates for the controller board (B) and power supply (E) were of little consequence. The controller board required 10 service calls during the year and the power supplies only 7.

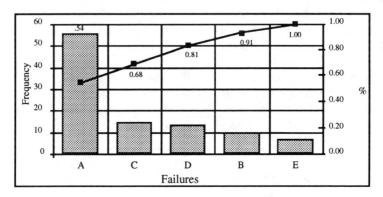

Example Figure 6-3. LWCI 1587 System Pareto Analysis.

The Pareto analysis provided the team with a clear picture of the most frequently occurring service calls. The service department could use this information to be better prepared to respond to calls, and to plan on what tools, training, and personnel would provide the best service for the LWCI 1587 customers.

➤ **Central Drive Shafts**   **Failures 56**
                               Cumulative 0.55

➤ **Drive Motors**   **Failures 15**
                               Cumulative 0.70

➤ **Hydraulic System**   **Failures 14**
                               Cumulative 0.83

➤ **Controller Boards**   **Failures 10**
                            Cumulative 0.93

➤ **Power Supplies**   **Failures 7**
                            Cumulative 1.00

The picture concerning the service requirements for the LWCI 1587 was becoming much clearer, and the department was better able to plan and organize the actions needed to control the service process. One element that highlighted itself very clearly was the proportion of service calls associated with the central drive shaft (significant few, insignificant many). The team wanted to analyze the failures causing these service calls corrective action. The team, with the concurrence of the management steering committee formed another team to perform cause and effect analysis.

This team included personnel from the production and design departments of the manufacturing equipment division, as well as engineers and production personnel from the machine tool division, where the drive shafts were produced. The cause and effect analysis team, after some initial training and team building, decided to use the random method of cause and effect analysis. Shaft failures were caused by physical damage to the shafts; they were worn on the ends connecting them to the drive motor, and in some cases were actually warped. The team brainstormed the possible causes of failure of the drive shaft and constructed the cause and effect analysis shown in Example Figure 6-4.

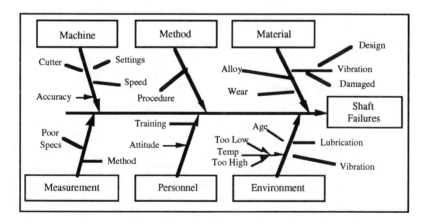

Example Figure 6-4. LCWI 1587 System Drive Shaft
Cause and Effect Analysis.

The analysis clearly indicated the cause of that the failures was the "quality" of the shafts coming from the machine tool division. This problem affected the service department directly, since the shafts are the primary cause of failure for this system. Further action was required by the machine tool division as a product and process improvement.

The service department also wanted to control its responsiveness to the customers by better forecasting of customer needs. The team decided to look at the service data relative to the age of the systems fielded and determine if any service requirements were influenced by age-related degradation of the systems. Data was available from the service records and from the date associated with LWCI 1587 serial numbers. The data for the 725 systems produced in the last four years and currently in use is available in existing records. The machines were produced at the rate of about 180 per year during that period, and the service calls for that period are listed in Example Figure 6-5. The figure also shows the number of maintenance calls based upon the age of the systems, stated in months. The team used data in this Figure to create the scatter plot in Example Figure 6-6.

Age (Months)	Service Calls	Age (Months)	Service Calls	Age (Months)	Service Calls	Age (Months)	Service Calls
1	3	13	5	25	6	37	5
2	0	14	6	26	4	38	6
3	0	15	5	27	6	39	9
4	2	15	7	28	7	40	6
5	1	17	5	29	7	41	7
6	0	18	6	30	6	42	8
7	2	19	6	31	7	43	9
8	4	20	6	32	6	44	8
9	3	21	4	33	7	45	9
10	2	22	5	34	7	46	8
11	3	23	6	35	8	47	10
12	4	24	5	36	7	48	10

Example Figure 6-5. LWCI 1587 Data

From the scatter plot, the team was able to determine that there was a positive correlation between the dependent (Y) and Independent (X) variables. The number of service calls is related to system age in months: as age increases, the number of service calls increases. The team therefore predicted that, as the systems aged there would be more service calls from the customers. This was not a surprise, but the analysis enabled them to understand those relationships much better and to understand how to control the service requirements to a much better degree.

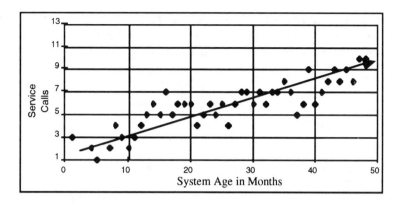

Example Figure 6-6. LWCI 1587 System Service Calls.

The team decided to perform a trend analysis on the scatter plot data, to forecast the requirements for the next year. They made trend analysis data Figure and evaluated it using the linear trend equation. The data Figure is presented in Example Figure 6-7, on the facing page. The team then proceeded to use the information from the data Figure to determine the equation of the trend line:

$$Y = aX + b$$

To evaluate the slope of the line (a):

$$a = \frac{\Sigma (X_i - \overline{X}) \ (Y_i - \overline{Y})}{\Sigma (X_i - X)^2} = \frac{1455.5}{9212} = 0.158$$

To evaluate the constant value of (b):

$$b = \overline{Y} - a\overline{X} = 5.48 - (0.158)(24.5) = 1.608$$

Therefore, the equation of the trend line is:

$$Y = aX + b$$
$$Y = (0.158) \ (X) + 1.61$$

The equation could be used to forecast service calls for a system of any age (in months). In the equation below the team evaluated the maintenance requirements based upon the 49th month with the current population of 725 systems.

$$Y = aX \pm b$$

$$Y = (.16)(49) + 1.57$$

$$Y = 9.41$$

The result was 9.41, or nine service calls. But how accurate is this estimate? Does the team want to use this equation to forecast maintenance requirements? To determine the answer, the team performed a correlation analysis using the data from Example Figure 6-7. They evaluated the coefficient of determination (r^2) using the equation:

$$r^2 = \frac{a \Sigma (X_i - \overline{X})(Y_i - \overline{Y})}{\Sigma (Y_i - \overline{Y})^2}$$

$$r^2 = \frac{(.158)(1455.5)}{299.98} = \frac{229.97}{299.98}$$

$$r^2 = .77$$

The r^2 value of .77 indicated a strong correlation between the age of systems and the service calls received. It showed that the equation was sufficiently representative of this relationship to be used for forecasting. Using this data, the team forecasted the service requirements for the next 12-month period. The division production schedule would remain the same as in previous years; therefore, the forecast needed to account for maintenance calls for the existing systems for months 49 to 60, and new systems with ages of 1 to 12 months. This information is presented in Example Figure 6-8.

The forecast provided fact based information for the service division to control its service call process. This information, and the data from the previous evaluations, provided a projection of the number of service calls that would be needed and the approximate proportion of the calls for each specific assembly (for example, 55% drive shafts). In addition to the frequency and types of calls, this analysis also provided geographic information regarding the service calls. At this point, the department was ready to consider using control charts.

	Age X	Service Y	$(X-\overline{X})$	$(Y-\overline{Y})$	$(Y-\overline{Y})^2$	$(Y-\overline{Y})(X-\overline{X})$	$(X-\overline{X})^2$
	1	3	-23.48	-2.48	6.15	58.23	551.31
	2	0	-22.48	-5.48	30.03	123.19	505.35
	3	0	-21.48	-5.48	30.03	117.71	461.39
	4	2	-20.48	-3.48	12.11	71.27	419.43
	5	1	-19.48	-4.48	20.07	87.27	379.47
	6	0	-18.48	-5.48	30.03	101.27	341.51
	7	2	-17.48	-3.48	12.11	60.83	305.55
	8	4	-16.48	-1.48	2.19	24.39	271.59
	9	3	-15.48	-2.48	6.15	38.39	239.63
	10	2	-14.48	-3.48	12.11	50.39	209.67
	11	3	-13.48	-2.48	6.15	33.43	181.71
	12	4	-12.48	-1.48	2.19	18.47	155.75
	13	5	-11.48	-0.48	0.23	5.51	131.79
	14	6	-10.48	0.52	0.27	-5.45	109.83
	15	5	-9.48	-0.48	0.23	4.55	89.87
	15	7	-9.48	1.52	2.31	-14.41	89.87
	17	5	-7.48	-0.48	0.23	3.59	55.95
	18	6	-6.48	0.52	0.27	-3.37	41.99
	19	6	-5.48	0.52	0.27	-2.85	30.03
	20	6	-4.48	0.52	0.27	-2.33	20.07
	21	4	-3.48	-1.48	2.19	5.15	12.11
	22	5	-2.48	-0.48	0.23	1.19	6.15
	23	6	-1.48	0.52	0.27	-0.77	2.19
	24	5	-0.48	-0.48	0.23	0.23	0.23
	25	6	0.52	0.52	0.27	0.27	0.27
	26	4	1.52	-1.48	2.19	-2.25	2.31
	27	6	2.52	0.52	0.27	1.31	6.35
	28	7	3.52	1.52	2.31	5.35	12.39
	29	7	4.52	1.52	2.31	6.87	20.43
	30	6	5.52	0.52	0.27	2.87	30.47
	31	7	6.52	1.52	2.31	9.91	42.51
	32	6	7.52	0.52	0.27	3.91	56.55
	33	7	8.52	1.52	2.31	12.95	72.59
	34	7	9.52	1.52	2.31	14.47	90.63
	35	8	10.52	2.52	6.35	26.51	110.67
	36	7	11.52	1.52	2.31	17.51	132.71
	37	5	12.52	-0.48	0.23	-6.01	156.75
	38	6	13.52	0.52	0.27	7.03	182.79
	39	9	14.52	3.52	12.39	51.11	210.83
	40	6	15.52	0.52	0.27	8.07	240.87
	41	7	16.52	1.52	2.31	25.11	272.91
	42	8	17.52	2.52	6.35	44.15	306.95
	43	9	18.52	3.52	12.39	65.19	342.99
	44	8	19.52	2.52	6.35	49.19	381.03
	45	9	20.52	3.52	12.39	72.23	421.07
	46	8	21.52	2.52	6.35	54.23	463.11
	47	10	22.52	4.52	20.43	101.79	507.15
	48	10	23.52	4.52	20.43	106.31	553.19
Sum	1175	263			299.98	1453.98	9229.98
Avg	24.48	5.48					

Example Figure 6-7. Trend Analysis Spreadsheet.

Next 12 Month Period			
Month	Existing System Calls	New System Calls	Total System Calls
1	9.41	1.73	11
2	9.57	1.89	11
3	9.73	1.57	11
4	9.89	2.21	12
5	10.05	2.37	12
6	10.21	1.57	12
7	10.37	2.69	13
8	10.53	2.85	13
9	10.69	3.01	14
10	10.85	1.57	11
11	11.01	3.33	14
12	11.17	3.49	15
Total	123.48	26.71	150

Example Figure 6-8. LWCI 1587 System Service Call Forecast.

7

Statistical Process Control Charts

CONTROL CHARTS ALLOW ANY PROCESS TO ACHIEVE HIGH QUALITY, LOWER COST AND HIGHER CAPABILITY .

CONTROL CHARTS PROVIDE A GRAPHIC DEPICTION of the quantifiable characteristics of process, process element or work activity. Control charts display the plotted values of the process and indicate if the process is approaching an established limit. In everyday business applications, control charts have five uses:

➢   **Determine if a process is trending**

➢   **Determine if a process is in control**

➢   Achieve statistical process control

➢   **Reduce process variability**

➢   Forecast requirements

CONTROL CHARTS

The use of control charts focuses on the prevention of defects, rather than their detection and rejection. In business, government, and industry, economy and efficiency are always best served by prevention. It costs much more to produce an unsatisfactory product or service than it does to produce a satisfactory one. There are many costs associated with producing unsatisfactory goods and services. These costs are in labor, materials, facilities, and the loss of customers. The cost of producing a proper product can be reduced significantly by the application of statistical process control charts.

Control Charts and the Normal Distribution

The construction, use, and interpretation of control charts is based upon the normal statistical distribution as indicated in Figure 7-1. The centerline of the control chart represents the average or mean of the data ($\overline{X}$). The upper and lower control limits (UCL and LCL) respectively represent this mean plus and minus three standard deviations of the data ($\overline{X}$ +/- 3s).   Either the lower case s or the Greek letter σ (sigma) represents the standard deviation for Control Charts.

The normal distribution and it's relationship to control charts is represented on the right of the Figure. The normal distribution can be described entirely by its mean and standard deviation. The normal distribution is a bell shaped curve (sometimes called the Gaussian distribution) that is symmetrical about the mean, slopes downward on both sides to infinity and theoretically has an infinite range. In the normal distribution 99.73% of all measurements lie within $\overline{X}$+3s and $\overline{X}$-3s, this is why the limits on control charts are called three sigma limits. We will discuss how to establish these statistics for control charts as we proceed in this chapter.

Some data encountered in our daily operations is not normally distributed. However, due to the contributions of Dr. Walter Shewhart we can still use a control chart based upon the normal distribution. Dr. Shewhart developed the method of subgrouping and sampling process data such that, even though individual process values are not normally distributed, the values of the subgroups demonstrate a normal distribution. Using the same basic theory we can use the sub-grouped ranges to control process variation. For variable control charts, the recommended sample size for each subgroup is five, and for attribute control charts sample size should be ten. Each of these control charts should be established using 20 or more subgroups as baseline data. You will see this theory in practical application as we develop the different types of flowcharts.

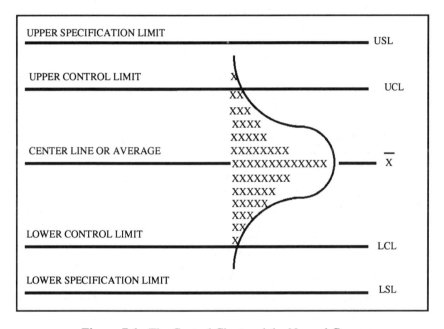

Figure 7-1. The Control Chart and the Normal Curve

Common Cause Variation and Special Cause Variation

Control chart analysis determines whether the inherent process variability and the process average are at stable levels; one or both are out of statistical control (not stable); or that appropriate action needs to be taken. Another purpose of using control charts is to distinguish between the inherent, random variability of a process and the variability attributed to an assignable cause. The sources of the random variability are often referred to as common causes. These are the sources that cannot be changed readily, without significant restructuring of the process. Special cause variability, by contrast, is subject to correction within the process under process control.

➣   **Common Cause Variability:** This source of random
variation is always present in any process. It is that
part of the variability inherent in the process itself.
The cause of this variation can be corrected only by a
management decision to change the basic process.

➣   **Special Cause Variability:** This variation can be
controlled at the process level. Special causes are indicated by a point on the control chart that is beyond
the control limit or by a persistent trend approaching
the control limit.

To use process control measurement data effectively, it is important to understand the concept of variation. No two product or process characteristics are
exactly alike, because any process contains many sources of variability. The
differences between products may be large, or they may be almost immeasurably
small, but they are always present. Some sources of variation in the process can
cause immediate differences in the product, such as a change in suppliers or the
accuracy of an individual's work. Other sources of variation such as tool wear,
environmental changes or increased administrative control, tend to cause
changes in the product or service only over a longer period of time.

To control and improve a process, we must trace the total variation back to
its sources. Again the sources are common causes and special causes variation.
Common causes are the many sources of variation that always exist within a
process that is in a state of statistical control. Special causes (often called
assignable causes) are any factors causing variation that cannot be adequately
explained by any single distribution of the process output, as would be the case
if the process were in statistical control. Unless all the special causes of variation are identified and corrected, they will continue to affect the process output
in unpredictable ways.

The factors that cause the most variability in the process are the main factors found on cause and effect analysis charts: people, machines, methodology,
materials, measurement, and environment. These causes can either result from
special causes or be common causes inherent in the process.

➣   **The theory of control charts suggests, that if the source**
of variation is from chance alone, the process will re-
main within the three sigma limits.

➣   **When the process goes "out-of-control", special causes**
exist. These need to be investigated, and corrective
action must be taken.

Control Chart Types

Just as there are two types of data, continuous and discrete, there are two types of control charts: variable charts for use with continuous data and attribute charts for use with discrete data. Each type of control chart can be used with specific types of data. Figure 7-2 provides a brief overview of the types control charts and their applications.

VARIABLE CHARTS	ATTRIBUTE CHARTS
$\overline{X}$ and R charts: To observe changes in the mean and range (variance) of a process.	p chart: For the fraction of attributes nonconforming or defective in a sample of varying size.
$\overline{X}$ and s charts: For a variable average and standard deviation.	np charts: For the number of attributes nonconforming or defective in a sample of constant size.
$\overline{X}$ and s^2 charts: for a variable average and variance.	c charts: For the number of attributes nonconforming or defective in a single item within a subgroup, lot, or sample area of constant size.
	u charts: For the number of attributes nonconforming or defective in a single item within a Subgroup, lot, or sample area of varying size.

Figure 7-2. Types of Control Charts and Applications

Variable Charts Control charts for variables are powerful tools that we can use when measurements from a process are variable. Examples of variable data are the diameter of a bearing, electrical output, or the torque on a fastener.

As shown in Figure 7-2, $\overline{X}$ and R charts are used to measure control processes whose characteristics are continuous variables such as weight, length, ohms, time, or volume. The p and np charts are used to measure and control processes displaying attribute characteristics in a sample. We use p charts when the number of failures is expressed as a fraction, or np charts when the failures are expressed as a number. The c and u charts are used to measure the number or proportion of defects in a single item. The c control chart is applied when the sample size or area is fixed, and the u chart when the sample size or area is not fixed.

Attribute Charts Although control charts are most often thought of in terms of variables, there are also versions for attributes. Attribute data have only two values (conforming/non conforming, pass/fail, go/no-go, present/absent), but they can still be counted, recorded, and analyzed. Some examples are: the presence of a required label, the installation of all required fasteners, the presence of solder drips, or the continuity of an electrical circuit. We also use attribute charts for characteristics that are measurable, if the results are recorded in a simple yes/no fashion, such as the conformance of a shaft diameter when measured on a go/no-go gauge, or the acceptability of threshold margins to a visual or gauge check.

It is possible to use control charts for operations in which attributes are the basis for inspection, in a manner similar to that for variables but with certain differences. If we deal with the fraction rejected out of a sample, the type of control chart used is called a p chart. If we deal with the actual number rejected, the control chart is called an np chart. If articles can have more than one non-conformity, and all are counted for subgroups of fixed size, the control chart is called a c chart. Finally, if the number of nonconformities per unit is the quantity of interest, the control chart is called a u chart.

The power of control charts (Shewhart technique) lies in their ability to determine if the cause of variation is a special cause, that can be affected at the process level, or a common cause that requires a change at the management level. The information from the control chart can then be used to direct the efforts of the engineers, technicians and managers to achieve preventive or corrective action.

The use of statistical control charts is aimed at studying specific ongoing processes in order to keep them in satisfactory control. By contrast downstream inspection aims to identify defects. In other words, control charts focus on prevention of defects rather than detection and rejection. It seems reasonable, and it has been confirmed in practice, that economy and efficiency are better served by the prevention rather than by detection.

Control Chart Components

All control charts have certain features in common (Figure 7-3). Each control chart has a centerline, statistical control limits, and the calculated attribute or control data. Additionally, some control charts contain specification limits.

The centerline is a solid (unbroken) line that represents the mean or arithmetic average of the measurements or counts. This line is also referred to as the X Bar line ($\overline{X}$). There are two statistical control limits, the upper control limit for values greater than the mean, and the lower control limit for values less than the mean.

Specification limits are used when specific parametric requirements exist for a process, product or operation. These limits usually apply to the data and are the pass/fail criteria for the operation. They differ from statistical control limits in that they are prescribed for a process, rather than resulting from the measurement of the process.

The data element of control charts varies somewhat among variable and attribute control charts. We will discuss specific examples as a part of the discussion on individual control charts.

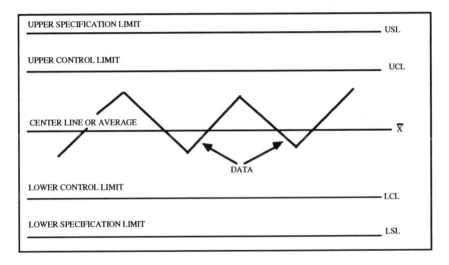

Figure 7-3. Control Chart Elements

CONTROL CHART INTERPRETATION

There are many possibilities for interpreting various kinds of patterns and shifts on control charts. If properly interpreted, a control chart can tell us much more than simply whether the process in or out of control. Experience and training can lead to much greater skill in extracting clues regarding process behavior, such as that shown in Figure 7-4. Statistical guidance is invaluable, but an intimate knowledge of the process being studied is vital in bringing about improvements.

A control chart can tell us when to look for trouble, but it cannot by itself tell us where to look, or what cause will be found. Actually, in many cases, one of the greatest benefits from a control chart is that it tells when to leave a process alone. Sometimes the variability is increased unnecessarily when an operator keeps trying to make small corrections, rather than letting the natural range of variability stabilize. The following paragraphs describe some of the ways the underlying distribution patterns can behave or misbehave.

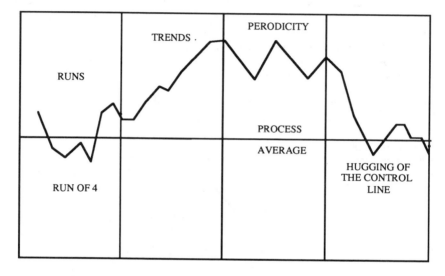

Figure 7-4. Control Chart Interpretation

Runs

When several successive points line up on one side of the central line, this pattern is called a run. The number of points in that run is called the length of the run. As a rule of thumb, if the run has a length of seven points, there is an abnormality in the process. Figure 7-5 demonstrates an example of a run.

Trends

If there is a continued rise or fall in a series of points, this pattern is called a trend. In general, if seven consecutive points continue to rise or fall, there is an abnormality. Often, the points go beyond one of the control limits before reaching seven. Figure 7-6 demonstrates an example of trends.

Periodicity

Points that show the same pattern of change (rise or fall) over equal intervals denote periodicity. Figure 7-7 demonstrates an example of periodicity.

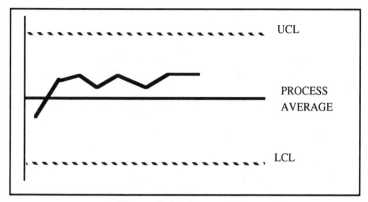

Figure 7-5.   Process Run

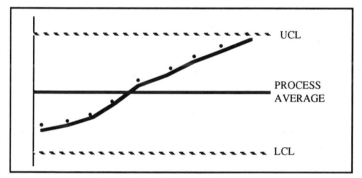

Figure 7-6.   Control Chart Trends

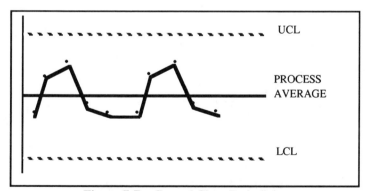

Figure 7-7.   Control Chart Periodicity

Hugging the Centerline or Control Limit

Points on the control chart that are close to the central line or to the control limit, are said to hug the line. Often, in this situation, a different type of data or data from different factors has been mixed into the subgroup. In such cases it is necessary to change the subgrouping, reassemble the data and redraw the control chart. To decide whether or not there is hugging of the center line, draw two lines on the control chart, one between the centerline and the UCL and the other between the center line and the LCL. If most of the points are between these two lines, there is an abnormality. To see whether there is hugging of one of the control limits, draw a line two-thirds of the distance between the center line and each of the control lines. There is abnormality if 2 out of 3 points, 3 out of 7 points, or 4 out of 10 points lie within the outer one-third zone. The abnormalities should be evaluated for their cause(s) and corrective action taken. Figure 7-8 demonstrates data hugging the LCL.

Out-of-Control

An abnormality exists when data points exceed either the upper or lower control limits. Figure 7-9 illustrates this occurrence.

In-Control

No obvious abnormalities appear in the control chart. Figure 7-10 demonstrates this desirable process state.

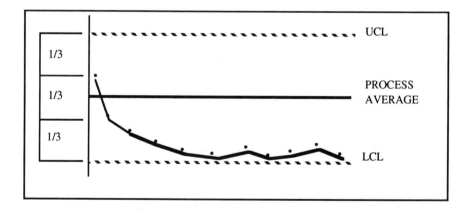

Figure 7-8. Control Chart Hugging

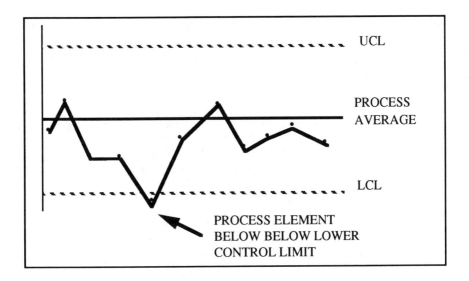

Figure 7-9. Control Chart Out of Control

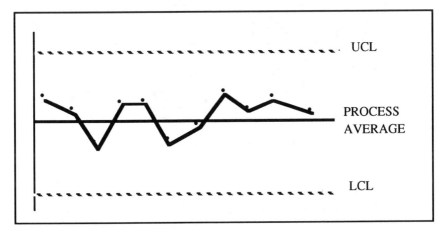

Figure 7-10. Process in Control

$\overline{X}$ AND R CONTROL CHARTS

The $\overline{X}$ and R chart (Figure 7-11) is a powerful tool used when measurements from a process are available. These measurements can be mechanical (diameter, length, width), electronic (resistance, RF output), or related to time (process time, on time, waiting time). The $\overline{X}$ and R variables control chart is used to describe process data in terms of its variation (item-to-item variability) and the process average (location). $\overline{X}$ is the average value in each group and is a measure of location. R is the range of values within each group and is a measure of variability. UCL_X and LCL_X represent the limits for the process averages, and UCL_R and LCL_R are the control limits for the ranges.

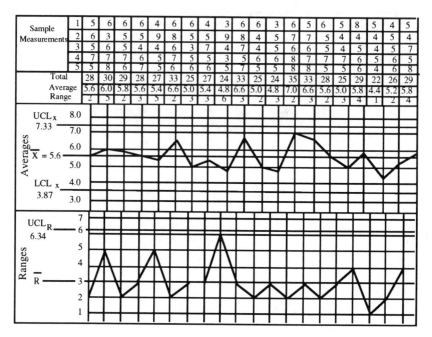

Sample Measurements	1	5	6	6	6	4	6	6	4	3	6	6	3	6	5	6	5	8	5	4	5
	2	6	3	5	5	9	8	5	5	9	8	4	5	7	7	5	4	4	4	5	4
	3	5	6	5	4	4	6	3	7	4	7	4	5	6	6	5	4	5	4	5	7
	4	7	7	7	6	5	7	5	5	3	5	6	6	8	7	7	7	6	5	6	5
	5	5	8	6	7	5	6	6	6	5	7	5	5	8	8	5	5	6	4	6	8
Total		28	30	29	28	27	33	25	27	24	33	25	24	35	33	28	25	29	22	26	29
Average		5.6	6.0	5.8	5.6	5.4	6.6	5.0	5.4	4.8	6.6	5.0	4.8	7.0	6.6	5.6	5.0	5.8	4.4	5.2	5.8
Range		2	5	2	3	5	2	3	3	6	3	2	3	2	3	2	3	4	1	2	4

Figure 7-11. $\overline{X}$ and R Chart

A key element in the construction of control charts of all types is the selection and collection of data. Data must be selected, gathered, recorded, and plotted on a chart for a specific purpose and according to a plan. The placement of data into rational subgroups according to date, time, lot, size, run, or other variable is an important step in variables control charting.

For an initial study of a process, each subgroup should typically consist of five or more consecutive actions representing only a single process factor. The measured actions within a subgroup should all be produced in a very short time interval. Sample sizes must remain constant for all subgroups when using $\overline{X}$ and R Control Charts.

During an initial process study, the subgroups themselves are often taken consecutively or at short intervals, to detect whether the process can shift or show other instability over brief time periods. As the process demonstrates stability (or as process improvements are made), we can increase the time between subgroups. Subgroup frequencies for ongoing production monitoring could be twice per shift, hourly, or at some other feasible rate.

In some cases, existing data may be available which could accelerate this first phase of the study. However, the data should be used only if it is relatively current and known to satisfy the rational subgrouping criteria noted above.

Constructing $\overline{X}$ and R Control Charts

Upon completion of data selection and collection, we are ready to start constructing the control chart in the following nine steps:

1 **Compute $\overline{X}$ and R**

2 **Plot Averages Data**

3 **Plot Regression Data**

4 **Compute and Draw R**

5 **Compute and Draw $\overline{X}$**

6 **Compute and Draw UCL$_R$ and LCL$_R$**

7 **Compute and Draw UCL$_X$ and LCL$_X$**

Step-1 Compute $\overline{X}$ (Mean) and R (Range) For Each Subgroup   Compute the mean and range of each subgroup as indicated in Figure 7-12 below. The letter $\underline{n}$ represents the number of observations within each subgroup.

The mean (sometimes called the average) is the $\overline{X}$ element of the chart; it is the summation of the readings in each cell of the subgroup divided by the number of cells. The range is determined by subtracting the lowest reading in the subgroup from the highest reading in the subgroup. The equations for calculating the X-BAR and R factors are:

$$\text{Mean} = \overline{X} = \frac{X_1 + X_2 + X_3 \ldots + \ldots X_i}{n}$$

$$\text{Range} = X_{Max} - X_{Min}$$

Where:

X = The individual reading from each cell in the subgroup.

n = The number of cells.

$\overline{X}$ = The average of the individual readings

R = The range between the highest reading in a subgroup and the lowest reading in the same subgroup.

In Figure 7-12 the mean ($\overline{X}$) and the range R are calculated as follows using subgroup 21 as an example:

$$\text{Mean} = \overline{X} = \frac{8 + 7 + 10 + 8 + 11}{5} = \frac{44}{5} = 8.8$$

$$\text{Range} = R = 11 - 7 = 4$$

Variable Data Table													
Part No:	Operation					Chart Type				Chart No:			
Stock No:	Dept:					Sample Size:				Frequency:			
	Metric:					Specification:							
Subgroup	1	2	3	4	5	6	7	8	9	10	11	12	13
1	8	8	9	7	9	7	6	9	12	6	9	8	9
Sample 2	9	6	8	12	11	8	11	11	7	8	9	10	8
Measures 3	8	6	8	7	9	10	7	10	7	8	9	9	8
4	7	8	10	8	10	8	6	8	9	9	12	10	10
5	8	8	9	8	9	9	9	10	8	8	11	11	8
Total	40.00	36.00	44.00	42.00	48.00	42.00	39.00	48.00	43.00	39.00	50.00	48.00	43.00
Average	8.00	7.20	8.80	8.40	9.60	8.40	7.80	9.60	8.60	7.80	10.00	9.60	8.60
Range	2	2	2	5	2	3	5	3	5	3	3	3	2
Subgroup	14	15	16	17	18	19	20	21	22	23	24	25	26
1	8	8	9	8	11	8	7	8	9	7	6	9	7
Sample 2	10	10	8	7	7	7	8	7	11	8	8	10	8
Measures 3	9	9	8	7	8	7	8	10	9	10	8	9	10
4	10	10	10	10	9	8	9	8	10	8	9	11	8
5	11	11	8	8	9	7	9	11	9	9	8	11	9
Total	48.00	48.00	43.00	40.00	44.00	37.00	41.00	44.00	48.00	42.00	39.00	50.00	42.00
Average	9.60	9.60	8.60	8.00	8.80	7.40	8.20	8.80	9.60	8.40	7.80	10.00	8.40
Range	3	3	2	3	4	1	2	4	2	3	3	2	3

Figure 7-12. $\overline{X}$ and R Data Table

Step-2 Plot Averages Data First it is necessary to establish the scales for the $\overline{X}$ and R charts respectively. These general rules for establishing the control chart scales are helpful, although they may need to be modified in particular circumstances. In most cases the control chart program you select will provide the proper scales. For $\overline{X}$ charts, the difference between the highest and lowest values on the scale should be at least twice the difference between the highest and lowest sub group average. For the r charts the scale should extend from zero to about 1.5 times the largest range encountered.

Plot the data from the averages table on the chart as indicated in Figure 7-13. In the below example data from a portion of the data table in Figure 7-12 has been used to demonstrate application and connection of the data points for the $\overline{X}$ chart.

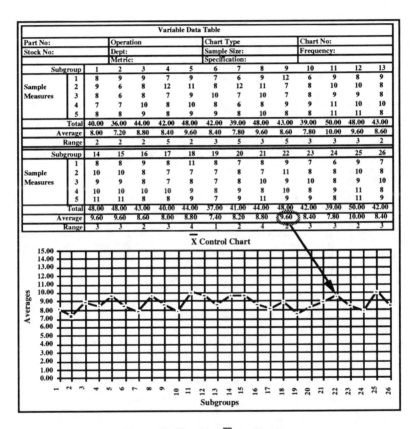

Variable Data Table													
Part No:		Operation				Chart Type				Chart No:			
Stock No:		Dept:				Sample Size:				Frequency:			
		Metric:				Specification:							
Subgroup		1	2	3	4	5	6	7	8	9	10	11	12	13
Sample Measures	1	8	9	9	7	9	7	6	9	12	6	9	8	9
	2	9	6	8	12	11	8	12	11	7	8	10	10	8
	3	8	6	8	7	9	10	7	10	7	8	9	9	8
	4	7	7	10	8	10	8	6	8	9	9	11	10	10
	5	8	8	9	8	9	9	8	10	8	8	11	11	8
Total		40.00	36.00	44.00	42.00	48.00	42.00	39.00	48.00	43.00	39.00	50.00	48.00	43.00
Average		8.00	7.20	8.80	8.40	9.60	8.40	7.80	9.60	8.60	7.80	10.00	9.60	8.60
Range		2	2	2	5	2	3	5	3	5	3	3	3	2
Subgroup		14	15	16	17	18	19	20	21	22	23	24	25	26
Sample Measures	1	8	8	9	8	11	8	7	8	9	7	6	9	7
	2	10	10	8	7	7	7	8	7	11	8	8	10	8
	3	9	9	8	7	8	7	8	10	9	10	8	9	10
	4	10	10	10	10	9	8	9	8	10	8	9	11	8
	5	11	11	8	8	9	7	9	11	9	9	8	11	9
Total		48.00	48.00	43.00	40.00	44.00	37.00	41.00	44.00	48.00	42.00	39.00	50.00	42.00
Average		9.60	9.60	8.60	8.00	8.80	7.40	8.20	8.80	9.60	8.40	7.80	10.00	8.40
Range		3	3	2	3	4	1	2	4	2	3	3	2	3

Figure 7-13. Plot $\overline{X}$ on the chart

Step-3 Plot Ranges Data Plot the data from the range table Figure 7-12. Connect the data points as indicated in Figure 7-14 below.

Step-4 Compute and Draw the Range Average $\overline{R}$ Calculate the average of the ranges ($\overline{R}$) from the data table in Figure 7-12 The average $\overline{R}$ is calculated by summing ($\sum$) the individual value of R (R_i). Then dividing that sum by the total number (n) of subgroups.

$$\bar{R} = \frac{\sum R}{n} = \frac{R_1 + R_2 + R_3 \cdots + \cdots R_i}{n}$$

$$\bar{R} = \frac{78}{26} = 3$$

Where:

$\bar{R}$ is the average value of R

R_i are the individual values of R

n is the number of subgroups.

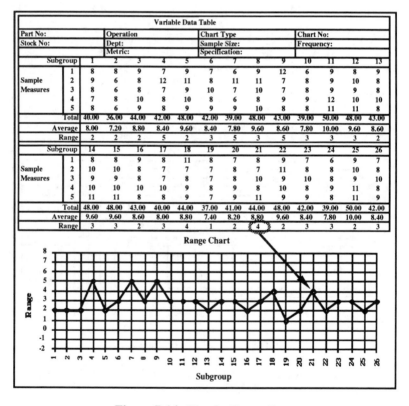

	Variable Data Table												
Part No:		Operation			Chart Type				Chart No:				
Stock No:		Dept:			Sample Size:				Frequency:				
		Metric:			Specification:								
Subgroup		1	2	3	4	5	6	7	8	9	10	11	12	13
	1	8	8	9	7	9	7	6	9	12	6	9	8	9
Sample	2	9	6	8	12	11	8	11	11	7	8	9	10	8
Measures	3	8	6	8	7	9	10	7	10	7	8	9	9	8
	4	7	8	10	8	10	8	6	8	9	9	12	10	10
	5	8	6	9	8	9	9	9	10	8	8	11	11	8
Total		40.00	36.00	44.00	42.00	48.00	42.00	39.00	48.00	43.00	39.00	50.00	48.00	43.00
Average		8.00	7.20	8.80	8.40	9.60	8.40	7.80	9.60	8.60	7.80	10.00	9.60	8.60
Range		2	2	2	5	2	3	5	3	5	3	3	3	2
Subgroup		14	15	16	17	18	19	20	21	22	23	24	25	26
	1	8	8	9	8	11	8	7	8	9	7	6	9	7
Sample	2	10	10	8	7	7	7	8	7	11	8	8	10	8
Measures	3	9	9	8	7	8	7	8	10	9	10	8	9	10
	4	10	10	10	10	9	8	9	8	10	8	9	11	8
	5	11	11	8	8	9	7	9	11	9	9	8	11	9
Total		48.00	48.00	43.00	40.00	44.00	37.00	41.00	44.00	48.00	42.00	39.00	50.00	42.00
Average		9.60	9.60	8.60	8.00	8.80	7.40	8.20	8.80	9.60	8.40	7.80	10.00	8.40
Range		3	3	2	3	4	1	2	4	2	3	3	2	3

Figure 7-14. Plot the Range Data

After calculating the average of the ranges, use the resulting value of $\bar{R}$ to draw the centerline of the Range Chart, as indicated in Figure 7-15.

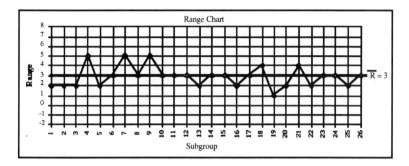

Figure 7-15. Calculate and Draw the Average Range

Step-5 Compute and Draw $\overline{\overline{X}}$ Calculate the grand average ($\overline{\overline{X}}$) of the process measurement data from the data table in Figure 7-12. by summing (Σ) each subgroup average ($\overline{X}$) from the data table and dividing this sum by the total number of Subgroups.

$$\overline{\overline{X}} = \frac{\Sigma X_i}{n} = \frac{\overline{X}_1 + \overline{X}_2 + \overline{X}_3 \cdots + \cdots \overline{X}}{n}$$

$$\overline{\overline{X}} = \frac{225}{26} = 8.64$$

Where:

$\overline{\overline{X}}$ The average value of $\overline{X}$

X_i The individual values of $\overline{X}$

n The number of subgroups.

After calculating the grand average of the process measurement data, use the resulting grand average ($\overline{\overline{X}}$) to draw the centerline of the $\overline{X}$ control chart as indicated in Figure 7-13.

Step-6 Compute and Draw UCL_R and LCL_R Calculate and draw the upper and lower control limit for the range using the equation below, the $\overline{R}$ calculated in Step 4, and the factor, (for subgroup size five) from the table in Figure 7-17.

$$UCL_R = (UCL_R \text{ Factor}) (\overline{R})$$

$$LCL_R = (LCL_R \text{ Factor}) (\overline{R})$$

$$UCL_R = (2.114)\,(3) = 6.35$$
$$LCL_R = (0)\,(3) = 0$$

After calculating the upper and lower control limits of the R charts apply the limits to the charts, as indicated in Figure 7-16 below.

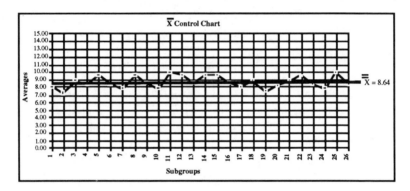

Figure 7-16. Calculate and Draw the Process Average

CONTROL LIMIT FACTOR CHART				
SUBGROUP SIZE (n)	RANGES (R) LCL	UCL	AVERAGES LCL & UCL	SIGMA (s)
2	–	3.267	1.880	1.128
3	–	2.574	1.023	1.693
4	–	2.282	0.729	2.059
5	–	2.114	0.577	2.326
6	–	2.004	0.483	2.534
7	0.076	1.924	0.419	2.704
8	0.136	1.864	0.373	2.847
9	0.184	1.816	0.337	2.970
10	0.223	1.777	0.308	3.078

Figure 7-17. Control Limit Factor Chart

Step-7 Compute and Draw UCL$_X$ and LCL$_X$ Calculate and draw the upper and lower control limit (Figure 7-19) for the process measurement averages using the equation below, the $\overline{\overline{X}}$ calculated in Step 5, and the factor (for subgroup size five) , from the table in Figure 7-17.

$$UCL_X = \overline{\overline{X}} + (UCL_X\ Factor)\ (\overline{R})$$

$$LCL_X = \overline{\overline{X}} - (LCL_X\ Factor)\ (\overline{R}))$$

$$UCL_X = 8.64 + (0.577)\ (3) = 10.3$$

$$LCL_X = 8.64 - (0.577)\ (3) = 6.9$$

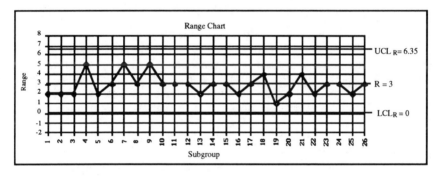

Figure 7-18. Upper and Lower Control Limits $\overline{R}$ Chart

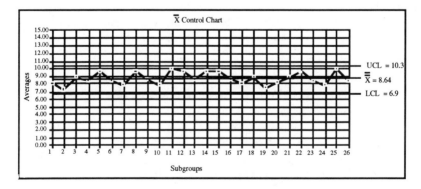

Figure 7-19. Upper and Lower Control Limits $\overline{X}$ Chart

The variable control chart is now complete and ready for interpretation. Figure 7-20 below is a completed control chart; we will now review how to interpret that control chart.

INTERPRETATION OF VARIABLE CONTROL CHARTS

We can interpret the completed $\overline{X}$ and R control chart to determine if the process is in control and we can maintained it as a tool for process control, improvement, and forecasting. In the control chart we have just completed, the process piece-to-piece variability and the process average remain constant at their present levels, as estimated by $\overline{R}$ and $\overline{X}$ respectively. The individual subgroup ranges (R) and averages ($\overline{X}$) would vary by chance alone, but they would seldom go beyond the control limits (less than 1% of the time for ranges and only .27% of the time for averages) for the limits calculated above. Likewise, as indicated in the completed chart in Figure 7-20, there would be no obvious trends or patterns in the data beyond what would likely occur due to chance.

The objective of control chart analysis is to identify any evidence that the process variability or the process average is not operating at a constant level, that one or both are out of statistical control, and to take appropriate action. The $\overline{X}$ and R charts are analyzed separately, but comparison of patterns between the two charts sometimes give added insight into special causes affecting the process.

Since the ability to interpret either the subgroup ranges or the subgroup averages depends on the estimate of piece to piece variability, the R chart is analyzed first. We compare the data points are compared with the control limits in order to observe any points out of control or any unusual patterns or trends.

Points Beyond the Control Limits

The presence of one or more points beyond either control limit is evidence of being out of control at that point. Since points beyond the control limits are very rare, any point beyond a control limit is the signal for analysis of the process to determine the special cause. Points above or below the control limit for range may indicate:

> **The control limit or plot point has been miscalculated or misplotted.**

> **The piece to piece variability has increased.**

> **The measurement system has changed.**

Even when all ranges are within the control limits, the presence of unusual patterns or trends can be evidence of non-control or a change in process spread during the period of the pattern or trend. This change could give the first warning of unfavorable conditions that should be corrected, even before points occur beyond the control limits. Conversely, certain patterns or trends could be favorable and should be studied for possible permanent improvement of the process. Comparison of patterns between the range and $\overline{X}$ charts give added insight.

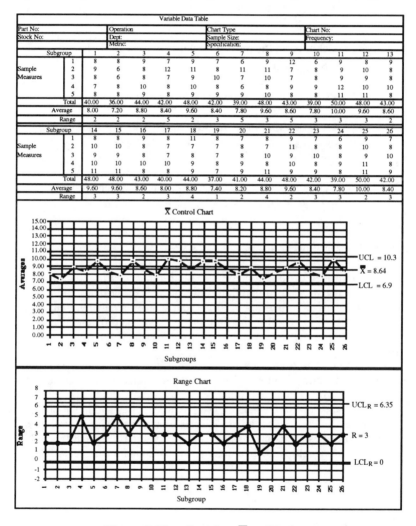

Variable Data Table												
Part No:	Operation				Chart Type				Chart No:			
Stock No:	Dept:				Sample Size:				Frequency:			
	Metric:				Specification:							

Subgroup	1	2	3	4	5	6	7	8	9	10	11	12	13
Sample Measures 1	8	8	9	7	9	7	6	9	12	6	9	8	9
2	9	6	8	12	11	8	11	11	7	8	9	10	8
3	8	6	8	7	9	10	7	10	7	8	9	9	8
4	7	8	10	8	10	8	6	8	9	9	12	10	10
5	8	8	9	8	9	9	9	10	8	8	11	11	8
Total	40.00	36.00	44.00	42.00	48.00	42.00	39.00	48.00	43.00	39.00	50.00	48.00	43.00
Average	8.00	7.20	8.80	8.40	9.60	8.40	7.80	9.60	8.60	7.80	10.00	9.60	8.60
Range	2	2	2	5	2	3	5	3	5	3	3	3	2

Subgroup	14	15	16	17	18	19	20	21	22	23	24	25	26
Sample Measures 1	8	8	9	8	11	8	7	8	9	7	6	9	7
2	10	10	8	7	7	7	8	7	11	8	8	10	8
3	9	9	8	7	8	7	8	10	9	10	8	9	10
4	10	10	10	10	9	8	9	8	10	8	9	11	8
5	11	11	8	8	9	7	9	11	9	9	8	11	9
Total	48.00	48.00	43.00	40.00	44.00	37.00	41.00	44.00	48.00	42.00	39.00	50.00	42.00
Average	9.60	9.60	8.60	8.00	8.80	7.40	8.20	8.80	9.60	8.40	7.80	10.00	8.40
Range	3	3	2	3	4	1	2	4	2	3	3	2	3

$\overline{X}$ Control Chart — UCL = 10.3, $\overline{X}$ = 8.64, LCL = 6.9

Range Chart — UCL_R = 6.35, R = 3, LCL_R = 0

Figure 7-20.   Complete $\overline{X}$ and R chart

Runs, Trends and Cycles

Runs are a clear sign that a process shift or trend has started. These runs can be used to forecast when a process will require adjustment before the control limits are violated. Seven points in a row on one side of the process average constitute a run. Mark the last point on the run, and extend a reference line back to the beginning of the run. Consider using the seven Quality Control Tools to evaluate the run. A run might signify any of several things affecting your process.

> A change in the output variable, which could be a special cause.

> A change in the measurement system.

> A smaller spread in output values, which is usually a good condition that should be studied for wider application.

> A change in the measurement system, which could mask real performance changes.

Find and Correct Special Causes

For each occurrence of special cause variation in the control chart, conduct an evaluation of the process to determine the cause. Bring that condition under control, and take the proper action to prevent it from recurring. The patterns, runs, and trends of the control chart are the keys to this problem analysis. The chart provides information on when the condition began and how long it has continued.

We must emphasize that corrective action, problem solving, and improvement often constitute the most difficult and time consuming phase of process and product control. Statistical input from the control chart is only the beginning. The explanation for the behavior of the process lies within the process and people involved with it. That is why a cross-functional team is vital to all improvement processes. It requires teamwork, thoroughness, patience, insight, and understanding to develop effective, long term solutions for process problems.

Recalculate Control Limits

After establishing the initial control chart, accounting for any special cause variation, and taking corrective action, we need to recalculate the control chart, excluding the effects of any subgroups affected by the special cause variation.

Excluding subgroups representing special cause variation provides a better estimate of the common cause variation of the process, and thus provides the most
appropriate data to establish control limits. The control chart should then be
maintained on a continuing basis. We need to recalculate the control limits each
time the number of subgroups exceeds the number required to establish the original control chart.

p CHART

The p control chart is applied to quality characteristics that are attribute data
(pass/fail, present/absent). This chart provides the capability to evaluate processes when we can take consistent samples with the same sample size.

This chart is used to control processes by evaluating the percentage rejected
as nonconforming to some specific requirement or specification. It is applied to
quality characteristics or to processes that produce variables data (such as measured dimensions) with pass/fail criteria. The chart has its best application in
measuring inspection results during a process.

Since this chart has a shape and characteristics different from the normal
distribution, the methods of calculating control limits look different, but we still
use the same concept of placing the control limits ± 3s on each side of the centerline.

Construction of the p Control Chart

Upon completion of a process analysis, election of the critical process elements
and their metrics, you are ready to collect data and construct a p control chart.
The construction of p control charts involves six steps:

❶ Selecting the size, frequency and number of sub
   groups.

❷ Compute and record the percent failing.

❸ Determine scales for the p chart.

❹ Compute and plot the values for each group p and the
   average failing $\bar{p}$.

❺ Compute and draw the process average.

⑥   **Compute and draw the process upper and lower control limits UCL and LCL.**

Step 1. Select the Size, Frequency and Number of subgroups For the subgroup sizes must be sufficient to determine moderate shifts in performance. A sample of fifty (50) actions must be taken for each subgroup. To enable the analyst/manager to interpret the chart for trends and patterns and to identify a process that is not in control. The p̄ control chart provides the capability to analyze subgroups of differing sample sizes; however, it is recommended that sample sizes do not vary by more than 25% .

The subgroup frequency (how often sample data is acquired) must be correlated with production periods. The analyst needs to understand the relationship between the frequency and the production periods (work shifts, machine runs, reporting cycles). To provide a reliable estimate of process performance, the data acquisition period should be long enough to capture likely sources of variation and to contain at least 25 subgroups. This number of subgroups enables the manager or analyst t to determine if the process is in control, and if the cause of being out of control is special or random.

Step 2. Compute and Record the Proportion Failing To compute the percent failing we need the following data: the number of items inspected or tested (n) and the number of failing items (d). Calculate the proportion failing as follows:

$$p = \frac{d}{n}$$

Record all data and the computed percent failing on a data table, as indicated in Figure 7-21.

Attribute Data Table												
Part No:	Operation				Chart Type				Chart No:			
Stock No:	Dept:				Sample Size:				Frequency:			
	Metric:				Specification:							
Subgroup	1	2	3	4	5	6	7	8	9	10	11	12	13
Date/Time	1-Jun	4-Jun	5-Jun	6-Jun	7-Jun	10-Jun	11-Jun	12-Jun	13-Jun	14-Jun	16-Jun	17-Jun	18-Jun
n	450	475	450	500	450	450	500	425	500	450	450	500	460
d	11	14	10	12	9	10	13	11	23	10	17	21	11
p	0.024	0.029	0.022	0.024	0.020	0.022	0.026	0.026	0.046	0.022	0.038	0.042	0.024
Subgroup	14	15	16	17	18	19	20	21	22	23	24	25	26
Date/Time	19-Jun	20-Jun	22-Jun	23-Jun	24-Jun	25-Jun	26-Jun	29-Jun	30-Jun	1-Jul	2-Jul	3-Jul	
n	475	500	465	450	500	480	475	450	500	460	450	475	
d	13	12	11	9	11	10	11	12	16	13	13	14	
p	0.027	0.024	0.024	0.020	0.022	0.021	0.023	0.027	0.032	0.028	0.029	0.029	

Figure 7-21. p Chart Data Table

Step 3 Determine Scales for the p Chart The horizontal scale of the p control chart identifies the subgroup by increments in hours, days, shifts, runs and other appropriate units of measure. The vertical scale represents the percentage failing and extends from zero 0 to 1.5 times the highest percentage failing in any subgroup. Figure 7-22 displays a properly drawn p control chart.

Step 4 Compute and Plot the Values for Each Group p and the Average Failing p From the data in table in Figure 7-21 plot the values for each subgroup. Connect the points to visualize patterns and trends.

Step 5 Compute and Draw the Process Average p̄ Calculate and draw a line for the process average (p̄), using the following equation and the data from figure 7-21:

$$\text{Process Average} = \bar{p} = \frac{\sum np}{\sum n} = \frac{\text{Total Defective}}{\text{Total Inspected}}$$

$$\text{Process Average} = \bar{p} = \frac{317}{11740} = .027$$

Draw the process average (p̄) as a solid horizontal line on the p Control Chart as indicated in Figure 7-24.

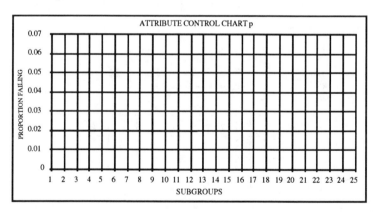

Figure 7-22. Scales for p Control Chart

Step 6 Compute and Draw the Process Upper and Lower Control Limits UCL and LCL The process control limits are the process average plus and minus the 3s allowance for common cause variation inherent in any process. The limits determine the parameters within which the process is in statistical control. When p̄ is low and/or n is small, the lower control limit can be a negative number. In these cases, the lower control limit is zero; (essentially) there is no lower limit. The p control chart upper and lower control limits are calculated as follows:

$$UCL_p = \bar{p} + 3 \sqrt{\bar{p}\ (1 - \bar{p})}\ /\ \sqrt{n}$$

p Chart Control Limits:

$$LCL_p = \bar{p} - 3 \sqrt{\bar{p}\ (1 - \bar{p})}\ /\ \sqrt{n}$$

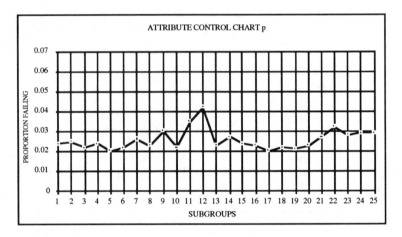

Figure 7-23. Plot the Values and Connect the Points

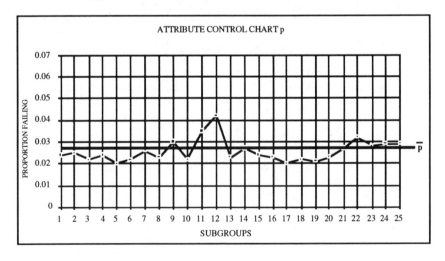

Figure 7-24. Compute and Draw the Process Average

Using the data from Figure 7-33 we can calculate the Upper and Lower Control Limits.

p Chart Control Limits:

$$UCL_p = 0.027 + 3\sqrt{0.027(1-0.027)} / \sqrt{309} = 0.054$$

$$LCL_p = 0.027 - 3\sqrt{0.027(1-0.027)} / \sqrt{309} = 0$$

The completed p control chart is displayed in Figure 7-25.

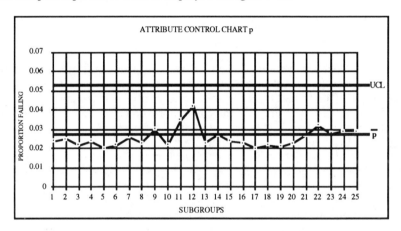

Figure 7-25. Completed p Control Chart

np CHART

We use the np control chart when the actual number of items failing is a better indicator of the process than the percent failing. One essential requirement for this use of the np chart is that the sample sizes for the subgroups must all be the same. (This is a limitation that does not apply to the use of p charts.)

The np chart is used to control processes by evaluating the number failing to conform to some specific requirement or specification. It is applied to quality characteristics, or to processes that produce variables data such as measured dimensions when measures as a pass/fail criteria. The chart has its best application in measuring discrepancies for an inspection lot, such as during the receipt of material.

Construction of the np Control Chart

The construction of np control charts involves five steps:

❶ **Select the standard sample size for lots, and record the number failing**

❷ **Determine scales for the np chart**

❸ **Plot the number failing**

❹ **Compute and draw the process average.**

❺ **Compute and draw the process UCL and LCL**

Step 1. Select the Standard Sample Size for the Lots and Record the Number Failing The calculations used for np charts are based on the binomial distribution. The centerline is the average number of rejects per subgroup, denoted by np. After dividing this value by n, the number of items per subgroup, we get the value to use for p in the control limit formulas.

The lot sampling frequency (how often sample data is acquired) must be correlated with receipt, production, or inspection periods. It is necessary to understand the relationship between the frequency and the production run. For effective control of process performance, the data acquisition increment or period should be long enough to capture likely sources of variation. The sample size for each subgroup must be sufficient and contain 25 or more subgroups during the production run. The selection of this number of subgroups will provide the manager or analyst to determine if the process is in control, and if the cause of being out of control is special or random.

Record all data and determine number failing on a standard data table as indicated in Figure 7-26.

Attribute Data Table														
Part No: Eng Assy		Operation	A.T.	Chart Type	np		Chart No:		1					
Stock No: B765		Dept:	Mfg	Sample Size:	200-Lot		Frequency:		Lot					
		Metric:	P/F Insp	Specification:	ANSI-771									
Subgroup	1	2	3	4	5	6	7	8	9	10	11	12	13	14	15
Date/Time	1-Jun			6-Jun			11-Jun			14-Jun			18-Jun		18-Jun
n	200	200	200	200	200	200	200	200	200	200	200	200	200	200	200
nd	2	12	10	10	8	4	4	6	4	6	4	2	6	2	8
Subgroup	16	17	18	19	20	21	22	23	24	25	26	27	28	29	30
Date/Time	22-Jun			23-Jun				29-Jun			2-Jul				
n	200	200	200	200	200	200	200	200	200	200	200	200	200	200	200
nd	10	8	2	12	30	24	12	6	8	6	6	4	10	14	8

Figure 7-26. np Chart Data Table

Step 2. Determine Scales for the np Chart The horizontal scale of the np control chart identifies the subgroups as increments and lot samples. The vertical scale represents the number failing. The vertical scale extends from 0 to

1.5 times the highest number failing in the subgroups and lot samples. Figure 7-27 below displays a properly drawn np control chart.

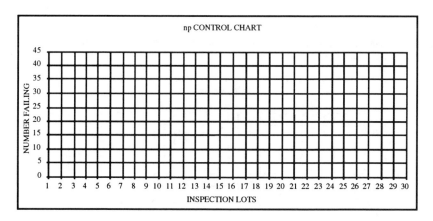

Figure 7-27. np Control Chart Scale

Step 3. Plot the Number Failing   From the data in the table in Figure 7-28, plot the value for each subgroup.   Connect the points to visualize patterns and trends.

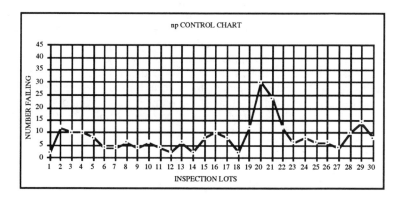

Figure 7-28. Plot the Number Failing

Step 4.   Compute and Draw the Process Average   Calculate and draw the process average as indicated below:

$$\text{Process Average} = n\bar{p} = \frac{\Sigma d}{\Sigma k} = \frac{\text{Total Defective}}{\text{Number of Lots (Samples)}}$$

Using the data from Figure 7-26 above calculate the process average.

$$\text{Process Average} = n\bar{p} = \frac{248}{30} = 8.27$$

Draw the process average as a solid horizontal line on the p Control Chart as indicated in Figure 7-29.

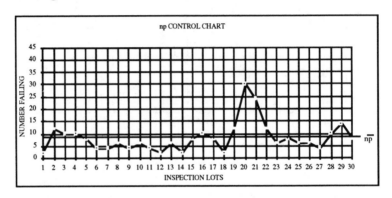

Figure 7-29. Compute and Draw the Process Average

Step 5. Compute and Draw the Process Upper and Lower Control Limits UCL and LCL The process control limits are the process average plus and minus the three standard deviation allowance for common cause variation inherent in any process. The limits determine the parameters within which the process is in statistical control. When $\bar{p}$ is low and/or $\bar{n}$ is small the lower control limit may be a negative number. In these cases the lower control limit is zero, because the lower control limit of the number failing cannot be less than zero. Therefore we will compute only the upper control limit for all np charts.

$$\text{UCL for np Charts} = n\bar{p} + 3\sqrt{n\bar{p}(1 - \frac{n\bar{p}}{n})}$$

Using the data from Figure 7-26 and the process average calculated in the previous step, we can calculate the Upper and Lower Control Limits.

$$\text{UCL for np Charts} = 8.6 + 3\sqrt{8.6(1 - \frac{8.6}{200})} = 16.7$$

The completed np control chart is displayed in Figure 7-30.

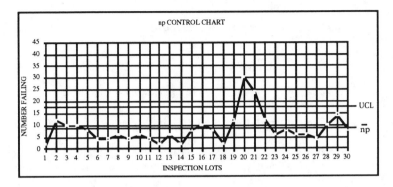

Figure 7-30. Completed np Control Chart

c CHART

The c control chart is used to measure the number failing in an inspection item when we are concerned with the variance between items. This chart also requires a constant sample or lot size. The chart is applied in two specific process control situations:

> ➤ **Where there is a continuous flow of product and the failures can be expressed as a ratio to total product.**

> ➤ **Where failures of different types can be found in a single inspection procedure.**

In a c chart, the sample size remains fixed (constant) and the chart shown the total number of defects per item in a sample or subgroup. The c chart is very easy to construct, but it requires that all subgroups be the same size. First, find the average number of defects per group, using at least 25 groups. Call this average c and use it for the centerline on the control chart. Then compute the control limits.

The best use for c charts is in short studies to ascertain the variation in quality of a characteristic or piece. These have been used for periodic sampling of production where a certain number of defects per unit is tolerable. The c chart can be used successfully for 100 percent inspection, where the primary aim is to reduce the cost of rework or scrap. Another good application of c charts is for acceptance sampling procedures based on defects per unit.

Construction of the c Control Chart

The construction of np control charts is accomplished in five steps:

❶   **Determine sample size and frequency**

❷   **Determine scales for the c chart**

❸   **Determine and plot the number failing**

❹   **Compute plot and draw the process average $\bar{c}$**

❺   **Compute and draw the UCL and LCL**

Step 1 Determine Sample Size and Frequency   The method of calculation used for c control charts is based on the Poisson distribution. The central line is an average number denoted by $\bar{c}$. After dividing this value by n, the number of items per subgroup, we get the value to for p in the control limit formulas.

The lot sampling frequency (how often data are acquired) must be correlated with receipt, production. or inspection periods. It is necessary to understand the relationship between the frequency and the production periods (work shifts, machine runs, reporting cycles). For effective control of process performance the data acquisition increment or period should be long enough capture likely sources of variation. The sample size from each subgroup must be sufficient and there must be 25 or more subgroups. The selection of this number of subgroups will provide the manager or analyst to determine if the process is in control, and if the cause of being out of control is assignable or random.

Record all data and determine the number failing on a standard data table, as indicated in Figure 7-31.

Attribute Data Table														
Part No:	Comp Tube	Operation	Prod, inprocess		Chart Type	c			Chart No:		1			
Stock No:	71B2	Dept:	Mfg		Sample Size:	10			Frequency:		Daily			
		Metric:	Holes/Part		Specification:	ANSI-631								
Subgroup	1	2	3	4	5	6	7	8	9	10	11	12	13	14	15
Date/Time	3-Jun	4-Jun	5-Jun	6-Jun	7-Jun	8-Jun	9-Jun	10-Jun	11-Jun	12-Jun	13-Jun	14-Jun	15-Jun	16-Jun	17-Jun
n	10	10	10	10	10	10	10	10	10	10	10	10	10	10	10
c	14	10	6	8	6	16	4	6	8	6	8	7	6	9	6
Subgroup	16	17	18	19	20	21	22	23	24	25	26	27	28	29	30
Date/Time	18-Jun	19-Jun	20-Jun	21-Jun	22-Jun	23-Jun	24-Jun	25-Jun	26-Jun	27-Jun					
n	10	10	10	10	10	10	10	10	10	10					
c	9	11	8	9	6	7	10	12	14	16					

Figure 7-31. c Control Chart Data Table

Step 2 Determine Scales For the c Chart scales   The horizontal scale of the c control chart identifies the subgroups as increments and lot samples. The vertical scale represents the number failing. The vertical scale extends from zero to 1.5 times the highest number failing in the subgroups and lot samples. Figure 7-32 displays a properly drawn c control chart.

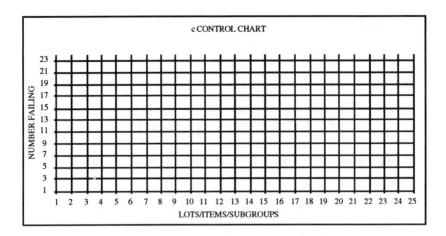

Figure 7-32. c Control Chart Scales

Step 3. Determine and Plot the Number Failing   From the data in table in Figure 7-31, plot the total number failing for each subgroup directly to the control chart, without calculating the mean of each subgroup. Connect the points to determine the patterns and trends, as indicated in Figure 7-33 below.

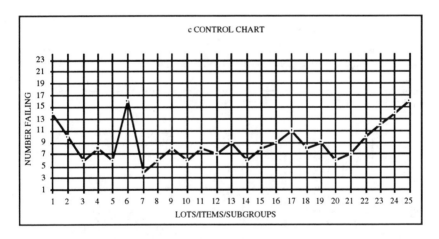

Figure 7-33. Plot the Total Number of Failures

Step 4   Compute and Draw the Process Average   The process average is calculated and applied to the control chart as follows:

$$\text{Process Average} = c = \frac{\Sigma c}{\Sigma k} = \frac{\text{Total Defective in All Subgroups}}{\text{Total Number of Subgroups}}$$

Using the data from Figure 7-31 above, calculate the process average.

$$\text{Process Average} = c = \frac{\Sigma c}{\Sigma k} = \frac{222}{25} = 8.88$$

Draw the process average as a solid horizontal line on the p control chart as indicated in Figure 7-34.

Step 5 Compute and Draw the LCL and UCL   The process control limits are the process average plus and minus the three standard deviation allowance for common cause variation inherent in any process. The limits determine the parameters within which the process is in statistical control. When $\bar{p}$ is low or $\bar{n}$ is small the Lower control limit may be a negative number. In these cases the lower control limit is zero, because the number failing cannot be less than zero. Therefore, we will compute only the upper control limit only for np charts.

$$\text{Upper Control Limit} = UCL_c = \bar{c} + 3\sqrt{\bar{c}}$$

Using the data from Figure 7-31 we can calculate the Upper and Lower Control Limits.

$$\text{Upper Control Limit} = UCL_c = 8.88 + 3\sqrt{8.88} = 17.82$$

The completed c Control Chart is displayed in Figure 7-35.

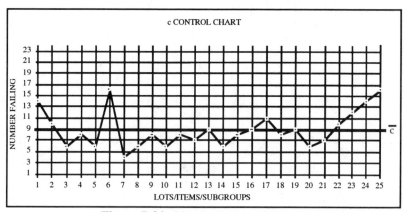

Figure 7-34. Plot the Process Average

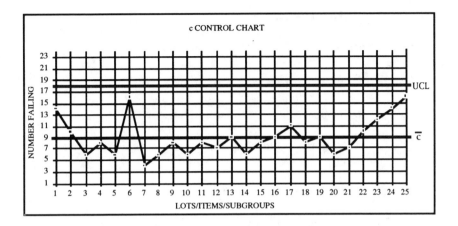

Figure 7-35. Completed c Control Chart

u Control Chart

The u control chart is used to measure the percent not conforming (failing) in an inspection subgroup when we are concerned with the variance between groups. This chart does not require a constant sample or lot size. It is applied in two specific process control situations:

➤ **Where there is a continuous flow of product, and the failures can be expressed as a ratio to total product.**

➤ **Where failures of different types can be found in a single inspection procedure.**

In a u chart, the sample size is flexible. The u chart, dealing with the proportion of defects in a sample or subgroup, is easy to construct. First, find the average number of defects per group (u). Next, calculate the process average ($\bar{u}$) and use it for the centerline on the control chart. Plot the process data and compute the control limits.

The best use of u control charts is to ascertain the variation in quality of a characteristic or piece. They are used for periodic sampling of production where a certain proportion of defects per unit are tolerable. The u chart can be used successfully in periodic or 100% inspection, where the primary aim is to reduce the cost of rework or scrap. Another good application of u control charts is for acceptance sampling procedures.

Construction of the u Control Chart

The construction of u control charts is accomplished in five steps:

❶ **Determine sample size and frequency**

❷ **Determine scales for the u control chart**

❸ **Calculate and plot the proportion (%) failing in each subgroup**

❹ **Compute plot and draw the process average u**

❺ **Compute and draw the UCL and LCL**

Step 1. Determine Sample Size and Sample Frequency   The sampling frequency (how often sample data are required) must be correlated with receipt, production, or inspection periods. It is necessary to understand the relationship between the frequency and the production periods (work shifts, machine runs, reporting cycles). For effective control of process performance, the data acquisition increment or period should be long enough to capture likely sources of variation. The sample size for each subgroup must be sufficient and there must be 25 or more subgroups. The selection of this number of subgroups enables the manager or analyst to determine if the process is in control, and if the cause of being out of control is special or random.

To compute the percent failing we need the following data: the number of items inspected or tested (n), and the number of failing items (d). Calculate the percent failing as follows:

$$u = \frac{d}{n}$$

Record all data and determine the number failing on a standard data table, as indicated in Figure 7-36.

Step 2. Determine Scales for the u Control Chart   The horizontal scale of the u control chart identifies the subgroups as increments and lot samples. The vertical scale represents the proportion failing. The vertical scale extends from zero to 1.5 times the highest number failing in the subgroups and lot samples. Figure 7-37 displays a properly drawn u control chart.

Step 3. Calculate and Plot the Proportion (%) Failing   From the data table in Figure 7-36, plot the value for each subgroup and connect the points, as indicated in Figure 7-38 below.

Attribute Data Table														
Part No: B-77 ENG	Operation	ACCEPTANCE		Chart Type	U		Chart No:		3					
Stock No: GM-B77-1	Dept:	RECEIVING		Sample Size:	15% LOT		Frequency:		LOT					
	Metric:	P/P+F		Specification:	INT 386/HP									
Subgroup	1	2	3	4	5	6	7	8	9	10	11	12	13	14	15
Date/Time	3-Jun	4-Jun	5-Jun	6-Jun	7-Jun	8-Jun	9-Jun	10-Jun	11-Jun	12-Jun	13-Jun	14-Jun	15-Jun	16-Jun	17-Jun
n	15	20	15	20	25	25	15	15	15	20	20	15	20	15	15
d	14	10	6	8	6	16	4	6	8	6	8	7	9	6	8
u	0.933	0.500	0.400	0.400	0.240	0.640	0.267	0.400	0.533	0.300	0.400	0.467	0.450	0.400	0.533
Subgroup	16	17	18	19	20	21	22	23	24	25	26	27	28	29	30
Date/Time	18-Jun	19-Jun	20-Jun	21-Jun	22-Jun	23-Jun	24-Jun	25-Jun	26-Jun	27-Jun					
n	25	15	20	15	20	20	15	15	25	15					
d	9	11	8	9	6	7	10	12	14	16					
u	0.360	0.733	0.400	0.600	0.300	0.350	0.667	0.800	0.560	1.067					

Figure 7-36. u Control Chart Data Table

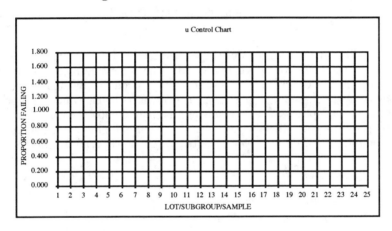

Figure 7-37. u Control Chart Scales

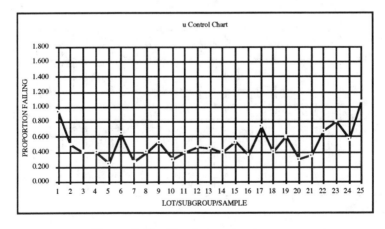

Figure 7-38. Plot the Process Averages

Step 4. Compute and plot the Process Average ū   Calculate and draw the process average as indicated below:

$$\text{Process Average} = \bar{u} = \frac{\Sigma d}{\Sigma n} = \frac{\text{Total Defects}}{\text{Total Inspected}}$$

Using the data from Figure 7-33 above calculate the process average.

$$\text{Process Average} = \bar{u} = \frac{224}{455} = 0.492$$

Draw the process average as a solid horizontal line on the u control chart as indicated in Figure 7-39.

Step 5. Compute and Plot the Upper Control Limit   We calculate the process control limits for the u control chart as the process average plus and minus three standard deviations (3s), to allow for common cause variation inherent in any process. These limits determine the parameters within which the process is in statistical control. When ū is low or n̄ is small the lower control limit can be a negative number. In these cases the lower control limit is set at zero, essentially no lower limit. The u control chart upper and lower control limits are calculated as follows:

Control Limits for u Charts:

$$UCL_u = \bar{u} + 3\sqrt{\bar{u}} \ / \ \sqrt{\bar{n}}$$

$$LCL_u = \bar{u} - 3\sqrt{\bar{u}} \ / \ \sqrt{\bar{n}}$$

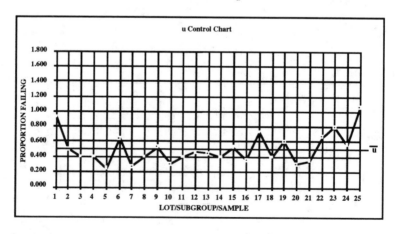

Figure 7-39. u Control Chart Process Average

Using the data from Figure 7-36 we can calculate the upper and lower control limits.

$$UCL_u = 0.492 + 3\sqrt{0.492} \;/\; \sqrt{18.2} \;=\; 0.986$$
$$UCL_u = 0.492 - 3\sqrt{0.492} \;/\; \sqrt{18.2} \;=\; 0$$

The completed u Control Chart is displayed in Figure 7-40

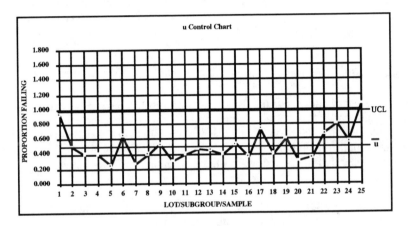

Figure 7-40. Completer u Control Chart

INTERPRETATION OF ATTRIBUTE CONTROL CHARTS

Our objective here is to identify any evidence that the process is no longer operating at the same level (that it is out of control) and take appropriate action. Points beyond control limits, or obvious trends or patterns in the data beyond what would likely occur due to chance, suggest the presence of special causes of variation.

Points Beyond the Control Limits

The presence of one or more points beyond either control limit is evidence of instability at that point. Since points beyond the control limits would be very rare if the process were stable and only common cause variation were present, we assume that special cause variation accounts for the extreme value. The special cause could be either unfavorable or favorable; in either case it bears immediate investigation. This is the primary decision rule for action on any control chart. Any point beyond the control limits should be marked.

A point outside a limit might indicate:

> **The control limit or plot point may be error**

> **A point above the upper control limit indicates that process performance has worsened.**

> **The measurement system has changed.**

> **A point below the lower control limit (here one is appropriate) indicates that the process performance has improved.**

Points Within the Control Limits

The presence of patterns or trends within the control limits can provide evidence of potential control problems, changes in levels of performance, and opportunities for variability reduction. When the average number of nonconforming items per subgroup is moderately large (nine or more), the distribution of the subgroup p values is nearly normal and we can trend analysis similar to that used for X.

Runs and Trends In a process under control, with np moderately large, approximately equal numbers of points should fall on either side of the average. Either of the following could be a sign that a process shift or trend has begun:

> **Seven points in a row on one side of the average**

> **Seven intervals in a row that are consistently increasing (equal to or greater than the preceding points) or consistently decreasing.**

Runs above and below the process average, or runs up generally signify one of the following:

> **The process performance has worsened, and may still be worsening,**

> **The measurement system has changed.**

> **The process performance has improved (the causes should be studied for permanent incorporation), or**

> **The measurement system has changed.**

Non-Random Patterns Other distinct patterns sometimes indicate the presence of special causes of variation, although care must be taken not to over-interpret the data. Among these patterns are trends, cycles, unusual spread of points within the control limits, and relationships among values within subgroups (for example, if all nonconforming items occur within the first few readings taken for the subgroup).

To test for unusual spread, determine the distance of points from the process average. In a process under statistical control, with only common cause variation present and np moderately large, about two thirds of the data points are within the middle third of the region between the control limits and about one third of the points will be in the outer two thirds of the region. Only about one in twenty data points will lie relatively close to the control limits (in the outer third of the region)

If substantially more than two thirds of the points lie close to the process average (for 25 subgroups if over 90% are within the middle third of the control limit region), this could mean one of the following:

> **The control limits or plot points have been miscalcu-**
> **lated or misplotted.**

> **The process or the sampling method is stratified so**
> **that each subgroup systematically contains measure-**
> **ments from two or more process streams with very**
> **different average performance (for example, the**
> **mixed output of two parallel production lines).**

> **The process capability is improving.**

Find and Correct Special Causes of Variation

When we identify an out-of-control condition is identified in an attribute chart we must evaluate the process to determine the cause. Analysis of the operations might reveal causes of variation that are within the ability of the operator or lo-cal supervision to correct. Problem-solving techniques, such as the Seven QC Tools and Process Analysis are always helpful.

For ongoing studies with real-time data, analysis of out-of-control condi-tions involves the timely investigation of the process operation, with emphasis on finding what, if any, changes occurred that might explain the abnormal per-formance. When this analysis results in corrective action, the effectiveness of the action should be reflected in the subsequent control chart.

For preliminary studies with historical data, the passage of time may make analysis of process operating changes more difficult, especially for symptoms that come and go. The analysis must be made as complete as possible under the circumstances to identify the condition and to prevent its recurrence.

Recalculate the Control Limits

When conducting an initial process study or a reassessment of the process capability, sometimes it is necessary to recalculate the trial control limits to exclude the effects of periods whose state of control was affected by special causes which have since been corrected. Recalculate the control limits excluding the points associated with these special causes, and plot them on the chart. This step prevents abnormal production periods from being included in the estimate of typical variability. Check the historical data against the revised limits to confirm that no further points suggest the presence of assignable causes.

Once the historical data show consistent performance within the trial control limits, we can extend the limits forward to cover future control periods. These limits become the operating control limits against which the future data will be evaluated as it is gathered and recorded, during the process.

PROCESS CAPABILITY

The basic statistical application in process control is to establish stability in the process and maintain that state of control over an extended period. It is equally important to adjust the process to the point where virtually all of the product meets specifications. The latter situation relates to process capability analysis.

Once we have established stability, it follows that we must adjust the process to a level where the output will conform to specifications. A state of control usually exists when process control charts do not show points out of control over an interval of 20 subgroups. Once this control is established, we can analyze process capability to determine conformance to specifications. The primary function of a process control system is to provide statistical signals when special causes of variation are present, and to enable appropriate action to eliminate those causes and prevent their reappearance.

Process capability is determined by the total variation that comes from common causes, the minimum variation that remains after all special causes have been eliminated. Thus, capability represents the performance potential of the process itself, as demonstrated when the process is operating in a state of statistical control.

We measure capability by the proportion of output that is within product specification tolerances. Since a process in statistical control can be described by a predictable distribution, we can express capability in terms of this distribution and evaluate the proportion of out-of-specification parts realistically. If this variation is excessive, actions are required to reduce the variation from common causes to make the process capable of consistently meeting customer requirements as indicated by the Upper and Lower Specification Limits (USL and LSL). Figure 7-41 demonstrates the relationship between process control chart limits (UCL and LCL), specification requirements and process capability.

CP Index[1]

The most commonly used capability indices are CP and CpK. CP, which stands for capability of process, is the ratio of tolerance to 6 sigma (σ). The formula is:

$$CP = \frac{TOLERANCE}{6\sigma}$$

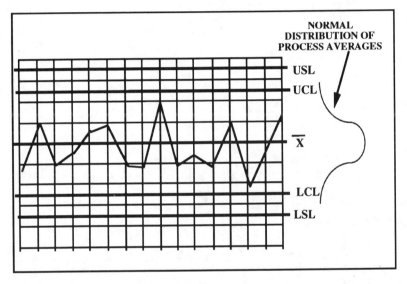

Figure 7-41. Process Capability and Control Chart and Specification Limits

The 6σ in the CP formula comes from the fact that, in a normal distribution 99.73% of the parts will be within a 6s (+/– 3s) spread when only random variation (common cause) is occurring. The CP for the data presented in Figure 7-42 is therefore:

$$CP = \frac{4.0}{3.0} = 1.33$$

As you can see from the CP formulas, values for CP can range from near zero to very large positive numbers. When CP is less than one, the process is said to be not-capable. The larger the number the better the CP index is.

Remember a CP index of 1.33 is considered required to be a world class competitor.

Cp only measures dispersion or spread of the distribution. It is not a measure of centeredness (where the distribution is in relation to the midpoint (nominal or target value). Figure 7-43 shows two distributions with the same specification limits and with the same CP index value. In the top distribution almost all product being produced is within specification: in the lower distribution a significant number of products would be out of tolerance. This is why CP in not used alone as a measure of capability. CP only demonstrates how good the process could be if it were centered. CP is usually used with CpK.

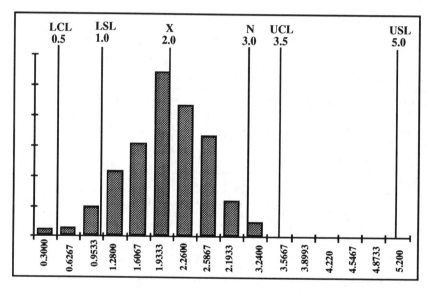

Figure 7-42. CP Index Relationships

CpK Index

While CP is only a measure of dispersion, CpK is a measure of both dispersion and centerdness. That is, the formula for CpK takes into account both the spread of the distribution and where the distribution is in regard to the specification midpoint, The formula is.

$$CpK = \frac{USL - MEAN}{3\sigma} \text{ or } \frac{LSL - MEAN}{3\sigma}$$

We choose the lesser of the two vales calculated as the CpK index. Using this value we find out how capable our process is on the worst side of the distribution. Using the example in figure 7-41 we calculate the value for CpK:

$$CpK = USL \frac{5.0 - 2.0}{1.5} = 2.0 \text{ or LSL } \frac{2.0 - 1.0}{1.5} = 0.67$$

The greater the value of CpK the better. A CpK value of greater than one means that the 6σ (+/- 3σ) spread of the data falls completely within the specification limits. A CpK between 0 and 1 means that part of the 6s spread falls outside the specification limits. A negative CpK indicates that the mean of the data is not within the specification limits.

KEY POINTS

In everyday business applications control charts are used to:

➤ **Determine if a process is trending**

➤ **Determine if a process is in control**

➤ **Achieve statistical process control**

➤ **Reduce process variability**

➤ **Forecast requirements**

Two types of control charts are used, depending on the nature of the data to be evaluated: variable and attribute.

VARIABLE CHARTS:

$\overline{X}$ **and R charts: To observe change in the mean and range (variance) of a process.**

$\overline{X}$ **and S charts: For variable average and standard deviation.**

$\overline{X}$ **and S^2 charts: for variable average and variance**

ATTRIBUTE CHARTS:

p Chart: For fraction of attribute nonconforming or defective in a sample of varying size.

np Charts: For number of attribute nonconforming or defective in a sample of constant size.

c Charts: For number of attribute nonconforming or defective in a single item within a Subgroup, lot or sample area of constant size..

u Charts: For number of attributes nonconforming or defective in a single item within a Subgroup, lot or sample area of varying size.

PROCESS CAPABILITY

Process capability provides a measure of the processes capability to produce a product within the customer expectations (specification).   There are two types of process capability index we have reviewed, Cp and CpK.

Cp Provides a measure of dispersion on the process compared to the specification limits and the upper and lower control limits of the process.

CpK Provides an additional measure of central tendency of the process indicating how close to monomial the process is.

A process capability must be 1.33 to be considered world class.

EXAMPLE

As indicated in a previous example the Machine Tool Division of LWCI produces the central drive shaft for the LWCI 1587 machine. The Manufacturing Equipment Division, Customer Service Department data and analysis of service failures and customer calls indicated that this shaft may be a contributing element to LWCI 1587 failures. The machine tool division, as a member of the team reviewing these failures, decided to review the control charts for the central drive shaft production. Specifically, since vibration is a contributing problem they will review the $\overline{X}$-R control chart for drive shaft concentricity. Example Figure 7-1 provides a sketch of the specifications for the drive shaft.

The overall shaft is 20 inches long plus or minus .01 inches. Thus the shaft is be between 19.99 inches and 20.01 inch long. The step-down part of the shaft is 2 inches long with an allowable tolerance of plus or minus .01 inch. The shaft is to be 1 inch in diameter, with an allowable tolerance of plus or minus .005 inch. The shaft is specified to be concentric from the centerline, with an allowable deviation of .002 as measured on the four points indicated on the shaft. The machine tool production department produces approximately 32 of these shafts during an 8-hour shift. The data for five shafts are sampled from each shift and the data used for the control chart.

The Machine Tool Division takes the measurements for the control charts from production with the shaft fixed to the centerline of the lathe. They use an automated measuring system to take the measurements for the shaft length for the control charts. The measurement for concentricity is taken using a dial gauge to measure the deviation from zero. This measurement is sampled and recorded on the $\overline{X}$-R chart. The chart UCL and LCL parameters are recalculated after each twenty Subgroups and the chart is maintained continuously during each shift. The process capability (C_p) is calculated for each new control chart. The resulting control chart is demonstrated in Example Figure 7-2.

The evaluation of these control charts indicated that the process is in control with all the data points for the $\overline{X}$ and the R charts within the statistical control limits. The process is exhibiting good process capability, with a CP of 1.66 this should be a very competitive process. Individually, the charts displayed runs, trends and cycles that could be considerations for variability reduction and continuous measurable improvement programs.

The team first evaluated the R control chart and annotated the chart as indicated in Example Figure 7-3. The R control chart exhibited a cycle of several readings below the line, followed by several readings above the line. This type of pattern is typical of a setup critical process element, where the process output can be affected by machine setup. This type of pattern also can be operator centric, caused by the different skill levels or training of the operators. Reviewing the data table associated with the control chart indicated that the shift in data was associated with the change of cutting tools. The team learned that the cutting tools were replaced as required, based upon the judgment of the operator. The operator was an experienced machinist, and as the cutting tool wore, he could judge by the chip size and temperature of the shaft that it was time to replace the tool. The control chart indicated that this change was consistently accomplished about every eight or nine shifts. Changing the cutting tool had the immediate result of reducing the range of data for the process.

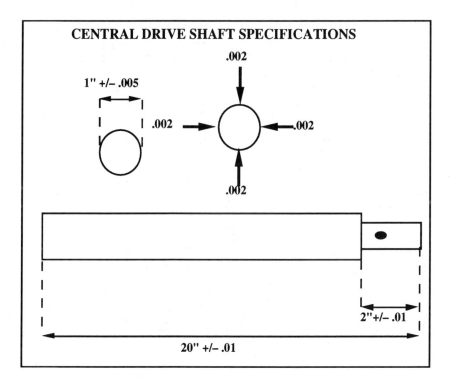

CENTRAL DRIVE SHAFT SPECIFICATIONS

Example Figure 7-1. Specifications

The team next evaluated the $\overline{X}$ control chart. Team members marked the control chart indicating any runs, trends, cycles, or separate distributions, as indicated in Example Figure 7-4. The $\overline{X}$ Control chart also exhibited cycles distributed in clear runs above and below the process centerline. The runs were normally distributed about a centerline. The overall chart demonstrated a bimodal distribution of the data. All of this activity coincided with the changing of cutting tools, just as it had done in the R control chart.

Variable Data Table													
Part No:	D.Shaft	Operation	Turning		Chart Type		X-R		Chart No:		1		
Stock No:	S-36A	Dept:	Mfg		Sample Size:		5		Frequency:		Shift		
		Metric:	.000 Inch		Specification:		ASI-3762D						

Subgroup		1	2	3	4	5	6	7	8	9	10	11	12	13
Sample Measures	1	0.71	0.61	0.79	0.64	0.90	0.85	0.78	1.00	0.75	0.80	0.66	0.88	0.85
	2	0.94	0.72	0.85	0.75	0.99	0.75	0.99	1.15	1.05	1.03	0.89	0.85	0.69
	3	0.78	0.85	0.97	0.85	0.92	0.91	1.04	0.78	1.19	1.02	0.72	0.99	0.61
	4	0.88	0.77	0.88	0.77	0.90	0.79	1.14	0.90	1.04	1.06	0.71	0.88	0.79
	5	0.80	0.69	0.71	0.71	0.78	0.63	0.94	1.01	1.00	1.20	0.69	0.75	0.72
Total		4.11	3.64	4.20	3.72	4.49	3.93	4.89	4.84	5.03	5.11	3.67	4.35	3.66
Average		0.82	0.73	0.84	0.74	0.90	0.79	0.98	0.97	1.01	1.02	0.73	0.87	0.73
Range		0.23	0.24	0.26	0.21	0.21	0.28	0.36	0.37	0.44	0.4	0.23	.24	0.24

Subgroup		14	15	16	17	18	19	20	21	22	23	24	25	26
Sample Measures	1	0.88	0.92	1.13	1	1.08	1.21	0.92	0.71	0.61	0.79	0.64	0.90	
	2	0.85	0.71	1.1	1.15	0.92	0.9	0.75	0.94	0.72	0.85	0.75	0.99	
	3	0.98	0.69	0.96	0.89	1.06	1.07	0.69	0.78	0.85	0.97	0.85	0.92	
	4	0.87	0.7	1.01	0.99	1.2	1.02	0.72	0.88	0.77	0.88	0.77	0.90	
	5	0.75	0.66	0.82	0.78	0.8	0.79	0.65	0.80	0.69	0.71	0.71	0.78	
Total		4.33	3.68	5.02	4.81	5.06	4.99	3.73	4.11	3.64	4.20	3.72	4.49	
Average		0.87	0.74	1.00	0.96	1.01	1.00	0.75	0.82	0.73	0.84	0.74	0.90	
Range		0.23	0.26	0.31	0.37	0.4	0.42	0.23	0.23	0.24	0.26	0.21	0.21	

X Control Chart

UCL = 1.04

X̄ = 0.87

LCL = 0.70

Range Control Chart

UCL = 0.64

R̄ = 0.30

LCL = 0.00

Example Figure 7-2. X̄ - R Control Chart and Data Table

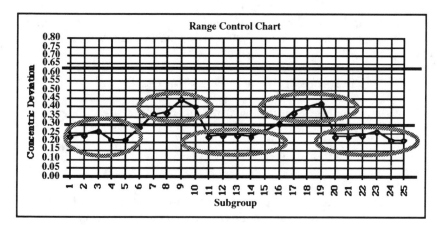

Example Figure 7-3.   Evaluation of the R Chart

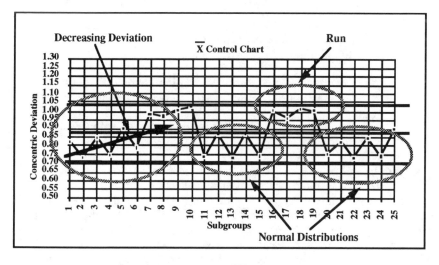

Example Figure 7-4.   X̄ Control Chart

The next consideration for the team was to attempt to correlate this information with the LWCI 1587 central shaft failures. Using the information and evaluation of the control charts, the team reviewed all of the LWCI 1587 service calls that were based upon central drive shaft failures. The documentation for the service calls included the serial numbers of the drive shafts from these serial numbers the team could determine what work shift and control chart subgroup the failing shafts came from. This information revealed that all failing shafts were produced in runs that were above the centerline of the control chart and therefore displayed the greatest deviation. The team then had the following facts to consider:

> **The process is in statistical control chart.**

> **The process is demonstrating a good process capability.**

> **The Range chart shows runs below and above the centerline.**

> **The $\overline{X}$ control chart has a bimodial distribution of two normal distributions above and below the centerline.**

> **The $\overline{X}$ control chart demonstrates an increasing concentric deviation, cyclically coincidental with the shifts in the distribution.**

> **The changes in the control charts are associated with the changing of the cutting tool.**

> **The changes in concentric deviation are directly associated with LWCI 1587 central drive shaft failures.**

> **No other equipment failures are associated with this shaft.**

The team had to make some decisions and recommendations based upon this data (fact-based decision making). The team determined that there were several options: Suspend use of this shaft in the LWCI 1587 until the process could be improved. 2) Continue to use the existing shafts and plan for the required service calls. 3) Segregate the production of central drive shafts by serial number and concentric deviation, allocating shafts from below the centerline to LWCI 1587 production and repair. 4) Review the process specifications and determine if they were properly established. 5) Optimize the replacement of cutting tools through a variability reduction program

The team decided to recommend the following:

> **Provide all shafts for the production and repair of LWCI 1587 equipment from shafts produces below the centerline of the control chart.**

➤ **Institute a Variability Reduction Program (explained in the following chapters) for the production of drive shafts that will:**

  Use customer requirements to establish specifications (QFD)

  Implement a Design of Experiments to test and Evaluate proposed process improvements

  Use the Taguchi Loss Function to determine the economic feasibility of the recommended process changes.

NOTE

1. DataMyte Handbook - A Practical Guide to Computerized Data Collection for Statistical Process Control- 5th Edition, DataMyte Division of Allen-Bradley Company Inc, 1993, used with permission.

8

The Seven Management and Planning Tools

THE 7 M&P TOOLS PROVIDE AN EFFICIENT
AND EFFECTIVE METHOD FOR ANALYZING
LANGUAGE DATA, RELIABLE PRIORITY
SETTING, AND CONTINGENCY PLANNING.

IN THE CHAPTERS ON PRODUCT AND PROCESS CONTROL, we discussed the tools and techniques used for Statistical Process Control (SPC) and Statistical Quality Control (SQC). The emphasis was on the collection, analysis, and interpretation of numerical data. In these activities, we count or measure things. We use the relationships of numbers, and the characteristics of mathematical distributions, to turn the data into information for decision making. In business planning processes, however, we must deal with large amounts of language data such as ideas, opinions, perceptions, or desires. The usual statistical methods do not work in the analysis of language data.

Recognizing the need for new tools and techniques, in 1972 the Society of Quality Control Technique Development, sponsored by the Japanese Federation of Science and Technology, began looking for ways to enhance planning activities. This exhaustive investigation culminated in a proposal for Seven New Quality Control Tools. In 1979 Shigeru Mizuno wrote a book entitled *Management for Quality Improvement, The Seven New QC Tools*. [1] GOAL/QPC had this book translated into English in 1983.[2] The English translation was published by Productivity Press in 1988.

GOAL/QPC and the American Supplier Institute began studying and teaching the Seven New QC Tools in 1983. Since that time, many others have refined the tools and contributed to their understanding. Some, like GOAL/QPC, refer to these tools as the Seven Management and Planning Tools (7 M&P Tools).

The 7 M&P Tools are:

❶ **Affinity Diagram**

❷ **Interrelationship Digraph**

❸ **Tree Diagram**

❹ **Matrix Diagram**

❺ **Process Decision Program Chart**

❻ **Arrow Diagram**

❼ **Matrix Data Analysis**

These tools are flexible in their application, and the output from one can be the input for another. In this manner we are able to leverage their power, thus increasing their value in all planning activities. The first two tools listed are for general planning, whereas the third, fourth, and seventh tools are for intermediate planning. The fifth and sixth tools are for detailed planning. When we integrate the application of the tools in a manner that is appropriate for the task at hand, the result is efficient, effective distillation of language data, rapid analysis of language data, reliable priority setting, and effective contingency planning.

DATA COLLECTION FOR THE 7 M&P TOOLS

The application of the 7 M&P tools begins with the collection of language data. This is the first step in all planning. As stated earlier, the term "language data" refers to ideas, opinions, perceptions, desires, and issues. These include requirements established by the leaders of the company, customer requirements and expectations, and ideas generated by the work team itself. The data are usually collected through brainstorming or surveys. Brainstorming is effective when the number of individuals, who possess the desired information, is small. In this instance every individual is involved in the data collection process.

There are several methods for brainstorming: multi-voting, nominal group technique, free association, and variations of all these. The recommended method for brainstorming is free association. A question is posed to the team, and each member is free to present his or her response. The question can relate to a problem, a desired result, a goal, or an objective. The ideas are not evaluated during the brainstorming. All discussion focuses on clarification and drawing out of additional ideas. Each idea or response is written on a single Post-it™ note.

If the topic is controversial, or the team members appear reluctant to offer ideas, or if one or two individuals dominate the discussion, we recommend the round robin method. This is a variation of the Nominal Group Technique (NGT). During round robin brainstorming, each individual has a turn to respond. No one may respond out of turn, nor is anyone allowed to criticize or evaluate an input. A member may, however, choose to pass. The round robin continues until the ideas are exhausted.

Surveys are appropriate when the population possessing the desired information is large. In this case, it is not practical to query every individual, so we select a sample of the population for the survey. Surveys use a set of structured questions to elicit responses from the sample. We analyze these responses to determine trends or to answer questions about a given or potential situation. Although surveys can be either written or oral, the results need to be documented in writing for further action.

AFFINITY DIAGRAM

Purpose

As stated above, the planning process begins with the collection of a large set of data regarding ideas, opinions, perceptions, desires, and issues. Initially, the relationships among these data elements will not be clear, although there may be a sense of where the team wants to go. The first task, then, is to distill the data into key ideas or common themes. The Affinity Diagram is a very effective tool for achieving this result. It organizes language data into groupings and determines the key ideas or common themes. The results can then be used for further analysis in the planning process.

Process

The development of an Affinity Diagram is a three-step process. This is a creative task, requiring analysis of ideas, association of common thoughts, and determination of patterns from large amounts of data. An individual can develop the Affinity Diagram, but because it is a creative process, a team often is more effective. The three steps for developing an Affinity Diagram are:

❶   **Group data.**

❷   **Select grouping titles.**

❸   **Refine groupings.**

Step 1. Group Data Begin by collating the ideas, opinions, perceptions, desires, or issues as individual data elements. Write each one on an individual piece of paper, such as a Post-it™ note. These then are arranged on a flat surface such as a wall, white board, or window. The objective is to cluster the ideas together in logical associations. Some people like to write tentative titles and cluster the ideas under them. We do not recommend this, because it can stifle creativity. Instead let the associations and patterns drive the title.

During this step, it is important that every member of the team participate. Begin by placing the data elements on the flat surface without regard to association. Then direct the team to arrange the notes in logical patterns. The team does this together, without discussion or evaluation of the choices. Each person is allowed to move the Post-it™ notes around at will. This may seem chaotic, but set a time limit (e.g. 15 minutes), encourage participation, and soon order and agreement will come out of the chaos (Figure 8-1).

Step 2. Select Grouping Titles The next step is to decide on a title for each grouping. The title needs to represent an action that reflects the main idea or theme of the grouping. The titles, therefore, need to be complete sentences, stated as actions.

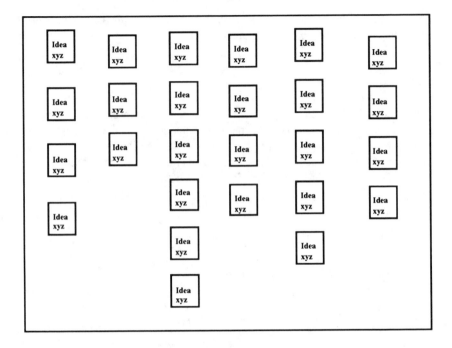

Figure 8-1. Associate Ideas.

In some instances, determining the title requires a compromise among the ideas in the grouping. Keep in mind that, at this point in developing the Affinity Diagram the title is important because it defines the action to be taken. Avoid evaluating the ideas in the groupings at this point in the process. The next step will further clarify the issues and the titles (Figure 8-2).

Step 3. Refine Groupings   After the groupings have appropriate titles, it is time to review each item under each title to see if it still fits or if it should be included under a different title. At the same time, review the titles to ascertain if any of the groupings can be consolidated. The resulting Affinity Diagram will bring order to the original collection of apparently unrelated ideas (Figure 8-3).

The Affinity Diagram is a very powerful tool for dealing with language data. It quickly and effectively distills the data into logical patterns that reveal emes and associations. It is also effective in dealing with old issues creative thinking is desired. Some practitioners argue against using Diagram when the situation is simple and requires quick results.

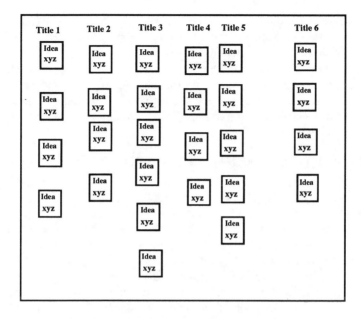

Figure 8-2. Title the Groupings.

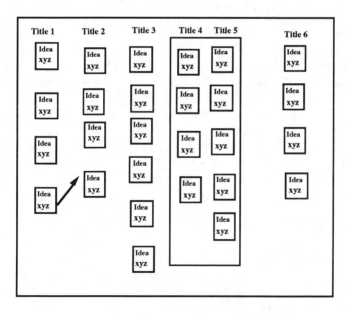

Figure 8-3. Refine Groupings.

In our experience the time and energy expended in developing an Affinity Diagram is amply rewarded by the resulting insights and consensus, regardless of the complexity of the situation or the quantity of data.

Application of the Affinity Diagram can extend from simple personal planning to the most complex industrial problems. A single individual or a team can use the Affinity Diagram as the starting point for planning. The results of this analysis become the input for the Interrelationship Digraph.

INTERRELATIONSHIP DIGRAPH

Purpose

The relationships among language data elements are not linear and they are often multidirectional. In other words an idea or issue can affect more than one other idea or issue, and the magnitudes of these effects can vary. Additionally, the relationships are often hidden or not clearly understood.

The Interrelationship Digraph is an effective tool for understanding the relationships among ideas and for mapping the sequential connections between them. The usual input for the Interrelationship Digraph is the results of an Affinity Diagram. The Interrelationship Digraph can, however, be used to analyze a set of actions or ideas without first developing an Affinity Diagram.

We use the information developed from the Interrelationship Digraph to establish priorities and to determine optimum sequencing of actions. Frequently, teams develop an Affinity Diagram, skip the Interrelationship Digraph, and go on to use another tool to develop their plan. This is a big mistake. The Interrelationship Digraph always provides an important understanding about the data you are analyzing.

There are three methods for accomplishing the Interrelationship Digraph. The original method is called the Arrow Method. GOAL/QPC teaches an alternate method referred to as the Matrix Method. There is a third method that we prefer. We call this the J-F Matrix Method. This is a cross between the Matrix Method and the Priority Matrix.

Arrow Method

To the Arrow Method, lay out the issues on a flat surface that you can write on (such as a white board). You can write them on the white board, attach cards or notes on the white board, or simply write them on a piece of paper. The Arrow Method consists of four steps:

❶ Determine causal relationships.

❷ Draw directional arrows.

❸ Sum arrows in and out.

❹ Set priorities for the issues.

Step 1. Determine Causal Relationships   The first step in preparing an Interrelationship Digraph is to determine the causal relationships among the issues. Take each issue, in turn, and ask the question "Does this issue cause or influence any other issue?" Ask the same question for every issue until all combinations have been examined.

This process works well if the question is the same each time, and if you move in one direction at a time; e.g. from issue A to B, from A to C, etc. If you change the wording of the question, or consider the relationships in a bi-directional manner, you will confound the issues and possibly miss a combination.

Step 2. Draw directional arrows   Draw an arrow from each issue to any issue it affects or causes (Figure 8-4). If issues have arrows going in both directions between them (a two way-arrow) determine which issue has the greater causal relationship and eliminate the other arrow.

One variation is to weight the causal relationship as strong or weak. Use a solid-line arrow to indicate a strong causal relationship, and dashed-line arrow to indicate a weak causal relationship.

Step 3. Sum Arrows In and Out   After exploring all possible combinations, sum the arrows in and out for each issue (Figure 8-5).   Record the results clearly next to each issue, indicating if the total is "in" (I) or "out" (O).

If you choose to discriminate between strong and weak causal relationships, give a half point value to a dash line arrow and a whole point to a solid line arrow (Figure 8-6).

Step 4. Set Priorities for the Issues   Review the results of Step 3. The issues with the largest sum totals, for arrows out, have the greatest impact on the other issues. These are typically the "critical few" issues. If we solve

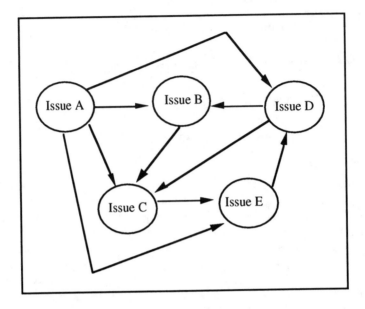

Figure 8-4.   Draw Directional Arrows

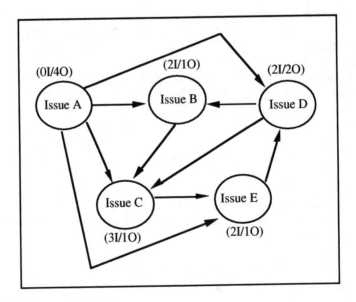

Figure 8-5.   Sum Arrows In and Out

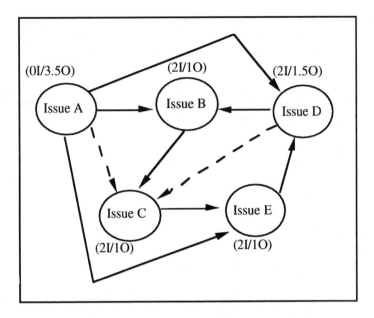

Figure 8-6. Strong and Weak Relationships

these problems, implement these actions, or provide these services, we will have the greatest influence on the problem, goal, or customer requirement. The totals are also an indication of the expected return on our investment in time, energy, and money for addressing a given issue.

The issues with the greatest number of arrows in are the ones affected by the greatest number of other issues. These are highly dependent on the accomplishment of the other actions or issues. These may, in fact, be bottlenecks or other critical issues to be analyzed. In our example above, Issue A clearly has the greatest impact on all the other issues. Issue C is clearly the most dependent issue and might be a bottleneck for the process, problem, or goal under evaluation.

GOAL/QPC Style Matrix Method[1]

The arrow method, as demonstrated, is easy to construct. Our example used only five issues, and the digraph is easy to understand. For those situations

---

[1] Adapted from *Memory Jogger Plus+* ™ by Michael Brassard, Boston: GOAL/QPC, 1989.

with more than five issues, however, the arrow diagram rapidly becomes very complex and virtually impossible to follow. GOAL/QPC teaches a simpler matrix method for developing the Interrelationship Digraph that makes it possible to deal with a large number of issues and ensures the methodical evaluation of each relationship. It is presented in their book *Memory Jogger Plus+* ™ and is presented as an alternative to the arrow method. The matrix method consists of five steps:

❶   **Develop L matrix of issues.**

❷   **Determine causal relationships.**

❸   **Draw directional arrows.**

❹   **Sum arrows in and out.**

❺   **Set priority for the issues.**

Step 1. Develop L Matrix of Issues   The first step in the matrix method is to develop an L matrix of the issues. This is a matrix with two axes. For this digraph, enter each issue on both the horizontal axis and the vertical axis. There is a column for the sum of the arrows in, one for the sum of the arrows out, and one for the combined total of arrows in and out (Figure 8-7).

Step 2. Determine Causal Relationships   The second step in developing the matrix is to determine the causal relationships among the issues. Take each issue on the vertical axis and compare it to each of the other issues on the horizontal axis. As in the Arrow Method, ask the question: "Does this issue cause or influence the issue on the horizontal axis?" or "Does Issue A cause or influence Issue B?".

The question needs to be worded the way same each time. Changing the wording of the question confounds the issues. Unlike the arrow method, however, you compare the issues in both directions each time and mark the direction accordingly.

Step 3. Draw Directional Arrows   Draw an arrow from each issue toward the issue it affects or causes. If a pair of issues has arrows going in both directions, determine which issue has the greater causal relationship and eliminate the other arrow.

	A	B	C	D	E	IN	OUT	TOTAL
Issue A								
Issue B								
Issue C								
Issue D								
Issue E								

Figure 8-7.   L Matrix

Step 4. Sum Arrows In and Out   After exploring all possible combinations, sum the arrows in and out for each issue.   Place the totals in the respective columns.   Then sum the total arrows in and out, and place that total in the last column (Figure 8-8).

Step 5. Set Priorities for the Issues   Review the results of Step 4. As in the arrow method the issues having the largest sum totals for arrows out have the greatest impact on the other issues.   These are the "critical few" issues.   Solving these problems, implementing these actions, or providing these services will have the greatest influence on the problem, goal, or customer requirement.   The issues with the largest total of arrows out are the issues that have the greatest impact on achieving your desired results.

J-F Matrix Method

The arrow method and the GOAL/QPC style matrix method are both effective methods for developing the Interrelationship Digraph to understand the relationships and sequential connections among ideas. Experience teaches that the application of the 7-M&P tools leads to new applications, and new ways of using them.   The frustration of applying the arrow method in very large, complex situations also led us to develop a new matrix method for preparing the

Interrelationship Digraph. To differentiate it from the GOAL/QPC style matrix method we call this method the J-F Matrix Method.

	A	B	C	D	E	IN	OUT	TOTAL
Issue A		↑	↑	↑	↑	0	4	4
Issue B	←		↑	←		2	1	3
Issue C	←	←		←	↑	3	1	4
Issue D	←	↑	↑		←	2	2	4
Issue E	←		←	↑		2	1	3

Figure 8-8. Completed Matrix

The J-F Matrix Method is a cross between the GOAL/QPC style matrix method and the GOAL/QPC Prioritization Matrix. It is similar to the GOAL/QPC style matrix method, but the symbols are different and the interrelationships are summed along both axes. The J-F matrix method consists of five steps:

❶ **Develop L Matrix of issues.**

❷ **Determine causal relationships.**

❸ **Mark the causal relationships.**

❹ **Sum the interrelationships.**

❺ **Set priority for the issues.**

Step 1. Develop L Matrix of Issues The first step in developing the Interrelationship Digraph using the J-F matrix method is to develop an L matrix of the issues. Enter each issue on the horizontal and vertical axes. Add a total column and a total row to the matrix, as shown in Figure 8-9.

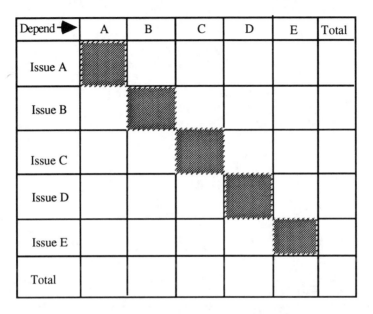

Figure 8-9. L Matrix of Issues

Step 2. Determine Causal Relationships The second step in developing the matrix is to determine the causal relationships between each pair of issues. Take each issue on the vertical axis and compare it to each of the other issues on the horizontal axis. For this method, the question is: "Does the horizontal issue depend on, or is it caused by the vertical issue?"

As in the other two methods, the question needs to be worded the same way each time. This method is like the arrow method, comparing the issues in only one direction at a time.

Step 3. Mark the Causal Relationships For this method we evaluate the extent of each causal or dependency relationship: strong, medium, weak, or none. The symbols used is the same as that used for Quality Function Deployment (Figure 8-10). Figure 8-11 is an example of a matrix with symbols added.

Step 4. Sum the Interrelationships After determining all the relationships, score them in both the vertical and horizontal axes. Place the totals in the appropriate column or row. As in Quality Function Deployment, the

weights for the associated symbols are as shown in Figure 8-12. Figure 8-13
shows the matrix with the scores added.

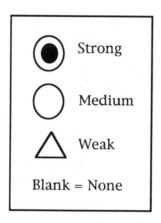

Figure 8-10.   Symbols for Causal Relationships

Depend ➡	A	B	C	D	E	Total
Issue A						
Issue B	◉			◉		
Issue C	△	◉		△		
Issue D	◉				○	
Issue E	◉		◉			
Total						

Figure 8-11.   L Matrix of Issues with Causal Relationships

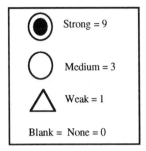

Figure 8-12.   Weights for Symbols.

Depend ➡	A	B	C	D	E	Total
Issue A	▨					0
Issue B	◉	▨		◉		18
Issue C	△	◉	▨	△		11
Issue D	◉			▨	◯	12
Issue E	◉		◉		▨	18
Total	28	9	9	10	3	

Figure 8-13.   L Matrix of Issues With Scores

Step 5. Set Priorities for the Issues   Review the results of Step 4. As in the Arrow Method the issues having the largest sum totals for arrows out have the greatest impact on the other issues. In this matrix this corresponds to the row totals at the bottom of the matrix.   These are the "critical few" issues. Solving these problems, implementing these actions, or providing these services will have the greatest influence on the problem, goal, or customer requirement.

The totals in the column, on the left side of the matrix, reflect the issues that are affected by the other issues. In this case the highest total indicates an issue is most affected by the other issues. It is, therefore, the most dependent.

In Figure 8-13 issue A has the highest independence score: 28. The next highest score is 10. Issue A, therefore, clearly warrants the highest priority of attention. Addressing this issue will have the greatest impact because of the extent that the other issues depend on it. It is also of interest that Issue A has the lowest dependence score. It is not affected by any of the other issues. Conversely, Issues B and E are tied for the highest dependence score: 18. These issues are affected the most by the other issues under evaluation.

You can use the insight provided by this evaluation to prioritize actions, or to determine the issues necessary for further planning. It is always valuable to perform this step even if all of the issues are to be acted on. The resulting understanding is always of value.

TREE DIAGRAM

Purpose

The Tree Diagram has many uses. It is a systematic tool for determining all of the tasks necessary to accomplish a goal. It can be used for determining key factors causing a problem, or to develop an action plan for a single event or a process. You can also use the Tree Diagram to decide on the priority for action.

Process

The Tree Diagram begins with the definition of a goal, task, or problem that we need to break into finite sub-elements. This definition is a statement of purpose, a problem statement, or some other fact. You can develop the statement from a previously developed Affinity Diagram, or Interrelationship Digraph, or from a new Affinity Diagram, a new Interrelationship Digraph, brainstorming, or some other means. This definition statement becomes the focal point for generating possible tasks, causes, or issues.

The development of the Tree Diagram is a logical task. It begins with a top-level statement, proceeding in a logical, step-by-step manner to lower and lower levels of detail. As each level is defined, these new statements become the focal point for further development. This process continues until you are satisfied with the level of information you have developed. Each level can also be provided by new or previously developed, Affinity Diagrams, Interrelationship Digraphs, or brainstorming.

The example in Figure 8-14 illustrates how a goal has been broken into four key tasks. Each task has been further broken into sub tasks, and each of these has been examined for further definition. For this illustration, sub tasks A-3 and C-2 have been broken down into further detail. Subtask C-2-c has been also broken into further detail.

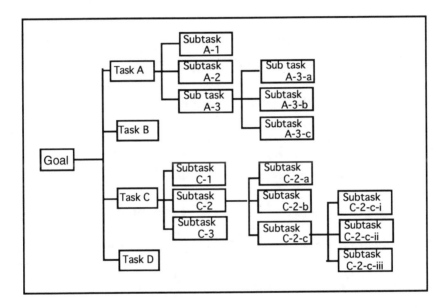

Figure 8-14. Tree Diagram.

The Tree Diagram uses linear logic to go from a broad statement to successive levels of detail. It is useful, therefore, when a task or problem is complex and when it is imperative to identify all key elements or subtasks.

MATRIX   DIAGRAM

Purpose

The Matrix Diagram is a tool for organizing language data (ideas, opinions, perceptions, desires, and issues) so that they can be compared to one another. The procedure is to organize the data on a vertical and a horizontal axis, examine the connecting points, and graphically display the relationships. The matrix diagram reveals the relationships among ideas and visually demonstrates the influence each element has on every other element.

Matrices are of two general types: two-dimensional and three-dimensional. A two-dimensional matrix is in the shape of an L or a T. A three-dimensional matrix is in the shape of an X, Y, or C. The L matrix is used for two sets of variables, the T, Y and C matrices for three sets of variables, and the X matrix is used for four sets of variables.

Process

The construction of a Matrix Diagram is a four step process:

❶   Select the matrix elements.

❷   Select the matrix format.

❸   Complete the matrix headings.

❹   Determine relationships or responsibilities.

Step 1. Select the Matrix Elements   The matrix elements fall into categories, which are sets of data. You can derive these elements from a new or previously developed brainstorming, Affinity Diagram, Interrelationship Digraph, or tree diagram.

Step 2. Select the Matrix Format   As stated above, the matrix format depends on the number of sets of data to be analyzed. The most common formats are the two-dimensional L and T matrices (Figure 8-15).

Step 3. Complete the Matrix Headings   After the language data is collected, sorted, and divided into sets, and the matrix format is selected, fill in the headings of the matrix.

Step 4. Determine Relationships or Responsibilities   Examine each of the interconnecting nodes in the matrix and determine if there is a relationship. As in the J-F Matrix Method for developing an Interrelationship Digraph, evaluate the relationships and mark the matrix accordingly (Figure 8-16). At this point, sum the rows and columns and interpret the matrix.

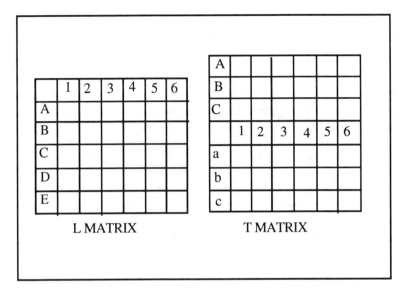

Figure 8-15. L and T Matrices.

Depend→	1	2	3	4	5	Total
Issue A						0
Issue B	◉			◉		18
Issue C	△	◉		△		11
Issue D	◉				◯	12
Issue E	◉		◉			18
Total	28	9	9	10	3	

Figure 8-16. Completed L Matrix

PROCESS DECISION PROGRAM CHART (PDPC)

Purpose

The Process Decision Program Chart (PDPC) is a tool that assists in anticipating events and in developing preventive measures, or countermeasures, for undesired occurrences. It is typically used when a task is unique, the situation is complex, and the price of potential failure is unacceptable. It is similar to the Tree Diagram. It leads you through the identification of the tasks and paths necessary to achieve a goal and its associated subgoals. The PDPC then leads you to answer the questions "What could go wrong?" and "What unexpected events could occur?" Next, the PDPC leads you in developing countermeasures. The PDPC provides very effective contingency planning by mapping out all conceivable events and leading to the development of appropriate countermeasures.

Process

The process for developing the Process Decision Program Chart (PDPC) is less structured than the 7 M&P tools discussed so far. The goal is to list and evaluate all possible subtasks or actions using the graphical method presented below, an outline or some other construct that you might develop. These steps listed, therefore, intended only as guidelines:

❶ Construct a Tree Diagram.

❷ Answer the questions "What can go wrong?" and "What unexpected events could occur?"

❸ Develop countermeasures.

Step 1. Construct a Tree Diagram As originally developed, the PDPC is a graphic chart. It begins with the development of a Tree Diagram of the process or activity under evaluation. For the PDPC, we prefer to orient the Tree Diagram vertically instead of horizontally (Figure 8-17). This convention is not a rigid requirement, but it does seem to provide a logical direction for the flow of activities when developing contingencies.

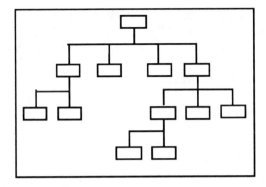

Figure 8-17. Vertical Tree Diagram as Basis for PDPC.

Step 2. Answer Key Questions   At each branch of the Tree Diagram two questions are asked:

> "What can go wrong at this point?"

> "What unexpected events could occur?"

The answers to the first question are documented on the chart. The alternate paths are added to the chart as well (Figure 8-18).

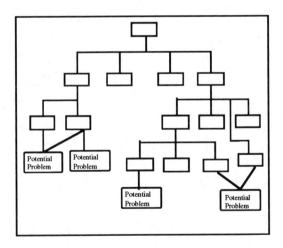

Figure 8-18. Potential Problems are Marked on the PDPC.

Step 3. Develop Countermeasures   Countermeasures are developed for each action that could go wrong. The development of the countermeasures may involve the application of one or a combination of the following tools:

➤   **Brainstorming**

➤   **Affinity Diagram**

➤   **Interrelationship Digraph**

➤   **Tree Diagram**

Annotate each countermeasure below the potential problems. Repeat the process until all branches or paths are exhausted. Then evaluate each counter-measure for feasibility, cost impact, quality impact, and schedule impact. This evaluation will enable you to make an informed decision when selecting the countermeasures to implement. As you evaluate the countermeasures, mark them to indicate if they are to implemented or not (Figure 8-19).

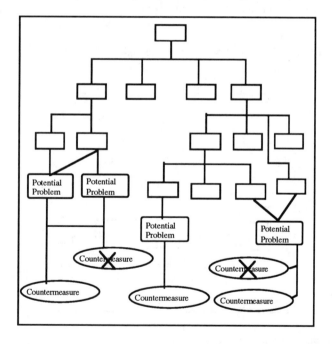

Figure 8-19. Countermeasures are Marked on the PDPC.

The PDPC is an efficient tool for evaluating a process or activity. It maps the conceivable activities or actions and contingencies in a methodical manner. The PDPC is very powerful when used in conjunction with the other 7 M&P tools.

ARROW DIAGRAM

Purpose

The Arrow Diagram is derivative of the Program Evaluation and Review Technique (PERT) developed in the United States in the 1950s. It is a tool for determining the optimum time for accomplishing a task, and for graphically displaying the activity flow. This tool is most effective when the subtasks for an activity are well known, and there is a high degree of confidence in that knowledge. Each subtask is plotted in sequence. The time to accomplish each task is indicated and used to determine the earliest time that a given subtask can begin.

An Arrow Diagram (Figure 8-20) clearly indicates which subtasks can be done in parallel and which subtasks must be done sequentially. In this manner, the optimum activity flow can be determined, and the minimum time to complete the entire task can be calculated. The Arrow Diagram can include the earliest and the latest start time for any given subtask. The Arrow Diagram aids in planning and in evaluating progress against the plan.

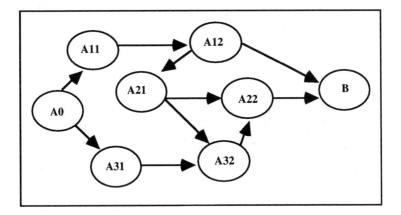

Figure 8-20. Arrow Diagram.

If the subtasks are not well known and understood, this is a very frustrating activity. In that case, the PDPC is a better tool for graphically displaying a task or project.

Process

The process for developing the Arrow Diagram is similar to that for developing the PDPC. It begins with defining all the subtasks or actions, and determining their sequence. Each subtask is evaluated, and the Arrow Diagram is drawn.

❶   **Define the subtasks for the activity.**

❷   **Evaluate each subtask.**

❸   **Construct the Arrow Diagram.**

Step 1. Define the Subtasks for the Activity   We begin by defining all the required subtasks. List each activity on a separate Post-it™ note, and number them for easy reference. Begin to arrange the tasks on a flat surface in the required sequence. Do this on the horizontal axis. The result is similar to the Tree Diagram, but the subtasks are arranged from right to left instead of from left to right (Figure 8-21).

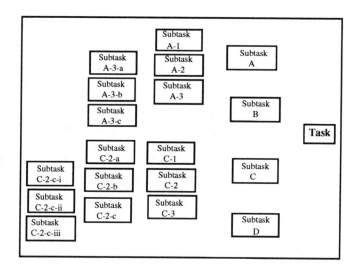

Figure 8-21.   Subtask Definition.

Step 2. Evaluate Each Sub-task Evaluate the sequence of the subtasks and modify the arrangement of the Post-it™ notes at this time. Carefully note those activities that can be performed in parallel with others. Mark the subtasks with the time duration that they require. At this stage, higher level subtask titles can be eliminated. These are subtask titles that are not actual actions themselves, but are accomplished by lower subtasks. Our goal is to leave only those subtasks on the diagram that are actual actions to be accomplished (Figure 8-22).

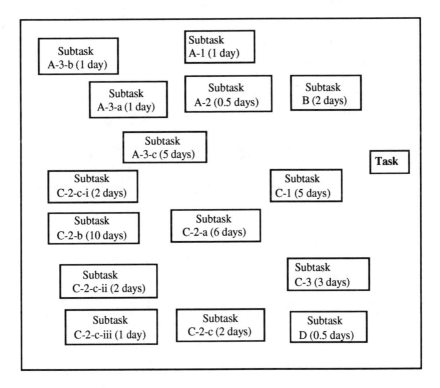

Figure 8-22. Subtask Evaluation.

Step 2. Construct the Arrow Diagram The final step in the construction of the Arrow Diagram is to finalize the arrangement of the subtasks, and to draw the appropriate arrows between the actions showing the flow of activity (Figure 8-23).

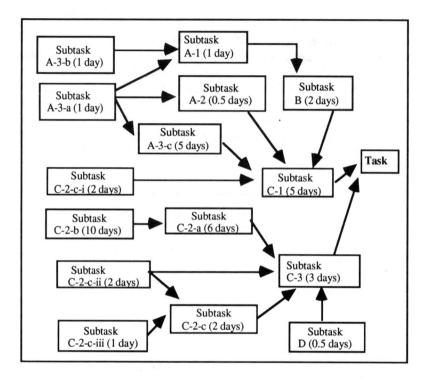

Figure 8-23. Arrow Diagram

In the example in Figure 8-23, there are four sets of subtasks that are performed in parallel:

❶   A-3-a, A-3-b, C-2-b, C-2-c-i, C-2-c-ii, and C-2-c-iii

❷   A-1, and A-3-c

❸   A-2, B, and C-2-c

❹   C-2-a and C-3

Mapping these subtasks in the Arrow Diagram reveals the optimum sequencing. The evaluation of the subtasks enables us to calculate that the task will take 16 days of elapsed time to complete.

MATRIX DATA ANALYSIS CHART

Purpose

The Matrix Data Analysis Chart is used primarily in market research for the development and planning of new products or services. It is a tool for graphically presenting a comparison of products or services. In this way, one is able to evaluate a market segment and determine the relationships among products, services, or companies based on representative characteristics.

Process

The process for developing the Matrix Data Analysis Chart consists of four steps:

❶   Determine the representative characteristics.

❷   Collect data.

❸   Calculate comparisons.

❹   Graphically display the results.

Step 1. Determine the Representative Characteristics   The first step in developing a Matrix Data Analysis Chart is to determine the representative characteristic(s) to be compared. These are the key parameters that are used to evaluate a product, service, or process. Some of these parameters are easily defined and measured, such as concentricity, hardness, footprint, or weight others are more obscure and difficult to measure: for example, gentleness, flavor, or ease of use. In all cases, however, the parameters need to be representative of how one would determine excellence for a product, service, or process.

Step 2. Collect Data   After determining the representative characteristic(s), collect data about the competing products, services, or processes.

Step 3. Calculate Comparisons   Calculate the comparisons for the products, services, or processes under evaluation.

Step 4. Graphically Display the Results   Display the results of Step 3 on a four-quadrant chart, as in Figure 8-24. In this chart you are able to compare how you perform against the competition with regard to two parame-

ters. In this specific case, company X is doing well in achieving attribute A
but not as well as company Y in achieving Attribute B.

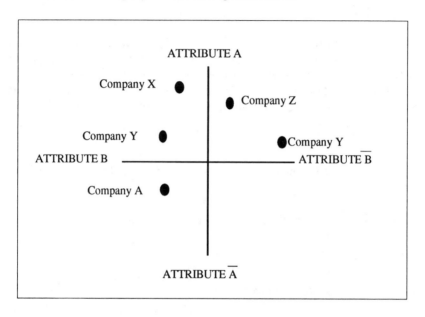

Figure 8-24 Matrix Data Analysis Chart.

PRIORITIZATION MATRIX

The Prioritization Matrix is not one of the original 7 M&P tools. It is an
innovation based on the Tree Diagram and the L-Shaped Matrix, and it is powerful enough to warrant discussion as a new 7 M&P tool.

The Prioritization Matrix is effective for sifting through a set of key issues
or criteria to focus priority of action. It begins with a broad set of data, and
uses Tree Diagrams to organize the information. The results of the Tree
Diagrams are used to develop an L-shaped matrix. The matrix is evaluated as in
the J-F Interrelationship Digraph. Figure 8-25 demonstrates the Prioritization
Matrix.

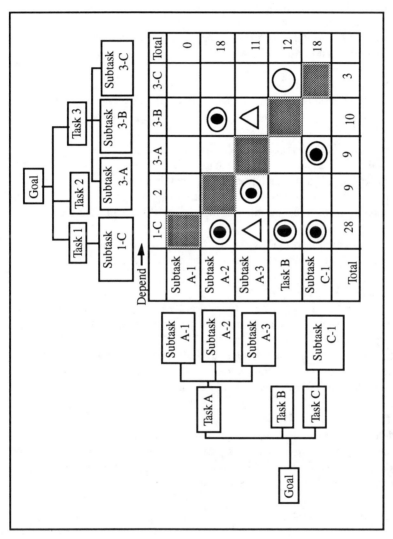

Figure 8-25. Prioritization Matrix

KEY POINTS

The 7 M&P Tools provide an efficient and effective method for analyzing language data. The output from one tool can be the input for another. In this manner we are able to leverage their power.

The application of the 7 M&P tools begins with the collection of language data through brainstorming or surveys.

AFFINITY   DIAGRAM

The Affinity Diagram quickly and effectively distills language data into logical patterns that reveal common themes and associations.

INTERRELATIONSHIP DIGRAPH

The relationships among the data elements are not linear, and are often times multi-directional. The Interrelationship Digraph is an effective tool for understanding the relationships among ideas and for mapping their sequential connections. The input for the Interrelationship Digraph is usually the results of an Affinity Diagram.

The information developed from the Interrelationship Digraph is useful in establishing priorities and determining optimum sequencing of action.

TREE DIAGRAMS

The Tree Diagram is a systematic tool for determining all the tasks necessary to accomplish a goal. It can be used for determining key factors causing a problem, and for developing an action plan.

The Tree Diagram uses linear logic to go from a broad statement to successive levels of detail. It is useful, therefore, when a task or problem is complex and when it is imperative to identify all key elements or subtasks.

MATRIX   DIAGRAM

The Matrix Diagram is used to organize language data (ideas, opinions, perceptions, desires, and issues) so that they can be compared to one another. The matrix diagram reveals the relationships among ideas and visually demonstrates the influence each element has on every other element.

PROCESS DECISION PROGRAM CHART (PDPC)

The Process Decision Program Chart (PDPC) is a tool that assists in anticipating events and developing preventive measures, or countermeasures, for undesired occurrences. It is used when a task is unique, the situation is complex, and the price of potential failure is unacceptable.

ARROW DIAGRAM
The Arrow Diagram is a tool for determining the optimum time for accomplishing a task and for displaying the activity flow. This tool is best used when the subtasks for an activity are well known, and there is a high degree of confidence in the knowledge about the subtasks.

MATRIX DATA ANALYSIS CHART
The Matrix Data Analysis Chart is used primarily in market research for the development and planning of new products or services. It is a tool for graphically presenting a comparison of products or services.

EXAMPLE

The Production Machinery Division of LWCI has embarked on a project to develop a new production machinery system. The new system will be designated the LWCI 1600. There will be a variety of models in the LWCI 1600 series. Each of the models will include features that are designed to address the particular requirements of a customer.

This new series of equipment will be the first product developed, by the Production Machinery Division, since LWCI established its vision:

> Leander Wiles Company Inc. will be a highly profitable enterprise producing world class quality products and services. We are focused on the design and production of manufacturing equipment. We will challenge the global marketplace, and do so while remaining committed to being a socially and civically responsible company.

The division's steering council established a product development team for the LWCI 1600 project. The product development team consists of representatives from Marketing, Engineering, Product Operations, Quality, Safety, Finance, and Procurement. The team also includes a representative from the Machine and Tool Division and Electronics Division. The mission of the product development team is to use the Management 2000 model to develop the LWCI 1600.

The team's first step was to perform a customer survey. This was done in two parts: a personal interview with customers of LWCI products, a survey of companies that currently do not use LWCI products but are potential customers. The goal of the survey was to collect information about customer requirements and expectations, for use in the design and development of the LWCI 1600.

The team analyzed results of the survey. The analysis yielded a list of customer requirements, desires, and expectations to be used in the development of the LWCI 1600 (Example Figure 8-1). The team developed an Affinity Diagram for this data and then developed and Interrelationship Digraph from the Affinity Diagram. These are presented in Example Figures 8-2 and 8-3.

The message from the "voice of the customers" is that they want and expect:

> A compact system that is low in cost, easy to use, and capable of highly accurate work.

This result was not a surprise to the team, but it was surprising to the team how customers defined those characteristics and their interrelationships. It was especially significant that support documentation and pre- and post-sales support are vital for satisfying the customers. In the past, these factors were not considered important. The analysis of the survey data has clearly stated otherwise.

The team developed a Tree Diagram for each of the broad characteristics of the customers' requirements. These diagrams ensure that the team understands the specific details for these characteristics. Example Figure 8-4 is the initial Tree Diagram that was developed for "System Easy to Operate & Maintain."

- Low cost
- Accurate schedule commitments
- Timely response to requests for information
- Reliability of System
- Low Mean Time Between Failures (MTBF)
- Low Mean Time To Repair (MTTR)
- Easy to use
- Good availability of training on system use
- Good availability of training on system maintenance
- Competent, knowledgeable salespeople/order takers
- Upward compatible system
- Downward compatibile system
- Easy to program
- Easy to incorporate modifications
- Good availability of upgrades
- Meet ommitements for quality, cost, & schedule
- Help line
- Good product documentation
- Accurate product documentation
- Product documentation easy to follow
- Setup instructions easy to understand
- Clear operating instructions
- Level of documentation appropriate for skill level of operators, maintenance personnel, etc.
- Minimum Special Test Equipment Required for Maintenance
- Easy to calibrate
- Calibration cycle better than average for the industry
- Small equipment footprint
- Equipment safe to use
- Equipment requires a minimum of hazardous material to operate
- Equipment generates a minimum of hazardous material
- Special tools not required for setup or operation
- System digitally controlled
- High tolerance system

Example Figure 8-1.   Survey Results.

High Degree of Compatibility
• Upward compatible system
• Downward compatibile system

Good Pre & Post Sales Support
• Good availability of training on system use
• Good availability of training on system maintenance
• Timely response to requests for information
• Competent, knowledgeable Salespeople/order takers
• Help line

High Degree of Safety to Personnel & the Environment
• Equipment safe to use
• Equipment requires a minimum of hazardous material to operate
• Equipment generates a minimum of hazardous material

Good Support Documentation
• Good product documentation
• Accurate product documentation
• Product documentation easy to follow
• Setup instructions easy to understand
• Clear operating instructions
• Level of documentation appropriate for skill level of operators, maintenance personnel, etc.

Ease of Operation & Maintenance
• Easy to calibrate
• Calibration cycle better than average for the industry
• Special tools not required for setup or operation
• Easy to program
• Easy to incorporate modifications
• Good availability of upgrades
• Reliability of system
• Low Mean Time Between Failures (MTBF)
• Low Mean Time To Repair (MTTR)
• Minimum special test equipment required for maintenance
• System digitally controlled
• Easy to use

High Tolerance System
• High tolerance system

Compact System
• Small equipment footprint

Low Cost, On Time Delivery
• Low cost
• Accurate schedule commitments
• Meet commitements for quality, cost, & Sschedule

Example Figure 8-2. Affinity Diagram of Survey Results.

Depend →	A	B	C	D	E	F	G	H	Total
A. High Degree of Compatibility	▨					◯			3
B. System Easy to Operate & Maintain	△	▨	◯		◯	⬤			16
C. Good Pre- & Post-Sales Support			▨			⬤			9
D. High Tolerance System		△		▨		△			2
E. System Provides High Degree of Safety to Personnel & the Environment		◯	△		▨	◯			7
F. Good Support Documentation						▨			0
G. Compact System							▨		0
H. Low Cost, On Time Delivery	△		⬤					▨	10
Total	2	4	13	0	3	25	0	0	

⬤ = Strong = 9   ◯ = Medium = 3   △ = Weak = 1

Example Figure 8-3. Interrelationship Digraph.

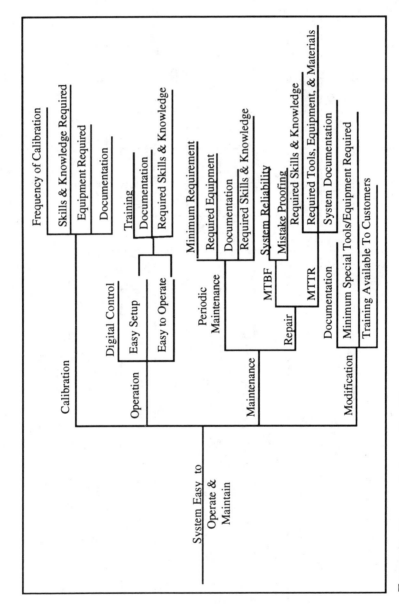

Example Figure 8-4. Tree Diagram

The design team decided that a critical target for the LWCI 1600 system was low cost but high tolerance accuracy. They evaluated their competitors' systems on that basis. They compared the results with the target they set for the LWCI 1600 system using a Matrix Data Analysis chart. The team chose the industry average cost and average tolerance accuracy as the 0,0 point. Each competitor's system was mapped in relation to the 0,0 point (Example Figure 8-5).

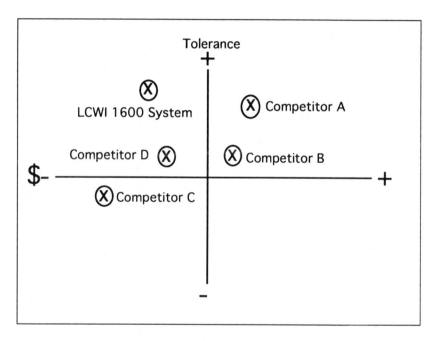

Example Figure 8-5.   Matrix Data Analysis.

The team concluded that the new system would provide an advantage over the competition. The LWCI 1600 would not be the cheapest in terms of acquisition cost, but it would be superior in accuracy for the cost. It would, therefore, provide superior value for the customers. The team's challenge is to meet the target for cost and accuracy, and to implement the other customer requirements as determined by the survey and subsequent analysis.

As the team members explored the requirements for customer support services, they discovered that LWCI had a history of errors in the customer orders. Initially, it was felt the errors resulted from the customers incorrectly completing the ordering documents. The team used a PDPC to evaluate the ordering process (Example Figure 8-6).

The Process Decision Program Chart for the Customer Orders Process was very revealing. When the team asked what could go wrong at each of the legs of the process, they were forced to face possibilities that were under their control (Example Figure 8-6). The team decided to implement several of the countermeasures they identified in the PDPC.

The LWCI 1600 development team realized that meeting delivery schedules was important to their customers. They also realized it was a vital element in making a profit. The team decided, therefore, to predict the cycle time based on past performance and knowledge about the technology for producing the LWCI 1600 systems. These predictions would then be used to develop process flows to meet the target cycle time. They used an Arrow Diagram was used to assist in the prediction of the production cycle time (Example Figure 8-7).

The Arrow Diagram showed that a system could take 64 to 94 days from receipt of an order until it was ready for packaging and shipping. This information will be used to develop work flows, establish ordering strategies, and establish warehouse requirements.

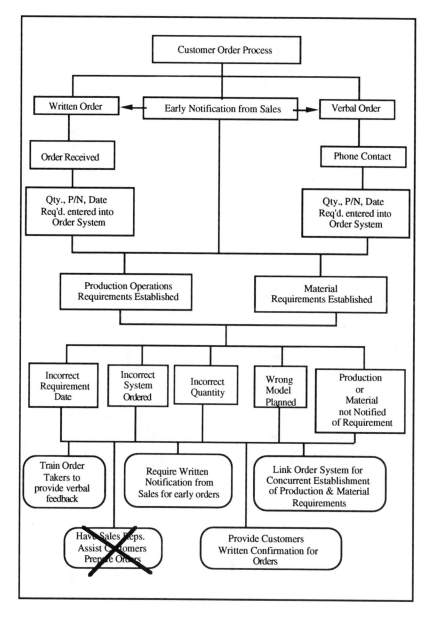

Example Figure 8-6. Process Program Decision Chart.

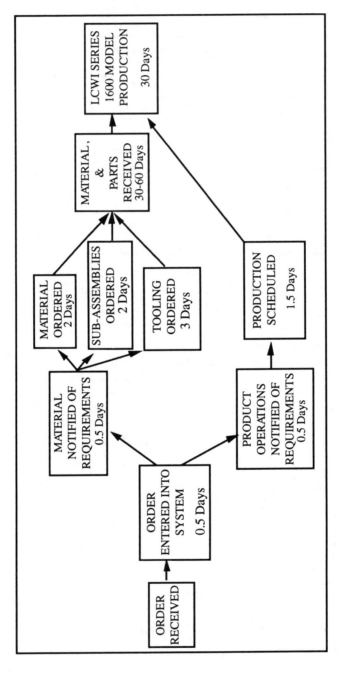

Example Figure 8-7. Arrow Chart.

9

Product Development Strategy

QUALITY FUNCTION DEPLOYMENT IS A STRUCTURED
METHOD THAT IDENTIFIES AND PRIORITIZES
CUSTOMER REQUIREMENTS, AND TRANSLATES THOSE
REQUIREMENTS INTO ENGINEERING REQUIREMENTS
FOR SYSTEMATIC DEPLOYMENT THROUGHOUT THE
COMPANY.

ALL COMPANIES - large or small, manufacturing or service, private or public, matrix or line - are organized by functional areas. These areas are often called departments, branches, sections, or groups. In most companies, each of these departments jealously guards its area of responsibility and authority.

The Management 2000 model calls for the breaking down of these artificial barriers, uniting all functions in a focused approach to achieve the goals of the company. In previous chapters, we focused on how each element of the organization develops its plans, and manages its processes, in a collaborative and sup-

337

portive manner to achieve the company's vision. In this chapter we will focus on how the company establishes the strategies for developing and improving the products and services it markets.

Regardless of the type of business, your company is in, its goal is to make a profit. Individuals who work for a government agency or a public institution may argue that their "company" doesn't make money. This is not true - they provide a value to the organization that gives them their funding. That organization will also benefit from increased effectiveness and efficiency. The value to the sponsor, and the increased effectiveness and efficiency, are forms of profit. This broader understanding of "profit" motivates us to implement the Management 2000 Model in all organizations.

The quickest and most reliable way to make money is to provide your customers the best value product or service, for the lowest cost in the shortest time frame. The customers define what "best value" is. We must, therefore, focus on understanding and satisfying their requirements. This strategy ensures that the customers will buy our products and services, thereby ensuring our market share.

Market share is meaningless if you lose money on your products or services. The method for developing and improving the products and services also needs to optimize activities to ensure that a profit is made. We need to minimize development and implementation cycle times, eliminate waste, and optimize all processes.

There are many benefits to be gained from a short development cycle:

> A longer product's sales life.

> Product in the marketplace longer.

> Customer loyalty due to the high cost of switching suppliers.

> Increased market share.

> Higher profit margins in the absence of competition.

> The perception of excellence resulting from the speed of introduction of new products or improvements.

Eliminating waste and optimizing processes clearly reduces operating expenses and leads directly to higher profit margins. The ideal situation is to have a very short development cycle time with a minimum of waste, in an environment of continuous measurable improvement.

The product and service development and improvement process needs to be an integral part of the company's strategy to become a world class competitor. This process needs to be an asset to competitiveness, not a liability.

THE SERIAL DESIGN PROCESS

The traditional method for developing products and services is a "serial approach," as depicted in Figure 9-1:

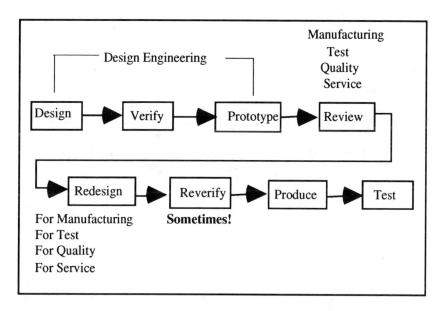

Figure 9-1. The Serial Design Process[1]

In this approach, the design engineers design the product and then hand it off to manufacturing. It is then up to the manufacturing and test engineers to figure out how to build it and test it. For a service, the "experts" decide what the service should be and design it according to their expert knowledge of what the customer needs. In both instances the designers do what they think is best, and use all their knowledge and talent to develop an excellent product or service. Unfortunately, they frequently develop a product or service that is innovative but difficult or impossible to produce without extensive redesign. The product or service design is frequently driven by technology and not by the customers' requirements or expectations.

The costs of detecting and repairing defects at various stages of product development, and integration increase greatly as you move through the design or production process, as shown in Figure 9-2 and 9-3.[2]

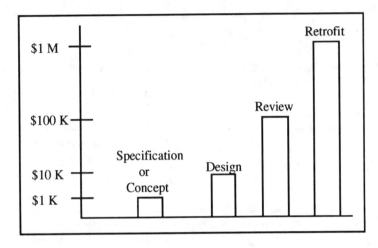

Figure 9-2. Cost to Detect and Repair a Defect at Various Stages of Product Development

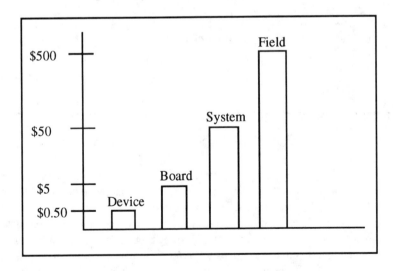

Figure 9-3. Cost to Detect and Repair a Defect at Various Levels of Product Integration

Recognizing these cost relationships, companies have developed various approaches to prevent the never ending cycle of design, redesign, and retrofit. Some have incorporated structured design reviews, formal hand-offs from design to manufacturing, and other systems to guarantee that the design is producible. Experience has proven that these are hollow actions. They miss the point. The product development process needs to be an integrated approach that addresses all of the factors early in the process and impacts productivity, quality, and customer satisfaction.

CONCURRENT ENGINEERING (CE)

Business needs new design process - one that ensures that all "downstream" product considerations are moved "up front."   The tradeoffs for producibility, testability, and serviceability need to occur in real time, during the design phase, not as a result of a design review or a problem detected in the manufacturing process. The design process must integrate the expertise from all the requisite engineering disciplines at the beginning of the design phase. These efforts need to continue throughout the life cycle of the product or service.

This improved design process is more a philosophy than a process. The common name for it in industry today is Concurrent Engineering or CE. This term refers to a systematic approach for the integrated, simultaneous design of products and their related processes including manufacturing, test, and support. The goal of CE is to optimize all critical product and process characteristics. This type of design process begins with the establishment of a cross-functional and multidisciplinary product development team. The goals of the team include:

> Shorter time to market.

> Lower product development costs.

> Higher quality.

> Lower manufacturing costs.

> Reduced service cost.

> Enhanced competitiveness.

> Improved profit margins.

To accomplish these goals, the design team needs to address, at least five specific, parallel design activities:

> **Design for performance.**

> **Design for manufacturability.**

> **Design for testability.**

> **Design for serviceability.**

> **Design for compliance.**

Each of these areas of concerns addresses a set of vital design requirements. Each set of requirements impacts another. It is this interrelationship that is ignored in a serial design. Concurrent design ensures that the design accounts for each set of requirements, resulting in a design that satisfies the customers' requirements, optimizes the manufacturability, and satisfies the regulatory requirements.

Each design team member each needs to represent her or his discipline actively to optimize the product or service, and all the associated processes, throughout each of these concurrent design phases. In order for the CE philosophy to become a reality we need a method for ensuring all of the design efforts are collaborative and focused on satisfying the customers' requirements. Quality Function Deployment is the method for implementing the CE philosophy.

QUALITY FUNCTION DEPLOYMENT (QFD)

Quality Function Deployment (QFD) was developed in Japan in the 1970s. It was first applied at the Kobe Shipyard of Mitsubishi Heavy Industries Ltd. Since that time it has become the accepted methodology for development of products and services in Japan. QFD has enabled businesses to successfully develop and introduce products in a fraction of the time required without it.

In the early 1980s, Dr. Don Clausing introduced QFD to Xerox. Since that time American business has shown growing interest in using QFD. The American Supplier Institute and GOAL/QPC have been the leaders in this movement. They have studied QFD, and helped businesses apply it, and they have contributed greatly to the development and innovation of QFD techniques.

QFD is a structured method that uses the 7 M&P tools to identify and prioritize customer requirements, and to translate those requirements into engineering requirements for systematic deployment throughout the company at each stage of product or process development and improvement. The implementation of QFD requires a multifunctional team with representatives from the functional organizations responsible for research and development, engineering, sales/marketing, purchasing, quality operations, manufacturing, and packaging.

QFD is driven by what the customer wants, not by technology. It demands, therefore, that we clearly identify who the customers are and what they want. This knowledge drives the need for new technology, innovations, improvements, new products, or new services. Collecting and analyzing this information increases the time necessary to define the project. This information enables the development team to focus only on the characteristics that are important to the customer, and to optimize the implementation of those attributes. The result is increased responsiveness to customer needs, shortened product design times, and little or no redesign. These improvements mean an overall improved product design cycle in terms of cost, quality, and time.

QFD uses the "what - how" matrix relationship demonstrated in Figure 9-3. This relationship generates a family of matrices in a matrix waterfall fashion. This family of matrices deploys the customer requirements, and related technical requirements, throughout all related design, and manufacturing processes for the development of a product or service.

There are five phases in the implementation of QFD. The appropriate tools or processes 7 M&P Tools, Failure Modes Effect Analysis, experiments, SPC, SQC, customer information systems, etc.) are used in each phase to ensure the systematic deployment of the customers' requirements throughout the design, manufacture, and service of the product. The Requirements Matrix which is also referred to as the House of Quality is the starting point for the QFD method. We deploy each matrix or activity from this starting point. This basic QFD approach is flexible and can be adapted to any given situation.

What - How Matrix Relationship

The words *goal* and *objective* are often used interchangeably. The dictionary definitions for these words are, in fact, similar enough to be considered the same. In practice, however, one is used to denote *what* is to be achieved, and the other *how* it is to be achieved. Confusion results when there is inconsistency in the application of the terms. It is important to establish a convention and to use it consistently.

Our convention is to use *goal* to designate *what* is to be achieved, and *objective* to designate *how* it is to be achieved. In a matrix, we list the goals on the vertical axis as the "Whats", and the objectives on the horizontal axis as the "Hows" (Figure 9-4).

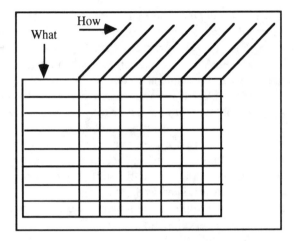

Figure 9-4. What - How Matrix Relationship

Matrix Waterfall Concept

If our goal is to make a profit, one objective might be to sell a product for more than it costs to produce. But then the question is raised: "How do we sell a product for more than it costs to produce?" This question contains a goal, that is, what we want to accomplish. The method that we use to achieve that goal is an objective. We see then that there are successive levels of goals and objectives. A top-level objective becomes a lower-level goal when we seek to determine the specific action that is necessary to achieve the top-level objective. Figure 9-5 presents a pair of partial matrices that illustrate the way these goals and objectives interrelate.

In this illustration, the Level 1 goal is to make a profit. One of the Level 1 objectives, necessary to make a profit, is to sell the product. This objectives translates into a Level 2 goal: sell the product. There are several Level 2 objectives necessary to sell product. Each of these can, in turn, be used as a Level 3 goal to determine the Level 3 objectives. In this fashion, we can start with a top-level goal and waterfall down the objectives until we have sufficient detailed action to achieve the Level 1 goal.

This waterfall method is especially powerful in developing products or services that satisfy and delight customers. It begins with the customer requirements, which are deployed in the waterfall fashion. Figure 9-6[3] illustrates this process through the design requirements and requisite engineering design to the product characteristics. Figure 9-7[4] shows how the organization deploys these product characteristics, through the manufacturing and purchasing operations to the production and quality controls.

This method yields the optimum design and is developed to satisfy the customers' requirements. The organization then implements the design, using the optimum materials, and processes. QFD thus provides a methodology for ensuring that the design and production of products and services is focused on achieving customer satisfaction. At each step, it leads us to select the optimum objective to achieve a goal.

Five Phases of QFD

There are five phases in Quality Function Deployment; Organizing, Product Planning, Product Design, Process Planning, Implementation. The complexity of the project will drive the level of detail at each phase, as well as the selection of tools and techniques. A simple task might require only one or two matrices and a few task sheets. A complex project (e.g., developing a system or complex machinery) might require a complete set of matrices, supplementary investigations, and designed experiments.

It is important, therefore, to plan the QFD project carefully and to tailor each application to your specific organization, product, and processes. We need to step through each phase and to make a conscious decision about its applicability. This means evaluating the required action for each phase, determining the most appropriate tools to be used, and deciding when to truncate the application of a tool. A facilitator skilled in the application of the improvement tools can greatly assist the design project.

In the Organizing Phase, we select the QFD project, establish a crossfunctional, interdepartmental team, and define the scope of the project. The selection of a QFD project is dependent upon the vision, goals, and objectives of the organization. The membership of the team is crucial to the success of the product development. The management team must, therefore, carefully select the design team members, ensuring that the appropriate disciplines and functional areas are represented. The design team needs to optimize the product or service, and all the associated processes, throughout each of the development phases. In establishing the scope of the QFD project, it is necessary to determine when the project must be accomplished, what resources are available, and the extent of the product life cycle. As a minimum, we must consider five areas: performance, manufacturability, testability, serviceability, and compliance.

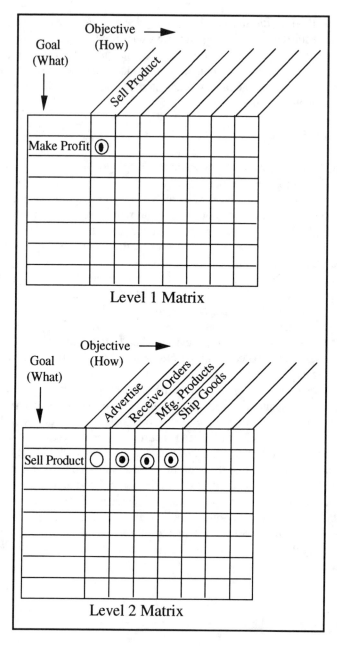

Figure 9-5. Level 1 to Level 2 Matrix Deployment

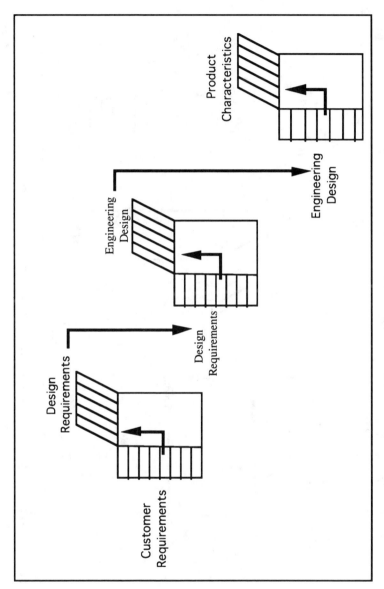

Figure 9-6. Deployment of Customer Requirements to Product Characteristics

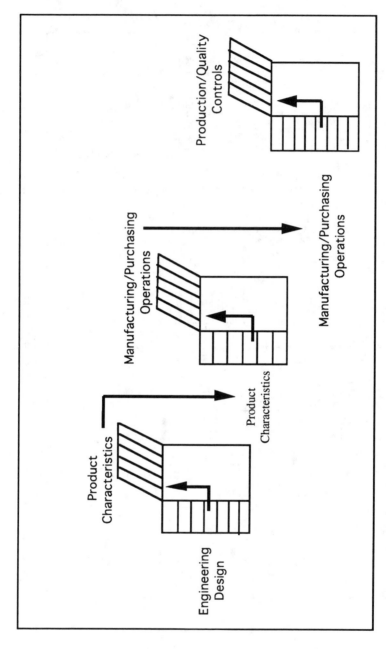

Figure 9-7. Deployment of Product Characteristics to Production/Quality Controls

After the project is organized, we begin the Product Planning Phase. In this phase the customers' requirements and desires are evaluated. We use this information to develop the Requirements Planning Matrix, also known as the House of Quality. This matrix defines the product in terms of the design requirements necessary to achieve customer requirements. The elements of the matrix can be developed using a variety of tools; e. g. Tree Diagram, Affinity Diagram, PDPC, Interrelationship Digraph, Pareto Diagrams, DOE, etc.

After the product is planned, we enter the Product Design Phase. In this phase we develop the Design Matrix and Product Characteristics Deployment Matrix. The Design Matrix identifies the engineering design activities required to achieve the product design requirements. The Product Characteristics Deployment Matrix subsequently identifies the product characteristics that satisfy the engineering design requirements. The product is defined at this point in terms of characteristics that satisfy the customers' requirements.

We then use the results of the Characteristics Deployment Matrix to develop the Manufacturing/Purchasing Matrix in the Process Planning Phase. At this point we select the manufacturing and purchasing operations needed to achieve the product characteristics. We also develop the Control/Verification Matrix to determine the necessary production and quality controls for the selected manufacturing and purchasing operations.

The final phase is the Implementation Phase. In this phase we are in production. As production proceeds, we implement SPC, conduct process capability studies, implement designed experiments, and achieve continuous measurable improvement. All process changes and product improvements are compared against the QFD matrices and the company's goals. If a change does not have a positive impact on satisfying customer requirements, or the company's goals it is not implemented.

House of Quality

The House of Quality is the starting matrix for QFD. It starts as a What - How Matrix that identifies the wants, desires, and needs of the customer. These customer requirements are translated into technical requirements as the "house" is constructed. The completed House of Quality is then used to start the matrix waterfall.

The process for developing the matrix clarifies the relationships between the objectives and the goals, thus ensuring that all of the customers' requirements are addressed. The process also provides a logical basis for determining the impact of each action on the other actions. Optional enhancements can be added to the House of Quality to provide greater understanding, and to facilitate the next phases of the product development project.

The construction of the House of Quality is a 5 step process:

❶   Establishing Customer Requirements.

❷   Determining Design Requirements.

❸   Developing the Relationship Matrix.

❹   Developing the Interaction Matrix

❺   Establishing Priorities for the Design Requirements.

Step 1. Establishing Customer Requirements The initial step in the development of the House of Quality is to establish the customer requirements. This is sometimes referred to as listening to the voice of the customer. The step involves defining what the customer needs, wants, and desires, in his own terms. First we need to identify who the customers are.

Organizations that have a wide variety of customers need to group the customers into natural categories. Next, stratify the customer groups using a Tree Diagram, Affinity Diagram, Pareto Diagram, or other method. This stratification enables you to categorize them according to their importance to your business. Thus you can consciously decide to satisfy all your customers, or only select groups of customers. A third alternative is to weigh their requirements according to their impact on the business.

After identifying and stratifying the customers it is time to learn their requirements. This is done by customer surveys, market research, analysis of service data, reviewing contractual requirements, or reviewing regulatory requirements. This data usually is not concise, and it may show no obvious patterns. It will require skill, and knowledge of your product, to make the data useful. An Affinity Diagram, Tree Diagram, or Pareto Diagram often is useful in distilling the data into a clear, concise statement of customer requirements.

These requirements fall into three categories: Musts, Wants, and Exciters. Musts are the basic requirements that are usually understood but frequently left unstated. Having them does not satisfy your customer, but *not* having them makes your product unacceptable, no matter how many of the other two types of attributes your product possesses. The Wants are characteristics that customers would like to have. These usually make your product more desirable in a linear fashion. Finally, the Exciters are unexpected features that delight the customer.

The relationships among these requirement categories can be illustrated by the automobile. Several features started out as Exciters, soon became Wants, and currently are Musts. Examples include the car radio, electric starter, and power brakes. It is important, therefore, to understand what category each customer requirement falls into, and the importance that the customer places on it. This information is valuable in determining the features for your product.

After identifying the customers' requirements, enter them on the vertical axis of the matrix. This can be a simple listing of requirements, or it may have two (or more) columns as secondary and tertiary requirements. In addition, enter the importance that the customers place on each feature on the matrix in the priority column. The importance is expressed as greatest, average, or least, depicted by a double circle, single circle, and triangle, respectively. Figure 9-8 illustrates these initial steps in developing the House of Quality and how the symbols are used for the customer importance rating.

Step 2. Determining Design Requirements The design requirements, sometimes referred to as the technical requirements, or the voice of the engineer, are the objective technical measurements that predict to what degree each customer requirement will be met. These establish how the customer requirements are met at the top level. They are global requirements and performance parameters. There needs to be at least one design requirement for each customer requirement.

The design requirements are developed in a manner similar to that used for the customer requirements. In this case, however, the source of the data is most likely the project team or other individuals within the company. The initial data may result from brainstorming. Affinity diagrams are helpful in organizing the data and giving it order. Tree diagrams are helpful for expanding and clarifying the information. After determining the design requirements, enter them on the horizontal axis of the House of Quality. Figure 9-9 illustrates this step.

Step 3. Developing the Relationship Matrix This is the body of the House of Quality. It visually displays the relationships between the customer requirements and the design requirements. The symbols quickly reveal patterns and identify weak points in the design requirements. Careful completion of the relationship matrix yields dividends in the form of reduced engineering changes later in the product's life cycle.

Identify the relationships by asking the question: "How well does this design requirement predict customer satisfaction for each requirement?" Do this for every intersecting point in the body of the matrix. It may seem to be a tedious exercise, but, it is extremely important that the entire team participate in order to develop a common understanding and ownership.

The matrix uses our standard symbology: a double circle for a strong relationship, single circle for medium, triangle for weak, and blank for none. Although we will assign numerical values to these symbols later in the process,

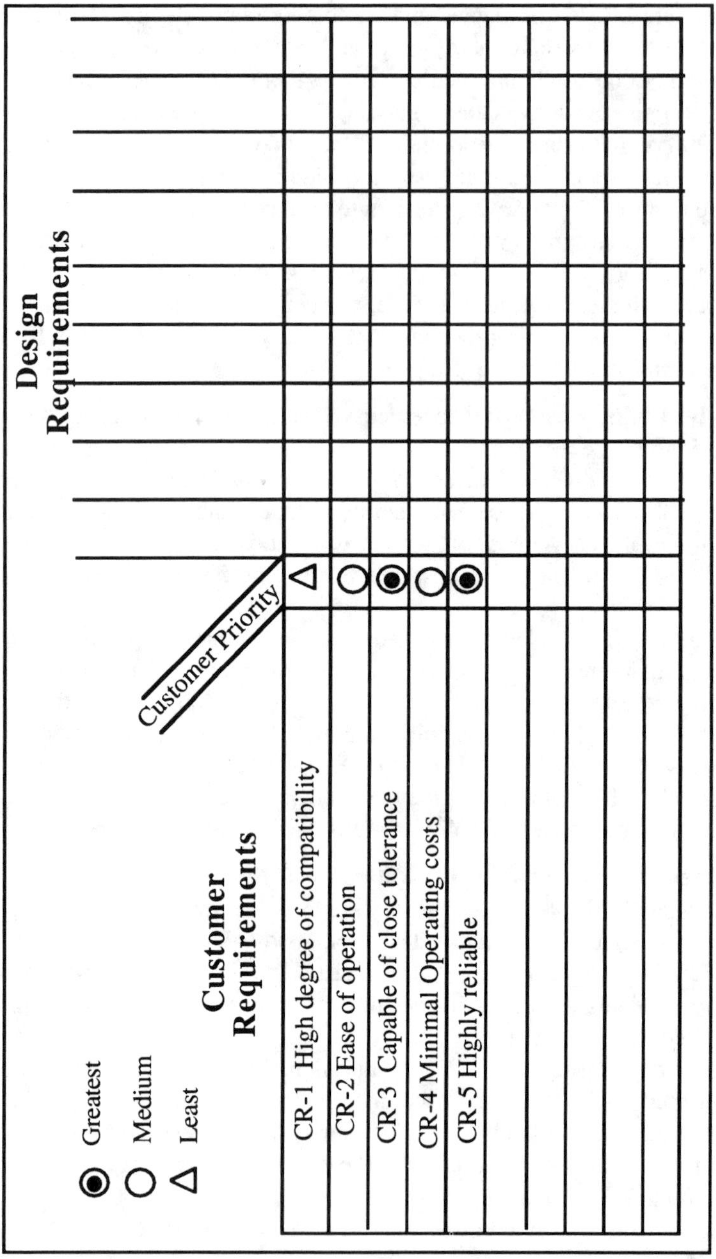

Figure 9-8. Initial Steps in the House of Quality

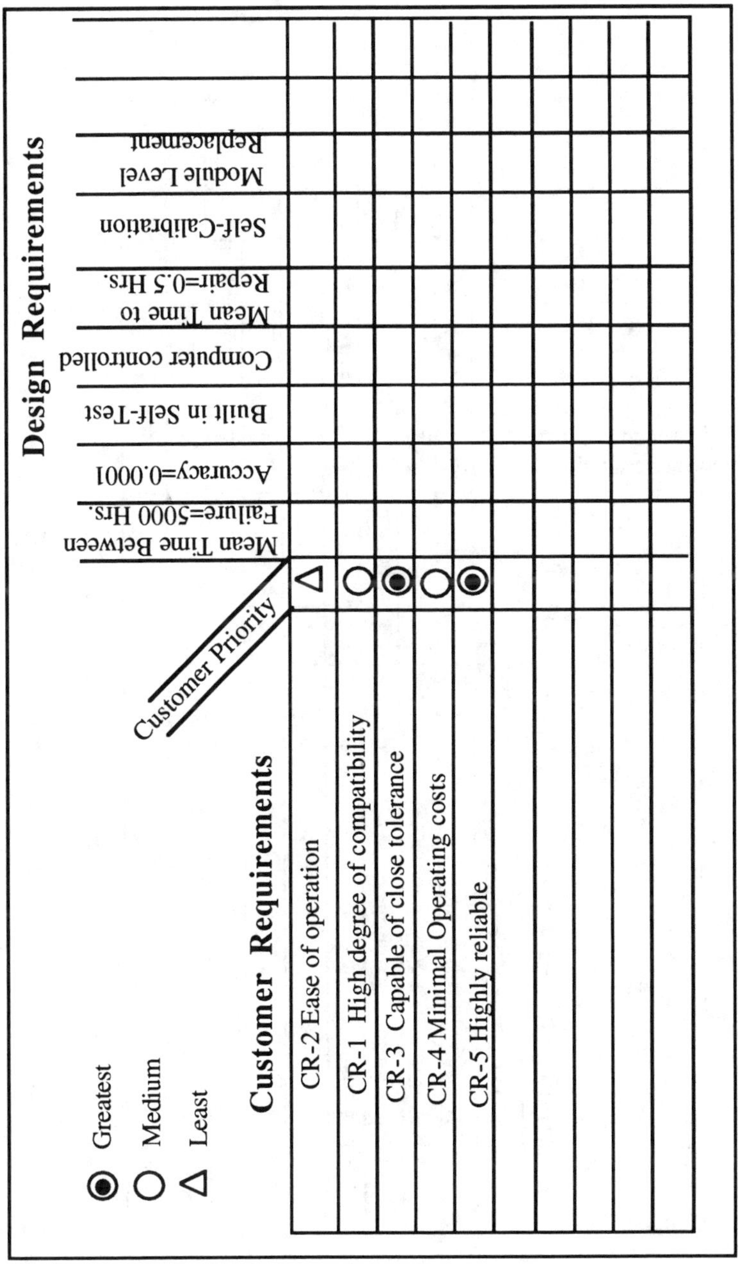

Figure 9-9. Step Two in the House of Quality

Design Requirements

Legend:
- ● Strong
- ○ Medium
- △ Weak

Customer Requirements

Customer Requirements	Customer Priority	Mean Time Between Failure=5000 Hrs.	Accuracy=0.0001	Built in Self-Test	Computer controlled	Mean Time to Repair=0.5 Hrs.	Self-Calibration	Module Level Replacement
CR-1 High degree of compatibility	△				○			△
CR-2 Ease of operation	○			●	●	△	○	△
CR-3 Capable of close tolerance	●		●		△		○	
CR-4 Minimal Operating costs	○	○		○			△	
CR-5 Highly reliable	●	●		○	△	△	△	△

Figure 9-10. Step Three in the House of Quality

it is important to use the symbols. They provide a quick visual indication of patterns, and quickly reveal holes in our planning. Figure 9-10 illustrates how the Relationship Matrix is developed.

Step 4. Developing the Interaction Matrix The Interaction Matrix, also known as the Correlation Matrix, is the "roof" on the House of Quality. This matrix is similar to the J-F Interrelationship Matrix from the 7 M&P tools. It is established to determine the technical interrelationships among the design requirements (Hows). This information is valuable as the basis for decisions regarding technical trade-offs.

We construct the roof by evaluating the interactions among the Hows and placing the appropriate symbol at each intersection point. This symbol reveals the impact of a change in a given characteristic. It answers the question: "Does this characteristic have an effect on another characteristic?" Repeat this question for each combination. Figure 9-11 illustrates how this matrix is developed.

Step 5. Establishing Priorities for the Design Requirements Establishing the priorities for the design requirements is necessary to identify the key elements. This understanding is valuable for making decisions about trade-offs, determining where to focus resources, and refining the design concept. It involves four steps: determining the risk, calculating the absolute weight, calculating the relative weight, and identifying the key elements.

To determine the risk for each design requirement, the team needs to assess the degree of difficulty associated with each requirement. The team needs to consider cost, technical difficulty, and the relationship to the other requirements. The team assigns a risk factor of greatest, average, or least to each requirement, using the same symbols as in the other parts of the matrix.

We calculate the absolute weights for each design requirement by assigning the associated values to the symbols in the appropriate column and adding them. Then enter the total in the associated cell for the absolute weight. Calculate the relative weight by multiplying the absolute weight by the value for the associated risk. Place the result in the associated cell for the relative weight.

The absolute and relative weights can be entered as raw scores, or the scores can be ranked and the corresponding ranks entered. In either instance, the results of these calculations provide three key pieces of data. The first is the risk associated with each How. The second is a ranking of the Hows according to the impact that each has on the overall achievement of the customer requirements based on the interaction of each How with all the What's. This is a valuable insight, as a given design requirement sometimes has an effect on several customer requirements.

The third piece of data, relative weights, ranks the design requirements in terms of their relationship to all the customer requirements, but also factors in the risk associated with each requirement. The combination of these two rankings gives a powerful insight into the importance of each design requirement. The key elements can now be determined from a comparison of the absolute and relative weights.

Figure 9-12 illustrates how the weighting is calculated and the key elements identified. This step completes the construction of the basic House of Quality. This Requirements Matrix is the first matrix in the implementation of Quality Function Deployment and serves as the source for the follow-on Design Matrix. This matrix is developed using the design requirements from the House of Quality. This step begins the waterfall of matrices and results in the full product design.

Bob King, in *Better Designs in Half the Time*, published by GOAL/QPC describes the "matrix of matrices" approach for QFD. This is an innovation of the QFD process. It is derived by looking at the matrix concept across the broad spectrum of the design process. The result is a set of 30 matrices that can be modified, or rearranged to fit the specific design goal. In this manner, the QFD process can be adapted to the complexity of the design task. Experience indicates that the initial application of QFD needs to be limited to the basic approach described here. This experience will enable the team to apply QFD to a complex design task and to use the powerful matrix of matrices.

Enhancements

The House of Quality depicted in Figure 9-12 is a very powerful tool for the product development team. There are several enhancements that can be added to the matrix to increase its effectiveness. These include Technical Benchmarking, Target Values and Competitive Benchmarking Figure 9-13 illustrates how these enhancements can be added to the House of Quality.

Technical Benchmarking Technical Benchmarking means determining how well the competition is fulfilling the customers' requirements in terms of the design requirements. We express this evaluation in terms of a score, which is plotted on the horizontal axis. Some score the design requirements on a scale of 1 to 5, with 5 being the best. This method results in a plot across the bottom of the House of Quality.

Target Values It is necessary to establish target values for each of the design requirements. This action establishes concrete goals for the design engineers and further defines the customer requirements. These values need to be measurable, and can be developed from historical records, designed experiments, or analysis of what the competition is doing. Once the team agrees on the target values, they are entered on the horizontal axis, below the row identifying the key elements.

Competitive Benchmarking A row is added on the right side of the House of Quality to reflect how well you and the competition are satisfying the customer requirements that are identified on the vertical axis on the left side of the matrix. As in the case of the technical Benchmarking, this evaluation is scored and plotted as a graph.

Comparing the results of the technical and competitive Benchmarking data should show a consistency. If your product scores high in the competitive comparison, it should also score high on the technical comparison. Inconsistencies are flags that there may be a problem with a design requirement.

We can add more columns to the right side of the matrix for including other information such as level of effort, cost, or priorities for the customer requirements. The possibilities are unlimited and should be driven by your imagination and capacity for innovation.

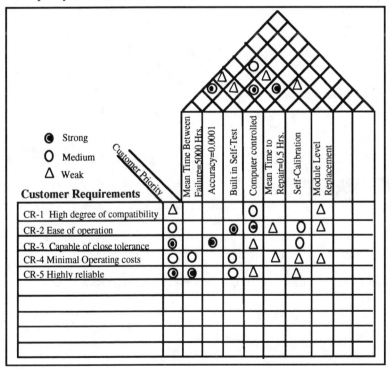

Figure 9-11. Benchmarking Enhancements

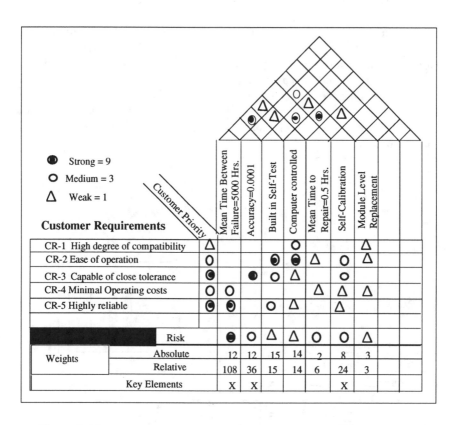

Figure 9-12. Benchmarking Enhancements (Identifying Key Elements)

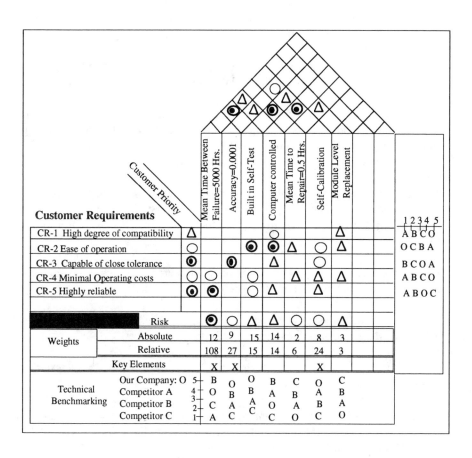

Figure 9-13. Benchmarking Enhancements

KEY POINTS

The product and service development and improvement process needs to be an integral part of the company's strategy to become a world class competitor.

The design process must integrate the expertise from all the requisite engineering disciplines at the beginning of the design phase.

 Concurrent Engineering is a systematic approach for the integrated, simultaneous design of both products and their related processes.

Quality Function Deployment is a structured method that identifies and prioritizes customer requirements, and translates those requirements into engineering requirements.   QFD results in increased responsiveness to customer needs, shortened product design times, and little or no redesign.

The Requirements Matrix, called the House of Quality, is the starting point for the QFD method.   There are five phases in Quality Function Deployment: Organizing, Product, Planning, Product Design, Process Planning, Implementation.

Organizing Phase: The QFD project is selected, a cross-functional, interdepartmental team is established, and the scope of the project is defined.

Product Planning Phase: The customers' requirements, and desires are evaluated.   The Requirements Planning Matrix is developed.

Product Design Phase: The Design Matrix and Product Characteristics Deployment Matrix are developed.

Process Planning Phase: The manufacturing and purchasing operations are selected to achieve the product characteristics.   In this phase the Control/Verification Matrix also is developed

Implementation Phase: As production proceeds, SPC is implemented, process capability studies are conducted, designed experiments are implemented, and continuous measurable improvement is achieved.

EXAMPLE

The Product Development Team, for the LWCI 1600 project, used Quality Function Deployment. They began by listening to the "voice of the customer" (Chapter 8 Example). The 7 M&P tools were used extensively to collect and analyze the customer information. The team used the results to identify the customer requirements. The information used to develop the Requirements Matrix included the customers' priority for each.

The customers' requirements and their priorities were entered on the vertical axis of a Requirements Matrix (Example Figure 9-1). Next, the Team identified the technical characteristics that the LWCI 1600 needed to satisfy the customers' requirements. These were entered on the top horizontal axis of the matrix.

The Team added the "roof," the risk row, and the weighting factors. The team decided that they would not use the technical comparison, or the competitive comparison enhancements on the matrix. They elected, instead, to use the Matrix Data Analysis Charts they had previously developed (Chapter 8 Example).

The team completed the matrix using the standard symbology: triangle for weak, open circle for medium, and concentric circles for strong. They evaluated each intersection in the body of the matrix for the relationship, and put the appropriate symbol in the box. They then evaluated the risk for each of the technical characteristics, in terms of financial, resource, or technical risk or difficulty. Again, they used the standard set of symbols to represent high, medium, or low risk.

The weight for each technical characteristic was first determined as an absolute value and then as a relative value. The team calculated the absolute value by assigning a value of 9 for strong, 3 for medium, 1 for weak, and 0 for none. The score was calculated by adding the individual scores in each column. The total was put in the corresponding absolute weight cell. The team calculated the relative weight by multiplying the absolute weight by the risk score, and placed the result in the corresponding relative weight cell.

The team decided to use actual scores instead of rankings. They felt this would give them an insight as to the magnitude of the differences between scores, which would be important to them in selecting the key characteristics. The key characteristics they identified were:

➤ Footprint <20 square feet.

➤ Minimum safety precautions required for operation, maintenance, and calibration

➤ Customer training program.

➤ Variability Reduction Program.

➤ Mean Time To Repair <0.5 hours.

➤ Accurate Operating, Maintenance, and Calibration Manuals.

These key elements then became focal points for the LWCI 1600 Development Team. The team did not abandon the remaining characteristics; rather the key elements became areas of special concern. They were judged as important and more difficult to accomplish, than the other characteristics. Therefore, these key elements warranted special consideration to ensure that they were accomplished.

Next, the roof of the House of Quality was completed. As discussed in the chapter this is a correlation matrix that demonstrates the interactions of the technical characteristics. A review of the Example Figure 9-2 demonstrates this correlation. As shown the Variability Reduction Program affects Mean Time Between Failures, accuracy of the system, accuracy of the manuals, Mean Time to Repair, synchronous manufacturing, and the compactness of the system.

The technical characteristics were used to develop the Design Matrix, which identifies the Engineering Design requirements for the technical characteristics. The team used the Engineering Design requirements to identify the Product Characteristics in the Product Characteristics Matrix. They used the Product Characteristics, in the Manufacturing/Purchasing Matrix, to define the Manufacturing and Purchasing operations needed to achieve the product characteristics. The Manufacturing and Purchasing operations were entered in the Control/Verification Matrix to determine the production and quality controls needed to accomplish the Manufacturing and/or Purchasing operations. Example Figures 9-3 through 9-6 follow one technical characteristic, MTBF (5,000 hours), through this process.

At each step of the QFD implementation, the team used the 7 M&P tools, and a variety of statistical tools and techniques, to develop and define the elements of the matrix. They also used these tools to execute the details of the LWCI 1600 development plan. The procedures used by the team included an extensive application of statistical process control and designed experiments.

The application of QFD provided the method for ensuring an integrated, concurrently engineered development of the LWCI 1600. In addition, the team identified numerous process improvements, such as the customer order process (Chapter 8). In each instance, an improvement was compared against the QFD matrices before implementation. If an improvement did not have a positive impact on achieving customer satisfaction, or on achieving the goals of the company, the team dropped it.

Technical Requirements →

Customer Requirements	Customer Priority	Industry Std. Software System	Std. LWCI Interface	Self-Test	Digital Control	Mean-Time-Between Failure: 5,000 Hrs.	Mean-Time-To Repair <0.5 Hrs.	Modular Design	Accurate Op., Maint., & Cal. Manuals	Customer Support Network	Customer Training Program	No Hazmat in process	Minimum Safety Precautions Req'd for Operation, Maintenance, & Calibration	Variability Reduction Program	Accuracy 0.0001 inch	Footprint: <20 sq. ft.	Synchronous Manufacturing
High Degree of Compatibility	●	●	●			△		○		△	△			△			
Easy to Operate	○	○	○	●	●		○	●	●				○				
Good Pre & Post Sales Support	○	△	△		△					●	●		△				
High Degree of Safety	●											●	●				
Capable of Close Tolerance Work	●			△	○									△	△		
Compact System	△	△	△	△	○	△	△	●								●	
Low Cost & On Time	○	△	△	△	○	△	△	△						●			●
Good Support Documentation	△	△		△	○	△	△		●	△	○		△	△			

Example Figure 9-1. Requirements Matrix

House of Quality matrix — relationship symbols: ◉ = strong, ○ = medium, △ = weak.

Customer Priority	Industry Std. Software System	Std. LWCI Interface	Self-Test	Digital Control	Mean-Time-Between Failure: 5,000 Hrs.	Mean-Time-To Repair <0.5 Hrs.	Modular Design	Accurate Op., Maint., & Cal. Manuals	Customer Support Network	Customer Training Program	No Hazmat in process	Minimum Safety Precautions Req'd for Operation, Maintenance, & Calibration	Variability Reduction Program	Accuracy 0.0001 inch	Footprint: <20 sq. ft.	Synchronous Manufacturing
High Degree of Compatibility	◉	◉	◉					○		△	△		△			
Easy to Operate	○	○	○	◉	◉	△	○	◉	◉				○			
Good Pre & Post Sales Support	○	△	△						◉	◉		△				
High Degree of Safety	◉		△	△							◉	◉	△	△		
Capable of Close Tolerance Work	◉			○										◉		
Compact System	△	△	△	○			◉								◉	
Low Cost & On Time	○	△	△	○	△	△	△							◉		◉
Good Support Documentation	△	△						◉	△	○		△	△			
Risk	△	△	△	△	◉	◉	○	△	○	○	○	○	○	○	◉	○
Weights — Absolute	13	15	12	19	2	4	22	18	11	13	9	14	12	10	9	9
Weights — Relative	13	15	12	19	18	36	22	54	11	39	27	42	36	30	81	27
Key Elements					X		X		X		X	X	X		X	

Example Figure 9-2. LWCI 1600 House of Quality

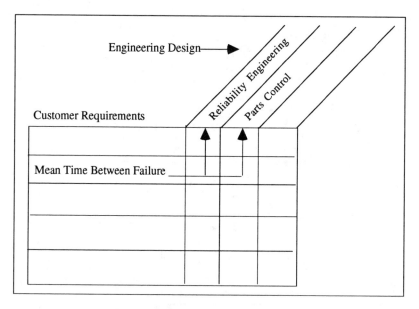

Example Figure 9-3. Design Matrix

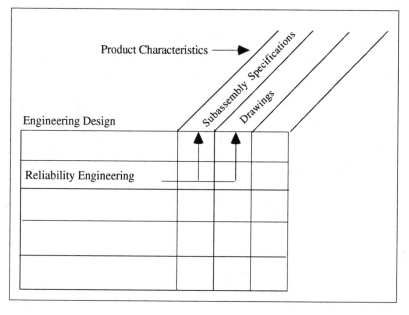

Example Figure 9-4. Product Characteristics Matrix

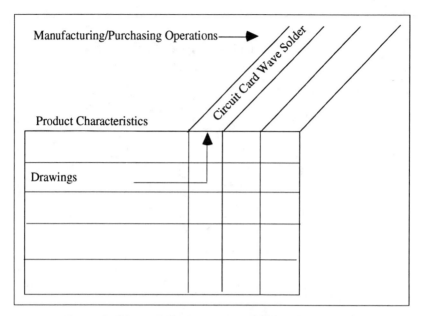

Example Figure 9-5. Manufacturing/Purchasing Matrix

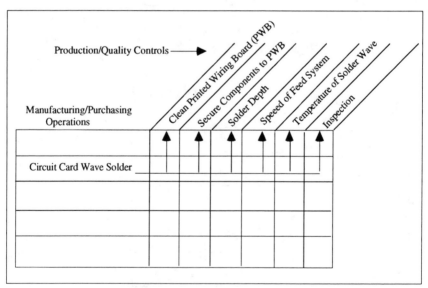

Example Figure 9-6. Control/Verification Matrix

NOTES

1. Jon Turino, *Managing Concurrent Engineering; Buying Time to Market.* Van Nostrand Reinhold, 1992
2. Ibid.
3. ReVelle, Dr. Jack, 1992, *The New Quality Technology,* pp. D-20. Los Angeles: Hughes Aircraft Company.
4. Ibid, pp. D-21.

10

Product Improvement Strategies

PROCESS AND PRODUCT IMPROVEMENT IS
THE KEY TO ACHIEVING AND MAINTAINING
WORLD CLASS COMPETITIVENESS

TO ACHIEVE AND MAINTAIN A WORLD CLASS COMPETITIVE STATUS for your products and services, you must continuously improve your processes. This program is frequently called Continuous Measurable Improvement CMI. The most direct route to Continuous Measurable Improvement is variability reduction. Reducing the variability of your process has a direct and immediate effect upon product defects, whether the products are goods, services, management or administration. This variability reduction lessens defect rates, improves yields, lowers scrap rates, reduces rework, expands market potential and reduced warranty costs. Figure 10-1 demonstrates the direct relationship between process variability and product quality.

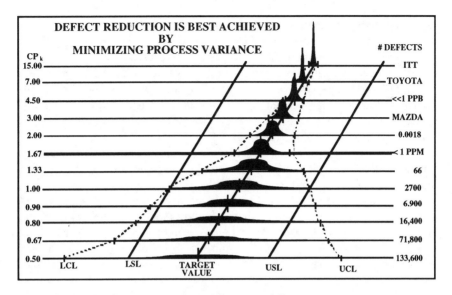

Figure 10-1   Minimizing Variability[1]

This figure demonstrates the effect of variability reduction compared to defect rates and specific world class competitors. If you have achieved a process capability (CP) of 1.00, your process is producing 2,700 failing parts per million (PPM). As we have indicated in Chapter 7, in today's competitive environment the minimum acceptable process capability is actually 1.33 to compete in the global marketplace. The best world competitors today are in the parts-per-billion (PPB) class. How can you be a contender in this very competitive and demanding global marketplace? Management 2000 has provided the basic tools for you to establish a world class organizational infrastructure, to know and understand your processes, and to measure and control them. Now you must implement continuous measurable improvement to capitalize on these achievements.

THE IMPROVEMENT PROCESS

The final decision for change is always a business decision. The business leader must, therefore, have confidence in the information used to make improvement decisions. The quality of the information used to make these decisions is very dependent on the structure of the improvement process, the validity of experimental design, and the analytical methods. Business people also must be able to address questions of experimental design and analysis in making the decisions to allocate resources and in designing the programs for improvement.

Here we will integrate the technical tools of Process Analysis and Product and Process Control with the new tools of Analysis of Variance (ANOVA) and Design of Experiments (DOE). These new tools will allow us to structure continuous measurable improvement efforts for new and existing products and processes. Figure 10-2 on the facing page provides the structured approach to Continuous Measurable Improvement (CMI).

All improvement programs to achieve world class competition must start with an in-depth understanding of the voice of the customer. It is crucial to understand what is expected in the marketplace and to establish the product and process parameters accordingly. The seven management tools can then be used to translate the voice of the customer to a quality function deployment, putting the marketplace language into technical terms such that engineers, analysts, and managers can design a process. By evaluating the resulting process, you can find the optimum parameters for the services or products and their associated processes.

The process is stabilized using the process control tools and further improved with process analysis. For these existing processes we recommend Analysis of Variance (ANOVA) to evaluate the existing data to find candidates for further improvement, and QFD and DOE to improve the process. The loss function enables you determine if the improvement to the process will result in a cost-effective change. Here we will explore the application and implementation of the improvement tools and how they fit into continuous measurable improvement.

In this chapter we will present new tools for the planning, management and evaluation of the improvement process. First, we will examine ANOVA. ANOVA is an advanced statistical technique that partitions variation and enables us to make decisions concerning its significance. We will review the implementation and application of ANOVA. The associated workbook contains a complete discussion and step-by-step ANOVA procedure, for academic purposes. For a more in-depth review of ANOVA we further recommend A Practical Guide to Statistical Quality Improvement by Beauregard, Mikulak, and Olson, available from Van Nostrand Reinhold.

We will then examine Design of Experiments (DOE). This section will include a brief review of the classical methods applied to Full Factorial, Fractional Factorial and Screening experiments, we will then present the Taguchi Method using the innovative applications derived by Dr. Jack B. Re Velle.

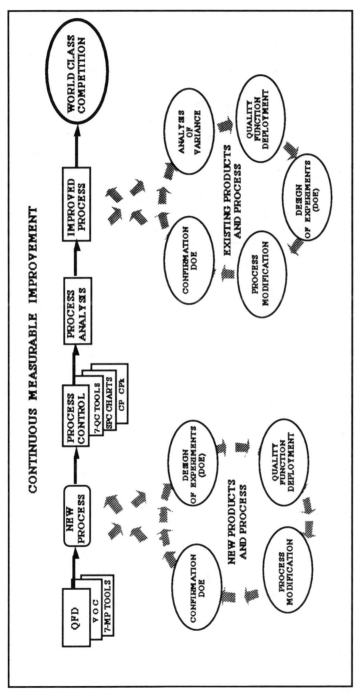

Figure 10-2. The Improvement Process

ANALYSIS OF VARIANCE

Analysis of Variance (ANOVA) is an important tool for making business and technical decisions. It tells us whether several different treatments (for example, different manufacturing processes) all have the same effect on the quality characteristics of interest. These treatments are specific values of an input (independent) variable. The variable(s) whose values are effected by these treatments are often called response variables, outcome variables or dependent variables. The best common-sense explanation of ANOVA that we have seen is from a 1939 book by a renowned scientist, Dr George Gaylord Simpson.

> "The purpose of analysis of variance, as its name implies, is to determine how much of the variation among observations is due to <u>variation</u> in each factor influencing the characteristic being studied."

The computation for ANOVA can be complex and tedious. In most cases, ANOVA is accomplished using an automated program such as MINITAB. We strongly recommend this approach. We have also simplified the manual approach to ANOVA by developing a generic computation and decision table, which shows all the intermediate steps in ANOVA (Table 10-3).

There are several aspects of ANOVA that we should understand when using this ANOVA for the evaluation of existing processes data or data from designed experiments. These factors are discussed in the following paragraphs. Here we will concentrate on understanding and implementing ANOVA for the continuous measurable improvement process.

➤ **Hypothesis testing**

➤ **Concept of variation**

➤ **Sum of the squares**

➤ **Degrees of freedom**

➤ **Mean squares**

➤ **Fisher's F statistic**

➤ **Level of significance**

➤ **Strength of statistical relationship**

➤ **Evaluating the results of ANOVA**

SOURCE OF VARIATION			SUM OF SQUARES	DEGREES OF FREEDOM	MEAN SQUARES	F RATIO	F' CRITICAL	STRENGTH
TREATMENTS	MAIN EFFECTS	A	SS_A	df_A	MS_A	F_A	F'_A	ω^2_A
		B	SS_B	df_B	MS_B	F_B	F'_B	ω^2_B
		C	SS_C	df_C	MS_C	F_C	F'_C	ω^2_C
	INTERACTIONS	AB	SS_{AB}	df_{AB}	MS_{AB}	F_{AB}	F_{AB}	ω^2_{AB}
		AC	SS_{BC}	df_{BC}	MS_{BC}	F_{BC}	F'_{BC}	ω^2_{AC}
		BC	SS_{AC}	df_{AC}	MS_{AC}	F_{AC}	F'_{AC}	ω^2_{BC}
		ABC	SS_{ABC}	df_{ABC}	MS_{ABC}	F_{ABC}	F'_{ABC}	ω^2_{ABC}
WITHIN			SS_{Within}	df_{Within}	MS_{Within}			
TOTAL			SS_{Total}	df_{Total}				

Figure 10-3 Analysis of Variance

Hypothesis Testing

When performing ANOVA, the assumption is always made that the population is homogeneous. Therefore, the null hypothesis is that the means of the data for all treatment groups are equal. Symbolically, the null Hypothesis is stated as:

$$H_O : \mu_1 = \mu_2 = \mu_3$$

The alternate hypothesis, therefore, is that at least one or more of the population means are not equal. Symbolically the alternate Hypothesis is:

$$H_A : \mu_1 \neq \mu_2 \neq \mu_3$$

$$H_A : \mu_1 = \mu_2 \neq \mu_3$$

To apply hypothesis testing to process and experimental data, we must first establish some basic facts about the data. We will use the data demonstrated in

Figure 10-4 for this purpose. There are four treatments. Each treatment is measured by 6 samples, repeats or replicates. Therefore there are 24 sample measurements.   The assumption of homogeneity indicates that the Null Hypothesis for this data is that the means of the data produced by Treatments A, B, C, and D are the same.

SAMPLE	TREATMENTS			
n	A	B	C	D
1	69	83	79	76
2	71	77	85	73
3	73	79	77	77
4	76	77	70	71
5	76	74	79	78
6	70	84	69	71

Figure 10-4 Basic ANOVA Data Table

When stating the null hypothesis for the sample data in the above example we use the symbol $(\overline{X})$ representing the mean of the sample data and the symbol (μ) represent the mean of the population or the true mean. The null Hypothesis (H_0) for this ANOVA is therefore that the means $(\overline{X})$ of the treatments are equal:

$$H_O : \overline{X}_A = \overline{X}_B = \overline{X}_C = \overline{X}_D$$

And the alternate Hypothesis (H_A) is that the means $(\overline{X})$ of at least one or more of the population means are not equal:

$$H_O : \overline{X}_A \neq \overline{X}_B \neq \overline{X}_C \neq \overline{X}_D$$

$$H_O : \overline{X}_A = \overline{X}_B \neq \overline{X}_C = \overline{X}_D$$

The Concept of Variation

Figure 10-5 illustrates the concept of variance between and within treatments. Variance between treatments A and B occurs when there is a significant difference between the means of the data for those treatments. The significance of these differences is measured using the F statistic as discussed in a following section.

NO VARIANCE BETWEEN OR
WITHIN TREATMENTS

A	B
75	75
75	75
75	75

VARIANCE ONLY BETWEEN TREATMENTS

A	B
75	77
75	77
75	77

VARIANCE BOTH BETWEEN
AND WITHIN TREATMENTS

A	B
75	77
73	77
76	72

Figure 10-5.   Concept of Variance

Sum of the Squares

The sum of the squares is the first calculation on the ANOVA table. For Main Effects and Interactions (SS_a, SS_{ab}), we summarize the squared values of the grand mean subtracted from the mean value of each treatment level and multiply that quantity by the sample size for each treatment combination. The equations for main effects and interactions are provided as generalized equations below.

$$SS_k = \Sigma \left[n_k \, \Sigma \left(\overline{X}_k - \overline{\overline{X}} \right)^2 \right]$$

$$SS_{kj} = \Sigma \left[n_k \, \Sigma \left(\overline{X}_k - \overline{\overline{X}} \right)^2 \right] + \Sigma \left[n_j \, \Sigma \left(\overline{X}_j - \overline{\overline{X}} \right)^2 \right] - SS_k - SS_j$$

The sum of the squares for the total variation SS_{Total} is calculated by subtracting the grand mean from the individual values of all samples, as indicated in the following equation.

$$SS_{Total} = \Sigma \left(X - \overline{X} \right)^2$$

In the ANOVA table the sum of the Squares for main effects, interactions and within are additive; therefore, the Sum of The Squares for within can be derived by subtracting the SS_{Total} from $SS_{Main \; Effects}$ and $SS_{Interactions}$.

$$SS_{Within} = SS_{Total} - SS_{Treatments}$$

Remember that these calculations are most frequently accomplished using a computer program. Before using such a program, however, it is important to understand the purpose and methods of the procedure.

Degrees of Freedom

Degrees of Freedom (*df*) are the number of independent comparisons available to estimate a specific treatment or level of a treatment. This is also an element of the Critical Value of F. Degrees of Freedom are used for both the numerator and denominator of the F statistic. The number of degrees of freedom for treatment main effects is $T_a - 1$ or the number of applicable treatment levels minus one. The degrees of freedom for treatment interactions is $(T_a - 1)(T_b - 1)$ or the degrees of freedom for each of the effects in the interaction. The total degrees of freedom are the total number of independent comparisons for all treatments, treatment levels and replicates N-1 or the total number of data elements in the sample minus one. The degrees of freedom applicable to variance within treatments (error) is the total degrees of freedom minus the degrees of freedom for treatments and treatment interactions.   This can be demonstrated using the data in Figure 10-6.

		TREATMENT A			
		A1	A2		
TREATMENT B	B1	.76, .81, .74	.78, .76, .77	C1	TREATMENT C
		.75, .71, .75	.76, .81, .74	C2	
	B2	.76, .71, .74	.76, .83, .77	C1	
		.78, .81, .76	.81, .79, .74	C2	

Figure 10-6. Sample Data to Illustrate Degrees of Freedom

Treatment Main Effects The degrees of freedom derived from this data, for the treatment main effects, are the number of treatment levels for each treatment minus one. In this example there are two treatment levels for each treatment, dfMain Effects are:

$$df \text{ Treatment A} = T_a - 1 = 2 - 1 = 1$$
$$df \text{ Treatment B} = T_b - 1 = 2 - 1 = 1$$
$$df \text{ Treatment C} = T_c - 1 = 2 - 1 = 1$$

Treatment Interactions The degrees of freedom derived from this data, for treatment interactions, are the multiplied degrees of freedom for the associated treatments.   In this example there are four possible treatment interactions, $A \times B$, $A \times C$, $B \times C$ and $A \times B \times C$, therefore, dfInteractions are:

$$df \text{ Interaction } A \times B = (T_a - 1)(T_b - 1) = 1 \times 1 = 1$$
$$df \text{ Interaction } A \times C = (T_a - 1)(T_c - 1) = 1 \times 1 = 1$$
$$df \text{ Interaction } B \times C = (T_b - 1)(T_c - 1) = 1 \times 1 = 1$$
$$df \text{ Interaction } A \times B \times C = (T_a - 1)(T_b - 1)(T_c - 1)$$
$$= 1 \times 1 \times 1 = 1$$

The degrees of freedom for within treatments (or error) is derived by subtraction of the dfMain Effects and dfInteractions form the dfTotal :

$$df\text{ Total} - df\text{ Treatments} - df\text{ Interactions} = 23 - 3 - 4 = 16$$

The total degrees of freedom for this figure are the total number of samples (24) minus one.

$$df\text{ Total} = N - 1 = 24 - 1 = 23$$

Mean Squares

The mean squares (MS) element of the ANOVA table is the quotient of the Sum of the Squares and the degrees of freedom (df):

$$MS_{\text{Main Effects}} = \frac{SS_{\text{Main Effects}}}{df_{\text{Main Effects}}}$$

$$MS_{\text{Interactions}} = \frac{SS_{\text{Interactions}}}{df_{\text{Interactions}}}$$

$$MS_{\text{Within}} = \frac{SS_{\text{Within}}}{df_{\text{Within}}}$$

F Ratio

The F_{Ratio} is the quotient of the $MS_{\text{Main Effects}}$, $MS_{\text{Interactions}}$ and MS_{within}:

$$F_{\text{Ratio}} = \frac{MS_{\text{Main Effects}}}{MS_{\text{Within}}} \qquad F_{\text{Ratio}} = \frac{MS_{\text{Interactions}}}{MS_{\text{Within}}}$$

Fisher's F Statistic

ANOVA determines if the means for several treatments are equal by examining population variances using Fisher's F Statistic. The F statistic is based upon the evaluation of the variance (S^2) of the data. ANOVA compares two estimates of this variance, one estimate attributable to the variance within treatments (S^2_{Within}) and one estimate from between treatment means $(S^2_{\text{Treatments}})$.

We calculate the first estimate from the variance within all the data from a single treatment (Univariant) or several distinct treatments or different levels of a treatment (Multivariant). This within treatment estimate is the unbiased estimate of variance that remains the same, whether the means of the treatments are the same or different. It is the average or mean of the variances found within the data.

The second estimate of the population variance is calculated from the variance between the treatment means ($S^2_{Treatments}$). This estimate is a true representation of the mean variance only if there is no significant difference between it and the variance within sample means (S^2_{Within}). Fisher's F statistic measures the difference in means based upon the ratio of the variance between and the variance within treatments, and compares that ratio to the critical value of F ($F_{Critical}$). The equation as it applies to our ANOVA application is therefore:

$$F = \frac{MS_{\text{Treatments}}}{MS_{\text{Within}}} \qquad F = \frac{MS_{\text{Main Effects}}}{MS_{\text{Within}}} \qquad F = \frac{MS_{\text{Interactions}}}{MS_{\text{Within}}}$$

We then compare this F ratio to the critical value of F ($F_{critical}$) to determine if the F ratio is significant. The critical value of F is determined by referring to the F table, (Table A-2 in Appendix A) for the applicable degrees of freedom and significance level selected for this evaluation. The degrees of freedom for the numerator is the degrees of freedom for Treatments, Main Effects or Interactions. The degrees of freedom for the denominator is the degrees of freedom for within or error.

$$F' \, df_{Numerator}, \, df_{Denominator}, \, \alpha$$

The variance is significant, therefore if means are significantly different, if the F_{Ratio} exceeds the $F_{Critical}$ value:

$$F_{Ratio} > F_{Critical} = \text{SIGNIFICANT}$$

$$F_{Ratio} < F_{Critical} = \text{NOT SIGNIFICANT}$$

Strength of Statistical Relationship

To evaluate the level of significance we will use the omega squared (ω^2) method. This method provides an estimate of the percentage of variation contributed by the treatment compared to the total variation of the process. From the computation and decision table we will use the equation:

$$\omega^2 = \frac{SS_{\text{Treatments}} - (T-1)(MS_{\text{Within}})}{SS_{\text{Total}} + MS_{\text{Within}}}$$

Level of Significance

The determination of the critical value of F (F_{Critical}) is dependent upon the selection of a level of significance (α) for the ANOVA. The level of significance applied to the analysis can be a very subjective choice where no specific standards exist. It is important that some standard for selection of significance level be implemented and applied to analysis uniformly throughout the business. The selection of the level of significance often reflects the consequences of the decision that will result from the analysis. A typical decision table for level of significance is provided in Figure 10-7.

DECISION	α LEVEL
CRITICAL SYSTEMS PARAMETERS System reliability System safety requirements System performance Systems competitive capability	0.01>
PROCESS EFFICIENCY OR EFFECTIVENESS Process improvement options Process selection Process differentiation Equipment selection	0.05 >
ADMINISTRATIVE/BUSINESS DECISIONS Payment of bonuses Return on investment Marketing decisions	0.10 >

Figure 10-7.   Significance Decision Table

For example if we are determining whether there is any significance between auto air bag manufacturers, we will tolerate only a very low probability of decision error. Therefore, we would select a significance level of .01. In decisions regarding the effectiveness or efficiency of equipment or processes for improvement purposes a significance level of .05 may apply. For routine business decisions, a significance level of .10 could be used.

Evaluating the Results of ANOVA

Now that we understand the basic principles of ANOVA we can apply them to the evaluation of a Multivariant Analysis of Variance (MANOVA). This type of ANOVA enables the manager, engineer and entrepreneur to evaluate multiple treatments of a product or process simultaneously. This capability is important to the ability to perform designed experiments with optimum effectiveness and efficiency. Multivariant ANOVA is a potent decision-making tool for improvement of existing processes, as well as, for the analysis of experiments for new and developing programs. We can now apply this last element to the example of a completed MANOVA Computation and Decision Table, as demonstrated in Figure 10-8.

We now use the completed table as a fact-based decision-making tool. A few of the important facts that we can extract from the table are listed below. These facts form the basis for business decisions concerning such things as material procurement, training, variability reduction programs, and management of further designed experiments.

SOURCE OF VARIATION			SUM OF SQUARES	DEGREES OF FREEDOM	MEAN SQUARES	F RATIO	F CRITICAL	SIGNIFICANCE
TREATMENTS	MAIN EFFECTS	A	SSa=2.55	$dfa = 1$	MSa = 2.55	Fa=2.71	F'a=4.08	0.01
		B	SSb= 30.08	$dfb = 1$	MSb = 30.08	Fb=32.00	F'b=4.08	0.22
		C	SSc=18.75	$dfc = 1$	MSc = 18.75	Fc=19.96	F'c=4.08	0.14
	INTERACTIONS	AB	SSab=1.78	$dfab = 1$	MSab = 1.78	Fab=1.89	F'ab=4.08	0.005
		AC	SSac=8.78	$dfac = 1$	MSac = 8.78	Fac=9.34	F'ac=4.08	0.06
		BC	SSbc=2.07	$dfbc = 1$	MSbc = 2.07	Fbc=2.20	F'bc=4.08	0.007
		ABC	SSabc=24.20	$dfabc = 1$	MSabc = 24.20	Fabc=25.74	F'abc=4.08	0.18
WITHIN			SSwithin = 37.71	$DFwithin = 40$	MSwithin= .94			
TOTAL			SStotal= 125.92	$DFtotal = 47$				

Figure 10-8. Completed Analysis and Decision Table

➤ The variability of the process is significant for treatments B and C and for the interaction of treatments $A \times C$.

➤ The Main Effect of Treatment B is contributing 22% to the total process variability.

➤ The Main Effect of Treatment C is contributing 10% to the total process variability.

➤ The Interaction of Treatments $A \times C$ is contributing 6% to the total process variability.

➤ The higher level interaction of AxBxC will be considered when approaching the problems associated with the main effects and lower level interactions

CLASSICAL METHODS OF DOE

Basic Concepts of DOE

Design of Experiments (DOE) is one of the most powerful tools for the design, characterization, and improvement of products and services. DOE is a group of techniques used to organize and evaluate experimentation to obtain the maximum data using the minimum assets. The language of DOE is colored by its genesis in the scientific, statistical, and engineering communities. Do not be intimidated by the verbiage; DOE is directly applicable to many types of businesses and can be effectively applied by the average business person with a little training. A "Designed Experiment" is no more than a test or trial program that has been well structured to measure the results (response variable) accurately in comparison to the inputs (treatments or input variables). Let's start with a brief survey of the basic concepts of DOE:

Experimental Matrix Figure 10-9 displays a typical DOE experimental matrix or test matrix. The matrix indicates the number of treatments, levels of the treatments and the treatment combinations for each Experimental Run (trial or test).

Orthogonal Array   The DOE experimental matrix translates directly to an orthogonal array. This matrix lays out the DOE in runs, indicating the levels for each run applied to the main effects and interactions of the treatments. In Figure 10-10 the treatment combination A2B1C1 is represented as experimental run 1, with main effects for A set as high (+), B set as low (-), and C set as low (-). The interactions for this experimental run are AB set as high (+), AC set as high (+), BC set as high (+), and the three-way interaction ABC set as Low (-).

Analyzing the results of a designed experiment includes calculating the mean effect of the levels of each treatment. To accomplish this result, it is necessary for the experiment to be balanced. A balanced set of experiments contains an equal number of experiments for each level of each treatment. The example in Figure 10-11 demonstrates this principle of a balanced experiment.

There are three criteria that can be applied to determine if a test array is orthogonal:

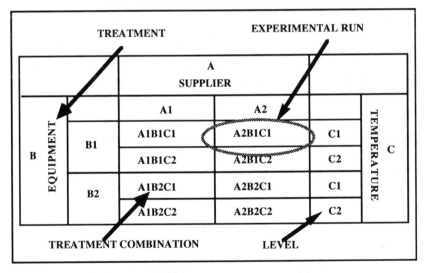

Figure 10-9 DOE Experimental Matrix

> **First:** Sum all the levels in each column. If there is an equal number of levels in each column, then we have passed the first test for an orthogonal array. In each column of Figure 10-11 the treatment has 4 plus level (+) and 4 minus level (-) values. The orthogonal array forms

the basis for many designed experiments, so it is important to recognize when a proposed test array is or is not orthogonal.

➤ **Second:** All rows having identical patterns in a given column must have an equal number of occurrences of settings in the other columns.

➤ **Third:** The selected matrix must have the least number of rows that satisfy the first two criteria for the selected number of treatments.

Main Effect   The main effect of a treatment is the measured change in the response as a result of changing that specific treatment. In Figures 10-10 and 10-11 above the Main Effects are for treatments A, B, and C.

Interaction   The measured change in the response as a result of the combined effect of two or more treatments. In Figures 10-10 and 10-11 above the Interactions are for treatment combinations AB, AC, BC, and ABC.

Treatment   Treatments are the controllable factors used as inputs to the products and processes under evaluation. These are the input variables (also called the independent variables) that can be varied to change the effect on the output or dependent variable. In Figures 10-10 and 10-11 above the treatments are (A) the supplier, (B) the equipment used in the process and (C) the temperature.

Level   Levels are the value of the treatments being studied. In most instances, designed experiments we can use two levels of the treatments: a high level symbolized by a (+) sign or the number 1 and a low level symbolized by a (-) sign or the number 2. In the figure above there are two levels for each treatment, Supplier A1 (+) and A2 (-), Equipment B1 (+) and B2 (-), and Temperature C1 (+) and C2 (-). There can be more levels than two, however, this makes the experiment much more complex and difficult to manage.

Treatment Combination   A treatment combination is the set of treatments and the associated levels used for an individual experimental run. In Figure 10-10 the treatment combinations are displayed for each experimental run. For instance A1B2C1 indicates that experimental run will be accomplished using material from Treatment A (Supplier) at level 1 (+), Treatment B (Equipment) at level 2 (-) and Treatment C (Temperature) at level 1 (+). These treatment combinations also describe the treatments and levels of an experiment and determine the number of experimental runs required.

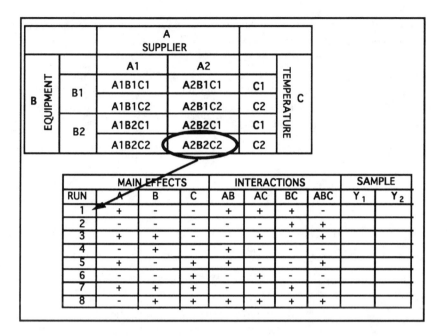

Figure 10-10 DOE Analytical Matrix

RUN	A	B	C	AB	AC	BC	ABC
1	-	-	-	+	+	+	-
2	+	-	-	-	-	+	+
3	-	+	-	-	+	-	+
4	+	+	-	+	-	-	-
5	-	-	+	+	-	-	+
6	+	-	+	-	+	-	-
7	-	+	+	-	-	+	-
8	+	+	+	+	+	+	+
+ -	4 4	4 4	4 4	4 4	4 4	4 4	4 4

Figure 10-11 Orthogonal Array

Experimental Run An experimental run is the accomplishment of a single trial (test or experiment) at a specific treatment combination. In the above example, there are three treatments at two levels (2^3) or eight experimental runs in this designed experiment. The number of experimental runs needed in a Designed experiment can be determined by the number of treatments and the levels of each treatment. These are stated as an exponential expression ($2^{t)}$, with the levels being the base number and the treatments being the exponent. We therefore, can calculate the number of experimental runs required for any combination of treatments and levels as indicated below:

$$2^2 = 4 \qquad\qquad 3^2 = 9$$
$$2^3 = 8 \qquad\qquad 3^3 = 27$$
$$2^4 = 16 \qquad\qquad 3^4 = 81$$
$$2^5 = 32 \qquad\qquad 3^5 = 243$$
$$2^6 = 64 \qquad\qquad 3^6 = 729$$
$$2^7 = 128 \qquad\qquad 3^7 = 2187$$

A designed experiment can have a few as four experimental runs (2^2) or as many as 2187 (three treatments with seven factors 3^7). This clearly demonstrates that DOE can cover a wide range of experimental combinations and levels of data. As we progress through this chapter we will describe DOE methods for dealing with large experiments.

Sample: The sample size is the number of times each Experimental Run is accomplished as a repeat or replicate. A repeat sample is used when the experiment is simply duplicated for each experimental run. A replicate sample is used when the experimental run is a measurement that is sensitive to setup, environment, or some other factor outside the sample treatments. The minimum sample size for a designed experiment is 2. This minimum is required to establish a variance about the mean of the response variable. The sample size then becomes dependent upon the levels of confidence needed in the experiment as indicated during our discussion on ANOVA. The sample size for each experimental run is indicated by a lowercase n, and the total sample size for the complete experiment is indicated by a upper case N. The samples for a designed experiment then can be described by $N = nL^T$.

It is apparent that we can use the sample size and number of experimental runs to plan our data management needs. If we run the simplest experiment, with the minimum number of samples there will be only eight resulting data points. In a (2^9) full factorial experiment with the minimum number of samples, there would be 4,374 data points.

$$(2)(2^2) = 8 \qquad (2)(3^2) = 18$$
$$(2)(2^3) = 16 \qquad (2)(3^3) = 54$$
$$(2)(2^4) = 32 \qquad (2)(3^4) = 162$$
$$(2)(2^5) = 64 \qquad (2)(3^5) = 486$$
$$(2)(2^6) = 128 \qquad (2)(3^6) = 1458$$
$$(2)(2^7) = 256 \qquad (2)(3^7) = 4374$$

Response: A response is a result of an experimental run. It is the dependent variable (also called the response variable). It is the measured effect, on the product or process, of using the specific combination of treatments and levels. In a 2^7 full factorial experiment there are 4,374 responses.

Randomization: We assign a treatment combination to an experimental run by random chance, using a randomization program or randomization table. Randomization prevents the influence of data in any test run due to any uncontrolled environmental variables. Randomization must always be used when the experimenter does not have total control over the environment, or when there are input variables outside the experiment that may affect the process. Figure 10-12 below has randomized the experimental runs first demonstrated in figure 10-11. The random order of the experimental runs is presented in the second column of the figure.

RUN	RAND	A	B	C	AB	AC	BC	ABC
1	3	-	-	-	+	+	+	-
2	5	+	-	-	-	-	+	+
3	4	-	+	-	-	+	-	+
4	7	+	+	-	+	-	-	-
5	2	-	-	+	+	-	-	+
6	8	+	-	+	-	+	-	-
7	6	-	+	+	-	-	+	-
8	1	+	+	+	+	+	+	+

Figure 10-12 Randomized Experimental Runs

DOE Process

The DOE process in Figure 10-13 applies to designed experiments for new product and process development and for existing processes. This process integrates many of the tools we have reviewed in previous chapters and introduces the use of ANOVA and the design of experiments. As with all of our technical tools, we first need to **define the process** in order to gain a clear understanding of what we desire to improve. The process and product must be understood at a very detailed level to determine all the treatments (input variables) that affect the product quality characteristics (output variables). We need to know what these parameters are, how they were set, what relevance they have to the customer needs, and how we can affect the end product. This understanding of the process provides us with the information to **identify improvement opportunities**.

If this improvement opportunity relates to existing process we can use **available data**. This data must be of sufficient quality and quantity to evaluate and determine which **response variables** and **treatments** can be subjected to **ANOVA** evaluation to further our improvement process. The availability of this data can significantly reduce the number of experimental runs that will be required by providing a priori information to reduce the number of screening runs required.

If no data is available concerning the process or product, we must use the **7-M Tools** and **T-Q Tools** to develop sufficient information to subject to a **brainstorming** session by an integrated team of subject experts, to **select treatments, levels** and **response variables**. The next step in the DOE process is to select the appropriate **experimental design**.

The selection of an experimental design is dependent upon the number of treatments that are to be evaluated, the level of data that is required and the cost associated with accomplishing the experimental runs. Since **full factorial** experiments are the most comprehensive, they are also the most costly and time consuming to run. **Fractional factorials** provide information only on a limited scope of data and are less costly; **screening experiments** (including Taguchi Designs) also provide a limited scope of data but, can provide some information concerning interactions. When many treatments are under consideration we recommend that you first perform screening experiments to identify the significant contributors to variance and then use fractional factorials or full factorials as **refining experiments**.

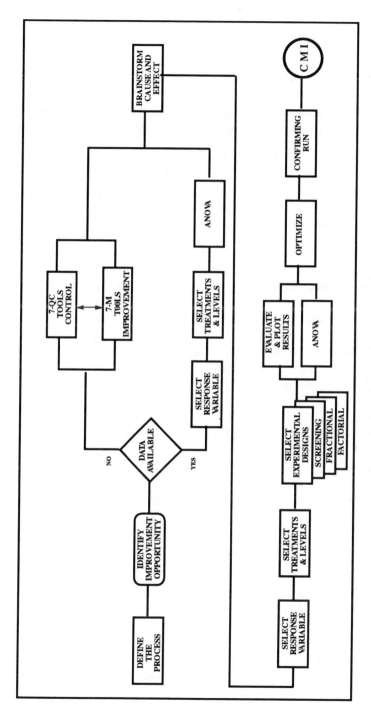

Figure 10-13. Improvement DOE Process

We evaluate the results of these experiments using two distinct methods. First, the data are evaluated for level effects and graphed for visual analysis. Second, we subject the data to ANOVA to determine if the effects are significant, which treatments are the most significant and (using ω^2) the percent contribution to overall variance from the treatments and their levels. We will review these methods as we develop full factorial designed experiments. A complete discussion and step by step procedure for accomplishing these analyses are contained in the work book associated with the text.

Several DOE methods have been developed by various factions, each proposing its particular model as the best or only solution. It is not our purpose to support or detract from the any of these approaches. That conflict is academic; we will focus upon applications. The following approaches to Design of Experiments apply most directly to management, industrial and administrative processes of concern to business.

> **Full factorial designs**

> **Fractional factorial designs**

> **Screening designs**

> **Taguchi designs**

We will discuss each one of these approaches to designed experiments in capsule form. For an in-depth understanding of the theory and other approaches to DOE we recommend *A Practical Guide to Statistical Quality Improvement*, by Beauregard, Mikulak, and Olson, 1992, published by Von Nostrand Reinhold, and we also recommend the forthcoming *A Practical Guide to New Product Development*, by ReVelle, Jackson and Frigon, also available from Von Nostrand Reinhold as part of the Management 2000 Series.

Full Factorial DOE

Full factorial experimental designs provide a comprehensive analysis of all treatments, levels, and interactions related to a selected quality characteristic. The full factorial designs we will discuss are commonly called the 2^f designs, where 2 is the number of levels and f represents the number of treatments. The orthogonal arrays for other designs such as 3^f are provided in Appendix B. These designs will be discussed only briefly due to their complexity. The analytical principles for all orthogonal arrays are essentially the same, and can be applied to all factorial experiments.

Selecting a Full Factorial Design   To select the appropriate full factorial design for your experiment, use the table of 2^f factorial designs demonstrated in Figure 10-14 below. The complete table is provided in Appendix A. The selected design is based upon the number of treatments and levels selected for the experiment. The figure demonstrates the full factorial designs for two-treatment (2^2), three-treatment (2^3) and four-treatment (2^4) experimental designs at two levels. If we were to select a design for three treatments (ABC) at two levels from this table, the resulting designed experiment orthogonal array would take the form of Figure 10-15, a full factorial for three treatments at two levels (2^3).

	DESIGN	TREATMENT COMBINATIONS														
RUN	2^f	A	B	AB	C	AC	BC	ABC	D	AD	BD	ABD	CD	ACD	BCD	ABCD
1		-	-	+	-	+	+	-	-	+	+	-	+	-	-	+
2		+	-	-	-	-	+	+	-	-	+	+	+	+	-	-
3	2^2	-	+	-	-	+	-	+	-	+	-	+	+	-	+	-
4		+	+	+	-	-	-	-	-	-	-	-	+	+	+	+
5		-	-	+	+	-	-	+	-	+	+	-	-	+	+	-
6		+	-	-	+	+	-	-	-	-	+	+	-	-	+	+
7	2^3	-	+	-	+	-	+	-	-	+	-	+	-	+	-	+
8		+	+	+	+	+	+	+	-	-	-	-	-	-	-	-
9		-	-	+	-	+	+	-	+	-	-	+	-	+	+	-
10		+	-	-	-	-	+	+	+	+	-	-	-	-	+	+
11		-	+	-	-	+	-	+	+	-	+	-	-	+	-	+
12	2^4	+	+	+	-	-	-	-	+	+	+	+	-	-	-	-
13		-	-	+	+	-	-	+	+	-	-	+	+	-	-	+
14		+	-	-	+	+	-	-	+	+	-	-	+	+	-	-
15		-	+	-	+	-	+	-	+	-	+	-	+	-	+	-
16		+	+	+	+	+	+	+	+	+	+	+	+	+	+	+

Figure 10-14 2^f Factorial Designs

RUN	RAND	A	B	AB	C	AC	BC	ABC
1	3	-	-	+	-	+	+	-
2	5	+	-	-	-	-	+	+
3	4	-	+	-	-	+	-	+
4	7	+	+	+	-	-	-	-
5	2	-	-	+	+	-	-	+
6	8	+	-	-	+	+	-	-
7	6	-	+	-	+	-	+	-
8	1	+	+	+	+	+	+	+

Figure 10-15 2^3 Orthogonal Array

Evaluation of Full Factorial Experimental Designs   Evaluating full factorial experiments includes: (1) the analysis of the effects of the treatments and treatment levels, (2) graphing these effects, (3) performing an ANOVA to determine the significance of the treatment and treatment levels and (4) determining the percentage of contribution of the variance at each level. To better visualize exactly how the effects are calculated, and how they relate to the test matrix and orthogonal array, we will apply the data directly to the orthogonal array as indicated in Figure 10-16.

		TREATMENT A				
		A+	A-			
TREATMENT B	B+	76, 81, 74	78, 76, 77	C+	TREATMENT C	
		75, 71, 75	76, 81, 74	C-		
	B-	76, 71, 74	76, 83, 77	C+		
		78, 81, 76	81, 79, 74	C-		

RUN	RAND	A	B	AB	C	AC	BC	ABC	Y_1	Y_2	Y_3	Ȳ	Range
1	3	-	-	+	-	+	+	-	81	79	74	78	7
2	5	+	-	-	-	-	+	+	78	81	76	78	5
3	4	-	+	-	-	+	-	+	76	81	74	77	7
4	7	+	+	+	-	-	-	-	75	71	75	74	4
5	2	-	-	+	+	-	-	+	76	83	77	79	7
6	8	+	-	-	+	+	-	-	76	71	74	74	5
7	6	-	+	-	+	-	+	-	78	76	77	77	2
8	1	+	+	+	+	+	+	+	76	81	74	77	7

Figure 10-16. Orthogonal Array With Data Applied

Effects   To calculate the effects of the treatment and treatment levels on our quality characteristic we must determine the difference that each of these is making. We previously applied the data to the orthogonal array in the above figure. Now we will apply the first calculation for effects to the same matrix. First we summarize the experimental data for each treatment and its associated level (Σ_k+, Σ_k-) at the bottom of the matrix as indicated in Figure 10-17.

The data summarized in the previous figure can now be applied directly to the equation to evaluate effects. The equation is:

$$\text{Effect}_K = \Sigma \frac{k+}{(+)} - \Sigma \frac{k-}{(-)}$$

RUN	RAND	A	B	AB	C	AC	BC	ABC	Y_1	Y_2	Y_3	$\bar{Y}$	Range
1	3	-	-	+	-	+	+	-	81	79	74	78	7
2	5	+	-	-	-	-	+	+	78	72	76	75	6
3	4	-	+	-	-	+	-	+	76	71	74	74	5
4	7	+	+	+	-	-	-	-	75	71	75	74	4
5	2	-	-	+	+	-	-	+	79	80	76	78	1
6	8	+	-	-	+	+	-	-	76	71	74	74	5
7	6	-	+	-	+	-	+	-	75	76	77	76	2
8	1	+	+	+	+	+	+	+	74	77	78	76	4
$\Sigma+$		299	300	306	304	302	306	304					
$\Sigma-$		306	305	299	301	303	299	301					

Figure 10-17. Summary of Experimental Data

Applying the data from Figure 10-17, we can calculate the effects for each main effect and interaction.

$$\text{Effect}_A = \Sigma\frac{A+}{+} - \Sigma\frac{A-}{-} = \frac{299}{4} - \frac{306}{4} = -1.75$$

$$\text{Effect}_B = \frac{300}{4} - \frac{305}{4} = -1.25$$

$$\text{Effect}_C = \frac{304}{4} - \frac{301}{4} = 0.75$$

$$\text{Effect}_{AB} = \frac{306}{4} - \frac{299}{4} = 1.75$$

$$\text{Effect}_{AC} = \frac{302}{4} - \frac{303}{4} = -0.25$$

$$\text{Effect}_{BC} = \frac{306}{4} - \frac{299}{4} = 1.75$$

$$\text{Effect}_{ABC} = \frac{304}{4} - \frac{301}{4} = 0.75$$

We can now graph the main effects and interactions to evaluate what effect the treatments and treatment levels are having on the quality characteristic. Figure 10-18 displays the graphs associated with the above effects.

Optimizing the quality characteristic depends upon the metric selected and the nature of the process. If we are measuring a process yield, maximum is best; for failure rates, minimum is best; for the deviation from a variable standard, nominal is best. The slope of the line for main effects indicates the significance of the effect. The steeper the slope, the more significant the effect is. The graph also indicates which treatment level is producing the desired effect of optimizing the process. If the lines of the graph are intersecting or converging, there is an interaction. If the lines run parallel there is no interaction.

This graph of the main effects and interactions indicates that the yield for this process can be maximized by selecting treatment A at the low setting,

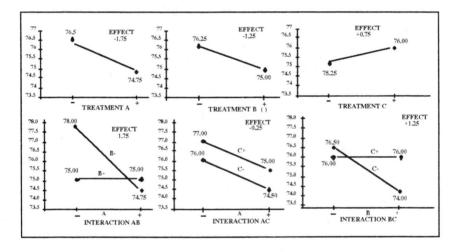

Figure 10-18. Effects Graphs

treatment B at the low setting and treatment C at the high setting. There are apparent interactions between A × B and B × C but no interaction between A × C.

Analysis of Variance: Analysis of Variance, applied within a designed experiment, indicates the significance of the main effects and interactions, and level of contribution as measured by ω^2 as we previously discussed in the Analysis of Variance section of this chapter. Figure 10-19 is an example of an ANOVA table used for that purpose.

This ANOVA Decision Table indicated that Treatment B is significant and contributed 22% to the overall process variation. This clearly indicates to us which treatment is to be the target of improvement processes such as CMI and Variability Reduction Programs. It also indicated to us which of the treatments in our experimental design has the most effect on our outcome.

Fractional Factorial DOE:

Factorial designs are the best designed experiments to use when evaluating all main effects and interactions. However, there may be too many factors for this type of experiment to be practicable. Conducting the full factorial experiments might be too costly or take too long, or the facilities and personnel might not be available.

SOURCE OF VARIATION		SUM OF SQUARES	DEGREES OF FREEDOM	MEAN SQUARES	F RATIO	F CRITICAL	ω^2
TREATMENTS / **MAIN EFFECTS**	A	SSa=2.55	dfa = 1	MSa = 2.55	Fa=2.71	F'a=4.08	.01
	B	SSb= 30.08	dfb = 1	MSb = 30.08	Fb=32.00	F'b=4.08	.22
	C	SSc=18.75	dfc = 1	MSc = 18.75	Fc=19.96	F'c=4.08	.14
INTERACTIONS	AB	SSab=1.78	dfab = 1	MSab = 1.78	Fab=1.89	F'ab=4.08	.005
	AC	SSac=8.78	dfac = 1	MSac = 8.78	Fac=9.34	F'ac=4.08	.06
	BC	SSbc=2.07	dfbc = 1	MSbc = 2.07	Fbc=2.20	F'bc=4.08	.007
	ABC	SSabc=24.20	dfabc = 1	MSabc = 24.20	Fabc=25.74	F'abc=4.08	.18
WITHIN		SSwithin = 37.71	DFwithin = 40	MSwithin= .94			
TOTAL		SStotal= 125.92	DFtotal = 47				

Figure 10-19. ANOVA Analysis and Decision Table

In such cases (which constitute the majority), fractional factorial designed experiments provide a reasonable alternative that still allows for the evaluation of main effects and key interactions, but requires fewer trial runs. To achieve this result we confound the higher order interactions (three or greater) with the main effect and two way interactions. Three way interactions often are insignificant, and to affect three way interactions we would alter the treatment main effects in any case. The fractional factorial technique enables the experimenter to reduce the number of runs needed by confounding these interactions with other design runs.

This method is easier to visualize if we use the already familiar 2^3 factorial. The treatment combinations (main effects and interactions) for this orthogonal array are given in figure 10-20. The higher-order interaction (ABC) here is the defining factor for confounding. The eight-run experiment can be separated into two four run-designs that separate the treatment combinations according to the sign (+ or -) conversion of interaction ABC.

We will separate the full factorial into two fractional factorials, each with four runs. Four runs designated by ABC are equal to minus, and four runs designated by ABC are equal to plus. The resulting two fractional factorial arrays are demonstrated in figure 10-21. This method creates aliases, that is more than one factor with the same treatment combination. The aliases result when more than one factor has the same treatment levels in the same run. In the upper portion of figure 10-21 the aliases are:

$$B = AC$$

$$A = BC$$

$$C = AB$$

RUN	A	B	AB	C	AC	BC	ABC
1	-	-	+	-	+	+	-
2	+	-	-	-	-	+	+
3	-	+	-	-	+	-	+
4	+	+	+	-	-	-	-
5	-	-	+	+	-	-	+
6	+	-	-	+	+	-	-
7	-	+	-	+	-	+	-
8	+	+	+	+	+	+	+

Figure 10-20. Fractional Factorial Design

By using the orthogonal array defined in the upper portion of Figure 10-21 we can accomplish the experiment in four runs instead of eight. The main effects are confounded with the interactions. This can be accomplished due to the assumption that interactions are unimportant. The main effects can still be estimated. This reduces the experimental burden (time, cost, facilities) by half. The effect of this becomes obvious when considering the following:

FULL FACTORIAL RUNS	1/2 FACTORIAL RUNS	1/4 FRACTIONAL RUNS
$2^3 = 8$	4	
$2^4 = 16$	8	4
$2^5 = 32$	16	8
$2^6 = 64$	32	16

We evaluate fractional factorial designs in the same way as full factorials using ANOVA and effects.

	A	B	AB	C	AC	BC	ABC
			ABC (+)				
1	+	-	-	-	-	+	+
2	-	+	-	-	+	-	+
3	-	-	+	+	-	-	+
4	+	+	+	+	+	+	+

ABC (+)

	A	B	AB	C	AC	BC	ABC
1	-	-	+	-	+	+	-
2	+	+	+	-	-	-	-
3	+	-	-	+	+	-	-
4	-	+	-	+	-	+	-

Figure 10-21. Fractional Factorial for 2^{3-1}

Screening Designs

Screening designs (form of factorial design) require some knowledge of the process variability. It is best, therefore, that screening be used to evaluate a controlled, stable process. Screening designs can identify and optimize process variability and help to improve process capability. In general, the concept behind screening designs is simple. We can represent it by a linear model of the form:

$$y = b_0 + b_1x_1 + b_2x_2 + ... + b_ix_i$$

We fit the data to determine the coefficients (b_i). Each variable (x_i) is studied at two levels (usually designated as +1 and -1), and the absolute values of the coefficients are ranked to determine the relative effects the treatments have on the response (quality characteristic). The sign of the coefficient determines the direction that the response moves as the factor is changed from the low level (-1) to the high level (+1). If the coefficient is positive, the response value increases; if the coefficient is negative, the response value decreases. Small coefficients indicate that the associated treatment does not have a significant effect on the response. We can screen out these factors at the next round of testing.

Screening experiments use predetermined designs, which must be randomized, repeated, and replicated as with any experimental design. The purpose of screening designs is to determine main effects. We will review the Plackett-Burman screening designs in this chapter. The predetermined designs for Placett-Burman arrays are in Appendix A.

Selecting a Screening Design   Based upon your detailed knowledge of the process, and using subject experts in a brainstorming session to produce a cause-and-effect analysis, choose the treatments and levels to be evaluated. It is better to have too many treatments than too few, but remember to keep the treatments practical, feasible and cost effective. When setting the levels, as with all experimental designs, be bold. The levels need to be far enough apart to detect their effect on the process.

Plackett-Burman experimental designs use predetermined matrices. We classify these designs by the number of runs in the experiment. Each design can evaluate one less factor than the number of experimental runs. For example, an eight-run design can evaluate seven factors. Select Blackett-Burman designs based upon the following:

TREATMENTS	PB ARRAY
2-7	8-RUN MATRIX
8-11	12-RUN MATRIX
12-15	16-RUN MATRIX
16-19	20-RUN MATRIX

The power of Plackett-Burman screening experiments is evident from the comparison of our 2^3 full factorial experiment with a screening design in Figure 10-22 below. The full factorial design (2^3) provides full evaluation of three treatments and their interactions, and the Plackett-Burman design provides the capability to evaluate the main effects of seven treatments, using the same number of runs.

Screening experiments assume that interactions are insignificant. Interaction columns are renamed for main effects as in the same method used for creating fractional factorials. Like all the experimental designs discussed in this chapter screening designs are orthogonal arrays.

When there are not enough treatments, dummy variables can be used to fill the Plackett-Burman matrix. For example, if there are six treatments you desire to test, that would require an eight-run matrix which would handle seven factors. This leaves one unassigned factor column which can be used as a dummy variable. The effect measured from a dummy variable is an estimate of the experimental error (variation within). As with the ANOVA used to evaluate other approaches to DOE, if the effect of error is significant it indicates that the variation is attributable to common cause rather than the sensitivity of the treatments or treatment levels. If, on the other hand, the dummy variable is not significant, it is an indication that the variation is caused by one of the selected treatments.

Executing the Experiment   As with all designed experiments, we must randomize the order in which the individual experimental runs are accomplished. Each replicate and each reflection of the experiment should be individually subjected to randomization. Remember, randomization reduces the effect of external sources of variation. Screening experiments should, to the greatest extent possible, be replicated and reflected.

Replication means repeating the experimental runs. To replicate, repeat the experiment, randomizing the treatment combinations once again. Replication optimizes the confidence in the resulting data and provides for an estimate of the amount of experimental error in the experiment. If dummy variables are used, there is less need for replication, because the effects of the dummy variable provide an estimate of experimental error.

Reflecting means reversing all the signs of the factor levels. Figure 10-23 is an example of an eight-run design, reflected and replicated. Reflecting screening experiments reduces the level of confounding, thus resulting in a higher level of confidence in the main effects being measured.

With the test planning completed, and the design matrix reflected, replicated, and randomized, it is now time to run the experiment and collect the data. As with other forms of DOE, you must collect a minimum of two data points for each set of conditions. For each run, set the treatment levels as indicated in the PB screening array. Then run each process and collect the data.

Determine the Treatment Effects To evaluate the results of the screening experiment, we will use the average value ($\overline{Y}$) for each treatment combination and multiply the mean by the sign (+ or -) in each column. We will then sum the data values for each treatment column and divide the sum by the total number of pluses in that column, to determine the effect. This procedure is demonstrated in the eight run (seven-treatment) Plackett-Burman Array in Figure 10-24.

FULL FACTORIAL 8 RUN ARRAY							
	A	B	AB	C	AC	BC	ABC
1	-	-	+	-	+	+	-
2	+	-	-	-	-	+	+
3	-	+	-	-	+	-	+
4	+	+	+	-	-	-	-
1	-	-	+	+	-	-	+
2	+	-	-	+	+	-	-
3	-	+	-	+	-	+	-
4	+	+	+	+	+	+	+

PLACKETT-BURMAN 8-RUN MATRIX							
	A	B	C	D	E	F	G
1	+	+	+	-	+	-	-
2	-	+	+	+	-	+	-
3	-	-	+	+	+	-	+
4	+	-	-	+	+	+	-
5	-	+	-	-	+	+	+
6	+	-	+	-	-	+	+
7	+	+	-	+	-	-	+
8	-	-	-	-	-	-	-

Figure 10-22. Comparison of Full Factorial and Screening Designs

8- RUN SCREENING ARRAY							
RUN	MEAN	A	B	C	D	E	F	G
1	+	+	+	+	-	+	-	-
2	+	-	+	+	+	-	+	-
3	+	-	-	+	+	+	-	+
4	+	+	-	-	+	+	+	-
5	+	-	+	-	-	+	+	+
6	+	+	-	+	-	-	+	+
7	+	+	+	-	+	-	-	+
8	+	-	-	-	-	-	-	-
REFLECTED ORIGINAL							
RUN	MEAN	A	B	C	D	E	F	G
9	+	-	+	+	-	+	-	-
10	+	+	+	+	+	-	+	-
11	+	+	-	+	+	+	-	+
12	+	-	-	-	+	+	+	-
13	+	+	+	-	-	+	+	+
14	+	-	-	+	-	-	+	+
14	+	-	+	-	+	-	-	+
16	+	+	-	-	-	-	-	-
REPLICATED ORIGINAL							
	MEAN	A	B	C	D	E	F	G
R1	+	+	+	+	-	+	-	-
R2	+	-	+	+	+	-	+	-
R3	+	-	-	+	+	+	-	+
R4	+	+	-	-	+	+	+	-
R5	+	-	+	-	-	+	+	+
R6	+	+	-	+	-	-	+	+
R7	+	+	+	-	+	-	-	+
R8	+	-	-	-	-	-	-	-
REPLICATED REFLECTED							
	MEAN	A	B	C	D	E	F	G
R9	+	-	+	+	-	+	-	-
R10	+	+	+	+	+	-	+	-
R11	+	+	-	+	+	+	-	+
R12	+	-	-	-	+	+	+	-
R13	+	+	+	-	-	+	+	+
R14	+	-	-	+	-	-	+	+
R15	+	-	+	-	+	-	-	+
R16	+	+	-	-	-	-	-	-

Figure 10-23. Screening Experiment Replicated and Reflected

RANDOMIZED PB SCREENING DESIGN									
RUN	RAND	A	B	C	D	E	F	G	Υ	RANGE
1	1	+	+	+	-	+	-	-		
2	4	+	-	-	+	+	+	-		
3	7	+	+	-	+	-	-	+		
4	6	+	-	+	-	-	+	+		
5	5	-	+	-	-	+	+	+		
6	3	-	-	+	+	+	-	+		
7	8	-	-	-	-	-	-	-		
8	2	-	+	+	+	-	+	-		

RANDOMIZED PB SCREENING DESIGN WITH DATA									
RUN	RAND	A	B	C	D	E	F	G	Υ	RANGE
1	1	(+)1.992	(+)1.992	(+)1.992	(-)1.992	(+)1.992	(-)1.992	(-)1.992	1.992	0.008
2	4	(+)1.990	(-)1.990	(-)1.99	(+)1.990	(+)1.990	(+)1.990	(-)1.990	1.990	0.008
3	7	(+)1.998	(+)1.998	(-)1.998	(+)1.998	(-)1.998	(-)1.998	(+)1.998	1.998	0.009
4	6	(+)1.995	(-)1.995	(+)1.995	(-)1.995	(-)1.995	(+)1.995	(+)1.995	1.995	0.005
5	5	(-)1.998	(+)1.998	(-)1.998	(-)1.998	(+)1.998	(+)1.998	(+)1.998	1.998	0.009
6	3	(-)2.000	(-)2.000	(+)2.000	(+)2.000	(+)2.000	(-)2.000	(+)2.000	2.000	0.007
7	8	(-)1.991	(-)1.991	(-)1.991	(-)1.991	(-)1.991	(-)1.991	(-)1.991	1.991	0.006
8	2	(-)2.001	(+)2.001	(+)2.001	(+)2.001	(-)2.001	(+)2.001	(-)2.001	2.001	0.005
	SUM	(-)0.015	(+)0.013	(+)0.011	(+)0.013	(-)0.005	(+)0.003	(+)0.017	R	0.0071
	EFFECT	(-)0.004	(+)0.003	(+)0.003	(+)0.003	(-)0.001	(+)0.001	(+)0.004		

Figure 10-24. Eight Run Plackett-Burman Array With Data

In the above example the mean of the response variables were positive. You must be cautious however; if the response variables are negative and positive, the rules of multiplication will apply when performing the multiplication c⁵ the mean by the sign in each column.

$$(-) \times (-) = (+)$$
$$(-) \times (+) = (-)$$
$$(+) \times (+) = (+)$$

The size of the effect relates to the change that can be expected in the process output due to the change in the treatment level (+ or -). The sign of the effect indicates the direction the response variable will change. A positive effect means that the response will increase when the treatment changes to a higher level. A negative effect means the response will decrease when the treatment level increases

Testing the Effects for Significance   We must now determine if the difference demonstrated by the effect is significant or is simply attributable to normal variation. To accomplish this, we will use a measure of variation called the two sigma effect (TSE). The two sigma effect for Plackett-Burman design analysis is a form of the Students t test. This form of Hypothesis test determines if the treatment effects are outside the normal control limits of the process. The test statistic used for this purpose is:

$$TSE = (t_{1-a/2,\ df}) \times (S_{eff})$$

If the TSE is larger than the treatment effect, then the factor effect is not significant. If the TSE is less than the treatment effect, then the treatment effect is significant.

$$TSE > Effect = Not\ Significant$$

$$TSE < Effect = Significant$$

To determine the TSE we must first calculate the experimental error S_{ee}. This is accomplished using the formula:

$$S_{ee} = \frac{\overline{R}}{d_2}$$

Using the data from figure 10-24 and table A-1 in Appendix A:

$$S_{ee} = \frac{\overline{R}}{d_2} = \frac{0.0071}{2.326} = 0.0031$$

Next we must calculate the standard deviation for the effects, S_{eff}, using the equation:

$$S_{eff} = \frac{2S_{ee}}{\sqrt{Tn}}$$

Using the data developed in the previous step from figure 10-24:

$$S_{eff} = \frac{2S_{ee}}{\sqrt{Tn}} = \frac{2(0.0031)}{\sqrt{(8)(5)}} = 0.00098$$

We calculate the degrees of freedom (df) using the equation:

$$df = T(n-1)$$

Based on the data from Figure 10-24 the number of test runs (T) is 8. Assuming we replicated the runs five times, the sample size (n) is 5. The Degrees of Freedom would be:

$$df = T(n-1) = (8)(5-1) = 32$$

Now we have the information we need to calculate the TSE. Using the students t statistical table in appendix A, with a α level of 0.05 and 32 df, the t-table value is 2.042. The TSE is therefore:

$$\text{TSE} = (t_{\alpha/2}, df)(S_{eff}) = (2.042)(0.00098) = 0.002$$

We can compare this value with the absolute value (no signs) of the individual treatment effects from Figure 10-24:

TREATMENT	EFFECT	TSE	SIGNIFICANCE
A	0.004	0.002	YES
B	0.003	0.002	YES
C	0.003	0.002	YES
D	0.003	0.002	YES
E	0.001	0.002	NO
F	0.001	0.002	NO
G	0.004	0.002	YES

This information can be used to select factors (screening) for further experimentation, or to select levels directly to attempt to optimize the response variable. Remember that you should always perform a confirmation run.

TAGUCHI METHODS OF DOE

Dr. Taguchi describes the engineering design and improvement cycle in three phases: System Design, Parameter Design, and Tolerance design. The system design phase occurs when the fundamental design and concept for a product or service are established. This phase is centric to the engineering and subject expert technologies.

In the parameter design phase we design the nominal specifications of the system. That is, we improve quality without controlling or eliminating the sources of variance that occur in the customer's environment. These sources influence the target dimensions, material properties, voltages, and other parameters. We set these parameters to make the product less sensitive to the causes of variation. Parameter design makes the product more robust to the causes of variation. Tolerance design reduces the product variation by tightening the tolerances. Dr. Taguchi's approach to the cost versus benefit is then applied to determine the cost effectiveness of the recommended improvements.

In the tolerance design phase designate the upper and lower specification limits for the parameters. The reduction in variability is accomplished by reducing the specification limits to make the product more robust and thus to reduce the cause of variation.

Taguchi designs are a special case of screening experiments. They provide for the evaluation of key two way interactions as well as main effects of the treatments. The Taguchi method uses orthogonal arrays that are condensed forms of the full factorial arrays previously presented in this chapter. We assume that there are no higher order interactions (3 interactions or more) that are critical. Key two-way interactions can be considered, based upon engineering and technical assessment, but they are assumed to be less significant than main effects. The focus of the Taguchi DOE methods however is clearly main effects, with interactions as a secondary consideration for the experimenter.

We will review the Taguchi tools that are the most widely applicable in business. These tools will be presented using the innovative approach developed by Dr. Jack Re Velle.[1]

> **Parameter Design DOE**

> **Tolerance Design DOE**

> **Taguchi approach to ANOVA**

Taguchi Parameter Design

The purpose of Parameter Design is to design a product or service that is robust against the working environment. Dr. Taguchi uses the term "signal to noise ratio" to describe the effect of the input parameters that cannot be controlled or are too costly to control. The best approach to this problem is to design your product or process to be robust against those environmental conditions.

There are certain environmental considerations that cannot be controlled. These include such considerations as temperature, vibration, humidity and use in the operating environment. Taguchi's parameter design process designs products and services to be robust to these considerations. DOE for Parameter aids in identifying the control factors (treatments) and levels that are most robust. Dr. Re Velle approaches the application of Taguchi parameter design in nine steps:

❶ **Identify a problem or an opportunity for improvement**

❷ **Perform a cause and effect analysis**

❸ **Select treatments, levels and values**

❹ **Determine how experimental results will be expressed**

❺ **Select a designed experiment**

❻ **Design a data acquisition and management system**

❼ **Conduct the experiment**

❽ **Calculate the main effects and interactions**

❾ **Graph the results**

Step 1.   Identify a Problem or an Opportunity for Improvement

The first step in parameter design is to identify the opportunity for improvement. The most effective way to accomplish this is the use of the Process Analysis, 7-MP tools and the 7-QC tools.   These opportunities can be derived from many sources in existing and new processes, products, and services. Examples include:

> Opportunities for variability reduction to improve the efficiency and effectiveness of existing processes

> Opportunities to improve products and services based upon customer requirements

> Opportunities to reduce reject and scrap rates

> Opportunities to improve the development of new products and services

Step 2.   Perform a Cause and Effect Analysis

Figure 10-25 below is an example of a fishbone diagram for cause and effect analysis. We will follow this example through our development of parameter design. To identify the opportunities for improvement four subject experts spent approximately one hour of their time to brainstorm the problem and create the cause and effect analysis.

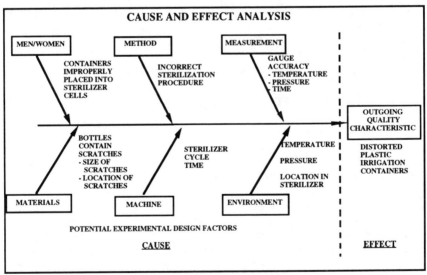

Figure 10-25. Potential Parameter Design Factors

Step 3.   Select Treatments, Levels and Values

Based upon the cause and effect analysis, select which factors will be tested. Determine the levels of the factors and assign a test value for each level. From our previous example the factors and levels are as indicated in Figure 10-26.

FACTORS	LEVELS		
	1	2	3
SCRATCH DIAMETER	0.020"	0.040"	0.060"
SCRATCH LOCATION ON BOTTLE	TOP	MIDDLE	BOTTOM

Figure 10-26. Selected Parameter Design Factors, Levels and Values

Step 4.   Determine How to Express the Experimental Results

Determine how the experimental results will be expressed. What quality characteristic will we try to measure? This is the output variable for the designed experiment. From the cause and effect analysis we have completed the quality characteristic will be quantified as follows:

UNACCEPTABLE DISTORTION   10 POINTS

MARGINAL DISTORTION   5 POINTS

ACCEPTABLE DISTORTION   1 POINT

Step 5.   Select a Designed Experiment

Based upon the number of treatments and treatment levels required to evaluate the output variable, select the appropriate Taguchi designed experiment from Appendix A. Remember the basic rules for selecting an experimental design: the design must be orthogonal, and must contain the minimum number of runs to satisfy the requirements. In our continuing example, we have two treatments (diameter and location) and three levels (3^2). The subject experts have also determined that it is desirable to measure the interaction between the treatments.

In the list of common orthogonal arrays in Appendix A there are three arrays that contain three levels:

ARRAY	NUMBER OF FACTORS	NUMBER OF LEVELS
L_9 (3^4)	4	3
L_{18} (3^7)	7	3
L_{27} (3^{13})	13	3

Our experiment, with three levels and two factors or treatments, is most closely represented by the L_9 Orthogonal Array. The array is presented with its associated interaction table in Figure 10-27.

The L_9 orthogonal array indicates that we will require nine test runs to evaluate the two treatments at three levels. We assign the two treatments (diameter and location) to columns 1 and 2. The interactions are assigned to related columns, using the triangular table to determine which columns in the L_9 array represent the interactions. The numbers in parentheses on the diagonal of the interaction table represent the column headings from the L_9 orthogonal array. The numbers across the top of the table also represent column headings. To determine which columns represent the interaction of the treatments use the number in parentheses on the diagonal and number on the heading. From the table, we can see that the interactions can be measured in columns 3 and 4. This is demonstrated in Figure 10-28.

L_9 ORTHOGONAL ARRAY

RUN \ COLUMN	1	2	3	4
1	1	1	1	1
2	1	2	2	2
3	1	3	3	3
4	2	1	2	3
5	2	2	3	1
6	2	3	1	2
7	3	1	3	2
8	3	2	1	3
9	3	3	2	1

TRIANGULAR TABLE

1	2	3	4
(1)	3 4	2 4	2 3
	(2)	1 4	1 3
		(3)	1 2

Figure 10-27. Selection of Orthogonal Array

COLUMN	DIAMETER	LOCATION	DIAM X LOC	DIAM X LOC
RUN	1	2	3	4
1	1	1	1	1
2	1	2	2	2
3	1	3	3	3
4	2	1	2	3
5	2	2	3	1
6	2	3	1	2
7	3	1	3	2
8	3	2	1	3
9	3	3	2	1

Figure 10-28. L9 Orthogonal Array for Main Effects and Interactions

Step 6. Design a Data Acquisition and Management System

Prepare a worksheet (automated or manual) to avoid errors in the collection and management of data from the designed experiment. In our example, there are nine test runs, and we have decided to sample each run 10 times, therefore there will by 90 data points coming from our experiment. We can design a data table directly from the orthogonal array, as indicated in Figure 10-29.

L9 ORTHOGONAL ARRAY				RESULTS									
COLUMN	1	2	3	4	1	2	3	4	5	6	7	8	9	10
RUN														
1	1	1	1	1										
2	1	2	2	2										
3	1	3	3	3										
4	2	1	2	3										
5	2	2	3	1										
6	2	3	1	2										
7	3	1	3	2										
8	3	2	1	3										
9	3	3	2	1										

Figure 10-29. Experimental Design Data Work Sheet

Step 7. Conduct the Experiment

Using the design formulated in Step 5, conduct the experiment. Measure the quality characteristic using the measure determined in Step 4. Record the results on your worksheet along with any notes on related circumstances that might provide information concerning the test results. The resulting data can be recorded as indicated in figure 10-30.

L9 ORTHOGONAL ARRAY					RESULTS									
COLUMN	1	2	3	4	1	2	3	4	5	6	7	8	9	10
RUN														
1	1	1	1	1	1	5	5	5	5	5	5	5	5	5
2	1	2	2	2	10	10	5	10	5	5	10	10	10	10
3	1	3	3	3	10	10	10	10	10	10	10	10	10	10
4	2	1	2	3	1	1	1	1	1	1	1	1	1	1
5	2	2	3	1	10	10	10	10	10	10	10	10	10	10
6	2	3	1	2	10	10	10	10	10	10	10	10	10	10
7	3	1	3	2	1	1	1	1	1	1	1	1	1	1
8	3	2	1	3	10	10	10	10	10	10	10	10	10	10
9	3	3	2	1	10	10	10	10	10	10	10	10	10	10

Figure 10-30. Record the Results of the Designed Experiment

Step 8.   Calculate the Main Effects and Interactions

Using the experimental results calculate the level mean (average) for each factor (treatment) and interaction. This calculation can be accomplished directly in the three rows beneath the orthogonal array, as indicated in Figure 10-31.

L9 ORTHOGONAL ARRAY					RESULTS										
COLUMN	1	2	3	4	1	2	3	4	5	6	7	8	9	10	TOTAL
RUN															
1	1	1	1	1	1	5	5	5	5	5	5	5	5	5	46
2	1	2	2	2	10	10	5	10	5	5	10	10	10	10	85
3	1	3	3	3	10	10	10	10	10	10	10	10	10	10	100
4	2	1	2	3	1	1	1	1	1	1	1	1	1	1	10
5	2	2	3	1	10	10	10	10	10	10	10	10	10	10	100
6	2	3	1	2	10	10	10	10	10	10	10	10	10	10	100
7	3	1	3	2	1	1	1	1	1	1	1	1	1	1	10
8	3	2	1	3	10	10	10	10	10	10	10	10	10	10	100
9	3	3	2	1	10	10	10	10	10	10	10	10	10	10	100
LEVEL 1	7.70	2.20	8.20	8.20											
LEVEL 2	7.00	9.50	6.50	6.50											
LEVEL 3	7.00	10.00	7.00	7.00											

Figure 10-31. Calculate the Main Effects and Interactions

Obtain the level means by adding all the observations at that level for each main effect and interaction, and dividing by the total number of observations for that level. The calculations for Factor 1 (diameter) are:

$$\text{LEVEL 1} = \frac{46 + 85 + 100}{30} = \frac{231}{30} = 7.70$$

$$\text{LEVEL 2} = \frac{10 + 100 + 100}{30} = \frac{210}{30} = 7.00$$

$$\text{LEVEL 3} = \frac{10 + 100 + 100}{30} = \frac{210}{30} = 7.00$$

Obtain the grand average by adding all the individual observations in the results columns and dividing by the total number of observations.

$$\text{GRAND AVERAGE} = \frac{1 + 5 + 5 + \ldots +10 \ +10 \ \ldots +1 + 1 \ldots +10}{90}$$
$$= \frac{651}{90} = 7.23$$

Obtain each level effect and total effect using the spread sheet in Figure 10-32. The level effect is calculated by subtracting the grand average (7.23) from each level mean. The total effect is calculated by subtracting the least level effect from the greatest level effect (the range).

Step 9.   Graph the Results

To confirm the information provided by the calculations, and to provide a graphical understanding of the effects upon the product and process, graph the results as shown in Figure 10-33.

Based upon the "smaller is better" criterion, to improve the distortion of plastic irrigation containers we need to minimize the distortion points allocated to the quality characteristic. Evaluation of the data in Figure 10-32 and the graphs, in Figure 10-33 indicates that Factor 2 (scratch location) has the highest positive correlation with distortion. The best results can be obtained by setting material Factor 1 at Level 3 (diameter 0.020) and Factor 2 at Level 1 (location top).

FACTOR	NAME	LEVEL	LEVEL MEAN	LEVEL EFF	TOTAL EFF
1	DIA	1 0.020" 2 0.040" 3 0.060"	7.70 7.00 7.00	0.47 -0.23 -0.23	0.70
2	LOC	1 TOP 2 MIDDLE 3 BOTTOM	2.20 9.50 10.00	-5.03 2.27 2.77	7.80
3	DIA × LOC		8.20 6.50 7.00	0.97 -0.73 -0.23	1.70
4	DIA × LOC		8.20 6.50 7.00	0.97 -0.73 -0.23	1.70

Figure 10-32. Level Effect & Total Effect Spread Sheet

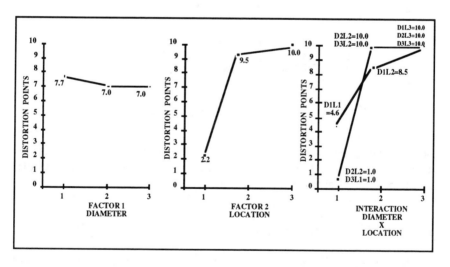

Figure 10-33. Graphing the Results

Predicting Optimum Results

To predict the optimum results based upon our evaluation in Step 9, insert the optimum treatment and level input variables into the equation to estimate the value of the optimized quality characteristic:

$$\hat{Y} = \frac{T}{n} + \left(A_X - \frac{T}{n}\right) + \left(B_X - \frac{T}{n}\right) + \ldots + \left(F_X - \frac{T}{n}\right)$$

Where:

$\quad$ T = Total of all Experimental Results

$\quad$ n = Number of Samples

$\quad \dfrac{T}{n}$ = Grand Average

$\quad$ Ax, Bx...Fx = Performance values at optimum level for each factor

Applying the data from our example to the optimization equation, we obtain:

$$\hat{Y} = \frac{T}{n} + \left(A_2 - \frac{T}{n}\right) + \left(B_2 - \frac{T}{n}\right)$$

$$= \frac{651}{90} + \left(7.00 - \frac{651}{90}\right) + \left(2.20 - \frac{651}{90}\right)$$

$$= 7.23 + (-0.23) + (-5.03) = 1.97$$

The predicted value of the distortion point is 1.97. We must now verify this prediction. The confirmation experiment is run using the optimum factor levels, based upon the "smaller is better" criteria.

Taguchi Tolerance Design

Tolerance design builds upon the gains of parameter design by further reducing variation. Tolerance design centers upon the relationship between the variance of the component or treatment and the overall variance of the response variable (quality characteristic). The variance of the overall response decreases in some proportion to a reduction in the variance of the component or treatment variability. This concept of variability transmission was evident during our study of ANOVA, when the total sum of the squares (SS_{total}) was derived from the treatment sum of the squares. The following equation describes this relationship:

$$S^2_{Total} = S^2_A + S^2_B + S^2_C + \ldots + S^2_x$$

The variance (S^2) indicated here is the variance of the quality characteristic "caused" by the variances of the contributing treatments or components. The greater the variance of any treatment or component, the greater the variation of the quality characteristic. The aim of Taguchi Tolerance Design is to reduce the tolerance variation of these contributing factors. After selecting the target component or treatment using parameter design of the Taguchi-Style ANOVA, then we can use DOE and/or ANOVA to define the improvement to that factor in the same manner as it was applied to parameter design.

Taguchi-Style ANOVA

Taguchi style analysis of variance uses several methods developed to facilitate the calculation and understanding of ANOVA. The basic rules of ANOVA apply here also, with regard to hypothesis testing, partitioning of variance, and measures of significance. One of the important elements of Taguchi-Style ANOVA is the integration of the percent contribution directly into the ANOVA calculations. The clear advantages of this method are the ease in performing the calculations and the integration of the percent contribution.

We have here encapsulated Dr. Jack Re Velle's approach to performing Taguchi Style ANOVA into nine steps:

❶   Calculate the grand average

❷   Calculate the level mean

❸   Calculate the effects

❹   Compute the sum of the squares

❺   Compute the mean squares

❻   Calculate the F_{Ratio}

❼   Determine the critical value of F (F_{Crit})

❽   Calculate the pure sum of the squares

❾   Determine the percent contribution

Step 1.   Calculate the Grand Average   The grand average is calculated by adding all the data observations and dividing by the total number of observations.

$$\text{Grand Average} = \frac{\text{Sum of Individual Observations}}{\text{Total Number of Observations}}$$

Using the three levels of data from the parameter design DOE as an example we obtain the following:

$$\text{Grand Average} = \frac{1 + 5 + 5 + \ldots + 10 + 10 + \ldots 1 + 1 \ldots + 10}{90}$$

$$= \frac{651}{90} = 7.23$$

Step 2. Calculate the Level Mean   The level mean is calculated by summarizing the observations at each level or treatment and dividing by the number of observations in that level.

$$\text{Level Mean} = \frac{\Sigma\,(\text{All Observations at Level } i)}{\text{Number of Observations at Level } i}$$

Using the three levels of data from the parameter design DOE with the diameter treatment as an example, we obtain:

$$\text{Level } 1 = \frac{46 + 85 + 100}{30} = 7.70$$

$$\text{Level } 2 = \frac{10 + 100 + 100}{30} = 7.00$$

$$\text{Level } 3 = \frac{10 + 100 + 100}{30} = 7.00$$

Step 3. Calculate the Effects   The level effect is calculated by subtracting the grand average from the level mean. The total effect is calculated by subtracting the least level mean from the greatest level mean:

$$\text{Level Effects} = \text{Level Mean} - \text{Grand Average}$$

$$\text{Total Effect} = \text{Greatest Level Mean} - \text{Least Level Mean}$$

Using the three levels of data from the parameter design DOE with the diameter treatment as an example, we obtain the following result:

FACTOR	LEVEL	LEVEL MEAN	LEVEL EFFECT	TOTAL EFFECT
DIAMETER	1	7.70	0.47	
	2	7.00	−0.23	0.70
	3	7.00	−0.23	

Step 4. Calculate the Sum of the Squares   The next step is to calculate the sum of the squares for each of the following elements:

Sum of the Squares Total: SS_{Total} = [Distance of individual observations from the grand average]^2

Sum of the Squares for Factors/Interactions: SS_{Factor} = [Level Effects at each level]^2 × [Number of Observations at each level]

Sum of the Squares for Replications: SS_{Rep} = Sum of [Grand Average − Average of each replication column]^2 × Number of test runs.

Sum of the Squares for Error: $SS_{Error} = SS_{Total} -$ [$SS_{Factors} + SS_{Interactions} + SS_{Replications}$]

Using the three levels of data from the parameter design DOE with the main effects and interactions for diameter and location, we get:

$$SS_{Diameter} \quad = \quad 9.60$$

$$SS_{Location} \quad = \quad 1143.60$$

$$SS_{Dia \times Loc} \quad = \quad 45.60$$

$$SS_{Dia \times Loc} \quad = \quad .6045$$

$$SS_{Total} \quad = \quad 1244.40$$

$$SS_{Error} = 1311.84 - 1244.40 = 67.44$$

Step 5.   Calculate the Mean Squares Next we calculate the mean squares (MS) for each factor, interaction, replication and error. The mean squares are the sum of the Squares divided by the Degrees of Freedom:

$$MS = \frac{SUM\ OF\ THE\ SQUARES}{DEGREES\ OF\ FREEDOM}$$

Using the three levels of data from the parameter design DOE using the main effects and interactions for diameter and location.

$$MS_{DIAMETER} = \frac{9.60}{2} = 4.80$$

$$MS_{LOCATION} = \frac{1143.60}{2} = 571.80$$

$$MS_{DIA\ X\ LOC} = \frac{45.60}{2} = 22.80$$

$$MS_{ERROR} = \frac{67.44}{81} = 0.83$$

Step 6.   Calculate the F_{Ratio} Calculate the F_{Ratio} for each treatment and interaction by dividing the mean square for the factor or interaction by the mean square for error.

$$F_{Ratio} = \frac{Mean\ Squares\ for\ Factors/Interactions}{Mean\ Squares\ for\ Error}$$

Using the three levels of data from the parameter design DOE using the main effects and interactions for diameter and location.

$$F_{DIAMETER} = \frac{4.80}{0.83} = 5.78$$

$$F_{LOCATION} = \frac{571.80}{0.83} = 688.92$$

$$F_{DIA \times LOC} = \frac{22.80}{0.83} = 27.47$$

Step 7.   Determine the critical value of F (F_{Crit}) Using the F Table in Appendix A for each factor and interaction at the 0.05 or 0.01 level of significance (95% or 99% confidence level) respectively. The F Table columns represent the degrees of freedom in the numerator, and the rows represent the degrees of freedom in the denominator:

$$F_{Crit} = F_{\alpha}, df$$

Using the data from the parameter design DOE, for the main effects and interactions for diameter and location, we get the following:

Factor	F Ratio	F Critical		Significance
		.95	.99	
Diameter	5.78	3.11	4.90	Significant
Location	688.92	3.11	4.90	Highly Significant
Diam × Loc	27.47	3.11	4.90	Highly Significant

Step 8.   Calculate the Pure Sum of the Squares Calculate the pure sum of the squares (SS') as indicated in the following equation:

$$SS' = SS_{Factor} - [MS_{Error} \times df_{Factor}]$$

Using the data from the parameter design DOE, for the main effects and interactions for diameter and location, we obtain these results:

$$SS'_{Diameter} = 9.60 - [0.83 \times 2] = 9.60 - 1.66 = 7.94$$

$$SS'_{Location} = 1143.60 - [0.83 \times 2] = 1143.60 - 1.66 = 1141.94$$

$$SS'_{Diam \times Loc} = 45.60 - [0.83 \times 2] = 45.60 - 1.66 = 43.94$$

Step 9. Determine the Percent Contribution   Calculate the percentage of the contribution to variability for each factor, interaction and replication using the following equation:

$$\% \text{ Contribution} = \frac{\text{Pure Sum of the Squares}}{\text{Total Sum of the Squares}} \times 100$$

To calculate the percent contribution for error ($\% \text{CONT}_{Error}$), use the following equation:

$$\% \text{ CONT}_{Error} = 100 - \Sigma [\% \text{ Contribution of all}$$
$$\text{Factors/Interactions/Replicates}]$$

Using the data from the parameter design DOE, for the main effects and interactions for diameter and location, we obtain:

$$\% \text{ CONT}_{DIAMETER} = \frac{7.94}{1311.84} \times 100 = 0.61\%$$

$$\% \text{ CONT}_{LOCATION} = \frac{1141.94}{1311.84} \times 100 = 87.05\%$$

$$\% \text{ CONT}_{DIAM \times LOC} = \frac{43.94}{1311.84} \times 100 = 3.35\%$$

$$\% \text{ CON}_{Error} = 100 - [0.61 + 87.05 + 3.35 + 3.35]$$
$$= 100 - 94.36 = 5.64\%$$

Now that we have completed all the calculations for a Taguchi-Style ANOVA, we can place the information into a familiar ANOVA table. This ANOVA table looks much like the ones we have seen in the classical approach to DOE, and

can be interpreted in much the same way. Figure 10-34 demonstrates the
Taguchi ANOVA Table for the data we have used in developing the steps.

SOURCE OF VARIATION	df	SUM OF SQUARES	MEAN SQUARES	F	CONF LEVEL	PURE SUM OF SQUARES	% CONT
1. DIAMETER	2	9.6	4.8	5.78	99%	7.94	0.61%
2. LOCATION	2	1143.6	571.8	688.92	99%	1141.94	87.05%
3. DIAM X LOC	2	45.6	22.8	27.47	99%	43.94	3.35%
4. DIAM X LOC	2	45.6	22.8	27.47	99%	43.94	3.35%
ERROR	81	67.44	0.83				5.64%
TOTAL	89	1311.84					100.00%

Figure 10-34. Taguchi ANOVA Table

With the Taguchi ANOVA Table fact-based decision making becomes almost effortless. It is clear that all factors are making significant contributions to
variation, but the degree of that contribution is clearly greater for location. The
location factor is contributing 87.05% of the total variation.

KEY POINTS

The most direct route to Continuous Measurable Improvement is variability reduction. Reducing the variability of your process has a direct and immediate effect upon product and service defects, whether the products are goods, services, management or administration. The business leader must, therefore, have confidence in the information used to make improvement decisions. All improvement programs to achieve world class competition must start with an indepth understanding of the voice of the customer. It is crucial to understand what is expected in the marketplace and to establish the product and process parameters accordingly.

THE IMPROVEMENT PROCESS

To integrate the technical tools of Process Analysis and Product and Process Control with the new tools of Analysis of Variance (ANOVA) and Design of Experiments (DOE), we use the improvement process model presented in Figure 10-2. These tools will allow us to structure continuous measurable improvement efforts for new and existing products and processes. This is best accomplished by usine the model to integrate the improvement tools of:

➤ **Process Analysis**

➤ **Process Control**

➤ **Quality Fubction Deployment**

➤ **Analysis of Variance**

➤ **Design of Experiments**

ANALYSIS OF VARIANCE

Analysis of Variance (ANOVA) is an important tool for making business and technical decisions. It tells us whether several different treatments (for example, different manufacturing processes) all have the same effect on the quality characteristics of interest. "The purpose of analysis of variance, as its name implies, is to determine how much of the variation among observations is due to *variation* in each factor influencing the characteristic being studied."

METHODS OF DOE

The several methods of performing Design of Experiments provide specific capabilities and have specific limitations. The following approaches to Design of Experiments apply most directly to management, industrial and administrative processes of concern to business.

> ➤ **Full factorial designs:** Full factorial experimental designs provide a comprehensive analysis of all treatments, levels, and interactions related to a selected quality characteristic.

> ➤ **Fractional factorial designs:**   In such cases (which constitute the majority), fractional factorial designed experiments provide a reasonable alternative that still allows for the evaluation of main effects and key interactions, but requires fewer trial runs. To achieve this result we confound the higher order interactions (three or greater) with the main effect and two way interactions.

> ➤ **Screening designs:** The purpose of screening designs is to determine main effects. Screening designs can identify and optimize process variability and help to improve process capability.

> ➤ **Taguchi designs:** Taguchi designs are a special case of screening experiments. They provide for the evaluation of key two way interactions as well as main effects of the treatments. The Taguchi method uses orthogonal arrays that are condensed forms of the full factorial arrays previously presented in this chapter.

EXAMPLE

The QFD manufacturing/purchasing matrix for the LWCI 1600 series manufacturing equipment, stated MTBF as a critical engineering design element of the new system. The benchmark requirement for this system MTBF is 3000 hours as stated in the QFD (Chapter 9). The Electronic Control Division of LWCI was tasked to provide a digital control assembly that met this basic system requirement.

A team consisting of the LWCI 1600 program management, design engineers, service personnel and analysists met to determine the approach to providing the needed assembly. The team first evaluated all the available process data for the existing assembly. From this data, they determined that the controller A12 board was the most significant contributor to MTBF for the digital control assembly. The customer service department's historical data, on this board indicated that it currently exhibited an MTBF of 2750 operating hours in the customer's environment.

The team then performed a Cause and Effect Analysis, using additional subject experts, to determine what factors contributed to the A12 board MTBF. The resulting analysis is demonstrated in Example Figure 10-1.

Based upon this Cause and Effect Analysis and the knowledge of the subject specialists, the team selected three factors or treatments that could contribute most significantly to MTBF:

Board Supplier LWCI is using two board suppliers for existing digital controllers. The boards had the same performance characteristics, but the suppliers produced them using different methods and technologies. Both boards had previously met all LWCI supplier quality requirements and were one-to-one interchangeable. These treatments will be Supplier A1 and Supplier A2.

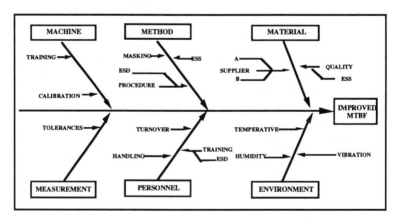

Example Figure 10-1. Cause and Effect Analysis

Vibration Protection The vibration induced upon the assembly by the equipment itself and by the customer's environment was a concern to the subject specialists and the system engineers. The existing controller assembly and its associated boards are assembled to the system without any special vibration damping. The treatments will be called, Vibration Protection (Damper) B1 and No Vibration Protection B2.

Electro-Static Discharge (ESD) Sensitivity to ESD had not been very well defined in the past. LWCI is currently using ESD standards that are acceptable in the industry. There was very little information on the effects of ESD, and no known correlation between ESD and customer service calls for the existing systems. The engineers and subject experts wanted to determine if, in fact, ESD had any effect on system service life. Improved ESD protection standards, devices and training are available. The treatments selected for this evaluation are, Existing ESD Standards C1 and Improved ESD Standards C2.

The team determined that the experimental results would be expressed (quality characteristic, output variable, dependent variable) as hours MTBF. The experimental process would be incorporated at the end of the ESS cycle as an accelerated life cycle test and the systems would be tested to failure or to the equivalent of 3,750 hours (125% of requirement). There was a consensus among the team members no interactions would be significant. Therefore, the designed experiment considered the following factors:

➤ **Treatment A:** Supplier

➤ **Treatment B:** Vibration Protection

➤ **Treatment C:** ESD Protection

➤ **Experimental Results:** Hours MTBF

The resulting design matrix is demonstrated in Example Figure 10-2. To evaluate this experiment completely for main effects and interactions would require a 2^3 full factorial experiment or eight test runs. The expense and time requirements for accelerated life cycle testing are significant and are of concern to the team and management. Therefore a Taguchi L_4 orthogonal array was selected as meeting these needs and the requirements for orthogonality. Example Figure 10-3 demonstrates the orthogonal array for the MTBF improvement experiment.

The team next prepared a worksheet for the experiment to manage the data more effectively and to estimate the data management requirements. The resulting worksheet is demonstrated in Example Figure 10-4.

The experiment was then run, using the data from four samples after initial ESS was completed. The resulting data table is shown in Example Figure 10-5

		A SUPPLIER			
		A1	A2		
B DAMPING	B1	A1B1C1	A2B1C1	C1	ESD PROTECTION C
		A1B1C2	A2B1C2	C2	
	B2	A1B2C1	A2B2C1	C1	
		A1B2C2	A2B2C2	C2	

Example Figure 10-2. Test Matrix

COLUMN	TREATMENT		
	1	**2**	**3**
RUN	**SUPPLIER**	**VIBRATION**	**ESD**
1	+	+	+
2	+	-	-
3	-	+	-
4	-	-	+

Example Figure 10-3. MTBF Experiment Orthogonal Array

COLUNM	1	2	3	RESULTS			
RUN				1	2	3	4
1	+	+	+				
2	+	-	-				
3	-	+	-				
4	-	-	+				

Example Figure 10-4. MTBF Experiment Work Sheet

COLUMN	1	2	3	RESULTS				
RUN				1	2	3	4	TOTAL
1	+	+	+	5365	5791	4902	5523	21581
2	+	-	-	4615	5110	4790	4988	19503
3	-	+	-	5112	4976	5378	5500	20966
4	-	-	+	5045	4798	5110	4811	19764
LEVEL 1	5135.5	5318.38	5168.13	GRAND AVERAGE = 5113				
LEVEL 2	5091.25	4908.38	5058.63					

Example Figure 10-5. MTBF Data Table

The next step in evaluating the Taguchi DOE for improving MTBF is to determine the level effects and total effects. To accomplish this, the team used the spreadsheet in Example Figure 10- 6.

TREATMENT	NAME	LEVEL	LEVEL MEAN	LEVEL EFFECT	TOTAL EFFECT
A	SUPP	+	5135.5	22.5	
		-	5091.25	-22.5	
B	VIB	+	5318.38	205	410
		-	4908.38	-205	
C	ESD	+	5168.13	55	
		-	5058.63	-55	

Example Figure 10-6. MTBF Level and Total Effect

Example Figure 7 provides a graphical representation of the level effects and total effects calculated from the Taguchi DOE. To determine the level of significance of the effects and the percent contribution the team then performed a Taguchi-Style ANOVA. The first three steps of the Taguchi ANOVA can be extracted directly from the calculations for the DOE in Example Figure 10-6.

Grand Average From Example Figure 10-5, the grand average for this data is 5113.

Level Mean: From Example Figure 10-6, The level means are:

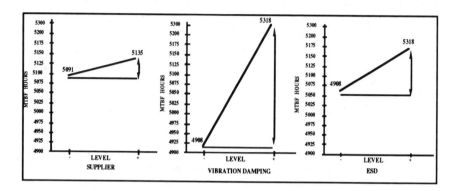

Example Figure 10-7. DOE Graph

LEVEL MEANS

LEVEL	TREATMENT A	TREATMENT B	TREATMENT C
LEVEL +	5135.50	5318.38	5168.13
LEVEL -	5091.25	4908.38	5058.63

Effects: From Example Figure 10-6, the level and total effects are, as shown below:

LEVEL EFFECTS

LEVEL	TREATMENT A	TREATMENT B	TREATMENT C
LEVEL +	22.5	205	55
LEVEL -	-22.5	-205	-55

TOTAL EFFECT 410

Sum of the Squares Total   The total Sun of the Squares was calculated using the spreadsheet in Example Figure 10-8 .

Sum of the Squares Treatments   The sum of the squares for treatments was calculated as shown in Example Figure 10-9.

Sum of the Squares for Replicates All samples taken for this DOE were repeats, there are no replicates.

Sum of the Squares for Error The sum of the squares for error can now be calculated. Recall that interactions are not being studied and that there were no replicates in this experiment.

$$SS_{Error} = SS_{Total} - SS_{Treatments}$$

$$SS_{Error} = 1,537,602 - 8,100 - 674,895 - 49,515 = 805,092$$

SAMPLE	X	X–5113	$(X-5113)^2$
1	5365	252	63504
2	4615	-498	248004
3	5112	-1	1
4	5045	-68	4624
5	5791	678	459684
6	5110	-3	9
7	4976	-137	18769
8	4798	-315	99225
9	4902	-211	44521
10	4790	-323	104329
11	5378	265	70225
12	5110	-3	9
13	5523	410	168100
14	4988	-125	15625
15	5500	387	149769
16	4811	-302	91204
		$\Sigma (X-5113)^2 = 1537602$	

Example Figure 10-8. SS_{Total}

Mean Squares The mean squares can now be calculated. As explained previously in the chapter the degrees of freedom are N-1=15 for total, T-1=1 for each treatment and by subtraction for error. Therefore we can calculate Mean Squares as:

$$MS_A = \frac{8,100}{1} = 8,100$$

$$MS_B = \frac{674,895}{1} = 674,895$$

$$MS_C = \frac{49,515}{1} = 49,515$$

$$MS_{Error} = \frac{49,515}{12} = 67,691$$

F Ratio The next step in the ANOVA is the calculation of the F_{Ratio} for each treatment:

$$F_A = \frac{8100}{67,091} = 0.121$$

$$F_B = \frac{674,895}{67,091} = 1.100$$

$$F_C = \frac{49,515}{67,091} = 0.738$$

F Critical To determine the critical value of F (F'), the team needed to determine the level of significance to be applied to this ANOVA. Since this was a process improvement effort a level of significance of .05 ($\alpha = .05$) was used. From the F Table in Appendix A the critical value of F was determined to be:

$$F' = 4.75$$

Pure Sum of The Squares The pure sum of the squares (SS') was the next calculation the team needed to perform. The SS' for treatments were calculated as following:

$$SS'_A = 8,100 - (67,091 \times 1) = -58,991$$

$$SS'_B = 674,895 - (67,091 \times 1) = 607,804$$

$$SS'_C = 49,515 - (67,091 \times 1) = -17,516$$

SUM OF THE SQUARES TREATMENT A			SUM OF THE SQUARES TREATMENT B		
	LEVEL +	LEVEL -		LEVEL +	LEVEL -
LEVEL MEAN	5135.5	5091.25	LEVEL MEAN	5318.38	4908.38
LEVEL EFFECT	22.5	-22.5	LEVEL EFFECT	205.38	-205.38
(LEVEL EFFECT)2	506.25	506.25	(LEVEL EFFECT)2	42180.94	42180.94
OBSERVATIONS	8	8	OBSERVATIONS	8	8
SS LEVELS A	4050	4050	SS LEVELS B	337447.6	337447.6
SS TREATMENT A = 8100			SS TREATMENT B = 674895.1		

SUM OF THE SQUARES TREATMENT C		
	LEVEL +	LEVEL -
LEVEL MEAN	5168.63	5058.63
LEVEL EFFECT	55.63	55.63
(LEVEL EFFECT)2	3094.697	3094.697
OBSERVATIONS	8	8
SS LEVELS C	24757.58	24757.58
SS TREATMENT C = 49515.15		

Example Figure 10-9. $SS_{Treatments}$

Percent Contribution   The percent contribution is the next Taguchi ANOVA element to be calculated:

$$\% \, Cont_A = \frac{58,991}{1,537,602} \times 100 = 3.84\%$$

$$\% \, Cont_B = \frac{607,804}{1,537,602} \times 100 = 39.53\%$$

$$\% \, Cont_C = \frac{17,516}{1,537,602} \times 100 = 1.14\%$$

% ContError $= 100 - 3.84 - 39.53 - 1.14 = 55.49\%$

The team then placed all this data into the Taguchi ANOVA Table in Example Figure 10-10 to evaluate the results. The team evaluated the results of the analysis and was able to make the following "fact-based decisions"

> **Treatment B is making a significant contribution to the MTBF of the A12 Board in this experiment.**

> **Treatments A and C are not significant.**

> **Treatment B is contributing 39.34% of the total variation in MTBF.**

> **Due to the relatively large SS, MS and percent contribution for error, there may be significant contributors to MTBF that were not considered in this DOE or that are attributable to common cause variation.**

SOURCE OF VARIATION	df	SS	MS	F	F'	SS'	% CONT
A	1	8100	8100	0.121	4.75	58991	3.84
B	1	674895	674895	10.10	4.75	607804	39.53
C	1	49515	49515	0.738	4.75	17516	1.14
ERROR	12	805092	67091				55.49
TOTAL	15	1537602					

Example Figure 10-10. MTBF DOE Taguchi ANOVA Table

Based upon this information the team determined that optimization of the MTBF would occur with all treatments are set at the high level (+), based upon the "greater is better" principle. Therefore, the estimate of the results of the optimized function is :

$$\hat{Y} = 5113 + (5135.5 - 5113) + (5318.2 - 5113) + (5168.1 - 5113)$$

$$= 5133 + 22.5 + 205.38 + 55.13 = \mathbf{5416.01}$$

Based upon the results of this designed experiment the team determined that the QFD design and manufacturing matrix goal of 5000 hours could be met by the

A12 controller board with an optimized MTBF of 5416. The team also determined that there were other opportunities to improve MTBF based upon Treatments, Interactions, Environment and other factors not included in this study. The team recommended damping as a vibration protection as the most significant contribution to MTBF.

NOTE

1. The New Quality Technologies, Dr. Jack B Revelle, Hughes Aircraft Company 1992, used with permission.

Glossary

Accuracy: The deviation of measures or observed values from the true value.

Advanced Statistical Methods: A term used by statisticians, members of secret handshake societies and consultants to convince business people that they cannot survive without them.

Alias: The alternative factor(s) which could cause an observed effect due to confounding.

Analysis of Variance (ANOVA/AOV): In design of experiments, a method of investigation which determines how much each factor contributes to the overall variation from the mean. Also determines the amount of variation produced by a change in levels and the amount due to random error.

Analytical Approach (to management improvement): an approach based on learning from the evaluation of past experience.

Attribute Data: Pass/fail, qualitative data that can be counted binomially. These includes the presence or absence of specific characteristics such as conformance to a specification. pas or fail on a go-no go gauge.

Automation (Jidohka): A word coined to describe a feature of the Toyota production system whereby a machine is designed to stop automatically whenever a defective part is produced.

Average: The sum of a group of values divided by the number of values (n). The average is designated by the symbol ($\overline{X}$), the grand average of several groups of data is designated by the symbol ($\overline{\overline{X}}$).

Awareness: Understanding the interrelationship of quality and productivity. Knowing the management and technical tools needed to achieve continuous measurable improvement.

Balanced Design: An experimental design which has an equal distribution of levels within each factor.

Basic Statistical Methods: The applied theory of variation used for statistical process control, design of experiments, loss function, analysis of variance and many other useful evaluation tools.

Bigger is Better Characteristic: Performance characteristic that gives improved performance as the value of the characteristic increases, e.g., tensile strength.

Binomial Distribution: A discreet Probability Distribution for attribute data, that is applied to pass/fail and go/no go attribute data.

Block: A block is a stratum of data that is homogeneous.

Blocking: A technique to eliminate nuisance factors by setting them as extra factors in the experiment, often using up the higher order interaction columns to save resources.

Capability: Process Capability

Cause and Effect Diagram: A comprehensive tool used to focus problem solving. This is also called a fishbowl diagram or Ishikawa diagram.

Central Line: The line on a control chart that represents the average or median value of the items being plotted.

Characteristic: A distinguishing feature of a process or its output on which variables or attributes data can be collected.

Check Points and Control Points: Both check points and control points are used in measuring the progress of improvement-related activities between different managerial levels. Check points represent process-oriented criteria. Control points represent result-oriented criteria. What is the check point to the manager becomes a control point to the next-level manager. For this reason, check points and control points are also used in policy deployment.

Column Modification: Modifying an O. A. to allow for fewer (Column Degrading) or greater (Column Upgrading) number of levels to be evaluated.

Common Cause: A source of variation that affects all the individual values of the process output being studied: in control chart analysis it appears as part of the random process variation.

Comparative Experiments: An experiment whose objective is to compare the treatments rather than to determine absolute values.

Confirmation Experiment: A designed experiment which defines improved conditions of produce/process design. An experimental run at these conditions is intended to verify the experimental predictions.

Confounding: Confusing. Where two factors (or interactions) are inseparable in regard to their effect on the response. Used to advantage by confounding high order interactions which have no practical value.

Consecutive: Units of output produced in succession; a basis for selecting subgroup samples.

Control: See Statistical Control.

Control Chart: A graphic representation of a characteristic of a process, showing plotted values of some statistic gathered from that characteristic, a central line, and one or two control limits. It minimizes the net economic loss from Type I and Type II errors. It has two basic uses: as a judgment to determine if a process has been operating in statistical control, and as an operation to aid in maintaining statistical control.

Control: A line (or lines) on a control chart used as a basis for judging the significance of the variation from subgroup to subgroup. Variation beyond a control limit is evidence that special causes are affecting the process. Control limits are calculated from process data and are not to be confused with engineering specifications.

Cross-Functional Management: The inter-departmental coordination required to realize the policy goals of a KAIZEN and a Total Quality Control program. After corporate strategy and planning are determined, top management sets objectives for cross-functional efforts that cut laterally throughout the organization.

Cross functional management is the major organizational tool for realizing TQC improvement goals. (While cross-functional management may resemble certain Western managerial techniques, it is distinguished from them by an intensive focus on the follow-through to achieve the success of goals and measures.)

Degrees of Freedom (DF): The number of independent values associated with a given factor (usually the number of a factor levels minus 1).

Deming Cycle: The concept of a continuously rotating wheel used by W. E. Deming to emphasize the necessity of constant interaction among research, design, production, and sales so as to arrive at an improved quality that satisfies customers (See PDCA Cycle).

Design Approach (to management improvement): tries to build a better approach through predetermined goals. The design approach should receive greater attention in future applications of the management process.

Design of Experiments: The planned, structured and organized observation of two or more input/independent variables (factors) and their affect on the output/dependent variable(s) under study.

Detection: A past-oriented strategy that attempts to identify unacceptable output after it has been produced and then separate it from the good output (see also prevention).

Distribution: A way of describing the output of a common-cause system of variation, in which individual values are not predictable but in which the outcomes as a group form a pattern that can be described in terms of its location, spread, and shape. Location is commonly expressed by the mean or average, or by the median; spread is expressed in terms of the standard deviation or the range of a sample: shape involves many characteristics such as symmetry and peakedness, but these are often summarized by using the name of a common distribution such as the normal, binomial or Poison.

Effect: The change in level of the response variable due to the change in a factor; the average response at the high level of a factor minus the average response at the low level of a factor. There are both main effect (due to single factors) and interaction effects.

Effect of a Factor: The effect of a factor is the change in response produced by a change in the level of the factor. (Applicable only for factors at two levels each.)

Experiment: A planned set of operations which leads to a corresponding set of observations.

Experimental Error: Failure of two identical treatments to yield the same response; process standard deviation present during the experiment; sigma of the experiment.

Experimental Run: A combination of experimental conditions which is required to produce experimental results; a treatment combination; a cell in the design.

Experimental Condition: A specific combination of factors and levels to be evaluated in a designed experiment.

Experimental Unit: One item to which a single treatment is applied in one replication of the basic experiment.

F Test: A means for determining statistical significance of a factor by comparing calculated F values to those contained in an F Table.

F Value: A ratio of the factor effect to the random error effect within a designed experiment.

Factor: A processing variable whose level may change the response variable; a method, material, machine, person, environment, or measurement variable changed during the experiment in an attempt to cause change in a response variable; independent variable.

Factorial Experiment: An experiment in which at least one experimental observation is made for each distinct treatment combination.

Fractional Factorial: An abbreviated version of a full factorial designed experiment which reduces the minimum number of experimental runs, but which introduces confounding.

Full Factorial: A balanced, designed experiment which tests each possible combination of levels that can be formed from the input/independent factors.

Factor-Independent Variable: A feature of the experimental conditions which may be varied from one observation to another. May be qualitative or quantitative, fixed or random.

Homoscedasticity: Constant common cause variation across all levels of all factors.

Individual: A single unit, or a single measurement of characteristic.

Improvement: Improvement as a part of a successful KAIZEN strategy goes beyond the dictionary definition of the word. Improvement is a mind-set inextricably linked to maintaining and improving standards. In a still broader sense, improvement can be defined as leadership and innovation, where a leadership strategy maintains and improves the working standard through small, gradual improvements and innovation calls forth radical improvements as a result of large investments in technology and/or equipment.

A successful leadership strategy clearly delineates responsibility for maintaining standards to the worker, with management's role being the improvement of standards. The Japanese perception of management boils down to one precept: maintain and improve standards.

Inner Array: Used in parameter design, it is that portion of a designed experiment which contains the O. A. for the controllable factors.

Interaction: If the effect of one factor is different at different levels of another factor, the two factors are said to interact or to have interaction.

Interaction Effect: The effects on the output/dependent response variable caused by the combination of two or more factors, independent of their individual effects. An interaction exists between two or more factors if the response curve of one or more factors is dependent upon the level of other factor(s).

Just-in-Time: A production and inventory control technique that is part of the Toyota production system. It was designed and perfected at Toyota by Taiichi Ohno specifically to cut waste in production.

KAIZEN: Means improvement. Moreover it means continuing improvement in personal life, home life, social life, and working life. When applied to the workplace it means continuing improvement involving everyone-managers and workers alike.

Levels of a Factor: The various values of a factor considered in the experiment are called levels.

Linear Graph: A series of numbered lines and dots with one-to-one correspondence to the columns of a related O. A. Each linear graph is associated with one O. A., however, an O>A. can have several linear graphs. Linear graphs facilitate assignment of factors to specific columns of an O. A. See triangular tables which perform the same function.

Location: A general concept for the typical values or central tendency of a distribution.

Loss Function: See quality loss function.

Main Effect: The average effect of a factor is called the main effect of the factor.

Maintenance: Refers to activities that are directed to maintaining current technological, managerial and operating standards.

Mean: The average of values in a group of measurements.

Mean Square (V): The average deviation from the target value or nominal specification.

Nested Design: A n experimental design used to estimate the components of variation at various stages of a sampling plan or analytical test method.

Noise Factor: Any uncontrollable factor that causes a product's quality characteristic to vary is called noise. There are three types of noise:

1. Noise due to external causes, such as temperature, humidity, etc.

2. Noise due to internal causes, such as wear, deterioration.

3. Noise due to part-to-part variation.

Nominal is Best Characteristic: Performance characteristic that has an attainable target or nominal value, e. g., length, voltage, etc.

Non-Comparative Experiments: An experiment who's objective is the determination of the characteristics of a population.

Nonconforming Unit: A unit or units that do not conform to a specification or standard. These can also be called discrepant or defective units. p and np control charts are used to measure and analyze processes producing nonconforming units.

Nonconformity's: Specific occurrences of a condition which does not conform to specifications or other inspection standards: sometimes called discrepancies or defects. An individual nonconforming unit can have the potential for more than one nonconformity (a door could have several dents and dings; a functional check of a carburetor could reveal any of a number of potential discrepancies) c and u control charts are used to analyze systems producing nonconformity's.

Normal Distribution: A continuous, symmetrical, bell-shaped frequency distribution for variables data that underlies the control charts for variables. When measurements have a normal distribution, about 68.26% of all individuals lie within plus or minus one standard deviation unit of the mean, about 95.44% lie within plus and minus two standard deviation units of the mean, and about 99.73% lie within plus and minus three standard deviation units of the mean. These percentages are the basis for control limits and control chart analysis (since subgroup averages are normally distributed even if the output as a whole is not), and for many capability decisions (since the output of many industrial processes follows the normal distribution).

Nuisance: A nuisance factor affects the process but is not of interest in this experiment, e.g. ,a difference in raw materials which we are already managing.

Off-Line Quality Control: Methods which focus on product and process design and experimentation.

On-Line Quality Control: Methods which focus on production, corrective actions, and process control. Includes the use of the Seven QC Tools (statistical Process Control).

Operational Definition: A means of clearly communicating quality expectations and performance. It consists of (1) a criterion to be applied to an object or to a group; (2) a test of the object or of the group; (3) a decision: yes or no--the object or the group did or did not meet the criterion.

Optimal Condition: That combination of factors and levels that produces the most desirable results.

Orthogonal Array (O.A.): A matrix of numbers arranged in rows and columns. Each row represents the state of the factors in a given experiment, Each column represents a specific factor, variable or condition that can be changed between experimental runs. The array is called orthogonal because the effects of the various factors resulting from an experiment can be separated, one from the other.

Outcome (Response) Dependent Variable: The result of a trial with a given treatment is called a response.

Outer Array: Used in parameter design, it is that portion of a designed experiment which contains the O.A. for the uncontrollable, environmental or noise factors.

Parameter Design: The design stage where parameter (factor) levels of performance characteristic are determined so that a product functions at an optimal performance level (least variability/cost).

Pareto Diagram: An important tool for problem solving that involves ranking all potential problem areas or sources of variation according to their contribution to cost or to total variation. Typically, a few causes account for most of the cost (or variation), so problem-solving efforts are best prioritized to concentrate on the "vital few" causes, temporarily ignoring the "trivial many."

PDCA Cycle: Plan, Do, Check, Action—An adaptation of the Deming Wheel. Where the Deming Wheel stresses the need for constant interaction among research, design, production, and sales, the PDCA Cycle asserts that every managerial action can be improved by careful application of the sequence; plan, do check, action.

Percent Contribution: The amount of influence each factor contributes to the variation in the experimental results.

Performance Characteristic: The resultant of a designed experiment to be evaluated. Taguchi uses three criteria to evaluate performance characteristics; bigger is better, smaller is better, and nominal is best.

Poisson Distribution: A discrete probability distribution for attributes data applies to nonconformity's and underlies the c and u control charts.

Policy Deployment: The process of implementing the policies of a leadership program directly through line managers and indirectly through cross-functional organization.

Policy Prioritization: A technique to ensure maximum utilization of resources at all levels of management in the process of policy deployment. Top management's policy statement must be restated at all management levels in increasingly specific and action-oriented goals, eventually becoming precise quantitative values.

Pooling: Following an ANOVA/AOV, the combining of factors which have minimal percent contribution.

Precision: A measurement's precision is related to its repeatability in terms of the deviation of a group of observations from a mean value. While the terms accuracy and precision are often used interchangeably, they could be distinguished as accuracy being the measure of the approach to a true value, while precision is a measure of consistency or repeatability.

Prevention: A future-oriented strategy that improves quality and productivity by direction analysis and action toward correcting the process itself. Prevention is consistent with a philosophy of never-ending improvement. (see also Detection)

Problem-Solving: The process of moving from symptoms to causes (special or common) to actions that improve performance. Among the techniques that can be used are Pareto Charts, Cause-and-effect diagrams and statistical process control techniques.

Process: The combination of people, equipment, materials, methods, and environment that produce output--a given product or service. A process can involve any aspect of our business. A key tool for managing processes is statistical process control.

Process Average: The location of the distribution of measured values of a particular process characteristic, usually designated as an overall average, X.

Process Control: See Statistical Process Control.

Process-Oriented Management: A style of management that is also people oriented in contrast to one that is oriented solely toward results.

Process Spread: The extent to which the distribution of individual values of the process characteristic vary: often shown as the process average plus or minus some number of standard deviations (such as $X + 3$).

Pure Sum of Squares (S): A value not used in classical/traditional ANOVA/AOV, but used in Taguchi-style ANOVA/AOV, to account for the degrees of freedom and the mean square error when determining the percent contribution.

QC (Quality Control): A system of means to economically produce goods or services that satisfy customer requirements.

Qualitative: Levels of the variable may be changed only to discrete levels, e.g., off/on, machine A vs. B

Quantitative: Levels of the variable may be changed on some underlying continuous scale, e.g., pressure.

Quasi-interaction effect: A crude estimate of an interaction from a screening design.

Quality: Taguchi's Definition is "the minimum loss imparted by the Product to society from the time the product is shipped."

Quality Assurance: Quality assurance means assuring that the quality of the product is satisfactory, reliable, and yet economical for the customer.

Quality Characteristic: See Performance Characteristic.

Quality Deployment: A technique to deploy customer requirements (known as "true quality characteristics") into designing characteristics (known as "counterpart characteristics") and deploy them into such subsystems as components, parts, and production processes.

Quality Loss Function: Parabolic Approximation of the financial loss which results when performance characteristic deviates from its best (or target)value.

Randomness: A condition in which individual values are not predictable, although they may come from a definable distribution.

Randomization: Chance assignment of experimental units to treatment combinations so that any systematic trends do not bias the results.

Range: The difference between the highest and lowest values in a subgroup. The expected range increases both with sample size and with the standard deviation.

Reflection: A copy of the original design with "+" and "-" signs transposed. Retains attractive features when combined with the original design. Allows main effect estimates clear of two factor interactions.

Repeat: A additional experimental run which can be used to estimate part of the experimental error from the range between repeats but which does not include all sources of experimental error.

Repeatability: Describes the measurement variation obtained when one person measures the same dimension or characteristic several times with the same gage or test equipment (sometimes referred to as "equipment variation").

Replicate: An additional experimental run which can be used to estimate experimental error from the range between replicates; includes all sources of experimental error.

Response Variable: A characteristic whose distribution

you wish to change, i.e., its mean, variance, or shape: Dependent variable, quality output characteristic; usually one of the key variables identified in Step 2 of the Eight-Step Procedure.

Reproducibility:
A term popularized in the automotive industry as representing the variation in measurement averages when more than one person measures the same dimension or characteristic using the same measuring instrument.

Response: The numerical result of a trial based on a given treatment combination.

Results-Oriented Management:
This style of management is well established in the West and emphasizes controls, performance, results, rewards (usually financial), or the denial of rewards and even penalties. Criteria, or R Criteria, are easily quantifiable and short term. Western style management emphasizes R Criteria almost exclusively.

Robust: Products/process designs that function with reduced variability in spite of diverse and changing conditions of environment, wear or component-to component variations, i.e., insensitivity of product/process performance to the presence of noise.

Run: A consecutive number of points consistently increasing or decreasing, or above or below the central line. Can be evidence of the existence of special causes of variation.

Run Chart: A simple graphic representation of a characteristic of a process, showing plotted values of some statistic gathered from the process (often individual values) and a central line (often the median of the values), which can be analyzed for runs. (See also Control Chart).

Sample: In process control applications, a synonym with subgroup; this use is totally different from the purpose of providing an estimate of a larger group of people or items.

Shape: A general concept for the overall pattern formed by a distribution of values.

Sigma (σ): The Greek letter used to designate a standard deviation.

Signal Factor: With dynamic characteristics, a factor which controls responses in a specified or designed manner. In measurement studies, a factor used o generate different measurement results.

Signal-To-Noise Ratio (S/N): S/N is a metric used to project (from experimental results) field performance. S/N is calculated in decibels and depends on the type of characteristic being considered. See Performance Characteristic.

Smaller is Better Characteristic: Performance characteristics belonging to the category of characteristics having zero as a vest value, e.g., wear, deterioration.

Special Cause: A source of variation that is intermittent, unpredictable, unstable: sometimes called an assignable cause. It is signaled by a point beyond the control limits or a run or other non-random patterns of points within the control limits.

Specification: The engineering requirement for judging acceptability of a particular characteristic. A specification is never to be confused with a control limit.

Spread: A general concept for the extent by which values in a distribution differ from one another: dispersion.

Stability (for Gage Studies): The variation in the measurement averages when the measuring instrument values are recorded over a specified time interval.

Stability (for control charts): The absence of special causes of variation; the property of being in statistical control.

Stable Process: A process that is in statistical control.

Standard Deviation: A measure of the spread of the process output or the spread of a sampling statistic from the process (of subgroup averages): denoted by the Greek letter (sigma) (σ).

Statistic: A value calculated from or based upon sample data (a subgroup average or range), used to make inferences about the process that produced the output from which the sample came.

Statistical Control: The condition describing a process from which all special causes of variation have been eliminated and only common causes remain: evidenced on a control chart by the absence of points beyond the control limits and by the absence of non-random patterns or trends within the control limits.

Statistical Process Control: The use of statistical techniques such as control charts to analyze a process or its outputs so as to take appropriate actions to achieve and maintain a state of statistical control and to improve the process capability.

Subgroup: One or more events or measurements used to analyze the performance of a process. Rational subgroups are usually chosen so that the variation represented within each subgroup is as small as feasible for the process (representing the variation from common causes). and so that any changes in the process performance (special causes) will appear as differences between subgroups. Rational subgroups are typically made up of consecutive pieces, although random samples are sometimes used.

Suggestion System: The Japanese system emphasizes morale-boosting benefits and positive employee participation over the economic and financial incentives that are stressed in the American-style systems.

System Design: The first stage in product design where engineering knowledge is applied to select materials, parts, components and assembly systems so that a product/process functions at a desired target value.

Tolerance Design: The final stage in product design where allowable component tolerances are tightened if it is expected to result in greater loss avoidance than the cost of tightening.

TQC (Total Quality Control) Organized leadership activities involving everyone in a company-

managers and workers- in a totally integrated effort toward improving performance at every level. Feigenbaum describes TQC as an effective system for integrating the quality-development, quality-maintenance, and quality-improvement efforts of the various groups in an organization so as to enable marketing, engineering, production, ad service at the most economical levels which allow for full customer satisfaction.

Treatment Combination: The set of levels of all factors included in a trial in an experiment is called a treatment or treatment combination.

Triangular Table: A table designed to identify sets of interacting columns in an O. A. See Linear Graph which perform the same function.

Type Error: Rejecting an assumption that is true: taking action appropriate for a special cause when in fact the process has not changes: over control.

Type II Error: Failing to reject an assumption that is false: not taking appropriate action when in fact the process is affected by special causes: under control.

Uncontrollable Factor: A factor that is difficult, undesirable

or impossible to alter. See Noise
Factor.

Variables Data: Quantitative
data, where measurements are used
for analysis. Examples include the
diameter of a bearing journal in
millimeters, the closing effort of a
door in kilograms, the
concentration of electrolyte in
percent, or the torque of a fastener
in Newton-meters. X and R.X and
(X) median and individual control
charts are used for variables data.
(See also Attributes Data.)

Variation: The inevitable
differences among individual
outputs of a process: the sources of
variation can be grouped into two
major classes: common causes and
special causes.

Statistical Tables

TABLE A-1 FACTORS FOR CONTROL CHART AND STANDARD DEVIATION FORMULAS

SUBGROUP SIZE	FACTORS STANDARDS DEVIATION d_2	X̄ & R CHARTS FACTORS FOR			X̄ & S CHARTS FACTORS FOR			X̄ - Rm CHARTS FACTORS FOR		
		X̄-CHART CONTROL LIMITS A_2	R-CHART CONTROL LIMITS LCL D_3	UCL D_4	X̄-CHART CONTROL LIMITS A_3	S-CHART CONTROL LIMITS LCL B_3	UCL B_4	X̄-CHART CONTROL LIMITS E_2	Rm-CHART CONTROL LIMITS LCL D_3	UCL D_4
2	1.128	1.880	-	3.267	2.659	-	3.267	2.660	-	3.267
3	1.693	1.023	-	2.574	1.954	-	2.568	1.772	-	2.574
4	2.059	0.729	-	2.282	1.628	-	2.266	1.457	-	2.282
5	2.326	0.577	-	2.114	1.427	-	2.089	1.290	-	2.114
6	2.534	0.483	-	2.004	1.287	0.030	1.970	1.184	-	2.004
7	2.704	0.419	0.076	1.924	1.182	0.118	1.882	1.109	0.076	1.924
8	2.847	0.373	0.136	1.864	1.099	0.185	1.815	1.054	0.136	1.864
9	2.970	0.337	0.184	1.816	1.032	0.239	1.761	1.010	0.184	1.816
10	3.078	0.308	0.223	1.777	0.975	0.284	1.716	0.975	0.223	1.777
11	3.173	0.285	0.256	1.744	0.927	0.321	1.679	0.946	0.256	1.744
12	3.258	0.266	0.283	1.717	0.886	0.354	1.646	0.921	0.283	1.717
13	3.336	0.249	0.307	1.693	0.850	0.382	1.618	0.899	0.307	1.693
14	3.407	0.235	0.328	1.672	0.817	0.406	1.594	0.881	0.328	1.672
15	3.472	0.223	0.347	1.653	0.789	0.428	1.572	0.864	0.347	1.653
16	3.532	0.212	0.363	1.637	0.763	0.448	1.552	0.849	0.363	1.637
17	3.588	0.203	0.378	1.622	0.739	0.466	1.534	0.836	0.378	1.622
18	3.640	0.194	0.391	1.608	0.718	0.482	1.518	0.824	0.391	1.608
19	3.689	0.187	0.403	1.597	0.698	0.497	1.503	0.813	0.403	1.597
20	3.735	0.180	0.415	1.585	0.680	0.510	1.490	0.803	0.415	1.585
21	3.778	0.173	0.425	1.575	0.663	0.523	1.477	0.794	0.425	1.575
22	3.819	0.167	0.434	1.566	0.647	0.534	1.466	0.785	0.434	1.566
23	3.858	0.162	0.443	1.557	0.633	0.545	1.455	0.778	0.443	1.557
24	3.895	0.157	0.451	1.548	0.619	0.555	1.445	0.770	0.451	1.548
25	3.931	0.153	0.459	1.541	0.606	0.565	1.435	0.763	0.459	1.541

TABLE A-2 F TEST

DF DENOM	1−α	DF NUMERATOR									
		1	2	3	4	5	6	7	8	9	10
1	0.90	39.90	49.50	53.60	55.80	57.20	58.20	58.90	59.40	59.90	60.20
	0.95	161.00	200.00	216.00	225.00	230.00	234.00	237.00	239.00	241.00	242.00
2	0.90	8.53	9.00	9.16	9.24	9.29	9.33	9.35	9.37	9.38	9.39
	0.95	18.50	19.00	19.20	19.20	19.30	19.30	19.40	19.40	19.40	19.40
	0.99	98.50	99.00	99.20	99.20	99.30	99.30	99.40	99.40	99.40	99.40
3	0.90	5.54	5.46	5.39	5.34	5.31	5.28	5.27	5.25	5.24	5.23
	0.95	10.10	9.55	9.28	9.12	9.10	8.94	8.89	8.85	8.81	8.79
	0.99	34.10	30.80	29.50	28.70	28.20	27.90	27.70	27.50	27.30	27.20
4	0.90	4.54	4.32	4.19	4.11	4.05	4.01	3.98	3.95	3.94	3.92
	0.95	7.71	6.94	6.59	6.39	6.26	6.16	6.09	6.04	6.00	5.96
	0.99	21.20	18.00	16.70	16.00	15.50	15.20	15.00	14.80	14.70	14.50
5	0.90	4.06	3.78	3.62	3.52	3.45	3.40	3.37	3.34	3.32	3.30
	0.95	6.61	5.79	5.41	5.19	5.05	4.95	4.88	4.82	4.77	4.74
	0.99	16.30	13.30	12.10	11.40	11.00	10.70	10.50	10.30	10.20	10.10
6	0.90	3.78	3.46	3.29	3.18	3.11	3.05	3.01	2.98	2.96	2.94
	0.95	5.99	5.14	4.76	4.53	4.39	4.28	4.21	4.15	4.10	4.06
	0.99	13.70	10.90	9.78	9.15	8.75	8.47	8.26	8.10	7.98	7.87
7	0.90	3.59	3.26	3.07	2.96	2.88	2.83	2.78	2.75	2.72	2.70
	0.95	5.59	4.74	4.35	4.12	3.97	3.87	3.79	3.73	3.68	3.64
	0.99	12.20	9.55	8.45	7.85	7.46	7.19	6.99	6.84	6.72	6.62
8	0.90	3.46	3.11	2.92	2.81	2.73	2.67	2.62	2.59	2.56	2.54
	0.95	5.32	4.46	4.07	3.84	3.69	3.58	3.50	3.44	3.39	3.35
	0.99	11.30	8.65	7.59	8.01	6.63	6.37	6.18	6.03	5.91	5.81
9	0.90	3.36	3.01	2.81	2.69	2.61	2.55	2.51	2.47	2.44	2.42
	0.95	5.12	4.26	3.86	3.63	3.48	3.37	3.29	3.23	3.18	3.14
	0.99	10.60	8.02	6.99	6.42	6.06	5.80	5.61	5.47	5.35	5.26
10	0.90	3.28	2.92	2.73	2.61	2.52	2.46	2.41	2.38	2.35	2.32
	0.95	4.96	4.10	3.71	3.48	3.33	3.22	3.14	3.07	3.02	2.98
	0.99	10.00	7.56	6.55	5.99	5.64	5.39	5.20	5.06	4.94	4.85
15	0.90	3.07	2.70	2.49	2.36	2.27	2.21	2.16	2.12	2.09	2.06
	0.95	4.54	3.68	3.29	3.06	2.90	2.79	2.71	2.64	2.59	2.54
	0.99	8.68	6.36	5.42	4.89	4.56	4.32	4.14	4.00	3.89	3.80
20	0.90	2.97	2.59	2.38	2.25	2.16	2.09	2.04	2.00	1.96	1.94
	0.95	4.35	3.49	3.10	2.87	2.71	2.60	2.51	2.45	2.39	2.35
	0.99	8.10	5.85	4.94	4.43	4.10	3.87	3.70	3.56	3.46	3.37
30	0.90	2.88	2.49	2.28	2.14	2.05	1.98	1.93	1.88	1.85	1.82
	0.95	4.17	3.32	2.92	2.69	2.53	2.42	2.33	2.27	2.21	2.16
	0.99	7.56	5.39	4.51	4.02	3.70	3.47	3.30	3.17	3.07	2.98
40	0.90	2.84	2.44	2.23	2.09	2.00	1.93	1.87	1.83	1.79	1.76
	0.95	4.08	3.23	2.84	2.61	2.45	2.34	2.35	2.18	2.12	2.08
	0.99	7.31	5.18	4.31	3.83	3.51	3.29	3.12	2.99	2.89	2.80
60	0.90	2.79	2.39	2.18	2.04	1.95	1.87	1.82	1.77	1.74	1.71
	0.95	4.00	3.15	2.76	2.53	2.37	2.25	2.17	2.10	2.04	1.99
	0.99	7.08	4.98	4.13	3.65	3.34	3.12	2.95	2.82	2.72	2.63
120	0.90	2.75	2.35	2.13	1.99	1.90	1.82	1.77	1.72	1.68	1.65
	0.95	3.92	3.07	2.68	2.45	2.29	2.17	2.09	2.02	1.96	1.91
	0.99	6.85	4.79	3.95	3.48	3.17	2.96	2.79	2.66	2.56	2.47

TABLE A-2 F TEST (continued)

DF DENOM	1−α	DF NUMERATOR								
		12	15	20	30	40	50	60	100	120
1	0.90	60.70	61.20	61.70	62.30	62.50	62.70	62.80	63.00	63.10
	0.95	244.00	246.00	248.00	250.00	251.00	252.00	252.00	253.00	253.00
2	0.90	9.41	9.42	9.44	9.46	9.47	9.47	9.47	9.48	9.48
	0.95	19.40	19.40	19.40	19.50	19.50	19.50	19.50	9.48	19.50
	0.99	99.40	99.40	99.40	99.50	99.50	99.50	99.50	99.50	99.50
3	0.90	5.22	5.20	5.18	5.17	5.16	5.15	5.15	5.14	5.14
	0.95	8.74	8.70	8.66	8.59	8.59	8.58	8.57	8.55	8.55
	0.99	27.10	26.90	26.70	26.50	26.40	26.40	26.30	26.20	26.20
4	0.90	3.90	3.87	3.84	3.82	3.80	3.80	3.79	3.78	3.78
	0.95	5.91	5.86	5.80	5.75	5.72	5.70	5.69	5.56	5.66
	0.99	14.40	14.20	14.00	13.80	13.70	13.70	13.70	13.60	13.60
5	0.90	3.27	3.24	3.21	3.17	3.16	3.15	3.14	3.13	3.12
	0.95	4.68	4.62	4.56	4.50	4.46	4.44	4.43	4.41	4.40
	0.99	9.89	9.72	9.55	9.38	9.29	9.24	9.20	9.13	9.11
6	0.90	2.90	2.87	2.84	2.80	2.78	2.77	2.76	2.75	2.74
	0.95	4.00	3.94	3.87	3.81	3.77	3.75	3.74	3.71	3.70
	0.99	7.72	7.56	7.40	7.23	7.14	7.09	7.06	6.99	6.97
7	0.90	2.67	2.63	2.59	2.56	2.54	2.52	2.51	2.50	2.49
	0.95	3.57	3.51	3.44	3.38	3.34	3.32	3.30	3.27	3.27
	0.99	6.47	6.31	6.16	5.99	5.91	5.86	5.82	5.75	5.74
8	0.90	2.50	2.46	2.42	2.38	2.36	2.35	2.34	2.32	2.32
	0.95	3.28	3.22	3.15	3.08	3.04	3.02	3.01	2.97	2.97
	0.99	5.67	5.52	5.36	5.20	5.12	5.07	5.03	4.96	4.95
9	0.90	2.38	2.34	2.30	2.25	2.23	2.22	2.21	2.19	2.18
	0.95	3.07	3.01	2.94	2.86	2.83	2.80	2.79	2.76	2.75
	0.99	5.11	4.96	4.81	4.65	4.57	5.52	4.48	4.42	4.40
10	0.90	2.28	2.24	2.20	2.16	2.13	2.12	2.11	2.09	2.08
	0.95	2.91	2.85	2.77	2.70	2.66	2.64	2.62	2.59	2.58
	0.99	4.71	4.56	4.41	4.25	4.17	4.12	4.08	4.01	4.00
15	0.90	2.02	1.97	1.92	1.87	1.85	1.83	1.82	1.79	1.79
	0.95	2.48	2.40	2.33	2.25	2.20	2.18	2.16	2.12	2.11
	0.99	3.67	3.52	3.37	3.21	3.13	3.08	3.05	2.98	2.96
20	0.90	1.89	1.84	1.79	1.74	1.71	1.69	1.68	1.65	1.64
	0.95	2.28	2.20	2.12	2.04	1.99	1.97	1.95	1.91	1.90
	0.99	3.23	3.09	2.94	2.78	2.69	2.64	2.61	2.54	2.52
30	0.90	1.77	1.72	1.67	1.61	1.57	1.55	1.54	1.51	1.50
	0.95	2.09	2.01	1.93	1.84	1.79	1.76	1.74	1.70	1.68
	0.99	2.84	2.70	2.55	2.39	2.30	2.25	2.21	2.13	2.11
40	0.90	1.71	1.66	1.61	1.54	1.51	1.48	1.47	1.43	1.42
	0.95	2.00	1.92	1.84	1.74	1.69	1.66	1.64	1.59	1.58
	0.99	2.66	2.52	2.37	2.20	2.11	2.06	2.02	1.94	1.92
60	0.90	1.66	1.60	1.54	1.48	1.44	1.41	1.40	1.36	1.35
	0.95	1.92	1.84	1.75	1.65	1.59	1.56	1.53	1.48	1.47
	0.99	2.50	2.35	2.20	2.03	1.94	1.88	1.84	1.75	1.73
120	0.90	1.60	1.55	1.48	1.41	1.37	1.34	1.32	1.27	1.26
	0.95	1.83	1.75	1.66	1.55	1.50	1.46	1.43	1.37	1.35
	0.99	2.34	2.19	2.03	1.86	1.76	1.70	1.66	1.56	1.53

TABLE A-3 Students t Table

Degrees of Freedom	α				
	0.010 $t_{0.01}$	0.050 $t_{0.05}$	0.250 $t_{0.025}$	0.010 $t_{0.01}$	0.005 $t_{0.005}$
1	3.078	6.314	12.706	31.821	63.657
2	1.886	2.353	1.303	6.965	9.925
3	1.638	2.132	3.182	4.541	5.841
4	1.533	2.015	2.776	3.747	4.604
5	1.476	1.943	2.571	3.365	4.032
6	1.440	1.895	2.447	3.143	3.707
7	1.415	1.860	2.365	2.998	3.499
8	1.397	1.833	2.306	2.896	3.355
9	1.383	1.812	2.262	2.821	3.250
10	1.372	1.796	2.228	2.764	3.169
11	1.363	1.782	2.201	2.718	3.106
12	1.356	1.771	2.179	2.681	3.055
13	1.350	1.761	2.160	2.650	3.012
14	1.345	1.753	2.145	2.624	2.977
15	1.341	1.746	2.131	2.602	2.947
16	1.337	1.740	2.120	2.583	2.921
17	1.333	1.734	2.110	2.567	2.898
18	1.330	1.729	2.101	2.552	2.878
19	1.328	1.725	2.093	2.539	2.861
20	1.325	1.697	2.086	2.528	2.845
30	1.310	1.684	2.042	2.457	2.750
40	1.303	1.671	2.021	2.423	2.704
60	1.296	1.661	2.000	2.390	2.660
120	1.290	1.645	1.984	2.358	2.626

TABLE A-4 FULL FACTORIAL DESIGNS

RUN	DESIGN		A	B	AB	C	AC	BC	ABC	D	AD	BD	ABD	CD	ACD	BCD	ABCD	E
		TREATMENT COMBINATIONS																
1	2^2		-	-	+	-	+	+	-	-	+	+	-	+	-	-	+	-
2			+	-	-	-	-	+	+	-	-	+	+	+	+	-	-	-
3			-	+	-	-	+	-	+	-	+	-	+	+	-	+	-	-
4			+	+	+	-	-	-	-	-	-	-	-	+	+	+	+	-
5	2^3		-	-	+	+	-	-	+	-	+	+	-	-	+	+	-	-
6			+	-	-	+	+	-	-	-	-	+	+	-	-	+	+	-
7			-	+	-	+	-	+	-	-	+	-	+	-	+	-	+	-
8			+	+	+	+	+	+	+	-	-	-	-	-	-	-	-	-
9	2^4		-	-	+	-	+	+	-	+	-	-	+	-	+	+	-	-
10			+	-	-	-	-	+	+	+	+	-	-	-	-	+	+	-
11			-	+	-	-	+	-	+	+	-	+	-	-	+	-	+	-
12			+	+	+	-	-	-	-	+	+	+	+	-	-	-	-	-
13			-	-	+	+	-	-	+	+	-	-	+	+	-	-	+	-
14			+	-	-	+	+	-	-	+	+	-	-	+	+	-	-	-
15			-	+	-	+	-	+	-	+	-	+	-	+	-	+	-	-
16			+	+	+	+	+	+	+	+	+	+	+	+	+	+	+	-
17	2^5		-	-	+	-	+	+	-	-	+	+	-	+	-	-	+	+
18			+	-	-	-	-	+	+	-	-	+	+	+	+	-	-	+
19			-	+	-	-	+	-	+	-	+	-	+	+	-	+	-	+
20			+	+	+	-	-	-	-	-	-	-	-	+	+	+	+	+
21			-	-	+	+	-	-	+	-	+	+	-	-	+	+	-	+
22			+	-	-	+	+	-	-	-	-	+	+	-	-	+	+	+
23			-	+	-	+	-	+	-	-	+	-	+	-	+	-	+	+
24			+	+	+	+	+	+	+	-	-	-	-	-	-	-	-	+
25			-	-	+	-	+	+	-	+	-	-	+	-	+	+	-	+
26			+	-	-	-	-	+	+	+	+	-	-	-	-	+	+	+
27			-	+	-	-	+	-	+	+	-	+	-	-	+	-	+	+
28			+	+	+	-	-	-	-	+	+	+	+	-	-	-	-	+
29			-	-	+	+	-	-	+	+	-	-	+	+	-	-	+	+
30			+	-	-	+	+	-	-	+	+	-	-	+	+	-	-	+
31			-	+	-	+	-	+	-	+	-	+	-	+	-	+	-	+
32			+	+	+	+	+	+	+	+	+	+	+	+	+	+	+	+

TABLE A-4 (Continued) FULL FACTORIAL DESIGNS

DESIGN: 2^5

RUN	AE	BE	ABE	CE	ACE	BCE	ABCE	DE	ADE	BDE	ABDE	CDE	ACDE	BCDE	ABCDE
1	+	+	−	+	−	−	+	+	−	−	+	−	+	+	−
2	−	+	+	+	+	−	−	+	+	−	−	−	−	+	+
3	+	−	+	+	−	+	−	+	−	+	−	−	+	−	+
4	−	−	−	+	+	+	+	+	+	+	+	−	−	−	−
5	+	+	−	−	+	+	−	+	−	−	+	+	−	−	+
6	−	+	+	−	−	+	+	+	+	−	−	+	+	−	−
7	+	−	+	−	+	−	+	+	−	+	−	+	−	+	−
8	−	−	−	−	−	−	−	+	+	+	+	+	+	+	+
9	+	+	−	+	−	−	+	−	+	+	−	+	−	−	+
10	−	+	+	+	+	−	−	−	−	+	+	+	+	−	−
11	+	−	+	+	−	+	−	−	+	−	+	+	−	+	−
12	−	−	−	+	+	+	+	−	−	−	−	+	+	+	+
13	+	+	−	−	+	+	−	−	+	+	−	−	+	+	−
14	−	+	+	−	−	+	+	−	−	+	+	−	−	+	+
15	+	−	+	−	+	−	+	−	+	−	+	−	+	−	+
16	−	−	−	−	−	−	−	−	−	−	−	−	−	−	−
17	−	−	+	−	+	+	−	−	+	+	−	+	−	−	+
18	+	−	−	−	−	+	+	−	−	+	+	+	+	−	−
19	−	+	−	−	+	−	+	−	+	−	+	+	−	+	−
20	+	+	+	−	−	−	−	−	−	−	−	+	+	+	+
21	−	−	+	+	−	−	+	−	+	+	−	−	+	+	−
22	+	−	−	+	+	−	−	−	−	+	+	−	−	+	+
23	−	+	−	+	−	+	−	−	+	−	+	−	+	−	+
24	+	+	+	+	+	+	+	−	−	−	−	−	−	−	−
25	−	−	+	−	+	+	−	+	−	−	+	−	+	+	−
26	+	−	−	−	−	+	+	+	+	−	−	−	−	+	+
27	−	+	−	−	+	−	+	+	−	+	−	−	+	−	+
28	+	+	+	−	−	−	−	+	+	+	+	−	−	−	−
29	−	−	+	+	−	−	+	+	−	−	+	+	−	−	+
30	+	−	−	+	+	−	−	+	+	−	−	+	+	−	−
31	−	+	−	+	−	+	−	+	−	+	−	+	−	+	−
32	+	+	+	+	+	+	+	+	+	+	+	+	+	+	+

TREATMENT COMBINATIONS

TABLE A-5 8 RUN SCREENING DESIGN

RUN	MEAN	A	B	C	D	E	F	G
1	+	+	+	+	-	+	-	-
2	+	-	+	+	+	-	+	-
3	+	-	-	+	+	+	-	+
4	+	+	-	-	+	+	+	-
5	+	-	+	-	-	+	+	+
6	+	+	-	+	-	-	+	+
7	+	+	+	-	+	-	-	+
8	+	-	-	-	-	-	-	-

REFLECTED AND REPLICATED

RUN	MEAN	A	B	C	D	E	F	G
1	+	+	+	+	-	+	-	-
2	+	-	+	+	+	-	+	-
3	+	-	-	+	+	+	-	+
4	+	+	-	-	+	+	+	-
5	+	-	+	-	-	+	+	+
6	+	+	-	+	-	-	+	+
7	+	+	+	-	+	-	-	+
8	+	-	-	-	-	-	-	-
9	+	-	-	-	+	-	+	+
10	+	+	-	-	-	+	-	+
11	+	+	+	-	-	-	+	-
12	+	-	+	+	-	-	-	+
13	+	+	-	+	+	-	-	-
14	+	-	+	-	+	+	-	-
15	+	-	-	+	-	+	+	-
16	+	+	+	+	+	+	+	+
R1	+	+	+	+	-	+	-	-
R2	+	-	+	+	+	-	+	-
R3	+	-	-	+	+	+	-	+
R4	+	+	-	-	+	+	+	-
R5	+	-	+	-	-	+	+	+
R6	+	+	-	+	-	-	+	+
R7	+	+	+	-	+	-	-	+
R8	+	-	-	-	-	-	-	-
R9	+	-	-	-	+	-	+	+
R10	+	+	-	-	-	+	-	+
R11	+	+	+	-	-	-	+	-
R12	+	-	+	+	-	-	-	+
R13	+	+	-	+	+	-	-	-
R14	+	-	+	-	+	+	-	-
R15	+	-	-	+	-	+	+	-
R16	+	+	+	+	+	+	+	+

TABLE A-6 8 RUN SCREENING DESIGN

RUN	MEAN	A	B	C	D	E	F	G	H	I	J	K
1	+	+	+	-	+	+	+	-	-	-	+	-
2	+	+	-	+	+	+	-	-	-	+	-	+
3	+	-	+	+	+	-	-	-	+	-	+	+
4	+	+	+	+	-	-	-	+	-	+	+	-
5	+	+	+	-	-	-	+	-	+	+	-	+
6	+	+	-	-	-	+	-	+	+	-	+	+
7	+	-	-	-	+	-	+	+	-	+	+	+
8	+	-	-	+	-	+	+	-	+	+	+	-
9	+	-	+	-	+	+	-	+	+	+	-	-
10	+	+	-	+	+	-	+	+	+	-	-	-
11	+	-	+	+	-	+	+	+	-	-	-	+
12	+	-	-	-	-	-	-	-	-	-	-	-

TABLE A-7 16 RUN SCREENING DESIGN

RUN	MEAN	A	B	C	D	E	F	G	H	I	J	K	L	M	N	O
1	+	+	-	-	-	+	-	-	+	+	-	+	-	+	+	+
2	+	+	+	-	-	-	+	-	-	+	+	-	+	-	+	+
3	+	+	+	+	-	-	-	+	-	-	+	+	-	+	-	+
4	+	+	+	+	+	-	-	-	+	-	-	+	+	-	+	-
5	+	-	+	+	+	+	-	-	-	+	-	-	+	+	-	+
6	+	+	-	+	+	+	+	-	-	-	+	-	-	+	+	-
7	+	-	+	-	+	+	+	+	-	-	-	+	-	-	+	+
8	+	+	-	+	-	+	+	+	+	-	-	-	+	-	-	+
9	+	+	+	-	+	-	+	+	+	+	-	-	-	+	-	-
10	+	-	+	+	-	+	-	+	+	+	+	-	-	-	+	-
11	+	-	-	+	+	-	+	-	+	+	+	+	-	-	-	+
12	+	+	-	-	+	+	-	+	-	+	+	+	+	-	-	-
13	+	-	+	-	-	+	+	-	+	-	+	+	+	+	-	-
14	+	-	-	+	-	-	+	+	-	+	-	+	+	+	+	-
15	+	-	-	-	+	-	-	+	+	-	+	-	+	+	+	+
16	+	-	-	-	-	-	-	-	-	-	-	-	-	-	-	-

TABLE A-8 20 RUN SCREENING DESIGN

RUN	MEAN	A	B	C	D	E	F	G	H	I	J	K	L	M	N	O	P	Q	R	S
1	+	+	+	-	-	+	+	+	+	-	+	-	+	-	-	-	-	+	+	-
2	+	+	-	-	+	+	+	+	-	+	-	+	-	-	-	-	+	+	-	+
3	+	-	-	+	+	+	+	-	+	-	+	-	-	-	-	+	+	-	+	+
4	+	-	+	+	+	+	-	+	-	+	-	-	-	-	+	+	-	+	+	-
5	+	+	+	+	+	-	+	-	+	-	-	-	-	+	+	-	+	+	-	-
6	+	+	+	+	-	+	-	+	-	-	-	-	+	+	-	+	+	-	-	+
7	+	+	+	-	+	-	+	-	-	-	-	+	+	-	+	+	-	-	+	+
8	+	+	-	+	-	+	-	-	-	-	+	+	-	+	+	-	-	+	+	+
9	+	-	+	-	+	-	-	-	-	+	+	-	+	+	-	-	+	+	+	+
10	+	+	-	+	-	-	-	-	+	+	-	+	+	-	-	+	+	+	+	-
11	+	-	+	-	-	-	-	+	+	-	+	+	-	-	+	+	+	+	-	+
12	+	+	-	-	-	-	+	+	-	+	+	-	-	+	+	+	+	-	+	-
13	+	-	-	-	-	+	+	-	+	+	-	-	+	+	+	+	-	+	-	+
14	+	-	-	-	+	+	-	+	+	-	-	+	+	+	+	-	+	-	+	-
15	+	-	-	+	+	-	+	+	-	-	+	+	+	+	-	+	-	+	-	-
16	+	-	+	+	-	+	+	-	-	+	+	+	+	-	+	-	+	-	-	-
17	+	+	+	-	+	+	-	-	+	+	+	+	-	+	-	+	-	-	-	-
18	+	+	-	+	+	-	-	+	+	+	+	-	+	-	+	-	-	-	-	+
19	+	-	+	+	-	-	+	+	+	+	-	+	-	+	-	-	-	-	+	+
20	+	-	-	-	-	-	-	-	-	-	-	-	-	-	-	-	-	-	-	-

TABLE A-9

L-4 TAGUCHI DESIGN

RUN	FACTOR		
	1	2	3
1	1	1	1
2	1	2	2
3	2	1	2
4	2	2	1

TABLE A-10

L-8 TAGUCHI DESIGN

RUN	FACTOR						
	1	2	3	4	5	6	7
1	1	1	1	1	1	1	1
2	1	1	1	2	2	2	2
3	1	2	2	1	1	1	2
4	1	2	2	2	2	2	1
5	2	1	2	1	2	2	2
6	2	1	2	2	1	1	1
7	2	2	1	1	2	2	1
8	2	2	1	2	1	1	2

TABLE A-11 L-12 TAGUCHI DESIGN

RUN	FACTOR										
	1	2	3	4	5	6	7	8	9	10	11
1	1	1	1	1	1	1	1	1	1	1	1
2	1	1	1	1	1	2	2	2	2	2	2
3	1	1	1	2	2	1	1	1	2	2	2
4	1	2	2	2	2	1	2	2	1	1	2
5	1	2	2	1	2	2	1	2	1	2	1
6	1	2	2	2	1	2	2	1	2	1	1
7	2	1	1	2	1	1	2	2	1	2	1
8	2	1	1	1	2	2	2	1	1	1	2
9	2	1	1	2	2	2	1	2	2	1	1
10	2	2	2	1	1	1	1	2	2	1	2
11	2	2	2	2	1	2	1	1	1	2	2
12	2	2	2	1	2	1	2	1	2	2	1

TABLE A-12 L-16 TAGUCHI DESIGN

RUN	FACTOR														
	1	2	3	4	5	6	7	8	9	10	11	12	13	14	15
1	1	1	1	1	1	1	1	1	1	1	1	1	1	1	1
2	1	1	1	1	1	1	1	2	2	2	2	2	2	2	2
3	1	1	1	2	2	2	2	1	1	1	1	2	2	2	2
4	1	1	1	2	2	2	2	2	2	2	2	1	1	1	1
5	1	2	2	1	1	2	2	1	1	2	2	1	2	2	2
6	1	2	2	1	1	2	2	2	2	1	1	2	1	1	1
7	1	2	2	2	2	1	1	1	1	2	2	2	1	1	1
8	1	2	2	2	2	1	1	2	2	1	1	1	2	2	2
9	2	1	2	1	2	1	2	1	2	1	2	2	1	1	2
10	2	1	2	1	2	1	2	2	1	2	1	1	2	2	1
11	2	1	2	2	1	2	1	1	2	1	2	1	2	2	1
12	2	1	2	2	1	2	1	2	1	2	1	2	1	1	2
13	2	2	1	1	2	2	1	1	2	2	1	2	2	2	1
14	2	2	1	1	2	2	1	2	1	1	2	1	1	1	2
15	2	2	1	2	1	1	2	1	2	1	1	1	1	1	2
16	2	2	1	2	1	1	2	2	1	2	2	2	2	2	1

TABLE A-13 2 LEVEL INTERACTION TABLE

RUN	SECOND FACTOR FACTOR														
	1	2	3	4	5	6	7	8	9	10	11	12	13	14	15
	1	3	2	5	4	7	6	9	8	11	10	13	12	15	14
		2	1	6	7	4	5	10	11	8	9	14	15	12	13
			3	7	6	5	4	11	10	9	8	15	14	13	12
				4	1	2	3	12	13	14	15	8	9	10	11
					5	3	2	13	12	15	14	9	8	11	10
						6	1	14	15	12	13	10	11	8	9
							7	1	14	13	12	11	10	9	8
								8	1	2	3	4	5	6	7
									9	3	2	5	4	7	6
										10	1	6	7	4	5
											11	7	6	5	4
												12	1	2	3
													13	3	2
														14	1

TABLE A-14

L-9 TAGUCHI DESIGN (3 LEVEL)

RUN	FACTOR			
	1	2	3	4
1	1	1	1	1
2	1	2	2	2
3	1	3	3	3
4	2	1	2	3
5	2	2	3	1
6	2	3	1	2
7	3	1	3	2
8	3	2	1	3
9	3	3	2	1

TABLE A-15 L-27 TAGUCHI DESIGN (3 LEVEL)

RUN	\multicolumn{13}{c}{FACTOR}											
	1	2	3	4	5	6	7	8	9	10	11	12	13
1	1	1	1	1	1	1	1	1	1	1	1	1	1
2	1	1	1	1	2	2	2	2	2	2	2	2	2
3	1	1	1	1	3	3	3	3	3	3	3	3	3
4	1	2	2	2	1	1	1	2	2	2	3	3	3
5	1	2	2	2	2	2	2	3	3	3	1	1	1
6	1	2	2	2	3	3	3	1	1	1	2	2	2
7	1	3	3	3	1	1	1	3	3	3	2	2	2
8	1	3	3	3	2	2	2	1	1	1	3	3	3
9	1	3	3	3	3	3	3	2	2	2	1	1	1
10	2	1	3	3	1	2	3	1	1	3	1	2	3
11	2	1	3	3	2	3	1	2	2	1	2	3	1
12	2	1	3	3	3	1	2	3	3	2	3	1	2
13	2	2	1	1	1	2	3	2	2	1	3	1	2
14	2	2	1	1	2	3	1	3	3	2	1	2	3
15	2	2	1	1	3	1	2	1	1	3	2	3	1
16	2	3	2	2	1	2	3	3	3	2	2	3	1
17	2	3	2	2	2	3	1	1	1	3	3	1	2
18	2	3	2	2	3	1	2	2	2	1	1	2	3
19	3	1	2	2	1	3	2	1	1	2	1	3	2
20	3	1	2	2	2	1	3	2	2	3	2	1	3
21	3	1	2	2	3	2	1	3	3	1	3	2	1
22	3	2	3	3	1	3	2	2	2	3	3	2	1
23	3	2	3	3	2	1	3	3	3	1	1	3	2
24	3	2	3	3	3	2	1	1	1	2	2	1	3
25	3	3	1	1	1	3	2	3	3	1	2	1	3
26	3	3	1	1	2	1	3	1	1	2	3	2	1
27	3	3	1	1	3	2	1	2	2	3	1	3	2

TABLE A-16 3-LEVEL INTERACTION TABLE

	FACTOR												
RUN	1	2	3	4	5	6	7	8	9	10	11	12	13
	1	3	2	2	6	5	5	9	8	8	12	11	11
		4	4	3	7	7	6	10	10	9	13	13	12
		2	1	1	8	9	10	5	6	7	5	6	7
			4	3	11	12	13	11	12	13	8	9	10
			3	1	9	10	8	7	5	6	6	7	5
				2	13	11	12	12	13	11	10	8	9
				4	10	8	9	6	7	5	7	5	6
					12	13	11	13	11	12	9	10	8
					5	1	1	2	3	4	2	4	3
						7	6	11	13	12	8	10	9
						6	1	4	2	3	3	2	4
							5	13	12	11	10	9	8
							7	3	4	2	4	3	2
								12	11	13	9	8	10
								8	1	1	2	3	4
									10	9	5	7	6
									9	1	4	2	3
										8	7	6	5
										10	3	4	2
											6	5	7
											11	1	1
												13	12
												12	1
													11

Bibliography

Bernstein, Albert J. & Rozen, Sydney Craft, *Dinosaur Brains*. New York: John Wiley & Sons, 1989.

Beyer, William H., *Handbook Of Tables For Probability And Statistics*. 2nd Edition: CRC Press, 1991.

Bonoma, Thomas V., *(The) Marketing Edge, Making Strategies Work*. New York: The Free Press, 1985.

Bossert, James L., *Quality Function Deployment, A Practitioner's Approach*. Milwauki: Quality Press, 1991.

Brassard, Michael, *The Memory Jogger Plus+™*. Methuen: Goal/QPC, 1989.

Brownlee, K. A., *Statistical Theory And Methodology In Science And Engineering*. Second Edition, New York: John Wiley & Sons, Inc. 1967.

Byham, Dr. William C., with Cox, Jeff, *Zapp! The Lightning of EMPOWERMENT*. Pittsburgh: Development Dimension International Press, 1989.

Data Myte Corporation, *Data Myte Handbook*, Minnetonka: Data Myte Corporation, 1993.

Deming, W. Edwards, *Out of the Crises*. Boston: Massachusetts Institute of Technology, 1986.

Deming, W. Edwards, *Quality, Productivity, and Competitive Position*. Boston: Massachusetts Institute of Technology, 1986.8.

Eureka, William E. and Ryan, Nancy E, *The Customer Driven Company, Managerial Perspectives on QFD*. Dearborne: ASI Press, 1988.

Feigenbaum, Armand V, *Total Quality Control*. New York: McGraw-Hill, 1983.

Goldratt, Eliyahu M. & Cox, Jeff, *(The) Goal*. Croton-On-Hudson: North River Press, 1984.

Goldratt, Eliyahu M., *Theory of Constraints*. Croton-on-Hudson: North River Press Inc, 1990.

Grant, Eugene L. And Leavenworth, Richard S. *Statistical Quality Control* 6th Edition, New York: McGraw-Hill, 1988.

Hall, Robert W., *Zero Inventories*. Homewood: Dow Jones-Irwin,

Hall, Robert W., *Attaining Manufacturing Excellence*. Homewood: Dow Jones-Irwin, 1987.

Harrington, James, *(The) Improvement Process How America's Leading Companies Improve Quality*. Milwaukee: Quality Press, 1987.

Hazlewood Robert H, and Wheelwright, Steven C., *Restoring Our Competitave Edge, Competing through Manufacturing*. New York: John Wiley and Sons, 1984.

Fox, Ronald J. with Field James L., *The Defense Management Challenge*. Boston: Harvard Business School Press, 1988.

Hudiberg, John J., *Winning With Quality, The FPL Story*. White Plains: Quality Resources, 1991.

Hogg Robert V. and Craig, Allen T., *Introduction To Mathematical Statistics*. Third Edition , New York: The MacMillian Company, 1970.

Imai, Maska, *Kaizen* . New York: Random House, 1986.

Ishikawa, Kaoru, Translator Loftus, John H. *Introduction To Quality Control* . Tokyo: Juse Press Ltd,

Ishikawa, Kaoru, Translator Lu, D. J., *What is Total Quality Control* . Englewood Cliffs: Prentice Hall, Inc., 1985.

Jablonski, Josepk R., *Implementing Total Quality Management, Competing in the 1990's*, Albequerque: Technical Management Consultants Inc, 1991.

Juran, J. M., *Juran On Planning For Quality*. New York, The Free Press, 1988.

Juran, J. M., *Managerial Breakthrough* . New York: McGraw-Hill, 1964.

Juran, J. M. and Gryna, F. M. Jr., *Quality Planning & Analysis*. New York: McGraw Hill, 1980.

Ishikawa, Kaoru, *Guide To Quality Control*. White Plains: Quality Resources 1982.

Karastu, Hajime, *TQC Wisdom of Japan*, *Managing for Total Quality Control*. Cambridge: Productivity Press, 1988.

Kececioglu, Dimitri, *Reliability Engineering Handbook*, Volume 1 And Volume 2. Englewood Cliffs: Prentice Hall, 1991.

Kepner, Charles H. and Trego, Benjamin B., *The New Rational Manager.* Princeton: Kepner Trego Inc, 1981.

Khazanie, Ramakant, *Elementary Statistics In A World Of Applications.* Santa Monica: Goodyear Publishing Co. Inc., 1979.

King, Bob, *Better Designs In Half The Time - Implementing GFD In America..* Methuen: Goal/QPC, 1987.

King, Bob, *Hoshin Planning, The Developmental Approach.* Methuen: Goal/QPC, 1989.

Kerzuer, Harold, *Project Management, A Systems Approach to Planning, Scheduling and Controling.* New York: Van Nostrand Reinhold, 1992.

Levin, Richard I., *Statistics For Management.* Second Edition, Englewood Cliffs: Prentice-Hall, Inc. 1981.

Li Jerome C. R., *Statistical Inference .* Ann Arbor: Edwards Brothers, Inc., 1964.

Lubben, Richard T., *Just-in-Time Manufacturing, An Aggressive Manufacturing Strategy.* New York: McGraw Hill, 1988.

Marsh, S. Moran, J. W. Nakui, S., Hoffherr, G., *Facilitating And Training In Quality Function Deployment.* Methuen: Goal/QPC, 1991.

Mizuno, Shigeru, *Management for Quality Improvement - the 7 New Quality Tools.* Cambridge: Productivity Press, 1988.

Ohmae, Kenichic, *The Mind of the Strategist, The Art of Japanese Business.* New York: McGraw-Hill, 1982.

Orsburn, John D., Musselwhite, Ed, Zegler, John H., with Perrin, Craig, *Self-Directed Work Teams; The New American Challange.* Homewood: 1990

Ouchi, William, *(The) M-Form Society.* Reading: Addison-Wesley Publishing Co., 1984.

Ouchi, William G., *Theory Z.* New York: Avon Books, 1981.

Peters, Tom, *Thriving On Chaos .* New York: Alfred A. Knopf, Inc., 1988.

Re Velle, Jack B. Ph.D, *The New Quality Technology (An Introduction To Quality Function Deployment (QFD) And The Taguchi Methods).* Los Angeles: Hughes Aircraft Company 1990.

Rosander, A.C., *The Quest For Quality In Services.* Milwaukee: Quality Press, 1989.

Ross, Phillip J., *Taguchi Techniques For Quality Engineering.* New York: McGraw-Hill Inc., 1988.

Robson, George D., *Continuous Process Improvement, Simplifying Work Flow Systems.* Westport: The Free Press, 1991.

Rosander, A.C., *The Quest for Quality in Services.* Milwaukee: Quality Press, 1989.

Rubinstein, Moshe F. & Pfeiffer, Kenneth , *Concepts In Problem Solving.* Englewood Cliffs: Prentice-Hall, Inc, 1975.

Rubinstein, Moshe F., *Tools for Thinking and Problem Solving.* Englewood Cliffs: Prentice-Hall Inc, 1986.

Ryan Thomas P., *Statistical Methods For Quality Improvement.* New York: John Wiley & Sons, 1989.

Sanage, Charles M., *Fifth Generation Management,* Bedford: Digital Press, 1990.

Sandras, William A. Jr. *Just-In-Time: Making It Happen, Unleashing The Power Of Continuous Improvement.* Essex Junction: Oliver Wight Limited Publications, Inc., 1989.

Sanders, Donald H., Murphy, A. F., and Eng, Robert J. *Statistics A Fresh Approach.* Second Edition, New York: McGraw-Hill Book Co. 1980.

Satty, Thomas L, *Decision Making For Leaders, The Analytical Process For Decisions In A Complex World..* Pittsburgh: University Of Pittsburgh, 1988.

Scherkenbach , William W.; *Deming's Road To Continual Improvement.* Knoxville: SPC Press, Inc., 1991.

Schonberger, Richard J; *Building A Chain Of Customers.* Westport:The Free Press, 1990.

Schonberger, Richard J, *World Class Manufacturing & Casebook - Implementing JIT And TQC.* New York: The Free Press 1986.

Shetty, Y. K. & Buehler V. M, *Productivity & Quality Through People.* x Westport: The Free Press 1985.

Smith, Preston G., and Reinertsen, Donald G., *Developing Products in Half the Time.* New York: Van Nostrand Reinhold, 1991.

Stephanson, S. E. and Spiegl, F., *The Manufacturing Challenge From Concept to Production.* New York: Van Nostrand Reinhold, 1992.

Steudel, Harold J., and Desruelle, Paul., *Manufacturing in the Nineties.* New York: Van Nostrand Reinhold, 1992.

Sundararajan, C., *Guide to Reliability Engineering.* New York: Van Nostrand Reinhold, 1991.

Tenner, Arthur R. and De Toro, Irving J., *Total Quality Management, Three Steps to Continuous Improvement.* Reading Massachusetts: Addison-Wesley Publishing Co. Inc., 1992.

Thurow, Lester, *Head to Head.* New York: William Morrow and Co., Inc., 1992.

Tregoe, Benjamin B., Zimmerman, John W., Smith, Ronald A., and Tobia, Peter M., *Vision in Action, Putting a Winning Strategy to Work.* New York: Simon & Schuster, Inc., 1990.

Turban, Efraim, and Meredith, Jack R., *Fundamentals Of Management Science.* Plano: Business Publications, Inc. 1981.

Turino, Jon, *Managing Concurrent Engineering, Buying Time to Market*. New York: Van Nostrand Reinhold, 1992.

Weinberg, Gerald M., *Becoming A Technical Leader - An Organic Problem-Solving Approach*. New York: Dorset House Publishing, 1986

Walton, Mary, *The Deming Management Method*. New York: The Putnam Publishing Group, 1986.

Wriston, Walter B., *Risk & Other Four-Letter Words*. New York: 1987.

INDEX